Praise for *The Forgotten Rebels of*

WINNER, 2014 Stella Prize

WINNER, Nib: Waverley Library Award for Literature 2014

WINNER, Nib: People's Choice Award 2014

SHORTLISTED, Prime Minister's Literary Awards 2014

SHORTLISTED, NSW Premier's History Awards
Australian History Prize 2014

SHORTLISTED, WA Premier's Book Awards 2014

SHORTLISTED, Queensland Literary Awards USQ
History Book Award 2014

SHORTLISTED, Victorian Community History Awards 2014

LONGLISTED, Walkley Book Award 2014

'Immediately entrancing...recreates the landscape as one of bustling domesticity, commerce, theatre and constantly shifting authority...Wright challenges the traditional view of the stockade to create a much richer social history.' *Guardian*

'Beautifully written, her book takes readers on a vivid journey of what life was like for the families of the miners, merchants, prostitutes and police...It's a great story.' *Courier-Mail*

'Wonderful...Beautifully researched and full of vivid colour, engaging characters and dramatic reconstruction...A book with as much verve, energy and indomitable spirit as the digger women themselves.' *Independent* UK

'A style as racy and readable as that of any novel.'
Judges' comments, Nib: Waverley Library Award

'Lively, incisive and timely...an engrossing read. Essential reading for devotees of Australian history.' *Books + Publishing*

'Succeeds in bringing women's presence on the Australian goldfields vividly into focus...detailed and convincing...it is also a wonderful snapshot of the many issues Australian women might have found themselves confronted with.' *Sydney Review of Books*

'Her work fills an enormous gap…[and] supports her claim that women's presence does not just add colour to the picture, it changes the very outline.' *Australian*

'A career-defining work of scholarship and storytelling… Wright's history offers one of the richest social histories of the goldfields yet.' *The Conversation*

'A Eureka narrative like none other…It is exhilarating to encounter a historian who thinks that writing women into history is not about emphasising family life, or portraying women as victims of men, separate from the big struggles for democracy and justice.' *Marxist Left Review*

'Clare Wright asks a belated question on behalf of her schoolgirl self: "Where are *we* in this story?" It's a simple but disruptive question that has the power to stir the surface of even the most lacquered of Australia's founding stories.' Robyn Annear, *Monthly*

'A huge step towards a more truthful examination of the Stockade and its players…What this book does is lay down a new way…for all of us to understand our past through truth rather than reliance on myth.' *King's Tribune*

ALSO BY CLARE WRIGHT

Beyond the Ladies Lounge: Australia's Female Publicans

Clare Wright is a historian who has worked as an academic and broadcaster. She is a writer and presenter for television, with the ABC TV documentary series *Utopia Girls* and *The War That Changed Us* among her credits. She lives in Melbourne with her husband, three children and too many pets.

clarewright.com.au

The Forgotten Rebels of Eureka

CLARE WRIGHT

TEXT PUBLISHING
MELBOURNE AUSTRALIA

The Text Publishing Company
Swann House
22 William Street
Melbourne Victoria 3000
Australia
textpublishing.com.au

First published in 2013 by The Text Publishing Company
This edition 2014
Reprinted 2014 (twice), 2015, 2018

Typeset in Adobe Caslon 12.5/17.5 by J & M Typesetting
Book designed by WH Chong
Printed in Australia by Griffin Press

National Library of Australia Cataloguing-in-Publication entry

Author: Wright, Clare, author.

Title: The forgotten rebels of Eureka / by Clare Wright.

ISBN: 9781922182548 (paperback)
9781922148407 (ebook)

Subjects: Eureka Stockade, Ballarat, Vic., 1854.
Gold miners--Victoria--Ballarat--History.
Riots--Victoria--Ballarat--History.
Ballarat (Vic.)--History--1851-1901.

Dewey Number: 994.57031

This book is printed on paper certified against the Forest Stewardship Council® Standards. Griffin Press holds FSC chain-of-custody certification SGS-COC-005088. FSC promotes environmentally responsible, socially beneficial and economically viable management of the world's forests.

For my children,
Bernard, Noah and Esther

'That dreadful Eureka episode seems more like a disturbed dream than an actual historical reality.'

Age, 12 SEPTEMBER, 1856

'Every history of every country is a mirror of the author's own interests and therefore selective rather than comprehensive.'

GEOFFREY BLAINEY,
The Tyranny of Distance, 1966

'Well-behaved women seldom make history.'

PROFESSOR LAUREL THATCHER ULRICH,
HARVARD UNIVERSITY, 2007

CONTENTS

PREFACE

It was William Withers who first generated the myth of the Australian goldfields as an exclusively masculine domain. In his popular *History of Ballarat*, first published in 1870, Withers made arresting statements like this: the diggers were *young and wifeless for the most part*, to see a woman *was an absolute phenomenon*, the diggings were *womanless fields*. But Withers' unequivocal descriptions referred to the earliest days of the gold rush, that is, late 1851 and early 1852. It is a historical nicety conveniently overlooked by subsequent historians, eager to romanticise the digging life as one of unparalleled freedom and independence.

Such writers—there are many but we can finger Henry Lawson and practically anyone else coming out of the *Bulletin* and *Lone Hand* school of radical nationalism—sought to contrast the humdrum existence of their staid metropolitan lives with the bravery, adventurousness and risk-taking of the pioneers, symbolised by the classless (and womanless) diggers. In a lecture to the Australian Natives Association in 1889, John Francis Deegan, who had arrived at Ballarat as a nine-year-old boy in 1854, spoke of the diggers as bearing *a free and manly gait, and an aspect of self-reliance, begotten of their untrammelled life and independent habits.*[1] It was a muscular heritage that the inhabitants of an imperial metropolis on the verge of a depression longed to claim.

But is it still socially relevant to maintain the false premise of masculine independence and autonomy, particularly when the voices of women who were actually there can readily drown out the likes of Withers? A mature nation, surely, can continually resift, reconsider and reflect upon the implications of its creation stories.

There is a great body of international literature demonstrating the prevalence of women at the forefront of agitation for social and political change: in the American Revolution, the American Civil War, the French Revolution, the 1848 uprisings across Europe, the Spanish Civil War, the Russian Revolution and recent Latin American protest movements. Such works have charted the ways that traditional bounds of female and civic identity are transformed in times of upheaval and conflict.

Eureka, by contrast, has dovetailed with other Australian legends (Gallipoli, the bush, the 1890s shearers' and maritime strikes) with supposedly all-male casts and symbols of national potency to create an impermeable veneer of masculine dominion. Geoffrey Blainey was right to conclude that 'Eureka is like a great neon sign with messages that flick on and off with different messages for different people on different occasions'.[2] Yet the Eureka beacon has never before been used to illuminate issues of gender bias in our collective bedtime stories.

By examining the lives of women on both sides of the Stockade, we can begin to build an intricate portrait of the Ballarat goldfields in 1854. Instead of a rough and ready outpost of bachelors out for a quick buck, we find a heterogeneous and largely orderly community of 'working families' intent on building a new life of freedom and independence. Ultimately, as we'll see, it was the intimate, ambitious matrix of expectations, associations, disappointments and frustrations that culminated in the brief but bloody moment that aired miners' grievances and elicited official reprisals. Women's presence does not just add colour to the picture; it changes its very outline.

*

There is a vast scholarly literature on the gold rush era generally, and the Eureka Stockade specifically. I am indebted to the many fine historians who have worked over this terrain before me: Weston Bate, David Goodman, John Molony, the Geoffreys Serle and Blainey. You'll find the best of their work in the bibliography here included. I am also grateful for the pioneering archival work of local historians Dorothy Wickham, Laurel Johnson and Anne Beggs-Sunter, whose exhumation of information on Ballarat's early gold rush history, and especially its women, has been heroic.

I've tried, within narrative reason, to exclude from this book what you can readily locate in any bookshop or library. I have included, sometimes in great detail, that which you won't find anywhere else. In particular chapters focusing on women's participation in the social, economic and cultural life of the goldfields provide important data, not previously revealed.

Who knew that stores on the diggings sold breast pumps to ease the pain of lactation? Or that dances and balls provided paid childcare so that babies didn't need to be left in tents when their mothers went out for the night? This book is not simply a new inflection of an old story; it offers up a fresh body of scholarship for future dissection and, I hope, rampant expansion.

My aim is not to enter the usual interpretive controversies that have raged about Eureka for over 150 years: which side was to blame for the violence and bloodshed; whether the rebellion was a parochial tax revolt by small business or a republican insurrection; or whether Eureka even deserves the press it gets as a key landmark in Australia's democratic traditions. Nor am I looking to settle old empiricist scores: who fired the first shot; who amputated Lalor's shattered arm (historian Robyn Annear has called the rebel leader an octopus, given how many people claim their ancestor lopped off his limb); the exact topographic location of the Stockade site; whether Scobie was murdered by a blow to the head with a shovel or an axe; even who sewed the flag.

In this book, Eurekaphiles will discover previously unearthed factual details about key protagonists and events in the affair. And Eurekaphobes might reconsider their antipathy to a left-leaning legend once a more humane landscape re-emerges from the flames of political polarisation.

For Eureka is a story that is already so familiar and so emotive to Australians that successive political giants have seen fit either to make triumphant speeches on its anniversary or pointedly to scorn its relevance. On 3 December 1954, Victorian Premier John Cain Sr addressed the seventy thousand people who had flocked to Ballarat for the three-day centenary celebrations. *From Eureka came the crusading spirit against injustice*, he bellowed to the delirious crowd.[3]

On 3 December 1973, unveiling the newly restored Eureka Flag in Ballarat, Prime Minister Gough Whitlam hitched the spirit of Eureka to his own progressive agenda. *The kind of nationalism that every country needs*, intoned Whitlam, *is a benign and constructive nationalism [that] has to do with self-confidence, with maturity, with originality, with independence of mind.*[4] In 2004, national sesquicentenary events were incommoded by then Prime Minister John Howard's steadfast refusal to fly the Eureka Flag at Canberra's Parliament House.

It is neither my intention to undermine the centrality of the Eureka story in Australia's collective imagination, nor to elevate it beyond the ideological rubric of historical authenticity. But following women such as Catherine Bentley and Anastasia Hayes to *their* Eurekas has forced me to ask questions that will have wide-ranging repercussions, reaching beyond the picturesque frame of the Eureka narrative into the cultural and political heartland of Australian national identity. For the values and attributes that the Eureka Stockade has come to represent—independence, sacrifice, collectivism, unity, autonomy, dignity, dissent, resistance, self-government, the pursuit of democratic rights and freedoms in the face of oppression and humiliation—have largely been considered exclusively masculine aspirations and have been represented accordingly in our public culture.

But times have changed. Public accountability to a diverse Australian community requires socially inclusive models of institutional and popular representation. Knowledge about women's intrinsic role in the Eureka story will, from a concrete point of view, require our cultural and educational institutions to admit, respect and regard the political legacy of Australian women.

Beside the Eureka Obelisk, in the Eureka Stockade Memorial Park in the heart of Ballarat, a plaque is dedicated to *the honoured memory of the heroic pioneers who fought and fell on this sacred spot in the cause of liberty and the soldiers who fell at duty's call.* The names of twenty-eight white men follow.

Today, more than 150 years after the Eureka rebels raised their voices to demand justice and equality for the disenfranchised miner, there is a new plaque in Ballarat, at the entrance to the Museum of Australian Democracy at Eureka. Its language, thanks in part to discussions arising from the research for this book, is more inclusive:

> We honour the memory of all those who died during or because of the events at the Eureka Stockade on 3 December 1854—the men known to us, who are recalled below, as well as the other men and women whose names are unrecorded.

There is progress. But still we have to keep reminding the cultural gatekeepers that women were there too, and that their stories are just as vital, just as valid and just as vibrant as the stories of the men. This is not an 'either…or' predicament. It is a 'not only…but also' situation. We don't have to choose. We just have to respect the historical record.

*

Is it possible to imagine a nationalism that is not racist, sexist and otherwise xenophobic?

I do, and one of the reasons I can is because I have a picture in my head—indelibly inked there through my research—of men and women from many lands standing together beneath a new flag. The flag bore the symbol of the constellation that located and united them in their new home—the Southern Cross. That flag was almost certainly sewn by women of Ballarat. Under that flag the men of the Ballarat Reform League swore an oath to stand truly by each other and fight to defend their rights and liberties. Women were at that meeting too. At the time, they called that flag 'the Australian Flag'.

And not only men but also at least one woman died beneath that flag in defence of some basic democratic principles: freedom of speech, freedom of assembly and freedom of the press.

My goal, as I have said, is not to undermine the potency of the Eureka story in Australia's collective imagination. I have no desire to scoff at its centrality to our national mythology, or to deride those who have devoted themselves to the task of building a legend. Rather, I want to reinvigorate the story: to bring it with renewed relevance to a modern, diverse community for whom talk of 'democracy and freedom' should automatically raise questions of gender equity.

The great gift of Eureka—its beauty and, in a sense, its terror—is that the story of women's effort, influence and sacrifice is both politically correct and historically true.

Let's go down.

Let's go down to where it's dark and wet. The air is thick down here and our breathing gets shallow, impatient, restless with anticipation. The damp walls touch us, squeeze in close, pin us tight. Don't panic.

Let's dig down deep. Let's find that place where the light no longer gets in. There's another world down here, a place we enter with caution. But it promises so much, we can't let it be—and so we dig until we hit the core. Eureka!

Let's go down. Pick a random spot and start digging.

The past, as they say, is not dead. It's not even past.

INTRODUCTION

DUST AND RATTLING BONES

The ground is hard and dry. The dirt yields grudgingly as the gravedigger thrusts his shovel in. The summer sun blazes down, making thirsty work of a job that is grim enough without the intense heat. The crowd will be here soon, and there are still holes to dig. The gravedigger continues to jab and hack at the earth, grunting, choking on the dust; choking back the tears that threaten to join the course of his dripping sweat. It's lucky his hands are already callused.

Back down at the Eureka Lead, the people are gathering to perform their mournful task. They emerge solemnly from their tents, patting down rumpled clothes, straightening hats and bonnets, dusting off jackets and shawls usually kept for Sundays and subscription balls. They round up stray children, tether dogs and talk in muted whispers. When *will* these hot north winds ease? You'd think there'd be a change in the weather by now.

It's Monday morning, 4 December 1854. The township of Ballarat and its goldfields have woken to a strange dawn. A Monday morning on the richest auriferous basin in the world would ordinarily see a robust start to an energetic week. There are thirty-two thousand people on the Ballarat diggings, and none of them idle. Miners from every continent on the globe working their claims. Cartloads of goods arriving from Melbourne and Geelong to fill the stores with food and merchandise. Restaurants preparing victuals, grog shops dispensing their illicit wares, theatres preparing sets and wardrobes for the evening's farce or melodrama, newcomers erecting their tents and unloading their drays in wide-eyed fascination, children dodging and weaving through the tightly packed tents, campfires and washing lines. Everywhere the sights and sounds of a colonial frontier society going about its daily business, the din ferocious.

But this Monday morning is silent. Yesterday an inferno tore through the early hours of the still, moonlit morning, shattering the habitual rhythm of industry and domesticity.

It was a true Australian night, miner H. R. Nicholls later recalled of the Saturday evening that had just passed, *not a breath of wind stirred the leaves of the stringy-bark trees…the whole air was full of that fine haze…a haze which slightly veils but does not conceal, lending a ghostly yet beautiful appearance to all around.*[1]

What happened next has been taught to Australian school children for generations.

At 3am on Sunday 3 December 1854, a band of British troops and police stormed the rough barricades recently erected by a mob of armed miners. A few days earlier, the diggers had burned their mining licences in protest against the tyrannical rule of local authorities and pledged, in the words of their hastily appointed leader, Peter Lalor, *to stand truly by each other and fight to defend our rights and liberties*. The simple fortification of timber slabs, barrels and upturned carts was intended to protect unlicensed miners from arrest.

In the twenty-minute armed conflict that followed the surprise military attack, at least four soldiers and twenty-seven civilians were killed.[2] The rebel stronghold was taken, and their blue and white flag—bearing the symbol of the Southern Cross—hauled to the ground. Following the short-lived battle, authorities continued to harass people within close proximity to the barricades, fearing that renegades might be hiding in surrounding tents. Homes and businesses were torched, suspected rebels and their protectors were pursued and cut down, hundreds were arrested.

This event we have come to know as the Eureka Stockade.

Charles Evans was a twenty-six-year-old printer from Shropshire, England, who had kept a daily diary since arriving on the Ballarat goldfield in November 1853. He recorded what he saw on that shell-shocked Monday morning, when he too crept from his tent into the light of an altered reality. Amid the smouldering ruins of the Eureka goldfield, the bodies of those killed in and around the Stockade were being ceremoniously transported by horse-drawn carts to the nearby burial ground. This is what Evans wrote:

> I have witnessed today, I think, some of the most melancholy spectacles. A number of poor, brave fellows who fell in yesterday's cowardly massacre were buried…One of the coffins trimmed with white and followed by a respectable and sorrowing group was the body of a woman who was mercilessly butchered by a mounted trooper while she was pleading for the life of her husband. The mind recoils with horror and disgust from the thought that an Englishman can be found capable of an act so monstrous and cruel.[3]

Without the eyewitness account of Charles Evans, a young man whose moral universe had just been tipped upside down, we would never have known about the death of this woman.

For the name of the miner's wife with the white-trimmed coffin was not recorded in the official government lists of those killed and wounded at Eureka. It was not included on Peter Lalor's famous published list of heroes. Nor has it crawled down the haphazard wire of folk history. There are no inquest files. No newspaper reports. You certainly won't find it inscribed on the monument to *the sacred memory of those who fell in resisting the unconstitutional proceedings of the Victorian government* that looms over the Old Ballarat Cemetery. Nor do we know if this woman was defending the barricade or just a helpless onlooker, her tent randomly encircled by the hasty demarcation of the rebels' cordon.

There are no clues in the speeches delivered in Ballarat on the anniversary of the Stockade in 1856, when speakers eulogised the day *the first blood was shed for Australian liberty*. At that service, five hundred people met on the Stockade site to remember *the cause for which [the patriots] bled*. Leading citizen Dr Hambrook urged the crowd to remember those who *left the bosom of their families, the comfort of the domestic hearth*, to *live among strangers—dependent on their own manly energies for subsistence*, ruled over *by men increasing these sufferings and privations by arbitrary laws… goaded into resistance*.[4]

Hambrook concluded: *They would have been less than men if they had continued tamely to have submitted to it.* In that idea of manly defiance against oppression germinated the robust beanstalk that is the Eureka myth. Its tendrils have wound through every milestone moment in Eureka pageantry ever since. In countless books, poems, paintings, films and curricula, the Eureka Stockade has been portrayed as an essentially masculine episode in which male passions were inflamed, male blood was shed and, ultimately, manhood suffrage won.

Yet suddenly, one simple line in a young man's journal helps us to imagine the Eureka Stockade as a place populated by more than just a rabble of zealous male miners and their red-coated tormentors. Instead of an archetypal David and Goliath battle where, as the usually balanced historian Geoffrey Serle put it in 1954, 'the wavering Eureka men were compelled to write history with their blood', we are back in the land of the mortals.

We may never know her name, but the woman captured by Charles Evans' pen was not destined to lie mute in her rocky grave.

*

It was another woman's story that first brought me to Eureka. Catherine Bentley was a reluctant guide, her story a simple and a sad one; so well worn it was hardly worth telling. An Irish girl emigrates to Australia during the gold rush, marries an ex-convict, makes a fortune and loses the lot.

In 1854, when Catherine Bentley was the landlady of the Eureka Hotel, Ballarat, she was briefly the protagonist in a drama that attracted the attention of the times. Celebrity being a fickle creature even in 1854, her hour upon that stage passed quickly and she bowed out of the limelight seemingly without a trace.

But as I was to discover, the road to and from Eureka is littered with the documentary fallout from her heady rise and spectacular fall.

I first made Catherine's acquaintance when I was researching the history of women as hotel keepers in Australia. Female publicans have always been close to Australia's cultural, social, economic and political epicentre. My research about Ann Jones, the owner of the Glenrowan Inn, where Ned Kelly made his last stand, led me to look for other female publicans tangled up in Australia's iconic events. Reading C. H. Curry's 1954 staple *The Irish at Eureka* introduced me to Catherine. Here I found an account of the murder of the Scottish miner James Scobie outside the Eureka Hotel on the night of 7 October 1854, and the presumed involvement of the landlord James Bentley, two male associates and his wife. The wife remained anonymous in Curry's tale, but evidently aspersions were cast upon *her good name and character* by the drunken Scobie, and this was the singular motivation for the crime. I learned that Mrs Bentley was acquitted of a charge of murder for the miner's death, while her husband and the other men were convicted of manslaughter.

Tantalised by this chimeric glimpse of a female publican in the dock for murder, I set out to discover more about the exonerated Mrs Bentley. I read numerous secondary accounts of the Scobie murder and subsequent inquest in Ballarat; the torching of the Eureka Hotel by a riotous mob, indignant that official corruption had perverted the course of justice by absolving James Bentley; and the subsequent Melbourne trial in front of Justice Redmond Barry, the man who later sentenced Ned Kelly to death. But I could find no further details about the publican's wife, and so my initial foray into Eureka ended.

Later, through months of intense investigation of primary sources, I ascertained that twenty-two-year-old Catherine Bentley was just one of the 5165 women in Ballarat in December 1854. Her two-year-old son, Tommy, was one of 6365 children. Together, women and children accounted for thirty-two per cent of the entire Victorian goldfields population, and thirty-six per cent of Ballarat's restless, resourceful community.[5] Moreover, Catherine was seven months pregnant with her second child when her hotel was burned down by the mob. Young, recently married, pregnant and now impoverished, Catherine fitted Ballarat's dominant demographic to a tee. I also discovered this: Catherine was neither a silent witness nor a shrinking violet. There she is, in the letters and petitions she wrote, the court appearances she made, the births and deaths of babies she certified: the evidentiary fragments of an embattled woman dealt a perpetual raw deal.

And I realised I wasn't the only person trying to breathe life back into Catherine's deflated story.

Andrew Crowley is a man with a mission. His task is to recoup the £30,000 compensation his great-great-grandmother, Catherine Bentley, claimed in 1855 after her hotel was burned down while under the stewardship of the Victorian police. Andrew estimates that sum to be worth two million dollars today. His legal brief, which he has prepared and is pursuing himself, is as thick as a phone book. Some would call him a crank, a serial pest. The Victorian Government has long considered him a vexatious litigant and dismissed his claims.

To Andrew and his father Frank, the money would make a difference. But it is the Bentley family honour that they hope to resurrect. *The Eureka era is not over as most believe*, Andrew maintains, *and it won't be until the Bentleys are cleared once and for all time...it means our family's lives past and present vindicated!*[6] A few hours into our interview, Andrew broke down as he told me how important it was *to Catherine* that the truth be told.

And then he handed me a note written in Catherine's hand, dated 10 April 1892, sixteen years to the day after her husband James Bentley had taken his own life. It was one of those moments when the historian realises that the past really *isn't* past.

*

Ballarat winters are miserable. Anyone who has stood outside the majestic Craig's Royal Hotel in June knows the icy blast that blows up Lydiard Street, rattling bones and chilling you to the core. It is eye-popping, spirit-crushing cold. According to the Bureau of Meteorology, the winds blow harder and colder in Ballarat than any other place in Victoria.

I had left the cosy haven of the library to meet Anne Hall, the great-great-granddaughter of Anastasia Hayes, a Ballarat folk hero, reputed to have been one of three women to sew the Southern Cross flag. Anastasia, her husband Timothy and their five children arrived in Victoria in October 1852 aboard the *Mobile*, the same ship that was ferrying Charles Evans to his new homeland. Anne Hall and I had arranged to meet at the Art Gallery of Ballarat, where the Eureka Flag presently resides. I'd seen a million reproductions of the flag—I'd even bought my husband a souvenir Eureka Flag stubby holder—but this was my first visit to the real thing.

Anne led me into the darkened room that is designated to and dominated by the flag. The flag is pinned behind glass, but somehow still shimmers as if rippling in a wayward breeze. It is bigger than I expected, much bigger. The room has a grave aura; it calls for quiet murmurs and reverence.

Anne drew beside me as I stood gazing up at the giant blue and white standard. *I can't look at this without wondering which are her stitches*, she whispered. Her eyes darted from star to star, resting on the patch before her, clearly possessed by her ancestor Anastasia.

This was why I'd come to Ballarat today, an outsider and an ingénue. To be reminded, lest we forget, that what's done is not done. Neither forgotten nor lost, beyond hope and redemption and promise. Not for Andrew Crowley or Anne Hall, or for the hundreds of descendants who band together as Eureka's Children or the thousands of Australians who wear the image of the Eureka Flag on their hard hat or their bumper bar or their skin. For them, as for all of us, the past is a whisper away.

I have never met Ellen Campbell, but letters pecked out on her ribbon typewriter, dotted with liquid-paper corrections, regularly arrive in my mailbox. I first contacted Ellen after I learned of the precious family jewel she keeps guarded in her home in rural New South Wales: the diary of her grandmother, Margaret Brown Howden Johnston.

Newly married to Assistant Resident Gold Commissioner James Johnston and already pregnant with their first child, Margaret was living in the Government Camp in Ballarat during the time of the troubles. Later, when we had got to know each other better, Ellen sent me a photocopy of the diary. The real thing, rescued by her father from a backyard clean-up in the 1940s, never leaves her possession: *I guard this jealously as it is very fragile.*[7]

Margaret's diary would become as valuable to my research as it is to Ellen's family history. But it seems that not everyone has been as eager to embrace the Johnston legacy.

I must say I feel a bit frustrated, Ellen wrote to me on 4 December 2004, *as I would love to have been invited to celebrations conducted on 150th anniversary of Eureka—after all I am the granddaughter of the Ass. Gold Commissioner!!*

Ellen readily grasps the reason for her exclusion from the official festivities. *Much emphasis on the diggers, of course. Just a thought! Have a Happy Christmas.*

*

When the American historian Marilyn Yalom wrote her masterful *Blood Sisters: The French Revolution in Women's Memory,* she had more than eighty contemporary accounts penned by women on which to draw. These women had 'emerged from the Revolution with an urgent need to howl out their losses and cry for justice', writes Yalom. 'The more they had suffered, the more they felt compelled to chronicle the past.'

Having sifted through hundreds of gold rush diaries, private reminiscences and published memoirs, I have no doubt the women of Eureka endured exquisite suffering. But I have not found one contemporary account penned by a woman at the time of the tumultuous events. Unlike their French counterparts, the women of Ballarat apparently found their distress subsumed by the imperatives of material survival.

As we shall see, most of Ballarat's five thousand-odd women were young, newly married and raising small children. Many were illiterate. Almost all were working in some economic capacity. Unlike the French aristocrats and *bourgeoises* for whom 'the Revolution shaped their life trajectory more than any other historical event', it was dislocation, subsistence and sheer physical endurance in a tent city on a colonial frontier that characterised this Australian experience.

Psychologist Abraham Maslow's famous 'hierarchy of needs' theory imagines a pyramid bottom-heavy with the physiological needs: breathing, food, water, sleep and so on. Just above is the safety layer: economic security, property and freedom from threat. Self-actualisation—the opportunity for creative projects, moral judgment and personal expression—forms a needle-point summit, and the women of Eureka found themselves much lower down: floating somewhere between food and freedom.

It makes sense, then, that the women of Eureka did not begin, in Yalom's words, 'to create out of disaster an art of survival and transcendence' until much later in the nineteenth century, when permanent homes had been made, families reared and the institutions and social structures of colonial life firmly established.

By the thirtieth anniversary of Eureka, in 1884, some women made a conscious decision to cut a swathe through the masculinist rhetoric that filled the papers and strode the podiums. In July 1884, when Ballarat was in full swing planning for the biggest-yet Eureka commemoration and its associated civic boosterism, this appeared in the BALLARAT STAR:

> *The Eureka Stockade* (by a Lady who was there)
> Ballarat, the golden,
> Onward, onward go
> And may nothing ever
> Thy prosperity o'erthrow
> May all your sons and daughters
> A glorious future see
> And ne'er forget the old, old spot
> Where we fought for liberty.[8]

The Lady Who Was There wrapped her civic pride around a collectivist morality to which she clearly felt an abiding sense of kinship. The Eureka fight was her fight, and she publicly claimed a direct part in the spectacle of democratic progress.

On 28 November, another anonymous woman wrote a letter to the editor of the BALLARAT STAR with a less exalted but equally significant assertion. (The fact that these correspondents didn't commit their names to paper indicates both the strength of Victorian-era restrictions on women's public role and the intense local controversy that Eureka memory still evoked.) Identifying herself as *a Female of '54*, the woman disputed the memory of a previous correspondent—none other than Eureka hero, town father and Member of the Legislative Assembly J. B. Humffray—who declared, despite persistent rumours to the contrary, that no one had been shot by the authorities on that grim Monday when Charles Evans watched the funeral processions.

The woman wrote: *I for one was wounded on that night, and by the soldiers too.* A bullet fired from the Government Camp had grazed her head and *completely carried away hair and skin from the crown to the forehead*. She had waited thirty years to tell this story, and there was more:

> I felt stupid for a moment or so, I then caught my baby in my arms, and tried to run across the flat, having only my night-dress on. I tried to run with my child before me in a stooping manner, for the soldiers were still firing. My night-dress became entangled in my feet and I fell to the ground. At that moment, a cloud passed over the moon. It became dark instantly and the firing of the soldiers stopped.

This correspondent was in no doubt of the dramatic conclusion to her story: *Had the moon not clouded at the moment that it did, I should not have been here to tell you this.*[9]

Another woman was not so lucky. On the centenary of Eureka in 1954, thousands of people gathered in Ballarat on a weekend of torrential summer rain. Townsfolk who had braved the storm marched to City Hall, where a local actor, Mr Bernard D'Arcy, read 'the Lalor oration'. The ARGUS noted that one of the sodden attendees, Mr L. Moyle, had travelled from distant Upwey in order to honour his grandmother, Mrs Catherine Smith, who was shot in the side at Eureka and died three weeks later from her wounds.[10]

Was there more than one woman who died that brutal December day?

One thing is certain. The women of Eureka felt an unbreakable bond of belonging with an epic community and influential history, and they wanted their participation recognised and remembered.

*

Catherine Bentley, Anastasia Hayes, Margaret Johnston and the murdered wife of a Stockader are calling us across a century and a half. Forcing us to reimagine life on the Victorian goldfields and to interrogate the received wisdom of a masculinist Eureka. The material and documentary residue of their lives is everywhere: clinging to dusty files at the Public Record Office, trapped within the yellowing pages of newspapers, transmitted by generations of descendants. It demands that we ask new questions.

What if the hot-tempered, free-wheeling gold miners we learned about at school were actually husbands and fathers, brothers and sons? And what if their wives and families weren't far away across the watery wastes, but right by their sides? What if there were women and children inside the Eureka Stockade, defending their rights while defending themselves against a barrage of military-issue bullets?

And what if the soldiers who were firing upon civilians—including women—were themselves husbands and fathers, with wives and babies crouched not two miles away within a sand-bagged Government Camp?

How do the answers to these previously neglected questions change what over one hundred and fifty years of Eureka scholarship, commemoration and celebration have taught us about the so-called 'birthplace of Australian democracy'? Who, in fact, were the midwives to that precious delivery?

And if the birth attendants included ratbag women as well as reckless men, did their vision of democracy extend beyond the abolition of a poll tax to wider subversions of old-world tyranny? Did the unbiddable women of Ballarat claim a stake for themselves as members of the popular mass movement for political reform? Did they too want the vote? Tax relief? Justice?

This book asks these questions—and, like most works of history based on primary sources, the answers throw up many more conundrums besides. Why did Ballarat experience an explosive baby boom in the mid-1850s? Why was there a routinely observed spike in domestic violence on the Victorian goldfields, which garnered the ignominious laurel of 'the wife-bashing capital of the world'? Why were so many self-made women working alongside those famously entrepreneurial men? Why did Caroline Chisholm—the woman who once graced our five-dollar note—send a boatload of Jewish girls from London to Melbourne in 1853? And why were there so many men dressing up in female attire?

Then there are the elephant-in-the-room questions.

If there were women in and around the Eureka Stockade that brutal Sunday morning, what other outrages might have been perpetrated against them by the battle's frenzied victors?

And the big question, hanging over my checklist of challenges like a storm cloud: why haven't we gone down this road before? As students in an all-girls school, taught by a female history teacher, why didn't I or my classmates ever think behind the words in our textbooks? Why did not *one* of us ever think to ask, where are *we* in this story?

Like Henry Reynolds' ground-breaking *Why Weren't We Told?*, which shattered the myth that the colonisation of Australia was a benign and uncontested process, this is the first book to retell the Eureka story complete: as it was.

Women were there. They mined for gold and much else of economic value besides. They paid taxes. They fought for their rights. And they were killed in the crossfire of a nascent new world order.

PART 1

TRANSITIONS

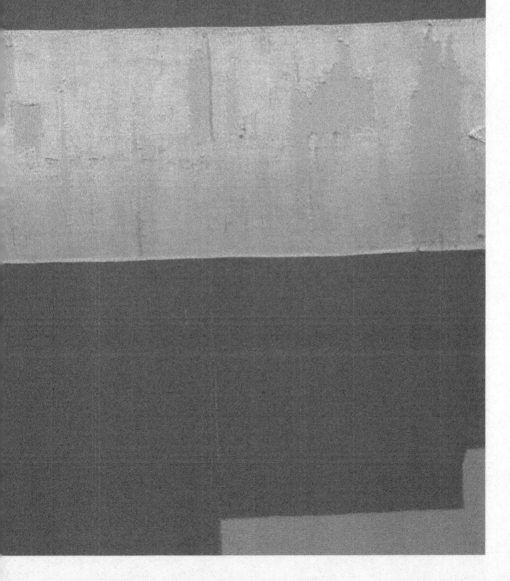

ONE

A VIRGIN COUNTRY

You could hear Ballarat before seeing it.

It took Charles Evans a full week to walk to the diggings. Leaving Melbourne on 9 November 1853, Charles, his brother George and travelling companion John Basson Humffray dragged a bullock dray up long steep hills and down treacherous ravines. The dray became mercilessly bogged on some stretches of the road; on others, it was all the Englishmen could do to keep the cart from overturning in potholes, sunk deep by the ambitions of thousands of hopeful immigrants. *The undertaking was far from pleasant*, wrote Charles in his diary. But there were compensations. Crossing a creek and preparing to camp for the night, Charles noted that:

> the scene from the hills was lovely beyond expression—the sun had set and a mellow twilight and the silvery rays of a full moon shed a soft light over the beautiful landscape...I can not remember any scene in my own country...to excel it—I was going to say, perhaps even to equal it.

A series of narrow ravines marked the long-awaited end to the ninety-mile journey from Melbourne. *We found to our alarm*, wrote Charles, *that we had one of the most dangerous and precipitous roads to descend which I ever saw attempted.* The final stretch of road ascended to a high tableland, and it was up this last incline that Charles Evans finally trudged, beckoned by the siren call of a scene he could hear but in no way envision. Atop the last gully, he was surrounded by eucalyptus and casuarina trees laced with wild cherry and honeysuckle. Another chronicler arriving in 1853, Thomas McCombie, recorded his first impressions of the Golden City:

> A confused sound like the noise of a mighty multitude broke upon our ears and a sudden turn of the road brought us in full view of Ballarat. I freely confess that no scene have I ever witnessed made so deep and lasting an impression on my mind.[1]

First, there was the barking of thousands of dogs chained outside tents and mine shafts, marking territory. Then there were the horse bells, the crack of whips, the shrill chorus of parrots and the mirth of the kookaburra. The *laughing jackass*, newcomers like young John Deegan called it—was the bird greeting or mocking them? There was nothing ambiguous about *the uproarious blasphemy of bullock drivers*, their oaths echoing across the basin. *Over all*, Deegan wrote years later, *that vague, indescribably murmurous sound, which seems to pervade the air where a crowd is in active motion* was his first impression, and it would never leave him. It was like a *genuine fairy tale*.

Charles Evans made his final approach in the morning, but the bewitching effect was particularly astonishing for those weary travellers who arrived at night. Henry Mundy, a twenty-year-old shepherd who had migrated from England with his parents in 1844, walked from Geelong to Ballarat to find his fortune. As Mundy later recalled, *the noises and scenes were indescribable.*[2] Standing on the ridge, he could see only the twinkle of a thousand campfires, like a mirror image of the night sky. Yet the noise was still bellowing. During the evening meal, *the talking and yelling was incessant*. Later, there was the ubiquitous firing of guns and pistols, a release of the day's pent-up emotion, and accompanying the firearms, the ever-present rolling choir of the dogs. After the ritual gunfire ceased, *accordions, concertinas, fiddles, flutes, clarionettes, cornets, bugles, all were set going each with his own tune*. The effect, said Mundy, was *deafening*.

Bug-eyed and prickle-eared, those who arrived during the prosperous months of late 1853 looked down upon a sprawling tent city. In the foreground lay the vast level diggings of East Ballarat. A creek wound through a valley of low, flat mounds and conical hills. Rising in the distance, Bakery Hill; and on the spur, the site of the original 1851 strikes, Golden Point. Perched on the plateau above the diggings was the Camp, home to *the aristocracy of the canvas city of Ballarat*. This is how Thomas McCombie described the officers of the Gold Fields Commission, police and assorted civil servants entrusted with administering the impetuous throng of gold seekers. Nestled beside the Camp on a neat grid of streets was an embryonic township of stores and homes, some confident enough to be constructed of timber.

Encircling the whole was a ring of green, the remnant fringe of a thick scrub that had once covered the entire basin. *The diggers*, observed English journalist William Howitt, *seem to have two especial propensities, those of firing guns and felling trees...Every tree is felled, every feature of Nature is annihilated.*[3] The majority of timber was used for tent poles and mine shaft supports, but in late 1853, Ballarat was also a ravenous camping ground, gorging on wood for heat, light and fuel. *The blue smoke of ten thousand campfires curled slowly upward*, observed John Deegan, *and blended with the haze of the summer evening*.

There were so many people going about their business, remarked Thomas McCombie from his ledge on the ravine, that *the ground actually appeared as if in motion.* From this distance, the people of Ballarat resembled a pulsating swarm. Henry Mundy too was struck by the *lively busy hive*, the throb of a community in constant motion, its kinetic charge heightened by the mad flapping of hundreds of flags. *Tents and stores in the flats, on the hills, in the gullies, everywhere one cast his eyes*, noted Mundy, *every store had two or three flags flying; flags of all nations but principally the Union Jack.* In the face of all the overwhelming novelty, a Ballarat greenhorn like Charles Evans could at least gravitate towards the familiarity of his national ensign.

It was like some grand dream...an entrance into fairy-land, wrote McCombie. He stood for a moment and watched the frenzied bustle. Listened to the din of thousands of cradles rocking gold out of clay on either side of a creek, startled as diggers popped in and out of holes like frantic moles. *It was a scene altogether so novel, unexpected and unlike the dull every-day world*, McCombie recorded. The view from the hill was so extraordinary that, once venturing into the basin—a taut geological drum vibrating with human enterprise—one could only anticipate *a new order of things.*

Indeed, gold rush immigrants like Dr Gillespie, who had arrived on the *Marco Polo* in the summer of 1853, would have expected nothing less. *A revolution commenced in Australia which has affected the whole civilised world*, he wrote in his role as editor of the ship's in-house journal, the MARCO POLO CHRONICLE.[4] What awaited the newcomer was no less than *a new chapter in the world's history.*

> Ages of tyrannous bungling and bad legislation had brought the continent of Europe to the verge

> of a terrific outburst. Every thinking mind looked anxiously onward to the next throb of outraged humanity. The unsolved problem of human happiness or misery found kindred echoes in the hearts of all men…The Australian goldfields have postponed the day of reckoning…
>
> It is a virgin country.

*

In August 1851 a blacksmith named Thomas Hiscock made a discovery in the rural backblocks of colonial Victoria that would change the lives of hundreds of thousands of the world's citizens, not least the hinterland's traditional owners, the Wathaurung people. Alert to the gold deposits recently unearthed in New South Wales, Hiscock went looking for payable gold in the hills of Buninyong, some 110 kilometres northwest of the port of Melbourne. And Eureka! There it was.[5] The alluvial leads were deep and seemingly endless, following the trails of ancient underground river systems—mute, furtive, auspicious. Victoria, only recently separated from its parent colony New South Wales, was suddenly the only place to be. Within days, news of the strike in the central highlands had spread to Melbourne and Geelong; within weeks, eager prospectors were making their way overland from all corners of Australia, from the garrison towns of Sydney and Hobart to the modest goldfields of New South Wales to the pastoral outstations of South Australia. Nobody wanted to miss the windfall; for Victorians and their neighbouring colonists, 1852 was the year when there was 'nothing but gold'.

Henry Mundy watched the sudden exodus to the new goldfields with a mixture of incredulity and excitement. *News of gold at Ballarat*, he later wrote in his reminiscences, *set the Geelong people and those of the surrounding district crazy.* Overnight, the workers of Australia had gone AWOL: farms, building sites, ships, police barracks, government offices, shearing sheds—all were deserted. Schools closed and postal services were disrupted as the public service staggered along on a skeleton staff. *The reports in the papers drove everyone mad*, explained Henry Mundy. *Every shepherd, hutkeeper, stockrider, every man, woman and child. All the world and his wife were looking for and examining quartz.* Journalist John Capper, embedded with the diggers, concurred that *society had become to a certain degree unhinged...the ordinary course of business deranged.*[6] Henry Mundy's own parents walked off their dairy and hiked to the diggings. It seemed a simple equation. *Who'll buy cows in these topsy-turvy times?* wondered Henry. Beef and mutton sold for nothing; digging equipment and transport cost a fortune.

The first on the ground were those closest to home. The township of Geelong became virtually divested of men overnight. Women banded together to draw water, chop wood, mind children and safeguard each other from the perceived dangers of being 'without natural protectors'. The famous 'grass widows' of the gold rush were left in the forsaken towns like the soapy ring around a bathtub. Sarah Watchwarn was one of a band of Melbourne mothers who *gathered at night in a central home, a faithful Collie dog being the only guard against blacks and outlaws*. Sarah had arrived with her husband Robert in 1849 and settled in the outlying seaside suburb of St Kilda. Sarah later recollected that on the news of gold, St Kilda found itself *devoid of menfolk.*[7]

But not all men wanted to leave their wives behind, and not all women would consent to be left. Anne Duke's parents,

James and Bridget Gaynor, had emigrated from Ireland to Australia in 1842, when Anne was four years old. The Gaynors moved from Melbourne, where they had witnessed the laying of the St Patrick's Cathedral foundation stone, to the mineral springs outstation of Mt Franklin, where they worked for the Aborigines Protection Society. They were well placed to be one of the first families to arrive on the goldfields. Anne was just sixteen years old when she married George Duke; the newlyweds went straight to Ballarat. So too did Jane Curnow when her life derailed. Cornish-born Jane immigrated to Adelaide with her husband William and their five children in 1848. Months after the Curnows' arrival, William died of sunstroke. In 1851, on news of the gold finds, fifty-two-year-old Jane trekked overland from Adelaide to Ballarat, where her oldest sons soon began providing handsomely for their widowed mother.

But the path to salvation in this *virgin country* was not as straightforward as it appeared. For one thing, the road was clearly signposted with the evidence of prior occupation. Every *kur* (tree), *yalluch* (river) *banyall* (valley), *woorabee* (fish) and *murrulbuk* (eagle)—every rock, plant and creature—was part of an integrated spiritual, political and economic system for the Wathaurung people, who had made the fertile hunting grounds of the Ballarat basin their ancestral home for tens of thousands of years. For them, the gold rush of the 1850s represented a second wave of dispossession; the first was the surge of pastoral expansion—often violent—into Victoria from the 1830s.

It is estimated that prior to European contact there were up to 3240 members of the twenty-five Wathaurung language groups. By 1861, 255 Aboriginal individuals remained in the Ballarat region. Among these survivors were 'Caroline', 'Queen Rose' and 'Old Lady'. What these three Indigenous women thought of the molten flow of white ghosts daily disgorging into their lands is not recorded. By the time Old Lady was buried according to customary rites in Ballarat in 1860, and Caroline and Rose died at Coranderrk Mission in the 1870s, the Aboriginal history of central Victoria was already considered a queer relic of an inevitably bygone era.[8]

Newcomers to the goldfields from 1851 often commented on the presence of Aboriginal family groups, their dwellings and activities. When eight-year-old Scottish lad William McLeish arrived at Ballarat in 1854 he was delighted to come upon some Aboriginal women hunting possums. *One was up a tree; another catching them as they dropped. She said something I did not understand*, William later wrote in his memoirs, *but gave me a kindly look that reassured me there was no danger. On looking up I saw another woman engaged in chopping a possum out of a branch.*[9] Many gold seekers were less sanguine about the Aboriginal presence than young William. Samuel Heape dismissed the Wathaurung as *poor helpless things*, while John James Bond was disgusted to hear *the howling of the lubras as their affectionate husbands drag them by their hair, dance on them or knock them on the head with their tomahawks.*[10] Few settlers and sojourners were prepared to concede, as C. Rudston Read did in his published account of his sojourn on the goldfields in 1853, *that white man has stepped in and taken possession of his land, nolens volens.* Early visitor W. B. Griffith recorded a glossary of Wathaurung language. He transcribed the most common nouns: words for sun, moon, water, fire, no, yes, old man, young girl. And he collected a handful of verbs: to walk, to run, to come, to go away, to rest, to know. And *pilmillally*. To steal.

Settlers might have been loath to acknowledge the Wathaurung as property owners, but many were aware of the extensive quarrying, and subsequent commercial transactions, being carried out by Victorian Aboriginal people prior to and after British colonisation. Gold was among the minerals extracted by Aboriginal people, as Captain Cadell, explorer of the Murray River, noted when in 1857 he registered a claim for the reward offered by the South Australian Government to discover a goldfield in that colony (in part to lure back its prodigal population). Cadell made his claim *conjointly with a black woman, or lubra, known as Betsy, who has resided at Cape Willoughby...for 30 years.*

> It appears that the latter recently informed the captain on being shown some nuggets from Ballarat, that she had seen plenty of 'dat yellow fellow tone'; and that when her son was a 'piccaninny' she, in company with another lubra, had beat out these stones, in her own words 'made 'em long'.[11]

Aboriginal people's superior knowledge of gold deposits, like their prior ownership of the land, was no secret.

Wathaurung people were initially bemused that white people would go to such frenzied lengths to take so much of the *yellow fellow tone* or *medicine earth* from the ground. After all, you couldn't eat it, cut with it or use it to hunt. But they were also wise to the opportunities for their own commercial and social advantage presented by the European lust for gold. To the Indigenous locals, gold only became a 'precious metal' when it was clear that the newcomers were so desperate to find it. Object exchange formed the basis of kinship relations, which were the backbone of Indigenous social, political and economic organisation. Wathaurung brought the white newcomers into their circle of influence, a fact demonstrated in the following exchange between two women whose paths had suddenly collided:

> My mother and wife and small boy that come out from England with us was standing at the tent one

> day all alone, no other tents near when they saw a mob of native Blacks and Lubrias [lubras] and a mob of dogs with them come across the gully so my wife said to Mother what ever will we do now so Mother said we must stand our ground and face them for there is no get away So up they come yabbering good day Missie. You my countary [country] woman now…the Blacks said You gotum needle missie you gotum thread you Gotum tea you Gotum sugar you Gotum Bacca [tobacco]. So Mother had to say yes to get rid of them and had to give them all they asked for to get rid of them. That was what was called the Bunyong [Buninyong] tribe and when they left they gave their usual salute. Goodbye missie and thankfull enough they was to see them disappear off into the bush.[12]

The white woman may have considered this would be the end of the affair, but to the Buninyong woman, initiating a new 'country woman' joined their families in a relationship of reciprocity and mutual obligation.

During the period of pastoral expansion, many *ngurungaeta* (elders) formed kinship alliances with squatters in order to gain permanent access to their ancient ceremonial and hunting grounds. With the sudden surge in population into their territory, Wathaurung quickly translated the principal of bilateral transactions from complex socio-political associations to a more purely economic function. One way to do this was for local Indigenous guides to point diggers in the direction of a new 'discovery' in exchange for money or goods.[13] Another was to supply the rapidly growing demand for *dallong*, heavy thick rugs or cloaks, made from *wollert* (possum), *goin* (kangaroo) or *tooan* (flying foxes). *Dallong* were prized by white fortune-seekers not only for warmth on frosty nights in a flimsy tent but also as a sartorial status symbol, due to the *majestic appearance* afforded to the wearer. A *dallong* could fetch as much as £5, and some indigenous makers sold enough to buy horses, as well as rice, sugar, bread, tobacco and alcohol. Other objects and consumables useful to the digging life, such as *biniae* (baskets) and *karrup* (spears) were also traded or sold. As historian Fred Cahir argues, Wathaurung were 'not outside the landscape in the development of modern economic institutions'; rather they successfully adapted to and exploited the commercial opportunities presented by the open, unregulated market of the early gold rush.[14] Ballarat's early residents soon came to rely on Indigenous knowledge and craftsmanship.

By Christmas 1852, a year after Thomas Hiscock's 'discovery', the luxuriant lands of the Wathaurung had been stripped of vegetation to become ravaged earth, honeycombed by holes and studded with calico tents. As Henry Mundy noted, the gullies were so crowded with people laying their small claims to river frontage that *there was not a shadow of a chance to edge in*.

But this was nothing compared to the avalanche of human endeavour that was about to descend.

*

It wasn't until early in 1853 that, as one early settler put it, *a huge tidal wave...the memorable rush from England and everywhere else* began in earnest.[15] If the first flood of inter-colonial gold seekers wasn't enough to change Victoria's fortunes—and alter things irrevocably for the land's first inhabitants—this inpouring of the world's schemers and dreamers was without doubt an immutable turning point.

News of Victoria's seemingly infinite supply of alluvial gold permeated the newspapers and market squares of London, Edinburgh, Dublin, Paris, Warsaw, Munich, Washington, Toronto and Shanghai. Entrepreneurial American George Francis Train was eager to volunteer as the Australian correspondent for the BOSTON POST. He wrote from New York on the eve of his journey in February 1853 that *the Australian fever seems to be raging here as well as Boston.* Twenty-four-year-old Train would later become a flamboyant presidential candidate, profligate financier and inveterate world traveller. But now, staring out over the wharf at Ellis Island, the dapper Bostonian was consumed by a singular mission: to capitalise on the mercantile potential of *a wonderful country where in a single hour the poorest beggar is worth his thousands, by a happy freak of fortune.* Train would not dig, but buy and sell.

By his side on the dock stood his new bride, Wilhelmina Wilkinson Davis. The couple were an odd match. Willie was ten years George's senior, and the daughter of Colonel Davis of Louisville, Kentucky—a slave owner and unlikely confidant of Abraham Lincoln. George was a voluble supporter of progressive causes, from Fenianism to women's suffrage; Willie was a southern belle. They were united by love and the grim memories they shared.

Willie and George were married in October 1851 and they had a new baby girl when they made the decision to reap the commercial rewards of what Willie termed *England's El Dorado.* But shortly before their departure tragedy struck, and it was with a grief-stricken heart that Willie hauled herself on board the *Batavia.*

Many and sad the changes through which I have passed, she wrote to a friend:

> our beautiful babe was too fragile to stem the current of life—and only a week before we were to sail for Australia we were called upon by God to 'render up to him the being that was his' and instead of a pleasant voyage with our little daughter to while away the weary hours we lied her in Mount—and turned our faces towards 'the Southern Cross' with hearts crushed almost to the earth.

For the Trains, a cruel twist of fate had turned a thrilling adventure into an odyssey of despair.[16]

If *the Australian fever* was raging across the globe, it seemed destined not to break. Reports of the continuing success of the early diggers confirmed that the gold in the hills of Victoria wasn't a mere flash in the pan. It would be worth it—well worth it, said correspondents like Train—to uproot families, dismantle homes, flee employers, abandon villages and join the mass movement of people to Australia. Gold was 'the lubricator of world trade during a period of great industrial and commercial expansion', as historian Weston Bate puts it.[17] As fiscal capital, gold was a pure currency, unsullied by the usual monetary trappings of borrowing, regulation and control. With gold, there was no middleman. The seemingly insatiable demand for the yellow mineral meant that prices remained high and stable. As social capital, gold symbolised the alchemic possibility of personal transformation. Anyone with the Midas touch was instantly master of his own domain.[18]

The viral spread of enthusiasm for gold's life-changing potential is most readily apparent in the population statistics for this era. In 1851, Victoria had a population of 77,000 people. That number skyrocketed to 237,000 by 1854 and 411,000 by 1857. By 1861, the population of Victoria was 540,000—half the total population of Australia. About a quarter of this meteoric multitude lived in Melbourne and the rest were scattered across the goldfields. In his official account for 1853, Victorian Government immigration agent Edward Bell reported that 77,734 unassisted immigrants had arrived that year: 33,032 from the United Kingdom, 35,834 from other colonies and 8868 from other countries. In addition to this, 14,578 people had arrived through the government assistance schemes that had been introduced in the late 1830s to rid Great Britain of its surplus labour and supply the colonies with an economically advantageous mix of settlers.[19]

A comparison with the population flows to the United States shows just how the tide of human ambition had turned towards Australia's shores. In 1845, 518,538 people emigrated from the United Kingdom to the United States. In the same year, only 830 found their way to Australia. By 1853, the number of people going to America had only increased by 21,183. Australia had received 87,424 new souls.

The glowing reports of the rivers of gold flowing through central Victoria couldn't have come at a better time for the world's fortune hunters: by 1853, the Californian gold rushes of '49 had buckled under the law of diminishing returns. The imagination of the world, ignited by the romance and adventure of gold seeking, now had somewhere else to blaze. In New York, according to George Francis Train, *Australia was the only topic on the street, on 'Change, at the club, or in the counting house.* The Victorian gold rush was nothing short of *a commercial revolution.* As Train breathlessly reported after his arrival in Victoria, nowhere else in the world did *such a go-aheadative* place exist.

*

What is most striking about the profile of gold rush immigrants is their youth. It was the world's young people who most readily grasped the opportunity to seek the wider horizons of Victoria's golden frontier. Going ahead—getting ahead—became the motto of the mid-1850s, as if the old world was a glutinous bog, dragging down aspirations and suffocating dreams. Now there was an empty land far from home where one could break free of the quicksand of economic stagnation and the mire of tradition. George Francis Train, at twenty-four, was typical. Not an upstart or an ingénue, but genuinely representative: young, newly married, starting out, getting ahead. He was also a man who would not be fazed by cataclysmic change. At the age of four, George had been orphaned when his parents and three sisters died in a yellow fever epidemic in New Orleans.

Charles Evans too felt the primal tug of new beginnings and was young enough to make the transition. Charles James Evans was born in 1827 in Ironbridge, Shropshire, a town that calls itself 'the Birthplace of the Industrial Revolution' and takes its name from the famous thirty-metre, cast-iron structure that was built across the River Severn in 1779. Charles was the second in his family of four boys: brother George Bassnet was senior by two years. Charles and George's father, Charles, worked as an excise officer, postmaster and printer. He was a learned man who raised his sons to value education and their Wesleyan faith.

But when Charles Sr died prematurely, the family's fortunes plunged. His widow Jane took her youngest sons and set up shop as a milliner in nearby Wellington. At fourteen, Charles was working as a farm labourer and sixteen-year-old George was down a coal mine. The Evans boys spent their adolescence in and out of the homes of relatives and friends: drapers, printers, stationers. On learning of the discovery of gold in Victoria, Charles and George were ready and willing to exchange a life of hard labour in the English midlands for the opportunity, as George recorded in his diary, to *make mother independent of others assistance.* The brothers were twenty-five and twenty-seven when they arrived in Melbourne on the *Mobile* in October 1852. Statistically, they were right on the money.

The Victorian Census of 1861 shows that approximately forty per cent of the population of Ballarat was between twenty and thirty-four years old. Another forty per cent were children aged under twenty. Visitors to Victoria often commented that there were no old people to be seen. Merchant Robert Caldwell noted that the gold rush cohort was one of *amazing energy, young, impulsive, generous and restless.* Leaving New York with his brother Davis in April 1853, twenty-two-year-old Dan Calwell assured his sisters back home in Ohio that they could not imagine *how our hearts bounded in anxious anticipation of soon overstepping the long limited boundaries.* Even in the Land of the Free the impatient Calwells felt the weight of family expectation and middle-class convention. *We are young*, reasoned Dan, *and must do something to give ourselves a start in the world. We have human hearts.*[20]

The restive hearts of the impetuous new arrivals remained buoyant in the giant open-air camp grounds of the early diggings. In 1851 there were 3851 births recorded and 2724 marriages officiated in Victoria. By 1855 these figures had more than trebled to 12,626 and 7816 respectively. In Ballarat, there were five babies born in 1851. In 1857 there were 1665 recorded births. Approximately one-fifth of the babies born in Ballarat in 1854 were ex-nuptial.[21] 'Boundary riders of modernity' is how historian David Goodman has characterised the Victorian gold diggers, a neat encapsulation of the mobility, vigour, liberalism and confidence of a generation of rule-breakers. For them, no barricade was too solid to penetrate.

*

Thomas and Frances Pierson, late of the Pennsylvania Olive Lodge, were, at thirty-nine and thirty-two years of age, swimming against the demographic tide. But surely they were not too old for an adventure. In fact, Thomas would write in his diary, *something novel* was just what they needed. In any case, the Piersons had always been a bit peculiar: only one child, fifteen-year-old Mason. And Frances with her photographic equipment and talk of setting up a daguerreotype studio in Victoria. On 30 September 1852, the 480-tonne clipper *Ascutna* left Staten Island *to shouts of hurahs, cheers, waveing handkerchiefs, hats tc tc fireing of pistols and farewell music.* With little else but news of Australia in the American papers for months now, Frances and Thomas were lucky to get a berth. One hundred and seventy other passengers and a mountain of merchandise joined the Piersons on the *Ascutna*.[22]

But as Thomas Pierson noted, even on the ships departing from New York, the passengers were not all of one hue. *Nearly every nation of the world is represented on our ship*, wrote Thomas.

One way or another, the racially and ethnically diverse bunch had all come for one thing. *We are beginning to see the elephant*, reported Pierson with pride, as land became a distant vision and the chill of a New York fall gave way to the untimely heat of the Caribbean. Frances and Thomas understood now why, in the Californian gold rush, it was said that prospectors went to 'see the elephant'. In the early nineteenth century, the arrival of a travelling circus in a small American town was a singular occasion. Folks would come from all parts to sample the bizarre attractions: wild beasts from Africa, fabled creatures like the Wolf Boy and other sideshow freaks. The major drawcard at these carnivals was the elephant: an animal larger than any native to North America.

By the 1830s, to 'see the elephant' had come to mean 'to experience all that there is to see, all that can be presumed, known and endured'. It spoke of deprivations, but also rewards. 'Did you see the elephant?' parents would ask their prodigal son. Did you go where you set out to go? Did you see what you set out to see? In time, the catchphrase acquired a military usage, suggesting a loss of innocence with first combat: a ritual transition from naivety to experience.

In the mid-nineteenth century—a time before passports, credit cards and rigorous records—innocence came in many guises. It could be refabricated too. Many of the women who came to Victoria had already lived a thousand colourful, capricious lives.

For Sarah Hanmer, the gold rush offered the chance to move back the hands of time. Born into a Protestant Scots–Irish farming family in County Down, Ireland, twenty-three-year-old Sarah Anne McCullough married Henry Augustus Leicester Hanmer at St James, Clerkenwell in 1844. Henry Hanmer was a widowed surgeon; Sarah was a single mother. Four years earlier, her affair with a London accountant, Frederick Ford, had produced a child but no ring. It's unclear how her marriage to Henry concluded, but by 1850, Sarah was living in Albany, New York, and possibly working as an actress. She appears to have gone to America without her daughter Julia, who perhaps lived with Sarah's brother William McCullough. Sarah may also have worked for a time at the Adelphi Theatre in San Francisco, which was located near to Rowe's Circus. She later returned to London, booked a passage on the *Lady Flora* for herself, Julia and William, and sailed for Victoria, arriving in August 1853.

John James Bond, a fellow passenger on the *Lady Flora*, noted in his ship journal that the voyage had been *discomfort from beginning to end.* There was no fresh meat, the coffee was burnt, the sea biscuits musty and all passengers staggered out at Port Phillip *three parts starved. We have been taken in*, Bond lamented.

But thirty-two-year-old Sarah Hanmer had her own conjuring trick up her sleeve. As if by magic, she took six years off her age, reporting to the immigration agent that she was twenty-six. Julia was twelve. Nobody stopped to do the maths. Mrs Leicester Hanmer, acclaimed London actress, had arrived, and her adopted home of Ballarat would soon know all about it.

Clara Du Val was another woman who could make husbands and birthdays disappear. Irish-born Clara Lodge was a tearaway from an early age. Popular legend (a story that Clara herself might have propagated) has it that Clara's ambitious father held a ball in her honour when his daughter turned seventeen, at which Clara appeared in a belt studded with seventeen sovereigns to wear around her seventeen-inch waist. After the ball, the story goes, Clara was presented to Queen Victoria but instead of moving smoothly into a good marriage, she eloped with French artist Claude Du Val. Together the love-struck couple sailed in 1847 for Victoria where, Claude having died, the grieving widow du Val provided for herself as an actress. It was a tale that no doubt played well when Clara began treading the boards in Ballarat's theatres. Shipping records reveal, however, that Clara arrived in Victoria on the *Marco Polo* in May 1853. She gave her age as twenty; she was in fact thirty-four. There is no evidence of a Claude Du Val arriving or dying in Australia. In fact, Clara had eloped in 1830 with her dancing teacher, George William Du Val, the brother of renowned portrait painter Charles Allen Du Val. Clara and George ran into trouble with the law in the Isle of Man and later Liverpool, where George was arrested as part of a gang involved in a botched kidnap. Moreover, when Clara sailed to Victoria, she brought two of her three children with her: nine year-old Oliver and one-year-old Francis. Francis's twin sister, Clara, was left in Ireland. Whether Clara Du Val had ever met Queen Victoria or not, she had certainly seen the elephant.

Margaret Brown Howden was one of perhaps few real innocents going abroad. As she stood on the wharf at Birkenhead in May 1854, twenty-three-year-old Maggie was thinking of one thing only: her fiancé, *dear Jamie*. The farewell dinners in her native Scotland, the last calls, the settling of accounts, the shopping and packing and getting of gifts, being driven to the station by tearful relations—these things were all behind her now. Maggie was sad, but stoic: *we cannot know what changes may take place*, she wrote in her diary, [but] *never shall I forget my dear home.* Margaret was reared among the god-fearing gentility of the Scottish borders, the third daughter of Francis and Sophia Howden. There is a touch of exotica about her belied by her sheltered upbringing: Margaret's mother was born on the Prince of Wales Islands, later to become Penang, to a Chinese mother, Ennui, and a Scottish planter father, David Brown. But this was Maggie's first time at sea. *Oh dear!* she wrote when the sails had been hoisted, the vessel was rolling and there was no turning back. *I wish things would go on well to take me to my Jamie.*

James Johnston, older brother of a dear friend, was waiting for Margaret Howden in Melbourne. James Johnston, Assistant Gold Commissioner at Ballarat: appointed in November 1853 with a salary of £400. James Johnston, nephew of George Johnston, famous in Australia for helping to arrest and depose Governor Bligh. Assistant Resident Commissioner James Johnston. Jamie. *My Jamie.*

*

By the time Charles Evans began his final descent into Ballarat on 16 November 1853, he had been in Victoria for just over a year. On his arrival at the ridge overlooking the diggings, after his week-long walk, he had but one shilling to his name. The great tent he and his brother George had purchased to start an auction house was safely loaded on the bullock dray, along with a few items to start knocking down. The night before, he and his companions had camped in a swamp, sharing a damper for their supper. *Everything was damp*, Charles wrote in his diary, *considerably damp—the ground, our beds, our bodies and our spirits.*

He and George had started many enterprises over the past twelve months: a confectioner's store, a coffee-roasting business, pie making, boarding house keeping, carting. All had failed to produce more than a hard day's work. He had been to the Ovens diggings and come back starving. He had seen men grow fat and others go mad. He should have known a thing or two about how this colony could turn pumpkins into carriages and just as readily change them back again. But still, when he at last walked onto the Ballarat digging, Charles was nothing short of flabbergasted.

We were astonished, wrote Charles, *to see the immense number of stores—every fourth or fifth tent was either a store or a refreshment tent.* He couldn't fathom how they all made a living until *the riddle was in a great measure solved... nearly all sold grog.* This was only the first revelation. *Contrary to our expectations*, Charles lamented, *there were several auctioneers carrying on business.* How would they ever sell their wares, and thus get a meal that was more sufficient than damper and tea? The Evans brothers took a punt. Asking some miners *as to the probable course of the diggings for the ensuing summer*, they chose a locality with very few tents; a quiet spot near the bridge on Commissioner's Flat. If the underground rivers of gold flowed their way, Charles reasoned, *it will soon be the busiest quarter on the diggings.*

Eugene von Guérard's famous painting *Old Ballarat as it was in the summer of 1853–54* hangs in pride of place at the Art Gallery of Ballarat. Austrian-born von Guérard painted his masterpiece in 1884 or '85, some thirty years after the time he spent living on Golden Point in Ballarat. His memory was surely encrusted with a sugar coating of nostalgia or, along with his own yellowing notes and sketches, he had a copy of James Bonwick's AUSTRALIAN GOLD DIGGER'S MONTHLY MAGAZINE AND COLONIAL FAMILY VISITOR at hand. Von Guérard, with his scene of verdant hills and corpulent sheep, draws on the same ideological palette as Bonwick, who, in January 1853 penned a profile of a *typical diggings home in the Ballarat valley.*

> Amongst the deep shade of the towering Eucalypts… [reside] the rosy cheeks of the little one, the contented smile of the matrons of the camp…the fret and fever of life have little place in the quietude and salubrity of this Diggings station…[there are] fuel and water for fetching, with no fear of a rent collector…privacy and security.

Bonwick could see nothing but *associations of the picturesque and beautiful.* Von Guérard's view of Golden Point depicts the same pastoral idyll: there are flocks of sheep being steered by a lone rustic, a scattering of whitewashed tents, a humble matron pegging out the wash, a solitary puff of smoke from a chimney. Green is the dominant tone; tranquillity is the message. The composition bears no resemblance to the many descriptions of Ballarat on the brink of that crucial moment between 1853 and 1854—when Charles Evans walked into Ballarat—or indeed to the many doleful sketches that von Guérard completed when he actually lived there. Von Guérard's painting is remarkable for its lyricism and elegance, but as history it's a sham.

Close up, newcomers who had heard Ballarat before they saw it were more shocked than awed. Diarists and letter-writers recorded their first impressions of the sheer ugliness of the diggings. To Mrs Elizabeth Massey, the goldfields had the appearance of *one vast cemetery with fresh made graves.*[23] Uncovered mine shafts pock-marked the surface, with mounds of earth heaped beside. By the beginning of 1854, Golden Point was, in the words of William Westgarth, *an upturned, unsightly mass.* There was not a tree or blade of grass to be seen. John James Bond travelled to the diggings after disembarking from the three-parts-starved *Lady Flora* in August 1853. *[Ballarat] is an immense circular plain of mixed yellow and red earth*, he recorded, *every bit had been turned topsy-turvy.* Alexander Dick, a Glaswegian teetotaller, was most struck by the Flat, that expanse of Ballarat East and its hub, the Eureka Lead. The Flat was covered with tents and 'flies' over mine shafts. Looked at from Golden Point or Black Hill *the Flat was a perfect sea of calico and canvas.*[24] This description is more benign than most, but all emphasise the conquest of culture over nature, the bulldozer urgency of conquest.

The turnover from ancestral homeland to pastoral runs had happened quickly, but the transformation of Ballarat from sheep station to thriving frontier town struck like lightning. In October

1851, only a few months after the discovery of gold, one visitor described Ballarat as being like the *encampment of an army.* That is to say, it was *orderly* and *peaceable*, a neatly contained collection of simple tents with diggers methodically working the gully creeks.[25] Before long, it was a riotous jumble of holes and mullock heaps.

One of the primary reasons for the sheer visual transformation of Ballarat by late 1853 was a shift in mining technology. In Ballarat, the shallow alluvial gold was quickly exhausted. But riches were still to be found below the deep basalt veins that followed ancient riverbeds under the surface. In fact, these deep lead deposits were larger and richer than ever found anywhere else in the world, but technological innovation was required to extract the exceptional nuggets. Deep sinking was the answer: a process by which 'a forest was taken under ground', as Weston Bate evocatively puts it. The subterranean shafts needed to be shored up, which meant great investments of time and labour, particularly to cut the timber slabbing for shaft supports. But the rewards could be magnificent. At some leads, an average of £2000 per claim was achieved for a period of several weeks running in 1853, and this was enough to entice punters to stick with the gamble of hand-digging shafts up to 160 feet deep for at least a year to come. But the whole pastime was costly in every respect, not least to the physical environment.[26]

Only at night, under the cover of darkness and after the ceremonial gunshot, did the pulse of activity gradually subside. A *vast city hushed in the arms of night*, the poetically inclined bureaucrat William Westgarth wrote from his vantage point at Bath's Hotel on the township hill. Especially if it was a Sunday night, for on the Sabbath, a truce was called with the demonic striving.

Sunday in Ballarat was washing day. *Scores of men could be seen in front of their tents with tin dish or bucket washing their weekly shirt and flannel*, recalled Henry Mundy. As a rule Sunday mornings were bathed in a reverential quiet, the time, noted James Bonwick, *consecrated to cookery*. A roast joint or plum pudding might be enjoyed, damper almost certainly baked. *It is here that the skill and economy of a woman are seen to advantage in a tent*, wrote Bonwick.

And by the summer of 1853, women were thick on the ground. *I did not fail to observe that the fair sex had ventured now on a large scale*, wrote Italian miner Raffaello Carboni on his second trip to Ballarat, at Easter 1854. On Sundays, some women put on their finest shawls to promenade around town or prepared picnics to enjoy in the bush. In the afternoon, stump preachers would be out, walloping bibles and singing hymns. The tents that accommodated the Catholic and Wesleyan congregations were full, the only Christian denominations to gain a toehold by 1854. Jews mustered a healthy quorum at the Clarendon Hotel for their Friday night Shabbat.

Who ever dreams in England that there is even the semblance of religion in the gold fields? asked Mrs Massey, *and yet amongst rough men, supposed to be the very scum of the earth, we found the Sunday more rigidly kept than in many far more civilised places.* The Sabbath: a day of rest, a cessation of industry, a time to reflect on the spiritual and indulge the domestic. Maybe von Guérard had a Sunday in mind when he immortalised the calm and stillness of a Ballarat summer.

Von Guérard's painting is accurate in at least one respect. Rising out of the ground like a flare was a remarkable circular tent, unlike any other structure on the diggings. This was Jones' Circus.[27] If weary travellers had left loved ones, crossed stormy seas and walked miles along a crooked road, surely here, finally, they would see the elephant. The Circus was both truth and metaphor. A fair dinkum illusion. For a shilling, you could be serenaded by a band of blackface minstrels, smudging their lily-white English skin with burnt cork. You could meet Signora Zephyrina, a Hobart girl, daughter of a housekeeper, who chose *the free and easy vagabonding life [of] bohemia*. (She borrowed her exotic name from a character out of a Madame de Staël novel.) You could see waxworks, wild beast shows, marionettes and dancing boys. You could watch a lion be tamed. You could ask Archie the Clown what it was like to be in Ballarat in the summer of 1853. He'd tell you it was a blast.

> The tents, theatres, bowling alleys, dancing saloons and hotels, all filled with a noisy, rough, restless crowd, feverish with the excitement of the great battle with the earth for her treasures, and the feeling that something was going to happen. There was a general presentiment of impending danger. It was, to use a hackneyed simile, as if we were sleeping over a volcano that we knew must, sooner or later, burst forth.[28]

In Ballarat, it was all *spangles and sawdust*, old circus terms for good business and bad. On any given day, life could go either way.

TWO

DELIVERANCE

It had not been a good year for the Nolan family of Monivea County, Galway. In 1846, the odds were stacked against carpenter Patrick Nolan and his wife, Margaret, a devout breeder of a dozen steel-eyed babes. First an old woman warned them the Nolan farm was built on a fairy path, then the cow died; by August, five-year-old James had suffered the same cruel fate. But still the pins kept falling. By 1849 eldest son Martin had taken the Queen's shilling and although the British army kept him in hot meals, he couldn't stomach his own rising gall. Martin soon deserted and fled back to the family farm, then gave himself up, fearing the repercussions if he were found. He was sent to India as penance.

These were the hungry years, the years of the Great Famine, and the Nolan family seemed as vulnerable to affliction as the mealy potatoes rotting in the ground. By 1851, nineteen-year-old Michael was on the run from the law for a different reason: he had refused to pay the family's English landlord his crushing rent on the farm. In a frank discussion, the landlord's agent had wound up with the prongs of Michael's pitchfork lodged in his backside. Aided and abetted by twenty-year-old sister Bridget, eldest of the remaining Nolan clan, Michael weighed up his chances with the courts and took to the road.

That's how, on 26 January 1852, Bridget and Michael Nolan found themselves standing on the docks at Birkenhead, about to board a ship bound for Geelong. On board the *Mangerton*, they met twenty-two-year-old Thomas Hynes, a farmer from County Clare, and thirty-year-old Patrick Gittins, a blacksmith and pike maker in his native Kilkenny. Less than two years later—on a honeycombed patch of dirt so remote it now seemed mythic—Bridget, Thomas and Patrick would forge a bond in blood.[1]

*

To comprehend what happened in Ballarat in the explosive year of 1854, we must first understand the tumult going on across the seas in the decade before that. It wasn't simply greed or poverty that pulled so many people away from the centres of their known universe—whether Pennsylvania or Paris, Limerick or London—and thrust them into uncharted waters. There were many reasons to join the exodus to the New El Dorado, as Victoria soon became known.

The 1840s had been a decade of extreme economic, political and social turmoil in Europe. In Ireland from 1845 to 1852 over a million people died in *an Gorta Mór* (the Great Hunger). At least another million refugees fled, sparking an unprecedented mass migration to the New World. The famine had wreaked most of its havoc on Ireland, but the potato blight that triggered the catastrophe also caused crop devastation throughout Europe. A subsistence crisis drove peasants and the urban working poor to join the rising tide of middle-class political reform across Britain and Europe.

Campaigns for a variety of political reform measures culminated in 1848, which has been called the Year of Revolution or the Springtime of the Peoples. Motivated by 'a chronic state of dissatisfaction', as British historian Jonathan Sperber has termed it, popular mass uprisings swept through France, Germany, Britain and Russia, ousting monarchs and fracturing the customary accord between church and state. In Paris, the overthrow of Louis-Philippe ushered in the Second Republic. In Munich, revolutionary uprising culminated in the storming of the Zeughaus in March 1849, forcing the abdication of Ludwig I. Chartism, an English mass movement for social and political reform that demanded a widening of the franchise to include working people, saw thousands take to the streets. In July 1848, just five months after Louis-Philippe had been removed from the French throne, the British Government so feared a popular uprising from Chartist demonstrators—six million of whom had recently signed a petition—that Queen Victoria was evacuated to the Isle of Wight.

The extent of the crisis was summed up by an editorial in the London TIMES on 23 October 1851: *England is threatened by two revolutions, the one political, the other social. The socialist, the extreme radical, are your true political bloomers.* Just two months after gold was found beneath the pastoral runs of central Victoria, the British press was talking up the prospect of mass civic upheaval. But despite the widespread nature of radical discontent, the victories of 1848 were mostly short lived; the forces of conservatism successfully restored the political status quo.

Yet the TIMES editor was expressing another topical anxiety in his carefully chosen bloomer metaphor. 1848 was also the year that a group of middle-class women, headed by an indefatigable mother of six named Elizabeth Cady Stanton, met in Seneca Falls, New York to address the problem of women's social and political oppression. Together these 'doctors' wives'—many of whom had cut their political teeth in the abolitionist movement, fighting to end slavery—penned the Declaration of Rights and Sentiments, based on the American Declaration of Independence.

First and foremost, the document claimed the right of women to have a say in determining the laws that governed them. The women's suffrage movement was born. (Early Chartists in England also endorsed equal voting rights for men and women in their push for universal electoral representation. By the late 1840s, however, leaders had lowered the bar in favour of the more politically expedient goal of manhood suffrage.[2])

At the same time, women's rights advocates on both sides of the Atlantic began a campaign of dress reform, advocating that political freedom should be expressed by emancipation from the sartorial constraints of corsets and crinolines, fashion items that not only distorted women's bodies but also ruined their health. A Seneca Falls woman devised a new 'rational dress' outfit, comprising a long tunic worn over billowing pants that were gathered at the ankle. The outfit became known as the Bloomer costume, after editor Amelia Bloomer, who publicised the costume in her magazine, THE LILY. Bloomers became an international smash, with women's rights advocates parading the costume in lecture tours across American and England. One such activist was English-born, French-educated, independently minded Caroline Dexter. Dexter became known as London's 'apostle of Bloomerism' when she began lecturing to packed audiences in 1851.

Just at the moment the TIMES editor summed up the dual crisis facing England, news of the riches at Ballarat began to trickle into the press. In the eyes of many, Victoria would provide a place of social and political renewal where the stains of old-world enmity could be washed away. In 1852 Caroline Dexter's idealist husband, William, left for the goldfields and two years later, Caroline too migrated permanently to Victoria.

For reform activists like the Dexters, Victoria was a political tabula rasa on which they might inscribe fresh ideas for the future, free from institutional and ideological impediments to progress.[3] For renegades like Bridget and Michael Nolan, here now was the chance for a clean start, free from economic hardship and ethnic prejudice. By the time newspapers in London and New York began carrying daily reports of the material riches to be found in Victoria, a restless generation of young men and women was united by one great notion: liberty.

In London, the headquarters of radical activism was Clerkenwell. It was at St James Church in Clerkenwell, hotbed of Chartist unrest, that a Hampshire poet named Ellen Warboy chose to marry her beloved, Frederick Young, a chemist from Shoreditch, in 1837. In the same church, Sarah Anne McCullough married Henry Augustus Leicester Hanmer in 1844, their marriage witnessed by Sarah's four-year-old daughter, Julia. These urban professionals and artists—with the exception of Henry, parted from the newly respectable Mrs Sarah Hanmer—would be in Ballarat by the beginning of 1854. A politically minded young Cornish man named Stephen Cuming and his wife, Jane, would join the caravan of progressive nonconformists. On 1 July 1848, the Cumings had christened their first daughter Martineau, after the liberal poet, writer and women's rights campaigner, Harriet Martineau. All of these women—Ellen Young, Sarah Hanmer and Jane Cuming—would play a vital role in the political future of their adopted homeland.

It was not only the English middle class who were dissatisfied with their lot. Anastasia Hayes (née Butler), who travelled to Victoria on the same ship as Charles Evans, was a devout Catholic from Kilkenny who, despite being educated and capable of holding her own against institutional oppression, was tired of treading water. At the age of thirty-four, she and her husband Timothy—a Wexford-born engineer and oil merchant who had been prominent in the Young Ireland movement—bundled up their five children and left for Victoria. The Irish dissidents had already fled their homeland as early as 1847; two of their children were baptised in Staffordshire, England. From her position of maternal and cultural authority within the Catholic community in Ballarat, Anastasia would become critical to the events at Ballarat.

Catherine Sherwin was another Irish lass on the move, but her momentum drew on a different sense of exclusion. Catherine was born in 1831 in County Sligo, Ireland. Sligo is famed for its mountainous Atlantic coastline, its favourite son W.B. Yeats and its massive rates of emigration; almost half of the County's population sailed from its renowned port between 1850 and the end of the nineteenth century. The Sherwin family was among the one per cent of Sligo's Protestant population. Literate and ambitious, Catherine would soon discover that, as the prosperous Mrs Catherine Bentley, it was not so easy to leave her deeply ingrained outlier status behind.

English teacher and historian James Bonwick, who arrived in Australia in 1841, recognised that the disaffected and dispossessed of Europe would not readily check their grievances at the door:

> Amongst the immigrants who were day after day pouring in from every quarter, there was no doubt many a chartist, many a democrat, escaped from the thralldom of aristocratic England, many a refugee and exile from the continent of Europe, who came in search not only of gold but of a refuge from the soul-and-body-grinding despotism of Europe.

The revolutions ripping at the fabric of Europe were not seamlessly elided in Victoria; rather, the ideas, aspirations and language of the old world seeped into the porous new cultural and political landscape. Seen from this angle, the Victorian gold rush doesn't represent a new dawn in Australia's young history so much as the long dusk of Europe's age of revolutions. Travelling south, the gold rush immigrants were sailing neither into nor away from the sunset. It would be their fate to be forever caught between old world antagonisms and new world expectations.

*

It was impossible not to have great expectations. The pull towards Victoria was overwhelming, the allure fervently communicated by the first arrivals of late 1851 and early 1852. These men and women sent heartfelt letters home to family members, wrote correspondents' reports for newspapers and published literary accounts of their travels. The WILTS AND GLOUCESTERSHIRE STANDARD regularly published letters from successful emigrants. One 'Elizabeth' had written to her mother: *I hope that all my brothers and sisters that are eligible for a free passage will apply immediately and be sure to apply as farm servants or dairymaids and they will be certain of a free passage to this our adopted country, the land of plenty.*[4]

The 'land of plenty' allegory is a common theme in these early reports. Victoria was *the Promised Land* and Ballarat, a Christian emigration society confidently announced in its promotional literature, *is the Ararat on which the ark of Victoria rested, and saved the colony.* Seventeen-year-old Scotsman Alexander Dick sought *a new, free and better life* and *deliverance from what I regarded as servile bondage.* Fanny Davis, an assisted immigrant from England, thought that as her ship prepared to depart: *We must have looked very much like the Children of Israel going out of Egypt.*[5]

Indeed, Fanny's reference to Exodus 3:1—God's decree to Moses to lead his people away out of affliction into the land *flowing with milk and honey*—explains a great deal about the aspirations of those immigrants in flight. The impending journey to Victoria was not simply about the lust for gold. The gold seekers were not sinners, but innocents abroad. Dreamers. Visionaries. Refugees. Like Alexander Dick, they sought deliverance.

The story of Victoria's gold dovetailed perfectly with the global liberation narrative that expressed the spirit of the times. If repression was the lock, gold was the key.

The picture painted of Victoria worldwide was as a land paved with gold, a yellow brick road to unlimited opportunity. Newspapers around the globe printed endless statements of gold returns, enumerating the breathtaking value of the gold in private hands, Melbourne banks and diggers' pockets. On 8 April 1852, the London TIMES reported the *astonishing results* achieved over the past three months: £730,242 worth of gold *and where it is to end no human being can guess. The field is reported to be illimitable.* This correspondent pressed readers to hurry to the land where *boundless plenty smiles side by side with countless wealth.* Just three months later, the total value of gold thus far found in Victoria was £1,647,810.

The promise of instant wealth is perennially attractive—as the vice-like grip of poker machines and lotteries on the pockets of today's punters still demonstrates—but how much more compelling when there are eye-witnesses to the Midas miracle:

> [Gold] lies on the surface and after a shower of rain, you may see it with the naked eye, and a child can put

> in a spade, and dig that with his little hands in one minute, which many of you in England wear out eyes and heart in getting.

That's how MURRAY'S GUIDE TO THE GOLD DIGGINGS, published in London in 1852, depicted the situation on the ground. Gold digging was simply child's play.

MURRAY'S GUIDE drew on a series of anecdotes to present a *true account* for prospective diggers. Like other guidebooks that promoted the attractions of the goldfields—the healthy air, beautiful scenery and the *glow of animal enjoyment peculiar to bush life*—MURRAY'S particularly encouraged *fathers of large families* to come, sowing the seed of aspiration in those husbands who, perhaps, had failed to bring home sufficient bacon in Manchester, Edinburgh or Cardiff. It was a well-publicised image: the victorious father arriving back in the mother country to a grateful wife and adoring children waiting patiently by the hearth.

According to John Capper, a man's children were, in England, *dead weights around his progress*, but a *true blessing* in Australia. Digger-turned-merchant Robert Caldwell agreed. *I enjoy the satisfaction of providing well for my family through my own exertions*, he wrote in his reminiscences, *a satisfaction I could never have felt in England.*

By late 1854, the time young William McLeish's family made the decision to try their luck in Victoria, British households were also suffering the material and psychological effects of the Crimean War. *Many of the working class found it a hard matter to obtain regular employment*, recalled William. Though the departing McLeish family was *surrounded by weeping friends who all believed they were bidding us a final good-bye, which indeed they were*, the promised restoration of masculine pride through honest toil beckoned like the Pied Piper.

Notions of 'manliness' were linked to another important incentive to gold seeking: independence. In mid-nineteenth-century Britain, manliness was a racialised concept imbued with assumptions about the civility of true British manhood, as against the brute stupidity or innate slovenliness of lesser beings.[6] For the labouring class, manliness was predicated on improving one's situation in life, and rested largely on the ability to become self-employed, and eventually self-made.

It is thus not surprising that the guarantee of autonomy resonates persistently in the letters of new immigrants to the family and neighbours they'd left behind. James Green conveyed this sentiment in a note to his sister, written on 24 July 1853, that answered her enquiry as to whether their brother George should also 'come out'. *Come here by all means*, entreated James; *a few years here and he would be an independent man, he is very simple if he stops at home digging potatoes when he might come here and dig gold.*

Robert Caldwell similarly emphasised the *perfect freedom and thorough independence* of a gold digger's life, particularly for the *youth of energy, adventure and courage.* Samuel Mossman evoked the image of a poor labourer and his family huddled around the *embers of a miserable fire*, surviving a northern winter, unable to improve his living conditions. In Australia, by contrast, there was *no snow and fuel was cheap and abundant. It's the poor man's country*, Mossman declared, *what independence would surround them! In Australia want and penury is unknown, daylight and darkness, heat and cold, are more equally distributed throughout the seasons.* Mossman steered clear of biblical allusion but referenced other mythological tales. Many Britons came to Australia as sickly and downcast, he argued, but under the bright southern sun and wholesome air the weak man rallied. With *health and strength before him, like a young Hercules, he commences the world anew.*

Images of heroic self-sufficiency reinforced the image of boundless personal space, both physical and psychic, to be found in Victoria. *I don't think I could breathe there now*, said one Englishman of his motherland, *it's always—you must do this, or you must not do that...it would fairly drive me mad.*[7]

The abolitionist movement had successfully campaigned to end slavery in the British Empire in 1833. Now a new generation was proclaiming that this was a time for white men to break free of their bonds, whether to exploitative employers, irksome family or a tyrannical state. *The land they are going to is neither formal nor exclusive*, wrote one booster, *working men need no introduction beyond industry and aptitude. Employers take no account of pedigree.*

For a man beaten down by generations of class consciousness, this chance to stand tall and proud, regardless of the cut of his cloth, seemed nothing short of redemptive. *Australia may well be considered the Paradise of Working Men*, struggling fathers and superfluous sons were told. *The Sweat of the brow—the time-worn badge of labour—bears with it no stamp of servitude, and to the patient worker success is no problem. For all willing hands there is labour, and for all labour there is liberal reward.*[8]

*

Historian David Goodman, in his classic comparative study of gold digging in Victoria and California, has persuasively elucidated what he calls the 'colonial narrative'—the story that contemporaries told about the effects of gold on society. One of the most significant elements of this story, Goodman argues, was 'the depiction of the human relationship to the environment as one of struggle and conquest, a relationship which allowed scope for masculine heroism'. Goodman understands the colonial narrative as 'a male story' because men's triumph over their circumstances—material and social—tapped into an atavistic desire for mastery.

But could this idea have appeal for women also? Did it have a *particular* appeal? This letter from Lucy Hart, written to her mother in England in May 1852, illustrates that autonomy was highly prized by women, too.

> I would not come back to England again unless I had enough to keep me without work on no account. Neither would my husband. I am speaking now the very sentiments of our hearts, but people must be saving, industrious and persevering. We have deprived ourselves of many things we might have had, but what was it for? All to try to do something for ourselves so that my husband should not always work under a *Master*, and happy I am to inform you that we have gained that point, he is now his own master.

Lucy's letter, like most personal correspondence and ship journals, would have been read out aloud at gatherings and passed around among family members, friends and acquaintances.[9] It would have become precious cultural capital, impressing other women with its pungent whiff of satisfaction, almost defiance. Its message: wives in Victoria could enjoy the ancillary benefits of a proud, upright husband and mutual reward for family labours.

But it's also clear that women were promoting the advantages of autonomy for their own personal fulfilment. May Howell wrote ardently of life at the diggings:

> I dare say it is an independent life, trusting to yourself, putting forth all your energy, no leaning on others, no one to control, or dictate to you, going where you

> like, doing what you like, no relation laying down the law, and chalking out your path in life.

Forty-two-year-old Mary Spencer, sailing on the *Arabian*, felt no ambivalence or anxiety as she looked back over her shoulder at *the receding shore* of her homeland. As her ship diary reveals, she saw only the miraculous prospect of liberation from suffocating drawing rooms and the endless minutiae of genteel etiquette. Mary revelled in the starry nights on deck *with everyone happy, no jarring world of cares to disturb us*. Her only woe was that there was so little to write about: *happiness is quiet and uninteresting in its detail*. For both men and women, the heady assumption of self-governance would come to have major socio-political implications once they reached the diggings.

MURRAY'S GUIDE held another prophetic image. This one relied on neither the promise of male breadwinning nor the intoxication of personal liberation. It involved the companionable mutuality of young husbands and wives making a new start together. This vision encouraged women to become the driving force behind emigration. *Wives should not allow their husbands to go without them if they have passage money for both* was the message, an inducement for women to assert command over proceedings. Other commentators exhorted women to come to the goldfields to *act as a stimulant to many fathers' yearning heart in this motley multitude*. Women, declared the ILLUSTRATED AUSTRALIAN MAGAZINE of September 1851, would give *a dash of humanity* to the *broad outline of savageism [sic]* that emerges when men congregate in sexual isolation.

The concept of women as civilising agents is endemic to transnational colonial history. According to this ideology, women are seen as agents of conservative restoration, bringing virtue to rough-and-ready frontier outposts. These angels of the imperial hearth would fulfil their 'natural' role in sweeping aside the detritus of frontier living, taming men with wholesome marriages, bearing children to send to nascent schools, and holding together a moral universe in which charity and benevolence would smooth the jagged edges of corruption and greed.

Nonconformist teacher and historian James Bonwick was chief proselytiser of the 'God's Police' archetype on the goldfields. It's a paradigm he laid out in his AUSTRALIAN GOLD DIGGER'S MONTHLY MAGAZINE AND COLONIAL FAMILY VISITOR, a magazine that ran from October 1852 to May 1853, sold in Melbourne and on the diggings, and sent back to be shared among family members and friends. To Bonwick, Victoria's golden gullies were *the gift of a God of gracious Providence* and he erected a special pedestal for women in his idealised rural scene. Bonwick wrote of the *sources of satisfaction* that awaited women who, with their husbands, set up happy, virtuous homes of honest toil. In the edition for February 1853, Bonwick described a pleasant weekend visit to Ballarat, where *no gold district has been so eminently rich as Eureka*.

> At no other diggings [was I] so struck with its order, propriety and comfort...The Sunday was strictly observed. A few parasols, veils and private arm-in-arm couples were encountered on our ramble. Many domestic scenes gave us a lively pleasure; as, the digger nursing his little babe, a mother reading to her children, family groups beneath bough porches, a roguish, tiny fellow pouring water into a plate for his puppy, a girl enticing a cow to be milked, with divers polka-jackets flitting to and fro in household duty.

It's not exactly Dodge City. Bonwick here imposes a pastoral idyll that historian Graeme Davison has called *the heart of*

England, a rhapsodic place of cultivated farmlands and compliant social relations.[10] This is the antithesis of Dickensian London, with its crowded streets, hungry waifs, toothless crones and worn-out factory fodder. But it's not the American Wild West either—all knife fights, saloon whores and lawless degeneracy. No, Bonwick's new frontier is the staging post of wholesome women, whose *presence is the harbinger, not only of comfort, but of moral progress.*

Was Bonwick aware of any contradiction between this smug polka-dotted duty and May Howell's vision of independence? The English rural idyll would prove to have little in common with Victoria's sunburnt hinterland, and even less relevance to its early intake of remarkably recalcitrant ladies.

*

It was not only pious ideologues who were promoting the advantages of female immigration to the goldfields. In September 1854, immigration agent Edward Bell reported to the colonial government on the success of its own recruitment drive:

> It will be gratifying to your Excellency to remark, that the recommendation of the late Lieutenant Governor, Mr La Trobe, that a large number of females should be imported in order to check the manifest disproportion in the sexes, consequent on the enormous addition to the male population which resulted from the opening of the Gold Fields in 1851, have been carefully attended by Her Majesty's Commissioners; and that the number of women, female children, and infants introduced, nearly doubles the number of males. The introduction of single men, except grown sons in large families, has been abandoned.

Bell's returns for 1853 reveal that 9342 females (of all ages) received assisted passage, compared to 5236 males. (By contrast, of the 77,734 unassisted passengers, 54,800 were adult men and 12,277 were adult women. The rest were children more or less equally spread between the sexes.) Demographic studies by historians have shown that this unprecedented pool of female government emigrants was largely drawn from small-farm and small-town environments, where extensive recruiting was carried out for young single women. A disproportionate number came from Ireland: between 1848 and 1860, fifty-one per cent of single immigrant women to Victoria were Irish.[11] English and Scottish girls proved more reluctant to leave established family circles and stable domestic service arrangements.

Much depended on the girl's place in the family. If an older (or younger) sister could stay behind to look after aging parents, then a spare daughter might see herself free. Some, like the letter-writer 'Elizabeth', became the family or village scout, judging the prospects before encouraging other siblings, aunts, cousins and neighbours to apply for passage. One lucky girl, who found work on an outstation near Geelong as a well-remunerated wet-nurse, wrote to her family: *I wish you were all here, there is room for you all, and wages too.* By such entreaties the process of chain migration began. Such refugees from the depressed economic and social landscape of Great Britain had no intention of making a return voyage.

Letters such as this one often ended up in the guidebooks for immigrants to Victoria that were a publishing phenomenon after 1852. These books recorded base wages for all grades of domestic servant and labourer, information on what to bring to the colony (mattress, bolster, blankets; knife, fork and mug) and, for single women, assessments of the marriage market. Of the roughly 7000 adult women who came as assisted emigrants in 1853, 4500 were single and 2500 were married. The average family size among the married emigrants was 1.5 children, which indicates the youth of the new arrivals: it was not uncommon for women of the time to bear seven or more children. A surprisingly large proportion was literate; only 2500 could neither read nor write, and this category included children and infants. (Even Edward Bell remarked on the unprecedented level of schooling among assisted emigrants.) Women were, clearly, making educated choices. The guidebooks, like the English journals of the time, were full of the *scarcity of wives* and *excellent matches* sure to be made in Australia, where *happy prosperous homes* could be created to erase the memory of *lives of struggling adversity at home*. The worst emigrants, all agreed, were those *genteel paupers* with *little money and much pride*. This for the simple reason that *the wealth of a colonist lies in work*. Similarly, young unmarried women intending to be brides but with *no experience of working* were advised to stay put:

> The drawing-room accomplishments of singing, dancing, painting and crochet would stand no shadow of a chance against the highly-prized virtues of churning, baking, preserving, cheese-making and similar matters.

The above examples, and the letter from our happy wet-nurse, all appear in PHILLIPS' EMIGRANTS' GUIDE TO AUSTRALIA, written by John Capper and published in Liverpool in 1855. The guidebooks were intended to be of practical value but there was also an imperial agenda. Colonial expansion required skilled migrants, male and female.

*

The British Government wasn't the only party with an interest in Victoria's extraordinary new attraction for the world's voluntary nomads. There were fortunes to be made from the traffic in human mobility: the costs of relocation and provisioning, the revenue generated by labour and taxes. The Colonial Office paid handsomely to reduce its surplus population through assisted immigration; private citizens also boosted the bank balances of the shipping magnates who were quickly (and cheaply) converting their ships to carry people instead of goods. There was a middle ground, too, between government assistance and commercial travel: the philanthropic societies to which a prospective immigrant could apply for financial aid to secure passage.

The Family Colonisation Loan Society established by the enterprising Caroline Chisholm, the woman on Australia's first issue five-dollar banknote, is the best known of the philanthropic organisations. Chisholm's endeavour to populate the inland of Australia with honest and industrious women who could infuse bush society with *permanent prosperity* began in 1840. *To break up the bachelor stations is my design*, Mrs Chisholm intoned, *happy homes my reward.* With the discovery of gold, Chisholm, now forty-four years old and wise to the vagaries of life under colonial conditions, saw the opportunity to extend her scheme to those families which could not afford passage and did not qualify for government assistance (because of the age or number of children). Keeping families together was her aim. Over three thousand immigrants were sponsored by the Family Colonisation Loan Society between 1852 and 1854.

An alternative solution was for a group of eager but impecunious emigrants—neighbours or acquaintances—to get together and charter a ship. Guidebooks often discouraged intending migrants from looking *to patronage or poor law guardians, or*

Government, for help, counselling them to form local committees and *do the work for themselves*. The ethic of self-help was strong among some communities, notably the Scots, whose religious or moral code disposed them to *earn* the rights and privileges of prosperity rather than being handed a better life on a platter. Here the covenant was struck between the parish or civic organisations that acted as benefactors and the recipients of that local largesse; wealth would flow back to the community in gratitude for its faith. Alexander Dick aligned himself to the Christian and Temperance Emigration Society, *a joint stock association*, which planned to buy a 470-tonne ship that could carry 250 passengers and sell it at the end of the voyage. Dick characterised his fellow travellers as *an interesting and virtuous band of voluntary exiles…run by a coterie of goody goody teetotallers and Methodists…a kind of modern Argonauts.* Still a teenager, Dick was delighted to find that his ship was full of intemperate young men like himself.

Chinese immigrants also favoured the self-help model. They formed triads—a culturally distinct form of friendly society—to send family and community members to Victoria. Immigration agent Bell's report noted that *a very large, though I fear not very profitable, addition to our population is now almost daily arriving from China.* Up to 30 June 1854, according to Bell, *no fewer than 2895 male Chinese had landed in Melbourne…and as rapidly removed to the Gold Fields. Their women,* Bell noted, *never emigrate.* (Bell was equally dismayed by the high number of Catholic immigrants from Ireland, a country he believed was relieving *a parish of its paupers.*) Bell would no doubt have been apoplectic to learn that by 1857 the Chinese population in Victoria would peak at 25,000.[12]

The majority of Chinese immigrants to Victoria came from one region, Guangdong Province, where they were largely involved in agrarian pursuits. Many were uninterested in cultural adaptation, even if the culture had been inclined to assimilate them, regarding Europeans as uncivilised and inferior beings—spiritual and cultural barbarians.[13] Chinese diggers hung together. They maintained close-knit social relations, both informally and in community organisations such as the See Yup Society.

Historian Anna Kyi has argued too that Chinese gold diggers can be characterised as having a 'sojourning mentality'; that is, their aspiration was to amass a quick fortune and return home to their wives and elders with wealth and respect.

The Chinese readily acknowledged that this was their primary motivation; most didn't want a fresh start, but a way to improve their financial, familial and social status at home. But leaders of the Chinese community were also eager to dispel the near hysteria that surrounded the fact that no Chinese women accompanied the male sojourners. A petition to the government written in 1857, protesting against a poll tax on Chinese arrivals, gave an explanation for this situation.

> The Chinese on first coming to this gold field thought the English very kind then the Chinese were glad to come digging gold and delighted in the mercy manifested. Now we learn that the news-papers complain that we Chinamen bring no wives and children to this country. Our reason is that we wish to leave some of the family to look after our aged parents as the climate there is very rough; our women too are not like English women, when they go into ships they cannot walk or stand and we cannot afford the passage money…as soon as we get a little money we will try to get home to our aged parents for our ancient books teach us that we must look after our parents.[14]

Another ethnic group prominent on the diggings, Jewish immigrants, were among the first to grasp the potential of Victoria for changing personal and collective fortunes. Long debarred from full commercial and civic participation, Jews from England and continental Europe hoped that in Victoria they would be free to integrate with mainstream society without compromising their cultural identity. In September 1853, the Family Colonisation Loan Society sent a boatload of passengers to Victoria, including a large party of girls recruited by the London Jewish Ladies' Benevolent Society on behalf of the Jews of Ballarat. They sailed on a newly built ship, making its maiden voyage: the *Caroline Chisholm*.

*

Echoing on both sides of the Atlantic, and reverberating through continental Europe and across Asia, there was one clear, resounding message. Fabulous wealth, a healthier, happier life, self-respect and limitless freedom were yours for the price of passage or your mark on a government paper. Whether you chose to come to the mountain, dig, make your pile and stay; or come, dig, make your pile and hightail it home, the route was unambiguous and unobstructed. The attraction was potent. The doomsayers were few.

But even in the early days of the miraculous gold rush, there was more realistic writing on the walls if you chose to read it. *Dysentery, cholera and ophthalmalgia are rife, and committing dreadful ravages*, testified the DAILY ALTA in April 1852. By July 1853 the DAILY ALTA conveyed reports of *deceptions practised in England to induce emigration to the colonies*. In Britain too, some journalists warned emigrants not to be deluded by exaggerated claims of prosperity. *Miserable homes, rags and filth, wives savagely beaten, children deserted and starved*, warned the London TIMES in October 1853, *all the evils to be found in the overcrowded centres of Europe may be seen in as great a proportion here.* Even some guidebooks were apprehensive about the possible backlash against a colonisation project based on flights of fancy. Should the emigrants *suffer privation*, if they could not *obtain from the stubborn soil sufficient for mere subsistence*, let alone *indulge in the refinements they have been accustomed to*, Samuel Mossman warned, there would be untold distress for those charged with governing these people. *The starved will revolt against all the laws of God and man however stringent.*

If the dream of independence was but a chimera—just wait and see *moral man revert into that of retrograde nature.* The spectre of savageism. The perils of a mixed multitude too hungry to keep its covenant.

THREE

CROSSING THE LINE

Two weeks out, and Louisa Timewell took it as a good sign that she had the strength to write in her ship journal: *make a loaf with sour leaven every day.* Details were beginning to come back into focus. *I save some of the dough for the next day's bread.* Louisa could even start to see the humour in it. Although the ship swayed like a hammock in the breeze, she and the other women still needed to go about their daily business. They held their babies on one hip while washing out clothes, trying to keep the basin steady. *It's very laughable to see them pitching about so.* Fortunately for Louisa Timewell, leaven and babies are strict taskmasters. *I got on deck all day with the children,* Louisa wrote after the morning's baking was complete, *and the time passed off very pleasantly watching the flying fish, sharks, whales, porpoises [and] fin backs.*[1]

For the fact is that no matter how devoutly some passengers held to the familiar markers of their former selves, by the time the gold rush immigrants reached Ballarat, they'd already endured a life-altering journey of colossal proportion. *A new era,* as one shipboard journal proclaimed grandly, for *men, women and children who had hitherto hugged the land.* These novice mariners *now committed their destinies to the wild world of water, seeking a far off land of Promise, where they may find wealth, social distinction and domestic happiness.*[2] A sourdough leaven might demand slavish reliability, but no ritual can hold together a universe that has burst apart at the seams.

Today it's hard to comprehend that the journey can be as transformative as the destination. We can cross the globe so fast that we might not even speak to the strangers in the seats around us. We might grimace when they belch or remove their shoes, but our lives and bodies will not connect in any meaningful way. Unless disaster strikes, the journey itself does not change us.

*

For most passengers, the first few weeks of the sea voyage seemed anything but promising. MURRAY'S GUIDE advised what to take on the three- to five-month journey: pickles, anchovies, potted herrings, smelling salts, camphor, perfumes to burn, musical instruments and *good humour, a close tongue about your own affairs, and a go-a-head spirit.* It seemed a practical kit, but no amount of sensible preparation could hold back the forces of physiology. Few first-timers took to the sea unscathed; even old hands felt the effects. Like war and childbirth, seasickness was a truly democratising experience. *Mal de mer. Seekrankheit. Mareo en barco. Wan syun long.*

With land disappearing astern and the waving handkerchiefs dwindling to specks in the distance, the body knows what the mind has yet to register. It has lost its bearings. Lines of sight no longer find fixed reference points. The equilibrium between eye and ear is disturbed. Even when the ship ceases to pitch and rock and sway, still there is the constant nauseating motion in the head and, as familiar visual anchors come unstuck, the brain adjusts to a new paradigm for balance. It helps to keep busy and concentrate on mechanical tasks, as Louisa Timewell discovered; the worst thing to do is stay below deck with no fresh air and no horizon.

Céleste de Chabrillan, wife of the new French consul to Melbourne, described the scene on the *Croesus* as it headed for open sea in 1854.

> It jolted and tossed about on the waves so much that passengers and objects all came tumbling down on top of each other...The famous line 'hare you sichowek' (are you seasick?) went from one passenger to the next, some escaping to their cabins, others leaning over the side. The only reply one hears is moaning, groaning and retching.[3]

Céleste herself felt the initial effects of this *horrible sickness*, but she refused to yield to its power: *I am fighting against it.* She stayed on deck—alone—for *all the passengers have disappeared as if by magic.* Her husband Lionel remained in their cabin with his head between two pillows and didn't emerge for three days. *I was distressed to see him suffer so and I could do nothing to bring him relief*, lamented Céleste. But neither would the headstrong Céleste, a former dancer and courtesan, keep vigil by his side in their dark, cramped cabin with the waves lashing against the sides of the ship, the planks, doors and masts cracking *as if thousands of woodcutters are cleaving them with axes.* Céleste was a fighter: *I prefer to face the enemy and I go back up on deck.* She stayed up all night, favouring fatigue to *the suffering I see endured around me.* Even her two dogs were curled up in the bottom of their wicker basket, *playing dead.*

Brave-faced Fanny Davis was mortified to discover that defiance alone was not enough. One week into her voyage she wrote, *It was a great mistake me being ill as I did not mean to be*;

it offended Fanny's dignity that crewmen needed to come down with mops and buckets to clean out her cabin. Agnes Paterson was, by her own admission, *reduced to a most pitiful condition.* Charlotte Spence *was a pitiable mess*, refusing all nourishment for days. Henry Nicholls distributed his recipe for *bilious pills*: four scruples compound extract of 'coloquth', one scruple powdered seammony, one scruple powdered 'soccolorine' aloes, six drops oil of cassia. The formula was probably more enterprising than effective. On the *Lady Flora* the doctor prescribed wine and porter for the invalids, which passenger John James Bond thought might explain why *some of the ladies are again disposed to faint.* Emma Macpherson worried at first that she *didn't have the necessary faith* for her homeopathic tincture to work; she was delighted to find it relieved her distress. Frances Pierson, sailing from New York with her husband Thomas, drank salt water and found that she was *a good deal better*.[4]

For Bethuel Adams, seasickness was his first reminder that leaving England meant forsaking the comforts of his mother's home. Popular mythology about male wanderlust would have us believe that men collectively revelled in the freedom from domestic constraints offered by frontier living; that women were but shackles on footloose masculinity. But listen to Bethuel Adams' anguish as he reflects on the privileges of the hearth:

> To be ill at sea is very dreadful, nothing but men to attend you and to perform those little kind offices which only come natural from a woman. Ah woman, we know not how to estimate your value until we are deprived of your presence!! Never before did I think so highly and with so much interest of the fair sex as I have since I have been at sea.

In his dismal queasiness, the future seemed to Bethuel not gloriously free but bleak and lonely. *How I shall be able to endure a bachelor life for half a score years in the solitary bush of Australia I don't know.* The poor fellow didn't have to worry for long. He arrived in Port Phillip on 3 January 1854 and died the following month in a shooting mishap, killed by his own gun.[5]

Only the most charmed of passengers avoided the gruelling initiation into life at sea. The rest may have failed to reflect, as they lay prostrate and retching, on the symbolic purging of old identities that seasickness represented. With heads reeling and stomachs churning, many immigrants prayed for death to deliver them from their misery.

Three weeks out, the passengers of the *Lady Flora*, the ship carrying Sarah Hanmer and her daughter Julia to their new home, petitioned the captain to put in to shore so they *could happily desert, so sick of the sea were they*. Poor winds meant the coast of England was still maddeningly in sight. One ship's surgeon-superintendent summed up the predicament of his charges:

> Unused to the sea, seasick, homesick, cold, wet, fearful and battened down, few aggregations of human wretchedness could be much greater than was to be found…in the close dark 'tween decks of an outward-bound emigrant ship.[6]

But when sufferers finally crawled out of the putrid cracks and cavities to face the light again, it was as if they were born anew. The first challenge had been overcome, and they were away. *In time I might make a brave sailor*, wrote Fanny Davis, marvelling at the new possibilities that suddenly seemed to arise before her.

*

For the vast majority of gold rush immigrants, those making their way from British ports, the early part of the journey proceeded in a southwesterly direction down the east Atlantic Ocean to the Equator. The English coastline might still be visible for weeks if conditions were poor, but eventually it receded into the distance. Then there was only the vast rolling ocean. The stars of the northern hemisphere constellations provided the last familiar markers. As Fanny Davis put it, the emigrants had entered *the pathless deep.* Heading south, the ship's route would descend past the Bay of Biscay, Lisbon, Madeira, the Canary Islands and the lumpy knob of West Africa, where the Tropic of Cancer was silently traversed.

The route for ships leaving the east coast of America, before the Panama Canal opened in the early 1900s, was south towards the Gulf of Mexico, then east across the Atlantic, joining up with the European clipper route in the tropics. Only six days after her departure, English schoolgirl Jane Swan noted it was *getting perceptibly warmer.*[7] Bethuel Adams finally had the strength to look around him and appreciate the vast beauty of the ocean, especially at night *when we can see the phosphoric lights dancing amid the spray like a shower of sparks from a blacksmiths anvil.* Thirteen-year-old Jane was less transfixed: *we get quite tired of having nothing to look at but the sea*, she complained to her diary. Perhaps adolescence and ennui are universal bedfellows.

When passengers had genuine grievances about their circumstances, they were not bashful about making their concerns public. The gold rush immigrants were either paying passengers or voluntary exiles. Their ships were neither penal hulks nor navy vessels. There was no debt of obedience or gratitude owing. On the *Lady Flora*, J. J. Bond read the mood of disquiet: *the 'tween deck people think they are living too much like pigs.* These disgruntled passengers petitioned the captain to land at the nearest port so as to *acquaint the owners of the ship* that facilities were *unequal to her crowded state.* The captain did not acquiesce, but asked the people to be considerate of each other and promised that all would settle down in time. It did not, and by the time the *Lady Flora* docked, a ship-wide subscription for the captain could only raise an insulting £4.

Living like swine was one thing, but being infested by deadly viruses and vermin was another. Passengers knew too well the destiny that could await the criminally neglected ship: they would all have heard of the *Ticonderoga.* This famous 'plague ship' had arrived at Port Phillip in November 1852, after a hell voyage in which one hundred of its 795 assisted migrants had died, over half of them children. Three hundred passengers were suffering typhoid fever and hundreds more dysentery. Almost seventy people died in quarantine at the Heads. No family aboard was left untouched; dreams of happiness and prosperity lay in tatters. A report by the Immigration Board in Melbourne later stated:

> The ship, especially the lower part, was in a most filthy state, and did not appear to have been cleaned for weeks, the stench was overpowering, the lockers so thoughtlessly provided for the Immigrants use were full of dirt, mouldy bread, and suet full of maggots, beneath the bottom boards of nearly every berth upon the lower deck were discovered soup and bouille cans and other receptacles full of putrid ordure, and porter bottles etc, filled with stale urine, while maggots were seen crawling underneath the berths.[8]

The plague ship's captain, American Thomas Boyle, continued in his globetrotting life as a successful privateer, despite the fact that barely one of his passengers arrived without the loss of a family member.

Jane Swan's family were immediately struck by the difference between the advertised and actual amenities on board the *William and Jane*. Just two days after departure, Jane recorded that *our water cashes turned out very bad. We signed a petition all round and were supplied with good water from the tanks.* Petitioning, like public meetings, had long been part of the political process at a local level. In English riots of the early eighteenth century, as historian John Bohstedt has shown, wherever people were bargaining over rights and bound together by geographical proximity, they formed a 'community' of interest, a local consensus, that had nothing to do with class cohesion or ethnic homogeneity.

The duration and conditions of the journey to Australia made the formation of a 'community', in Bohstedt's definition, quite straightforward. Authorities feared hostile crowds, and most ship captains, carrying large numbers of people in confined spaces, were willing at the very least to hear petitions and delegations without taking umbrage. Indeed, they expected to be held accountable for the safe and healthy passage of the ship. In 1853, there were over seventy prosecutions against captains of private passenger ships bound for Australia for breaches of the Passenger Acts, largely relating to substandard provisioning and the illegal sale of alcohol.

When the ship docked in Port Phillip, the harbour master would board and ask each family these three leading questions: *Have you any complaint against anyone on board? Have you been treated well on the voyage? Are you quite able to work?*[9] The stage was set early for the performance of individual and communal grievance.

By the time most gold seekers arrived on dry land, they had already made significant transitions, casting off old allegiances and forging bonds of sympathy based on a new understanding of shared space and common interest. Many passengers referred to the social organisation of the ship as being like *one well regulated family*. The MARCO POLO CHRONICLE put this clannish feeling down to *the depression that associates with 'goodbye'* followed by *the vast amount of physical suffering to be surmounted* through seasickness. The MARCO POLO CHRONICLE called the ship *our Floating World*. Thomas Pierson agreed: *You can have no idea how much we love our ship...we feel so much interested for each other and so free towards each other just like one family.*

This intense shipboard bonding, coupled with a sense of maverick privilege at having endured the ordeal, would become an important precursor to goldfields solidarity. And relationships forged on board could develop into important commercial and social associations on land. Charles and George Evans travelled on the *Mobile* with Henry Wright, Duke Paine and William Denovan, all men with whom they would later form business relationships in Ballarat. The Evans brothers' close friend from Shropshire, George Morgan, came out on the *Star of the East* with brothers John Basson and Frederick Humffray. Both in turn would also become business associates of the Evans brothers. Anne Keane, travelling with her two brothers and a sister-in-law on the *Star of the East*, would 'marry' shipmate Martin Diamond (de facto, if not before a priest) once the young sweethearts reached the relative permanence of Ballarat.

*

Shipboard relationships often led to important expatriate networks. But this didn't mean that everyone cohabited snugly, like peas in a floating pod. Where is the family that does not crack as much as it coheres? *Quarrels are quite the fashion*, noted Fanny Davis, *there is not an hour in the day but the doctor is fetched to quell some riot.* Indeed, it is one of the stubborn myths of the gold rush era that the months of fraternisation and friction on the sea voyage worked to dismantle old-world social structures irrevocably. In this widespread reading, ship society becomes a template for the new egalitarian society that will be re-created on the diggings. But, as many ship diaries reveal, the 'Floating World' embodied rudimentary signs of status demarcation, prejudice and snobbery. Community does not signify equality.

Englishman John Spence considered the *third class rabble* to be the scourge of the ship. These Irish poor *are the greatest nuisance we have on board*, ranted Spence. They were worse than vermin, stale biscuits, wild children or rank water. *The great majority are a dirty disagreeable lot*. Spence attributed the frequent robberies from insecure cabins to be the work of the Irish mob. *I expect before we reach Melbourne we shan't have a spoon left on us*, he lamented. *They are such expert thieves.*

Sectarianism was not debunked; indeed, its prejudices and comforts were likely to be enforced in close quarters. Spence, for example, attributed ethnic tensions to the excessive drinking of the Irish, and personally attempted to encourage the entire third-class cabin to take the Temperance Pledge until Melbourne. His evangelism was sorely misplaced. Spence would have done well to follow Emma Macpherson's resolution for shipboard sanity: *think charitably and associate sparingly.*

Religious intolerance surfaced too. During a fierce storm, James Menzies found just cause to disparage another denomination of his Protestant faith. *The Methodists*, he wrote, *went to prayers, thought they were going to the bottom, they were all oh Lord have mercy on my soul enough to give any one the belly ache*. Menzies

Queen Rose of the Wathaurung people in her possum-skin cloak, 1876.

Old Ballarat as it was in the summer of 1853–54: the golden vision that Eugene von Guérard painted in 1884.

One of von Guérard's more realistic sketches of Ballarat, from 1854.

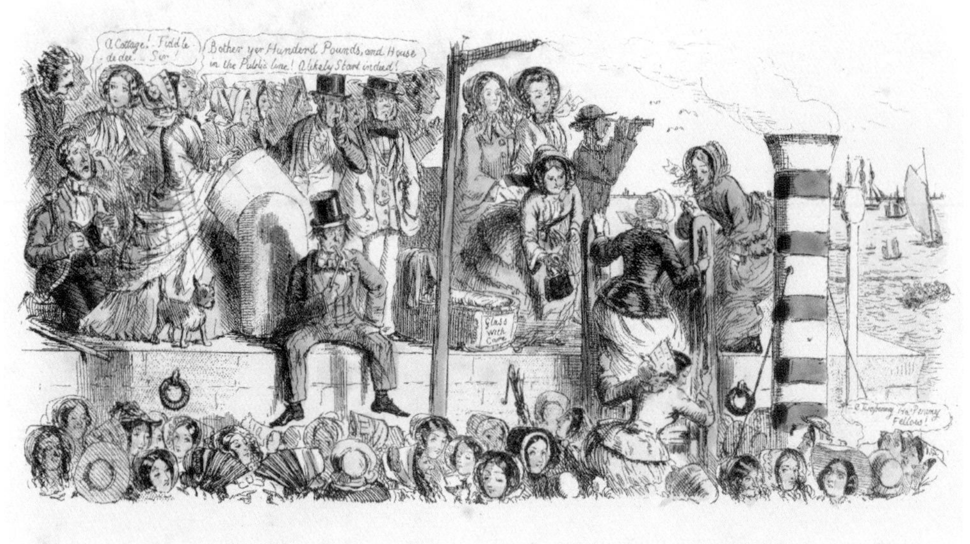

Alarming Prospect: all the single ladies. John Leech, 1854.

Head down, bum up on the road to Ballarat.
John Alexander Gilfillan, 1853.

Great expectations: the lucky digger returns. S. T. Gill, 1852–3.

Grass widows: the girls the diggers left behind and what they had to do (detail). William Strutt, 1851.

wasn't much for the Brotherhood of Man. Later in the voyage, he confided that he'd *sooner be among a lot of Irish for they are all Cornish people except two or three and a more ignorant set I never was with in my life.*[10] Bear in mind that in the mid-nineteenth century, the Irish, Welsh, Cornish and Scots were just as likely to communicate in their native languages as in English. Prejudice against non-English speakers would have provided another obstacle to egalitarian integration.

Fanny Davis, ever an eagle-eyed narrator, sketched a more piquant montage of her floating world. On 21 July 1858, six weeks out from home, she sat on deck on a warm, clear night. As she looked around, she saw in one corner *two dozen folks singing*. In another corner, there was a group *talking scandal about everyone*, making complaints about certain cabin-mates *that would make a cat laugh*. In another section of the deck, there were *a lot of Scotch girls dancing*—one imitating bagpipes—not *a one of them with shoes or stockings on*. Then there were the Irish. *The Irish will be squatting down under the boats talking over everybody's business but their own and vowing eternal hatred of the English*. Gossip, tittle-tattle, innuendo. Cultural kindling for the eternal flame of bigotry.

Ethnic and sectarian divisions weren't the only forms of demarcation. Discriminating between types of women based on their sexual conduct, always a favourite cultural pastime, was evident on passenger ships despite the literal loosening of stays. As ships sailed towards the tropics, and temperatures rose, women stripped back their layers of feminine restraints: corsetry was unlaced, hosiery removed. And, liberated from the prying eyes of kin, single women and men indulged in flagrant acts of exhibitionism. On clear nights there was dancing on the poop; in stormy weather there was always a dark corner for a liaison. *Of all the places of iniquity my eyes ever beheld*, wrote one passenger sailing on the *Star of the East* in September 1853, *an emigrant ship is the worst, men and women packed indiscriminately together, married couples and young girls, and I am sure some of the girls will have cause to remember the STAR OF THE EAST.*

Anne Keane was one Irish lass who may have arrived in Victoria with an unexpected souvenir of her trip. By the time twenty-seven-year-old Anne and partner Martin Diamond played a pivotal role in Ballarat's history just over a year later, they had already lost a baby.

Captains and surgeon-superintendents, particularly on government ships, had powers to keep the peace and could punish reprobates. Though women were ostensibly 'free', they were expected to conform to acceptable standards of respectable femininity. This was particularly true for the single ladies. On James Menzies' government-assisted ship, the doctor was fetched to see to some shenanigans going on in the women's quarters. *The single females were making a noise at night*, Menzies wrote, *and the doctor went down and told them to be quiet and some of them was saucy to him, he told them that he would have a prison made for some of them.* It wasn't a bluff. The ship's carpenters were called in. They used three-inch quartering to make uprights across the berths of the offending women. Menzies, who for some reason was a witness to this, chuckled that *it put me in mind of the wild beast cages at the Surrey Zoological Gardens.*

A farcical display of power aside, here was the contradiction that lay at the heart of the gold-seeking impulse: immigrants aspired to change their own lives yet expected that everyday social distinctions would remain the same. Could they have it both ways?

*

For some ships the danger was not over once seasickness passed and the saucy lasses had been given their comeuppance. Sexual misadventure might have been anticipated on a long journey of young, unchaperoned, often-intoxicated thrill-seekers, but some calamities were less predicable. Take the case of the *Sir William Molesworth*, the ship chartered by the Christian and Temperance Emigration Society with young Scot Alexander Dick on board. It was widely known that one child had been cleared of scarlet fever just in time to board. But others, it seems, had been incubating the disease. By the time the ship docked at Port Phillip a staggering five months later, ten per cent of her passengers were dead.

When Captain Watt ascertained the gravity of the situation in the mid-Atlantic, he stopped at the Cape Verde Islands off the coast of Senegal, effectively isolating the ship for a month. There was no pier or landing place, just the remains of an old Portuguese penal settlement and the islands' native population of mixed African and Portuguese descent. Cape Verde had once been central to the transatlantic slave trade, but by 1853 one of the primary *industries of the natives*, as Alexander Dick related, was carrying passengers from boats to the shore. The *Sir William Molesworth* arrived in considerable surf. Dick described the scene of moral pandemonium that ensued:

> The ladies in our boat were utterly horrified to find that the only means of reaching the shore was by being carried in the arms of a stalwart nigger as naked as the Apostle Belvidere and as black as Beelzebub.

Some refused to undergo the trial and returned to the ship. A few adventurous souls *resigned themselves half unwillingly to the clamorous niggers who soon set them down on the beach tousled and tumbled and blushing like peonies.*

How to read this remarkable scene? It's no accident that

historian Inga Clendinnen begins her classic work of contact history, *Dancing with Strangers*, on a beach, the archetypal boundary delineating fundamental states of being: water and land, here and there, coming and going. On Clendinnen's beach, the shores of Botany Bay, the British and the (Indigenous) Australians find common ground, dancing hand in hand like 'children at a picnic', mutually lowering their guard in an act of 'clowning pantomime'.

The scene on the Cape Verde coastline is analogous. Familiar sight lines are blurred, behaviours adapted, boundaries crossed. The women who are carried to shore by the islanders go only *half unwillingly*. They perform their scripted role as distressed damsels, but by letting themselves be carried away in the first place, they have engaged in an important theatre of inversion. No longer upstanding, they are tousled and tumbled and set down arse-about. The black demons are responsible for their fall, but also their rescue. Not all women jumped ship when the opportunity presented, but some relished the chance to throw off old vestiges of conventional femininity and surrender to this bewitching possession.[11] For some, the corollary of *roughing it* was going native.

Like the seasickness that reduced strong men to whimpering invalids or sentimental fools, this unexpected encounter on the cusp of sea and land was the first of many acts of reversal as immigrants headed south. 'Going south' was in itself an inversion. The Antipodes as the opposite of true north. Women themselves were constructed as a kind of vessel in the cultural armada of colonisation. As symbols of home, civilisation and order, women represented the goals of British expansionism, with the loyal wife and marriageable domestic servant cast as the good imperial subject. But as the unsettling episode at the Cape Verde Islands demonstrates, the authorised script could readily be abandoned for improvisation if necessary. How should a precious English rose act when suddenly thrust into the arms of a buck-naked black man, who is not her *bête noir* but her saviour? If the knight in shining armour is not a handsome prince but a savage, does a maiden blush, laugh or fervently embrace the startling possibilities of this altered reality? For many immigrants, the ship voyage fractured timeworn fairy tales abruptly.

Of course, you didn't need to be unexpectedly beached to experience the magnetic pull of limbo. The ship itself was a liminal space. Neither on land nor of the sea, neither leaving nor arriving, immigrants stood betwixt and between, caught in the vast hiatus of transhemispheric travel. It was a topsy-turvy time, when judging the distance between the real and the fantastic, the defensible and the inadmissible, was increasingly problematic.

Sometimes this disarray was literal. On the night of a tremendous storm, Fanny Davis described the effect of the mountainous waves like this: *It is like being in a great cradle only that instead of rocking us to sleep it rocks us more wide awake for every now and then it seems as if we're going to turn bottom upwards*. How frightening, that the hand that rocks the cradle might be malevolent, not maternal after all. Ever watchful for edifying details, Fanny also tells us that she observed a Catholic prayer service, below deck, *conducted by a young woman*. What had possessed this girl to subvert the strict institutional hierarchy of her faith?

Other moments of chaos were not so much quietly irreverent as madly entertaining. Alpheus Boynton, a young Canadian Episcopalian, described the scene on the promenade deck at night, where the ordinarily staid space *assumed the appearance of a dance hall*. There were fiddlers, tambourines, dancing. Folks stood in a ring, clapping and cheering. *Had it not been for a sober and quite respectable company*, wrote Boynton, *one might have imagined himself in an Ann Street gathering: in short, we had a regular break down*. The geographical reference here is to the red-light district of Boston, centred around Ann Street, where the city's blacks and whites would notoriously intermingle. So here is a vivid tableau of moral disintegration, as sexual and racial decencies are openly flouted. But for Boynton the prospect of a *break down* was not threatening; he enjoyed the bonhomie, the way he became encircled in a sphere of companionship and mirth.[12]

John Hopkins, travelling aboard the *Schomberg*, enjoyed a *silly affair* when the lads in his cabin put on a show: the star was *a 'beautiful young lady' with a beard*. And girls just wanted to have fun too. Fanny Davis described one of her ship's *full dress balls* where women went to pains to out-do each other's outfits. *Some of the girls*, she wrote, *dress in the Highland costume as men. It looks first rate*. Such carnivalesque gestures—overturning polarities—were a longstanding feature of going south. When women don men's clothes, argues cultural studies scholar Jean Howard, they become 'masterless women', signalling a breakdown of systems of control and compliance.

The collapse of sartorial superstructures was aided by geography. Six weeks out from London and Jane Swan's ship was lodged firmly in the dead calm of the intertropical convergence zone—otherwise known as the doldrums. *We can never get a night's rest for the heat*, she groused. The thermometer gauged an astonishing 108 degrees (42 degrees Celsius). With no breeze and no movement, the passengers were taking it in turns to row out to sea. *Some ladies ventured out*, tattled Jane, *so that you may judge what sort of day it was!* Strange days indeed. Fanny Davis, also stuck in the doldrums, was finding things most peculiar too. She could report that it was *very hot*, and they were almost completely becalmed. An awning had been rigged up on the deck for the ladies, but many did not use it. *The sun begins to turn the colour of our skins*, wrote Fanny, *we shall all be black soon.* The MARCO POLO CHRONICLE reported the same phenomenon: *fair faces brown rapidly.* What would James Hopkins have thought of this display of scorched flesh? Upon reaching the tropics, he was astonished to discover that *the ladies from the First Cabin had nothing upon their heads.* For sixteen-year-old Sarah Ann Raws, sailing on the *Bloomer* in 1854, reaching the tropics was a revelation. Although she and her brother could *scarcely sleep in our beds for the heat*, Sarah Ann delighted in lying on top of her mattress with only a thin sheet as cover, *sweat rolling off our faces*, sans stockings.[13] And it would have been an unearthly moment indeed when, traversing the Tropic of Cancer, Frances Pierson was asked by her dinner companions to carve the dolphin.

*

All the mashing up and breaking down was but a prelude to the foremost conceptual navigation: crossing the line. The line-crossing ceremony, steeped in maritime tradition and still practised today, is a customary initiation rite celebrating a sailor's first crossing of the equator and welcoming him into the Kingdom of Neptune. There is often an appearance by Neptune (Poseidon) and his wife, Amphitrite, a pantomime that provides an opportunity for sailors to compete for the accolade of being ugly enough to go in drag. The celebration is a ritual of reversal in which the inexperienced crew are permitted to take over the ship from the officers. If the full traditional fiasco is played out, a transition is made from the established order of the captain's regime to the controlled mayhem of the Pollywog Revolt, followed by a return to order as the 'Wogs' pass certain physical tests and earn their right to enlistment in Neptune's realm. Though the line-crossing ceremony is still honoured today, some of the more violent forms of 'testing'—such as beatings and sodomy—have been outlawed.

On immigrant ships, the line-crossing ceremony was practised as a rite of theatrical observance rather than brute harassment. Many journal-writers noted some aspect of the colourful proceedings. It took most ships at least five weeks to reach the equator, but a slow passage through the doldrums could delay that milestone by a month. Crossing the line was a symbolic mid-point in the journey, and crews and passengers alike enjoyed marking the occasion. On Sarah Hanmer's ship the *Lady Flora*, there was a *Grand Procession*. Neptune and his wife were drawn in a car with attendants dressed in unique costumes, carrying tridents and accompanied by dolphins. The event concluded with a hornpipe, much drinking, fist fights and squabbling, *as occurs on most days*. On James Menzies' ship, passengers were included in the ritual. *Neptune hailed the ship*, he recounted, *the water began to fly about, a great many got a wetting* as all who went on deck copped a bucketing. What came next was strictly for the sailors. Lathered with tar and muck, their heads shaved, they were festooned in *pills and wigs* and fine gowns. As the passengers looking on in delight knew by now, crossing the invisible lines of conformity, propriety and erstwhile identity could take many guises.

During those first weeks at sea when all that was solid melted into air, there were only two things the unmoored passenger could use for ballast: the watery horizon and the stars. Reading the map of the night sky (which everyone did, before electricity) kept passengers in touch with a familiar reality. There was Ursa Major. There was Pegasus. There was Leo. Constellations to orient oneself, to chart a known route towards an unknown destiny. And then, as ships sailed south through the layers of latitude towards the equator, even that stellar certainty was stripped away. At the equator you can see all the stars in the sky rise and set, giving access to the entire celestial sphere: another map begins unfolding. And as the weeks rolled by and the ship lurched further south towards Australia, it would provide a new reference point: passengers began to fix their mental compass on the Crux Australis. Matter-of-fact Fanny Davis recorded a single entry in her diary after crossing the equator on 15 July 1853: *Saw the Southern Cross at the Line. It is altogether different to an English sky.*

The Southern Cross was a beacon in more ways than one. It told of a new political identity, divested of old allegiances. But as a symbolic object—what Kleinian psychoanalysts might call 'a good object'—the Southern Cross offered new immigrants the reassuring embrace of affective belonging. Though the constellations ranged across the night sky, and the moon waxed and waned in primordial rhythm, they were permanent anchor points on an otherwise shifting shore. As the horizon is for disoriented seafarers, the Southern Cross became a hitching post for existential certainty when all else was in mortal flux. Before long, that simple constellation would come to have tremendous significance for the people of Ballarat, representing just how far their journey had taken them.

*

After skimming the equator and breaking free of the doldrums, ships plunged into the South Atlantic, following the natural circulation of winds and current, heading towards the Cape of

Good Hope and the roaring forties. The dancing and music making on deck came to an abrupt halt as ships entered the arctic trade winds of the Southern Ocean. Heavy seas and strong winds buffeted the ship. Passengers were forced to find their sea legs all over again. On a day that was blowing *a perfect hurricane*, Fanny Davis stayed below but one of her cabin-mates fell over trying to get on deck and knocked several teeth in. To avoid getting out of bed, Fanny and her friends huddled together under mantles and coverlets, *telling fortunes in teacups to pass the time.*

It was the little ones who suffered the worst in this final leg of the voyage. One boy on James Menzies' ship had a shocking fit. The doctor worked quickly to extract five worms from the lad's gut, each measuring eight inches long. On Fanny Davis's ship, one pregnant woman had lain in the hospital since departure. She delivered her baby in the middle of a fearsome storm only a week out from Port Phillip. It was *a night of terrors*, with waves flooding the berths and snow blanketing the deck. The baby died as soon as it was born; the mother followed not long after. Another traveller, Mrs Graham, witnessed the sea burials of a baby and toddler from the one family, dead within two days of each other, and wrote: *the body fell with a splash and all was over but the cries of the Parents who felt deeply the loss of the child.*[14] Four children died on John Spence's ship. The babies, he wrote pragmatically, *were nursed on the spoon, always more easily injured than those who nurse on the breast.*

Sarah Raws witnessed another morbid scene. *A lady died this morning in our cabin.* Her death came as a *great shock*; she had only been confined to bed for one day. The woman left ten grieving children. She was *much respected in our cabin* and had become *very intimate* with Sarah's mother and father. The woman's husband was a Baptist deacon, already settled in Australia. Sarah attended the funeral. *They sewed her up in canvas, and it was an effecting [sic] sight to see the bereaved family.* The woman's son offered £200 to the captain to bring the body to land, but the law prohibited this and so she was *consigned to the deep.* They had only three days left to sail.

It was grief and fear, not elation, that accompanied many passengers as they sailed into their dizzying futures.

*

When Louisa Timewell's ship docked at Sandridge wharf (now Port Melbourne), she was dumbstruck by the jetsam of prosperity. *Passing down the Yarra Yarra*, she wrote, *we saw thousands of bullocks' and sheep's heads lying at the edge of the river a little way from the slaughtering house, rotting in a heap. I thought how many poor families would be glad of them in England.* What an extraordinary land that would discard good meat as so much waste. As the anchor dropped from Sarah Raws' ship, shouts of joy rang out. *It appeared like coming out of Sodom into Paradise*, she remarked. Fanny Davis swore that her ship had experienced the worst passage in years: *We are all totally worn out in mind and body and want of sleep.* On the morning of the *Ascutna*'s arrival in Port Phillip, Mrs Dunn gave birth to a son in the stateroom adjoining Frances and Thomas Pierson. The ship's unassuming captain, George Pepper, named the boy George Pepper Ascutna Dunn.

*

The hours leading up to Margaret Howden's reunion with her *dear Jamie* prickled with tension. At just eighty-two days, the

Hurricane's voyage had been lightning fast, spared serious illness and blessed with agreeable company and generous conditions. But for Margaret the day of reckoning—the much-anticipated meeting that had kept her spirits buoyant all these weeks—was about to be realised. Was dear Jamie craving his young Maggie as much as she ached for him?

> July 29 Saturday
> A beautiful awakening at 4 o'clock. Saw from my porthole Cape Otway lighthouse, a most cheering sight, and at 6 o'clock saw land of the country we had so longed for weeks to behold. At last that comfort was granted us. My feelings were more than can be described. To think that my own beloved Jamie was residing in that land. I saw the sun rise for the first time on my new place of abode. Oh! I sincerely trust that the hour, God willing, is not far distant when I shall meet my Jamie again, in perfect health, and all I could desire.

It had been, after all, more than six months since the last communication with James. Anything could have happened since then. He might have been struck down by that fearful colonial fever. He might have left his government post. He might, God forbid, have found a currency lass to love. Margaret, for all she knew, could be alighting in a land where she knew no one but her shipmates—and they, surely, would scatter on the winds of their new destinies.

> July 31 Monday
> *A memorable day*. All the forenoon, walked on deck with Mr Robertson feeling very unsettled at the prospect of a termination to our voyage…Came down, then I put the cabin in order in fond expectations.

> We anchored at 5 o'clock. Oh! How thankful I feel. Several Scots came, but alas! my own Jamie was not among the number.

Margaret ran from one porthole to another trying to get a glimpse of her fiancé, but it was no use. He was simply not at the docks. So she returned to her neat berth and the routines of ship life: tea, walking, prayers, staring at the horizon.

> August 1 Tuesday
> A most anxious day as I was looking out for my *beloved* but alas! did not come.

By Wednesday, Margaret was compelled to leave the *Hurricane*. She packed up her *own dear cabin*, said farewell to new friends, and stepped onto the wharf at Sandridge. Margaret bravely walked to the Bedford Hotel. *Once again on dry land.*

> August 3 Thursday
> Oh! I long for my Jamie.
>
> August 4 Friday
> Thought of my Jamie first thing. In very low spirits. Another day passed.

Then, miraculously, mysteriously, Margaret's diary is missing the pages for August 5 to August 10. So we know nothing of how, where or when the day of reunion with James Johnston happened—but happen it did. Margaret and James were married on Wednesday 9 August 1854 at St Peter's Anglican Church, Eastern Hill. They were about to endure the honeymoon from hell.

✶

The *Lady Flora*, carrying Sarah Hanmer and her daughter, Julia, cruised through Port Phillip Heads on 13 August 1853. *We have been taken in*, complained Hanmer's shipmate J. J. Bond. *Nothing but discomfort from beginning to end.* The captain spent most of his time drinking below. The first mate was *mad with ill temper.* The steward and attendants were *insolent fellows who laughed at our misery.* The passengers were *three parts starved.* The salt beef was inedible, the sea biscuits musty, the coffee burnt. *Dirt, confusion and noise have prevailed in place of order and regularity*, Bond lamented.

How much more acutely must William Timewell have felt this sense of injustice, of being royally duped? His wife Louisa would contract colonial fever only months after their arrival, leaving William with a clutch of motherless children and a sourdough leaven in need of constant feeding.

For Sarah Hanmer, about to shed six of her thirty-two years when the immigration agent at Port Phillip asked for her age, the performance of grievance was poised to find a new and very public stage.

FOUR

THE ROAD

When the *Lady Flora* sailed into harbour in the spring of 1853, it was less than three short years since the Port Phillip District had been separated from its parent colony of New South Wales. Victoria officially became an autonomous colony on 1 July 1851, a month before gold changed its fortunes forever. Charles La Trobe was Victoria's first lieutenant governor, overseeing a town of fledgling institutions, a hinterland squired by a self-selected landed gentry (the 'squattocracy') and a measly 23,143 inhabitants.

Compared to sin-city Sydney, which had more than double the population, Melbourne before the gold rush was a country cousin. The inter-colonial influx following the discovery of gold, with a tsunami of immigrants hot on its heels, started an overnight boom in Melbourne. The mantle of inferiority was quickly thrown off, and Melbourne revelled in a carnival-like upheaval. According to John D'Ewes, a civil servant whose name would be forged in the fires of Eureka, *the streets wore a very holiday appearance.*[1]

By the census of April 1854, the city of Melbourne and its neighbouring seaport towns (Sandridge, Williamstown) recorded a population of some 65,000 males and 45,000 females. That represents a near five-fold increase in a mere three years. Just imagine if Melbourne's present-day population of 3.8 million quintupled to almost twenty million in less time than it takes to build, say, an Olympic stadium. Add to this phenomenal explosion the 52,000 males and 14,000 females packed onto the goldfields, which did not even exist when the census was taken in 1851, and the 49,000 males and 30,000 females in inland towns and districts including Geelong: this was a colony heaving under the weight of its own success. By August 1854, there were over 115,000 men, women and children on the goldfields alone. The official figures did not include the 'dying race' of Aborigines (estimated to be around 2500, a fraction of the 25,000 likely to have occupied the Port Phillip district prior to European occupation) or the Chinese, neither of whom were considered worth counting.

Like other cities that grow by magic, wrote American gold seeker Dan Calwell to his sisters at home in Ohio, *most of the buildings are temporary and they are already giving place to more capacious and costly ones.* Dan and his brother Davis had spent almost five months sailing from New York, arriving in the spring of 1853. *The quietness of ship life*, wrote Dan, *was superseded by the noise and confusion of a second Babel.* Melbourne reeked of wide-open possibilities, and the Calwell boys, only twenty and twenty-one years old, couldn't wait to cross the line that separated the mundane from the electrifying.

Nothing stayed still for long: taking a census at the feverish height of a gold rush was like trying to herd cats. The only piece of empirical data that refused to budge was the disproportion of the sexes: 193 males to every hundred females—a fact, said the statisticians, that *can scarcely fail to attract the attention of the legislature.* There was one demographic detail that was universally acknowledged. The proportion of people in the *prime of life*, aged between twenty and forty, was substantially higher than in Great Britain or in any other colony. Victoria's population was overwhelmingly young, male and mobile.

It was also surprisingly cosmopolitan, with all the associations of excitement and glamour, the sinuous interplay between cultures this sexy word conjures. Here is British merchant Robert Caldwell's pen picture of the populace of Melbourne:

> a most curious and picturesque exhibition of the people of all nations...the swart Briton walks shoulder to shoulder with the flat-faced Chinaman, the tall and stately Armenian, the lithe New Zealander or South Sea Islander, the merry African from the United States, the grave Spaniard, the yellow-haired German, the tall, sharp visaged Yankee, and the lively Frenchman. Every state in the world has its representatives

Among the religious denominations represented in Victoria, the 1854 census recorded three thousand *Mahometans and Pagans*. By the end of the year that figure had risen to ten thousand, about half of whom were Chinese.[2] On the other hand, noted Caldwell with little sense of alarm, *the wild animals and native inhabitants seem to have almost melted away.*

Commentators often noted the degree of dissimilarity, if not overt hostility, between the diverse ethnic groups, particularly the English and the Americans. Robert Caldwell believed the most *troublesome* part of the population came from America while the most *depraved* hailed from Britain via the Californian goldfields, where they had picked up the worst of American vices. The Americans' political creed, said Caldwell, was to *condemn everything British and with ignorant effrontery on British soil, to uphold as perfect everything American*. American Silas Andrews noted that the populace was a *mixture of all nations*, mostly English of the *lowest class, possessing none of that activity and capability of turning their hands to anything, which the 'Yankees' possess*. At the boarding house where Thomas and Frances Pierson, from the Pennsylvania Olive Lodge, eventually found a place to stay, there were three tables set up in the dining room: one was the *Britishers table*, another the *Yankey table*, and a third the *Experienced Colonials table*. We are accustomed to understanding anglophone ethnic tensions in Australia as an immemorial turf war between the English and Irish, but there was more than a hint of the Boston Tea Party about the parlours of 1850s Melbourne.

Where did Sarah Hanmer seat herself? Born into the McCullough clan in Scotland, Sarah was Anglo-Celtic. But like another actress of her generation, Lola Montez, Sarah had travelled to America during the Californian gold rush. In 1850, she was living in Albany, New York, raising enough capital to put herself in pole position when the magnetic pull of gold exerted its southward traction. Later, in Ballarat, Sarah would show that her allegiances were surprisingly *Yankey*.

*

Gold rush Melbourne—gateway to the diggings—was a city reeling. In the year following the first gold discoveries it became a virtual ghost town. *The reports in the papers drove every one mad*, wrote Henry Mundy, who had emigrated to Australia as a boy in 1844, *every shepherd, hutkeeper, stockrider, every man, woman and child. All the world and his wife were looking for and examining quartz.* Crews (and even captains) abandoned their ships in the harbour, leaving nothing more than a *forest of masts*, as Alexander

Dick described the Port of Melbourne. Construction sites were frozen in time, primed with potential but no labour to see it through. Postal services were disrupted. The police force was gutted. Roads could not be built for the lack of navvies. Schools closed and the public service staggered along on a skeleton staff. And husbands notoriously deserted their wives, creating the legendary grass widows of the gold rush, the discarded victims of male caprice. Some women expected their husbands to reappear with a pocketful of gold; others knew they were gone for good.

A year later, many of the original fugitives had returned, having either made their pile or realised there was now a more reliable and less backbreaking fortune to be made servicing the boatloads of immigrants being daily disgorged onto Melbourne's shores. Carpenters, stonemasons and other artisans found their skills were suddenly at a premium. Dubious lawyers and uncertified doctors, who had come to Australia to dig for wealth, discovered that their professional practices were lucrative regardless of talent or qualification. A publican's licence was a sure route to prosperity.

The social condition of the colony, and especially the city of Melbourne, wrote John Capper in his popular guidebook of 1854, *becomes every day more complicated and unmanageable*. Regulation of rents, prices, wages, sanitation and labour practices was a dream of the late nineteenth century's progressive thinkers. In the early 1850s, the guiding principle was adaptation, not control. By November 1853, on the eve of their departure for Ballarat and over a year since Charles and George Evans had stepped off the boat, George amused himself with the array of ventures he and his equally educated brother had embarked upon:

> Verily we have now got all the irons, poker, tongs and all: let me see, what are we? Confectioners, cooks,

> booksellers, dealers in cordials, fruiterers, lodging housekeepers, hay horners, storekeepers, carters, dealers in timber, et et et et

No one knew the value of adaptability better than women. What was needed in Victoria, far more than fine garments, letters of introduction and sterling protocols, wrote Elizabeth Ramsay-Laye in her advice manual for prospective female immigrants, *is a smiling face, and a firm determination never to look on the shady side of the picture but to make the very best of every cross, accident or discomfort*. There was no doubt that Melbourne was a pick-yourself-up, dust-yourself-off sort of a place.

It was also, thanks to the combination of dislocation and new money, a place of intoxicating experimentation. Commentators had endless fun describing the peculiarities of local dress. Diggers, draymen and labourers, reported Robert Caldwell, had adopted the 'uniform' of blue flannel shirt, brass-buckled belt, straw hat, knee-high boots and colourful *neckchief*. Large gold rings and flowing beards were also popular. It was a *worker's costume*, but adopted by all walks of life as a symbol of colonial authenticity. William Kelly, who had been in California before arriving in Australia in 1853, observed that in Melbourne it was de rigueur to dispense with coats, gloves and bell-toppers, and that the scorecard on neckties vs. bare necks was fifty-fifty. Kelly also enjoyed describing the attire of Melbourne's women who, he said, were *addicted to flowers and corn-stalks* worn in their bonnets. They also exhibited a *passion for parasols* (quite sensible, one would think, in the Australian sunshine). Warming to his topic, Kelly described how the *gentler portion of the [female] community* stayed indoors while the women who walked out in public were the *strong-minded class*...

> striking but unattractive women [who] jostled you on

> the flagways, elbowed you in the shops, and rattled through the streets in carriages hired at a guinea an hour, arrayed in flaunting dresses of the most florid colours, composed of silks, sarcenets and brocaded satins.

For Kelly, the most amusing detail of all was what these promenading women wore on their feet. Dressed to kill, they *buried their tiny feet and tapering ankles in lumbering Wellingtons.*

The journalist Charles Lyall had another expression for the peculiarities of women's dress in Victoria. *The prevailing costume of the Ladies*, he wrote, *is the chacun a son gout style*. The French phrase translates as 'each to his own', expressing individuality of taste or choice. John Capper put the *strange antics* of Melbourne's women down to the fact that many of the young wives had *never seen money before*, hence the fashion for white satin, ostrich feathers and pearls, which they exhibited proudly while *refreshing themselves with a pot of half-and-half.* The women of Melbourne might have been lampooned for their gaucheries, but they relished the opportunity to experiment with unorthodox appearances. For those women who were proceeding to the diggings, such aesthetic adventures were good preparation for the journey ahead.

*

The explosion in Melbourne's growth had far-reaching effects, and many immigrants, particularly those with families, were disheartened by what they saw when they left the relative security of their ship. The search for decent lodgings was the first challenge. Single young men like the Calwells could bed down in any nook or cranny, but fathers struggled to find accommodation for their dependants. Solomon Belinfante, a Jamaican-born London

Jew of Portuguese Sephardic ancestry, arrived on the luxurious *Queen of the South* in June 1854, the same journey that brought Governor La Trobe's replacement, Sir Charles Hotham, to his new home. Solomon had been assured a room in Melbourne by one of his brethren. He went ashore with his pregnant, twenty-one-year-old, Jamaican-born wife Ada, their infant daughter Rebecca and her nursemaid, after a comfortable seventy-eight days at sea under steam power. *We had lunch in a miserable place called Sandridge*, wrote Belinfante, aged forty, in his diary, *then walked to the omnibus ankle deep in mud...heartily sick of the Cohen promises to engage lodgings...heartily disgusted with the place.* Ada and Solomon soon settled in Collingwood, where he became a commercial broker and she got on with the business of having eleven more children.[3]

Genteel Martha Clendinning had a similarly tough time of finding lodgings. Thirty-two-year-old Martha was a member of the Anglo-Irish aristocracy, raised in Kings County. As a daughter of the Protestant Ascendancy class, it was fitting that she married a doctor sixteen years her senior. By the time Martha and her husband, George, arrived in Melbourne, they had already endured a long and monotonous voyage from England that ended in a calamitous shipwreck in Port Phillip Bay, just off Queenscliff. All the steerage passengers lost their entire belongings in the hold and lower deck, but the Clendinnings, in a first-class berth, got off lightly. They did lose their digging tools and almost lost their tent, which later became their Ballarat home for two years. But in Melbourne, Martha, her seven-year-old daughter, Margaret, and her sister, Sarah Lloyd, eventually found a room to rent—also in Collingwood—in the house of the *well known vocalist*, Mrs Tester. George Clendinning and Sarah's husband stayed at a pub, sleeping atop a billiard table.

At this stage, the suburb of Collingwood had no roads and the stumps of newly felled gum trees poked out of the ground. A four-foot-high gum stub protruded right at the entrance to the doctor's wife's new abode. Martha marvelled at the happy-go-lucky spirit of her young daughter *who remained free from all the anxieties and fears for the future that pressed on her parents.* The girl was *perfectly happy*, wrote Martha in her memoirs, *and enjoyed all the changes and chances we had passed through.* She probably slept well at night, too, unlike Martha, who found sleep *impossible.* It wasn't just apprehension that kept her awake; her restlessness was also *owing to the crowds of mosquitoes that attacked us.* Everyone complained about the mosquitos. Some newcomers reacted so badly to the insects' stings that they had to be hospitalised. And when they were not being monstered by mosquitos, neophyte Victorians were driven mad by flies.[4]

But if insects were irritating, there was a more menacing scourge. Colonial fever was a quaint name for a hideous disease: typhus, spread by head lice, and characterised by headaches, chills and the foul smell of rotting bodily fluids. It was sometimes known as *putrid fever.* Colonial fever was exacerbated by overcrowding and poor hygiene. It took out young and old, hearty and sickly alike, and it frightened even the Pollyannas among the immigrants. Women were known to shave their pubic hair to diminish the chances of lice infestation. To add to the lethal mix, influenza, scarlet fever, measles, tuberculosis and whooping cough all became endemic in Victoria in the 1850s, associated with high immigration, high birth rate and congested living conditions.

The housing shortage underlay many of Melbourne's social woes. Real estate prices had dropped in Melbourne when the town was emptied following the first gold discoveries, but now the rush was on to accommodate the daily delivery of new souls. All manner of temporary structures were erected to serve as lodging houses; so much the better if you could get a liquor licence and call it a hotel. Not surprisingly, disease spread like wildfire through these unsanitary and overcrowded hostelries. In 1854, the Legislative Council took action and passed the *Act for the Well-Ordering of Common Lodging Houses*, which required landlords and their houses to be registered and inspected for cleanliness and ventilation. The latter was theoretically easy in a wide-open country. The former was virtually impossible in a city that would not get a sewerage system until the 1890s. Lodging houses were also supposed to keep the unmarried sexes segregated. Like the ships captains, on this score the city fathers were truly beating against the wind.

Frances and Thomas Pierson could find neither a lodging house nor a hotel room. After debarking from the *Ascutna*, they pitched a tent on the beach at Sandridge. Hundreds more were doing the same thing. The beach was reduced to a campsite hugging the shore. One day soon after the Piersons' arrival, a hideous summer gale *blew a hurricane* for fourteen hours without reprieve. The *sand flew in clouds thicker than I ever saw it snow*, wrote Thomas. The sand stuck to the perspiration that dripped from their exposed skin. *All our faces was so black*, Thomas spat, *you actually could not tell a black man from a white one*. It took the Piersons two months to locate their more permanent accommodation in Collingwood. Thomas's antipathy did not abate with a roof over his head. Frances was *too unwell*, suffering from the debilitating dysentery that racked new arrivals. After witnessing several neighbours die of colonial fever, he wrote in his diary, *This is a very unhealthy place—all a Lie that we were told in History or the papers*. Thomas Pierson was scared for his wife's declining health and felt mightily ripped off. He was not reserving judgment on Australia: *This is the most God forsaken accursed country I could conceive of.*

Even more desolate for some: those too poor or unlucky to find accommodation were left with one grim place of last resort. Canvas Town was a tent city, authorised by Governor La Trobe in 1852 as a salve for the housing crisis, located on the south side of the Yarra River at Emerald Hill (now the site of the Melbourne Arts Centre). Like the township of Melbourne itself, Canvas Town was laid out in an orderly grid. Interspersed with tent dwellings were tent stores, bakers shops, butchers stalls, restaurants, sly grog shops and barbers shops. Inhabitants paid five shillings for a plot.

It sounds like a fine solution, but the way of life for its eight thousand inhabitants was anything but idyllic. The MARCO POLO CHRONICLE had warned immigrants about Canvas Town, *the epitome of misery and costliness.* The land here was unforgiving: boggy in winter, baked dry in summer. The only available water supply was the foetid Yarra River, downstream of the tanneries and soap factories of Collingwood and Richmond. Colonial fever, dysentery and crime were rife.

Martha Clendinning paid a ghoulish visit to Canvas Town one day, perhaps lured by what Charles Dickens called the 'attraction of repulsion'. The *begrimed and unrecognisable children* who roamed about in packs, dodging and weaving carts that were loaded with firewood, rumbling between the tents with their *wretched occupants*, horrified Martha. Everyone and everything was covered in dust. Henry Mundy provided the soundtrack: *children squalling, women shrieking and men shouting, the noise was uproarious.*

*

There may have been mud, filth, flies, teeming accommodation, gaudy dresses, drunken revellers, exorbitant prices, ominous diseases and absent husbands, but we should not confuse this bedlam with Hollywood's version of the Wild West. There is a significant difference. Melbourne was a far-flung but loyal satellite of the British Empire, built by and upon British institutions. By 1854, Melbourne already had a public library and a university. Within thirty years, it would become an exemplary international metropolis. And in the imperial metropolis, unlike Dodge City, one expected to be governed—and governed judiciously.

On the American frontier, Judge Lynch was the only paternal figure, and Darwinian logic—the survival of the physically and spiritually fittest—was remorseless. During the Californian gold rush, the ideology of order was based on the morality of the individual rather than the institutions established by the ruling elite: individual honour counted for more than an externally imposed social order. By contrast, British citizens expected to be governed by the organisations and ethos of British justice. As the MARCO POLO CHRONICLE reassured its readers, *the Genuine Spirit of British Generosity, Nobility and Earnestness exists in the brave young city.* They would not need to fend for themselves; the mother country had their back.

But prevailing British social mores would be tested. Tent living didn't only let the dust in. Like a sea voyage, mass camping brought unexpected, and potentially uninvited, familiarity. William Kelly described an *indelicate drawback* of tent living: *if your candle at bedtime happened to be extinguished first, you might probably be startled by the shadowy phantom of Mrs or Miss A B C, next door, in her night-dress, preparing for the stretcher.* There's a certain ribald piquancy to Kelly's sketch, but the fact is that camping life, like ship life, made for a community of intimate strangers.

Boundaries were as steadfast as the flicker of candlelight. In this, the material conditions of living reflected the metaphysical aspect of social change. One female sojourner wrote that Australian conventions were *quite an elastic, compressible thing, and give to the touch like anything.* William Westgarth reflected that such flexibility could catch a fellow off guard; over-weening aspiration lurked in the shadows and threatened customary notions of decency. *Ambition*, he observed, writing about the gold rush population, *may rear its head from any social grade, unchecked by conventional barriers.* It's no wonder that colonial anxiety did not turn on how to employ or house the restless throng daily washing up on the colony's shores, but rather on how to restrain this 'downside up community'.[5]

*

All a lie, thundered Thomas Pierson. He was merely committing to his diary what many people discussed over tea and damper. The crashing discord between expectation and reality quickly became apparent to most immigrants. Just think of those three months or more at sea. It's a long time to defer gratification. To stare at the horizon with only the wide-open future ahead. All those promises of prosperity—milk and honey and manly self-regard—conjured up at will to crowd out the oceanic stench of vomit, piss, maggots and death. And then, finally, you're there. Thomas Pierson was not the only new arrival with a gnawing sense that he'd been hoodwinked. And Martha Clendinning was but one of many chroniclers who spoke of their intense anxiety.

Anxiety, as today's psychiatrists will tell you, can be a symptom of the dissonance between two fundamental states of being: a clash between inner conception and outer manifestation, or between the idealised and the actual. Could we diagnose a mass emotional decompensation among Victoria's immigrants? Commentators certainly evoked the language of disease to describe the social pathology created by the cascade of gold rushes. The *yellow fever*, it was called. *Melbourne is a dreadful place*, wrote Henry Mundy, *everybody seems to be going mad either with too much money or too little.* The entire colony was *infected*, according to John Capper: *the gold fever raged here more generally and more violently than in New South Wales.*

George Evans analysed the root of the malady: *poor fellows who went up [to the diggings] with bright hopes and golden dreams are coming down with empty pockets and desponding hearts.* George Francis Train was apt to agree, despite the fact that he was well on his way to establishing one of Melbourne's most successful trading houses. *Lying reports. Yes—I repeat, lying reports*, Train wrote on 7 November 1853, *lying reports that went home from Melbourne and Sydney…reports made to catch the eye of every adventurer.* Train believed that the reports were planted by parties interested in land and sales commissions, then echoed by newspapers with an eye to their own profits. After six months in the colony, Train had decided that Victoria was not the Southern El Dorado, but the South Sea Bubble. *I know of no instance in commercial history*, he railed, *when so large a business has been transacted without any reliable information.*

Thomas Pierson also thought it was people *with interests* who trafficked in false hope; he fingered the shipowners—and merchants like G. F. Train.

Not everyone experienced their internal ructions as maddening. Willie Davis Train, a southern belle plucked from the plantation, might have been expecting to find life in the South

Sea Bubble arduous. But after a year in Melbourne, she wrote in a long letter to her father, Colonel George Davis, a friend of Abraham Lincoln: *The extraordinary change which has been effected in Melbourne within the past year can scarcely be credited by those who have not like myself witnessed the wonderful revolution.* For Willie, the external pace of change had swept through her like a tonic, tempering her grief at losing her only child just weeks before sailing. *As I advance in years and experience*, she wrote to her brother on the same day, *I find myself undergoing such a wonderful revolution that at times I marvel at my own thoughts.*

An inner riot; a symbiotic uprising of spirit and circumstance. Willie's only misgiving was the amount of time George spent at work, absorbed in business, building a new stone warehouse or clinching another deal. He was also infamous for occupying a personal chair in gin-slinging at the Criterion Hotel in Collins Street, run by American proprietor Sam Moss. *I rarely see him*, she confided, *but must I suppose make no complaints.* Willie would have known she was one of the lucky ones. For the majority of newcomers, even other well-heeled ladies of fine breeding and education, it was a struggle just to keep a toehold in an avalanche of adversity.

For every miner or merchant in the money, there was another down on his luck. And that very often meant a starving wife and children or a shelved fiancée or a fretful mother at home, waiting for news of a distant son's good fortune. In the case of Janet Kincaid, her husband's ledger was definitely in deficit. He had been gone for over two years, following the rushes around Victoria, while Janet was left in Glasgow with six children and a slew of unanswered letters. By the time she at last procured her husband's latest address from his father, she was heartily fed up. A rare archival find, here is Janet in her full glory:

> You left to better your family, you don't need to write that any more, we have had enough of that talk. You had better do something for *them*. You left the ship to better your *self* and to get your *money* to your *self*. You never earned much for your family, far less for your *Wife*, you sent five Pounds, two years and a half ago. You mention in a letter to me that you made more money at the digging than ever you made at home. You might have sent us the half of what you made. You are a hard hearted *Father* when you could sit down and eat up your *children's* meat your *self*. I was a poor unfortunate *Wretch*, little did I think when I was young what I had to come *through* with your *conduck*. We might have been the *happiest couple* in Greenock, you got a good *wife* and many a good job at home if you had been inclined to do well but folks that cante do well at home is not to be trusted *Abroad*...poor Duncan [child number five] does not know what sort of thing a Father is, he thinks it is something for *eating*...find a proper place where I will send my letters. No more at present from your *deserted Wife* Janet Kincaid.[6]

The ghosts of the past haunted new immigrants, reminding them of their righteous strivings and goading them with the too-often inadequate results.

Some single women fared better on arrival than their male counterparts, often because employment situations had been pre-arranged. When nineteen-year-old Irish girl Eliza Darcy arrived on the *City of Manchester* in July 1854, she went straight into the service of Mr Jeffries, on the Great Western Road, employed on a three-month contract for £18 with rations.[7] Eliza was born in Ennis, County Clare, in the parish of Killaloe, the second largest Catholic diocese in Ireland. Another branch of the Darcy family from Clare had arrived on the *Parsee* in June 1854: Anthony and Honora Darcy and their six children aged between fourteen and twenty-five. Eliza travelled alone to Victoria, but also sailing on the *City of Manchester* were members of the Howard family from Dublin. Devout Catholics, the Howard and Darcy lines would later unite in the passion-fuelled summer of 1854.

The Galway tearaways, Bridget and Michael Nolan, also secured employment as domestic servants soon after arriving in Geelong penniless, and, according to family tradition, shoeless. Bridget had a malformed arm and worried it would be counted against her, but the siblings found permanent work at a Mt Wallace grazing station without much trouble.

One girl, employed as a servant, twittered merrily to her sisters at home about her startling new prospects on the marriage market:

> I had an offer a few days after landing from a gold-digger, with £600–£700. Since that I have had another from a bushman, with £900; he has gone to the diggings again, to make plenty of money. That I have not decided on yet. I shall have a handsome house and garden and all I wish…I have so many chances, a midshipman for one, so you may guess how different things are here if you are respectable.[8]

Eligible women had a remarkable new power to pick and choose their mate, a fact that caused significant moral panic about the influence of truculent wives. Other single girls could get themselves an instant breadwinner. Eliza Lucus wrote home, *When immigrant ships came in, the Diggers came down to meet them, to try and induce women to marry them and go back to the diggings with them.*[9] Public servant William Westgarth, one of Victoria's earliest historians, corroborated Eliza's reminiscences. As soon as an immigrant ship arrived there was a rush to the docks, wrote Westgarth, *the wives for servants and the youth for wives.* (In Westgarth's opinion, the latter should always have taken precedence.)

The offer of marriage and a dray ride to the diggings was not every girl's idea of a good time, yet for many it was just another form of assisted passage. And single women had an alarming degree of autonomy, able to choose between domestic service and marriage. Even more disconcerting for bystanders, these newly empowered young women were choosing to go it alone and determine their own definition of freedom and independence.

But for married women, the insecurity of an unemployed male breadwinner and its accompanying disillusionment could be debilitating. After Jane McCracken and her husband Alex resolved to take up dairying as a means to self-sufficiency, Jane described her state of mind in a letter to her mother and eleven siblings back home in Auchencrosh in Scotland. *People give us great encouragement, of what it will do if we persevere,* wrote Jane, *but beginners in the world like us and everything new to us we likely have more anxiety than there is any use for.* As she suspected, the superfluous adrenaline did not serve Jane well, and her letters reveal a woman on the wrong side of a nervous breakdown.[10]

If uppity, anxious or aggrieved wives weren't enough to trouble a man, there was always the weather to complain about. *Where is the beautiful climate and the delicious fruits that every book on this country which I saw in the States pictured in such enthusiastic colours?* asked George Francis Train. The northerly wind, his wife Willie Davis wrote, *is more disagreeable than anything you can imagine.* After a full year in Victoria, the Calwell brothers had seen both sides of the seasonal coin. Dan bemoaned summer's *unsufferable heat, tormenting flies and whirl-winds of dust*, then winter's *Rain, rain, rain! Nothing but rain. Surely*, he lamented, *this is one of the most unpleasant climates in the world.*

What the Calwell boys didn't know was that, in the middle of one of the driest decades in the century, the winter of 1854 was one of the wettest on record. And that the meteorological crapshoot would make all the difference to the deluge of discontent about to prevail.

*

It was not just Victoria's barometric pressure that fluctuated wildly. In 1853, Victoria purchased £480,000 worth of British goods—about the same amount as Spain, and a quarter of what was bought by the sixty million people of the Russian Empire.[11] In 1851 Victoria imported £122 worth of American goods. A year later, that figure had reached £60,000, a measure of the sort of rapid expansion in American business interests that had George Francis Train jumping out of his long johns. In 1853, 134 ships arrived in Melbourne from the United States, bringing £1.7 million worth of goods. In 1852, bank deposits increased from £820,000 to £4,330,000.[12] *No such go-aheadative place exists elsewhere*, as Train put it. It was the sheer lunacy of the post-1852 market that persuaded contemporary observer John Capper to remark *society is to a certain degree unhinged.* Commercial transactions, to his mind, were completely *deranged.*

But by and large supplies were able to keep up with the exploding demand, and there were only two commodities that Victorians couldn't get enough of: women and alcohol. By the end of 1854, Melbourne merchant Robert Caldwell wrote that

80,000 wives are wanted—one of the few articles of export which is safe, if sent in good condition and warranted sound. As for grog, the statistics are eloquent. In 1851 Victorians drank £23,000 worth of brandy, £5000 of gin, £15,000 of rum, £3600 of whisky and £20,000 of wine. By 1853, these figures jumped to £630,000, £196,000, £149,000, £42,000 and £353,000 respectively.[13] You will notice that this jump in imports represents considerably more than the five-fold hike that would be commensurate with the population increase. (There were those, of course, who believed that the dearth of wives and profusion of alcohol were closely connected.)

But even liquor merchants were not doing as well as property owners. Those who had been in the colony prior to 1851, many of whom were now established professionals and merchants, were able to capitalise on the boom in real estate prices, selling for stupid prices land they had bought for next to nothing. Landlords could and did charge phenomenal rents.

Watching over the swirling eddies of fortune and famine from the heights of political office was the Victorian Government. In 1854 the government consisted of an Executive Council (comprising the lieutenant governor, the colonial secretary, the attorney general, the colonial treasurer and the collector of customs), the Legislative Council (eight members nominated by the governor and thirty-five by voters) and an understorey of clerks.

To exercise the privilege of a vote, a person had to be a British subject, male, over twenty-one and a free colonist. He had to be a freeholder of £100 or a leaseholder of £10 per annum value, or own a licence to depasture, or have occupied a house worth £10 per annum for six months previous. It was the property qualifications that effectively disenfranchised most of the new immigrant population. Wool had been replaced by gold as the most valuable commodity, but pastoralists lost none of their prerogative because of their entrenched position in the political economy of the colony. Even a gung-ho merchant capitalist like Robert Caldwell could see that volatile Victoria was governed by a system where the squatters had *more than their fair share of representation, while the diggers have none at all. At present*, wrote Caldwell, the diggers had no constitutional way *of calling attention to their grievances, real or fancied.* This was a big problem.

The trouble was, times had changed. Rapidly. The Victoria that greeted the arrivals of late 1853 and early 1854 was not the same place it had been in 1852 when people like Bonwick, Capper and Mossman were writing their breathless guidebooks and advice manuals. The sluggish communications of the mid-nineteenth century misrepresented the pace of change on the ground. It could take up to a year for a resident of Ballarat to send a letter home, receive a reply and write back again. In such time, several new rushes would have occurred, one town depleted of its fickle population while another tent city had mushroomed elsewhere. In such time, tens of thousands of new immigrants would be disgorged onto Melbourne's streets, all competing for the same small stock of housing, the same shallow pool of jobs, the same desire to kit themselves out and get on the road to the diggings.

What made this situation more ominous was the fact that the quantity of gold unearthed peaked in 1852. In that year the value of gold exported from Victoria was £14,866,799. In 1853 this sum fell to £11,588,782 and by 1854 the plummet continued, to £8,770,796. At the same time, the population of the goldfields had swiftly increased, from approximately 35,000 in

1852 to 73,000 in 1853 and 93,000 in 1854. This meant that there was much less gold to go around: from £425 worth per person per annum in 1852, it had dropped to only £87 worth by 1854 This change, wrote William Kelly in 1860, produced *a modified panic.*[14] Despite all the grandiosity, the simple fact was that by 1854, Melbourne was sliding into economic chaos. A glut of cheap imports meant there was no incentive for local manufacturing. An itinerant labour force moving between unemployment in the city and gruelling work for little reward on the diggings made for a fragmented population of disaffected migrants.

Governor La Trobe, who had resigned his commission in December 1852 but had to wait an agonising seventeen months for his replacement to arrive, was aware that he was in way over his head. Yet by mid-1853, the Executive Council had embarked on a spending spree of its own. In 1851 government expenditure on post offices, for example, was £11,165. In 1854, it was over £120,000. In 1851, spending on public works amounted to £32,600. By 1854 it was over £1.4 million. In 1851 policing received £24,000 and education £6000. In 1854 these services received £650,000 and £160,000 respectively.[15] A triumvirate of urban landowners, rural pastoralists and an unrepresentative administrative clique ruled Victoria. Buoyed by the land boom, the government borrowed freely.

It also taxed liberally. By the time Sir Charles Hotham arrived in June 1854, he would inherit not only a government deep in debt but also a populace chafing, as the centralised model of colonial government inherited from New South Wales ground up against a worldly populace expecting self-sufficiency and independence. As William Westgarth observed, the Victoria that welcomed the renegade Bridget Nolan, the adventurous Eliza Darcy, the go-getting Sarah Hanmer, the infatuated Margaret

Howden and the devout Anastasia Hayes was occupied by a *promiscuous multitude*: young, restless, indignant, over-invested, underfed—and smelling a rat.

*

Frances Pierson set out on the road to Ballarat on the first day of summer 1853 with her husband Thomas and son Mason. She had not travelled across the briny deep from her Pennsylvania home to be a grass widow in some flyblown Melbourne lodging house. Besides, she'd tried that once already. Back in April 1853, Thomas and Mason had ventured up to Bendigo to open a shop, and when that swiftly failed they went prospecting at the McIvor diggings. Left alone, Frances twiddled her thumbs for a moment or two, then applied for work at a stationer's business. She reasoned that *if they would employ her to help tend store she would rather be there than sitting in the Boarding House.* Frances was also earning a much-needed income, a fact upon which Thomas was reluctant to dwell. Less than two months later, the Pierson menfolk were back. Bendigo was *purgatory*, proclaimed Thomas, its population rife with disorder and antipathy towards the authorities. In June 1853, an anti-licence association was formed and a giant petition got up, decrying several aspects of the goldfields administration. Thousands of miners were wearing red ribbons as a symbol of unity and defiance.

By 1 September 1853, news of fresh gold strikes at Ballarat—110 feet deep, tens of thousand of pounds worth of gold per hole—came whistling down the wire. These spectacular finds were dubbed the 'Jewellers' Shops', so seemingly effortless was it to reach into the earth and pull out a fortune. The ensuing rush saw thousands of people suddenly throw in their jobs and head straight to Ballarat in the spring of 1853. Sparkling new evidence of Ballarat's untapped potential prompted a resurgence in intra-colonial travel to the diggings, as people ventured from South Australia and Tasmania to try their hand. George and Charles Evans left Melbourne on 11 November 1853, with John Basson Humffray in their travelling party. After an unsuccessful stint at mining on the Ovens goldfields, Charles Evans had decided that auctioneering, not digging, would be the key to future prosperity. J. B. Humffray was making his first trip to the goldfields—with no inkling, surely, that exactly a year from that date he would be at the forefront of a campaign for justice that would make the Bendigo Red Ribbon movement look like a fancy-dress party.

As for the Piersons, they too decided to go into commerce rather than industry. They planned to open a store at Ballarat, unperturbed by Thomas's recent failure at Bendigo. Frances carefully packed her camera and photographic apparatus. A daguerreotypist from Liverpool whom she had met in Melbourne assured her that her equipment was of impressive quality. And there would surely be a host of lucky diggers eager to commemorate their pristine nuggets. *Frances has some idea of her and the [Liverpudlian] Gent commencing the business*, Thomas wrote, with a hint of condescension, in his diary as they prepared to depart. What would the Worshipful Master back home at the Philadelphia Olive Lodge have thought of the idea? But Victoria was not Pennsylvania and Frances knew it.

The Piersons arrived in Ballarat on 6 December 1853. They were greeted by twenty thousand other hopeful supplicants at the altar of rampant ambition.

*

The road to Ballarat stretched west from Melbourne, through the outlying suburb of Flemington and on to the wide plains of Keilor and Melton. It's the same route that you would take today, without the tangle of ring roads, truck depots and tilt-slab factories. The modern-day industrial heartland takes advantage of the same topography that departing diggers appreciated: flat, open terrain, a carpet of basalt rolled out by ancient lava flows from the South Australian border to Port Phillip Bay. William Westgarth described these plains as *an ocean of grass*. Charles Evans saw it the same way: *stretching as far as the eye could reach were immense grassy plains undulating in emerald folds like the swell of the ocean.* It was fertile ground above as well as beneath: open hunting lands that had sustained the region's Indigenous inhabitants for tens of thousands of years.

The seventy-mile road to Ballarat—a well-worn track, really—marked the ragged course for a chaotic rush of fortune-seekers. Carts, drays, coaches and thousands of pairs of galloping hooves and plodding feet carried people and goods to the magnetic epicentre of Victoria's goldfields. *The fact is*, wrote one man in a letter home to Scotland in February 1852, *everybody, old and young, rich and poor, learned and illiterate are off to the diggings.* James Bonwick noted that the allure was physically impossible to ignore. *The Gold Fields have a most bewitching influence*, he wrote after his own visit to Ballarat in 1852, *the very name begets a spasmodic affection of the limbs, which want to be off.*[16] The road to Ballarat was akin to William Blake's 'crooked road of prophecy', a road washed smooth by the salvation that lay at the end.[17]

Thirty miles from Melbourne, in the low, fertile basin of Bacchus Marsh, travellers were forced to navigate a deep cut-out known as The Gap. This jagged landmark provided a lucrative winter industry for bullock drivers, who charged a king's ransom to haul out drays piled high with gear from the swollen river at the base of the gorge. Some mud-drenched parties were held up for days waiting to be dragged up the slippery face of the cut-out. (Today, cars whiz along this ravine on a nifty roller-coaster stretch of the Western Highway.) Back on flat land, the road snaked through a thick stringybark forest to Ballan and from there followed a gentle incline towards the only sizable peak on the landscape, Mt Buninyong, rising to the left. Once reaching that acme of achievement, you were almost there. A solitary messenger on horseback could make the journey in a day of furious riding. An average cart trip took three days (and cost £25 in dry weather—a princely sum). On foot, it was a week-long hike.

There are innumerable accounts of the epic journey to Ballarat. In most of them, after the muck, dust and overcrowding of Melbourne, the open road is a revelation. Twenty-two-year-old Emily Skinner, who travelled to the Ovens diggings in 1854, was immediately won over by *the beauty and healthiness of the country.* Mary Bristow was rendered speechless. *I cannot describe the bush*, she wrote. *It means such an extent of country covered with trees, some large, some small, no sign of human habitation except here and there a few camps or tents, some inhabited by blacks.* She found the scenery *beautiful* and the blacks *exquisitely made.* To her astonishment, Mary felt that the Australian bush was the incarnation of *Eden.* Mrs Mannington Caffyn, in her contribution to the compendium COO-EE: TALES OF AUSTRALIAN LIFE BY AUSTRALIAN LADIES, was also rhapsodic but observed a sting in the tail of Paradise. *Australian sunlight*, she wrote, *is quite original, and only flourishes in Australia. It is young and rampant and bumptious, and it is rather cruel, with the cruelty of young untried things.* Many women who travelled the roads in summer reported sitting out the midday sun under a stand of trees, taking their lead from the old hands, not to mention the cows and sheep.[18]

As early as March 1853, contemporary observers like James Bonwick were already commenting on the incontrovertible fact of the women: the diggings were attracting them like ants to honey. Bonwick wrote in his AUSTRALIAN GOLD DIGGER'S MONTHLY MAGAZINE that in just two days he counted *one hundred and twenty ladies, going up either with or to their lords of the pick and cradle*. Bonwick called it a phenomenon, this *feminine Exodus from our townships*. He also noted that *some husbands have taken uncommon care to prepare for the coming of their better halves* by forsaking their tents for log cabins with stone chimneys, floor coverings and even an iron bedstead.[19]

Some diggers were not so much tearaways as nest-featherers. Their wives accompanied them to keep families intact that would otherwise have fractured, but also in a genuine spirit of exploration. When James Watson determined to go to Ballarat, his wife Margaret, who had already survived several trials with James and their children, *decided that this was one more adventure for her*.[20] Emily Skinner knew that her husband William *would not go if I objected very much, etc. but*, she reasoned, *what a much better chance we should have of getting on [together]*. After thinking and talking it over a little, the couple determined that William would precede Emily, make enough money to build a comfortable tent home, then send for Emily to join him. This plan was realised surprisingly quickly.

There were hundreds of single women, too, on the road to Ballarat, some joining (or searching for) absent husbands or connecting with kin or kith from their old lives, others forging their own distinct paths in the world. Eliza Darcy, who left the employ of Mr Jeffries in October 1854, was one of them. Having seen out her pre-arranged contract, Eliza headed to Ballarat, where numerous members of her extended family had gathered. Anthony and Honora Darcy and their five children, probably Eliza's cousins, had recently arrived on the *Parsee*. Also sailing on the *Parsee* were six Dunne children, aged seventeen to twenty-three, and their mother Mary, Eliza's aunt. Other Dunnes had travelled on the *City of Manchester* with Eliza, as had several members of the Howard family. By the explosive spring of 1854, all these Darcys, Howards and Dunnes would be in Ballarat. By August 1855, Eliza would be married to Patrick Howard, a close friend of an Irish engineer named Peter Lalor who was engaged to her cousin, Geelong school teacher Alicia Dunne.

Bridget Nolan was also on the road to Ballarat. Life at the Mt Wallace station had been exciting for the Nolan siblings, with a visit from bushrangers and an old black woman coming to stay, but after eighteen months the call of the diggings could no longer be dismissed. Possibly Bridget had got word that her shipmate Patrick Hynes was in Ballarat and a reunion beckoned. Now that they had shoes, Bridget and her brother Michael walked the ten kilometres from Mt Wallace to Ballarat. She and Patrick Hynes would be married in the spring of 1854.

There is no account of how Clara Du Val or Sarah Hanmer, both single mothers of young children, made their way to Ballarat. Unlike Eliza Darcy, neither of the actresses appeared to have a network of family and friends to support them. But there were many women making the journey on their own. Emily Skinner met *two stout young women* on her journey to the Ovens. *They told me that they had many offers of a place [in Melbourne], as it was hard to get servants*, wrote Emily in her diary, *but the girls were determined to go to the diggings, where high wages and easy times awaited them.* Such was the unruly confidence of the times.

Forty-two-year-old spinster Mary Bristow was keen to go to the diggings *as a kind of bivouac*, and found three young women to accompany her. The party set off on foot almost immediately. The first night the women slept in a covered dray, but it rained in torrents. *I don't think I closed my eyes*, wrote Mary. In the morning, the women walked to a nearby brook *and completed our toilets*. Mary was relieved to note that *there is always due observance of respect* from the men in their travelling company. The first day, they walked fourteen miles, the next twenty-four miles. The women wore veils and large bonnets against the summer sun. They never ventured out in the middle of the day; it was *too dangerous to expose [ourselves] to the sun's burning rays.* But if the sun was hazardous, Mary found that the people of the road were not. *All strangers or travellers receive a welcome in this hospitable land*, she recorded: ladies could walk or ride long distances unattended and have nothing to fear. *I have never been so happy or free from care*, she wrote, calling to mind a line of Ralph Waldo Emerson's about 'the independence of solitude'. It was on a Victorian bush track that Mary Bristow discovered the sweetness of her own company and freedom from the crowded concerns of others. How curious that Emerson, the American champion of individualism, provided the guiding light for a woman forging a path to the Victorian gold diggings, the fabled home of radical collectivism.

Mrs Elizabeth Massey also found a change in herself on the road to Ballarat. She was not so much pulled by the allure of gold as pushed by the weight of duty. Back in England Mrs Massey had been married only a few weeks when her new husband *unexpectedly called on* her to accompany him to Australia. *Disgust*, she wrote in her memoir eight years later, *indeed is not a word strong enough to express my feelings at the moment, particularly as*

I had to wear a calm face and not distress my loving friends by any ebullition of feeling. Mrs Massey considered her journey banishment in place of a honeymoon. On arrival in Victoria, the Masseys went straight to the diggings to avoid the *filth, flies and expense* of Melbourne. It was on the road that Mrs Massey's expulsion began to take on a more optimistic quality. On the road, she found that people were more *warm-hearted and hospitable* than at home in England, more *compassionate and forgiving*. Her theory? *They themselves [have] passed through the fiery ordeal of expatriation and suspense.* A haphazard community of wanderers, a band of gypsies, no longer contained by a ship's hold or a social milieu of formality and diffidence.

Indeed, sudden outbursts of feeling, the likes of which Mrs Massey could not afford to affect at home, seemed the very order of the day in impulsive Victoria. Bonwick described this fashion for spontaneity in the February 1853 edition of his GOLD DIGGER'S MONTHLY MAGAZINE, a widely distributed publication that Mrs Massey may have consulted.

> Our gold fields, as a grand focus of moral magnetism, have drawn together a heterogenous multitude of all classes, climes and character. The ardent and impetuous form the vast majority...strong appeals are made to the sordid and animal passions of humanity.

Such unharnessed emotion would later fuel a tragedy, but for now Mrs Massey felt joyfully off the leash. What had initially settled upon her as a black cloud of submissive misery now seemed like *a party of pleasure*. True to her creed of feminine adaptation, Mrs Massey marvelled at the sights along the road: the gigantic fallen gums, the sweet-scented wattles and correas, a *fairyland* of magnificent new flowers to behold. She and other (unidentified) female travelling companions camped for the night in the Black

Forest, sleeping under the cart with their cloaks used to make a barricade against a looming storm. Mrs Massey revelled in the *sweet harmony of nature.* Every new thunderclap or lightning strike sent waves of electricity down her straitlaced back. *All is romance in this most romantic land*, she sighed.

Some women initially believed, like Elizabeth Massey, they were on the road to perdition but happily discovered they were actually on a path to unexpected release. Others yearned to be let loose and saw a journey to the goldfields as a credible flight path. Historians have long commented on the escape fantasies that, more than simple gold lust, stimulated men's rush to the diggings.... *[in] the days when men broke their bonds and dreamed of marvellous things to come.* It's always been at least implicit—sometimes aggressively obvious—that among the bonds from which men longed to be free were the harping women with their insufferable demands and bawling brats. There is no doubt that some men did see the goldfields as their ticket out of a domestic rut. Square this fact with all the late-nineteenth-century jingoism about frontier independence, and we have deadbeats like Janet Kincaid's husband reincarnated as national heroes.

But it's clear that many women also harboured their own aspirations of escape, not necessarily from spouses and children, but from the tedious and restrictive rituals of the feminine daily round. In particular, many educated and refined women (in the words of one emigrant who eloped with her brother's tutor and emigrated to Victoria) *thought the ease of their English life well left behind them.* High teas and calling cards were a subtle form of foot binding for many nineteenth-century British gentlewomen. The price of material comfort was conformity: it cost a lot of effort and anxiety to keep up appearances. Years later, Mrs Massey, who spent two years on the diggings between 1852 and 1854, would write *I look back with a grateful heart to my gipsy life*. But of course it is the women who disappeared into the slipstream of the nomads—the ones who didn't record their thoughts or movements for a reading audience—who truly abandoned genteel performance and enjoyed the colonial gift of insignificance.

*

Refugees from convention were joined on the road by fugitives from the law. The goldfields frontier offered rabbit warrens of protection for women who needed a fresh start. The predominance of ex-convicts from Van Diemen's Land on the goldfields became a political issue after 1853, but local currency lasses could also find themselves in trouble. Chief among such miscreants were 'fallen women', those who had drawn the short straw in the lottery of premarital sex. A Miss Smith, with her fatherless baby, could be reincarnated on the diggings as Mrs Smith, an apocryphal widow who'd lost her husband in a mining accident or maritime mishap.

For it was no joke to be 'caught out'. Reports of young women who killed or abandoned their newborns in an attempt to hide the evidence of sin are common. On 31 October 1854, for example, the colonial secretary was informed that a one-month-old child had been found in the grounds of St John's School on the corner of Elizabeth and La Trobe streets in Melbourne. The babe, *who was in good health*, was wearing a long white frock, white cap and white flannel hood and was wrapped in a blue and green checked shawl. The GOVERNMENT GAZETTE posted a reward for the apprehension of the mother.

The POLICE GAZETTE was also replete with reports of female runaways. On 27 February 1854, information was distributed about one Sarah Wilson, who had left the hired service of Mr Smith in Collingwood before the expiry of her contract. Wilson was nineteen years old, slightly under five foot, with a dark complexion and small, regular features. *She has left her clothes behind her and has no relatives in Melbourne*, noted the GAZETTE. In March 1854, Ann Plummer escaped from the residence of her husband in Fitzroy Crescent. Ann had been tried for an undisclosed offence at the Central Criminal Court in 1849 and given a fifteen-year sentence, to be served at the premises of her husband. Ann was described as aged twenty-five years, a fancy-box maker, five foot one inch tall, with a *fresh complexion, brown hair, blue eyes, native Burnley, nose has been smashed.*[21] Women had many pragmatic reasons to seek the anarchic embrace of the goldfields.

For Catherine Sherwin, Ballarat would be the place to build a dynasty from ignominious beginnings. Literate and ambitious, Catherine and her sister Mary had sailed to Australia as free immigrants in 1850. At five foot one, of slight build with a dark complexion, black hair and grey eyes, Catherine would have had some capital in the colonial marriage market. If the Sherwins followed typical patterns of Irish family chain migration, it's possible that Catherine's elder brothers came to Victoria first, followed by the unmarried sisters and finally the parents, with younger siblings in tow. There were certainly other Sherwins residing in Victoria, with whom Catherine later regrouped when her life course was derailed.

Like other Irish immigrant girls of the Famine generation, Catherine and Mary married soon after their arrival in the colony. Catherine was witness at Mary's wedding to Everard Gadd at the Wesleyan Methodist Church in Melbourne in April 1852. Five months later, Catherine exchanged her vows with James Francis Bentley at St Peter's Anglican Church. James was a thirty-four-year-old native of Surrey, England, running a confectionery business in Elizabeth Street, North Melbourne. Thirteen years her elder, James had experienced far more of colonial life than his young bride, not least because he had been transported to Norfolk Island on a ten-year sentence in 1844.

Of average height and stoutly built, with dark hair, a fair complexion, a mole on the back of his neck and a slight limp caused by a mutilated right foot, James nonetheless caught Catherine's eye. According to family oral history, the couple married for love.[22] In 1852, newly wedded to a merchant with good connections in Melbourne society—and pregnant within a few months of her marriage—Catherine's colonial star was only rising. Her first son, Francis Henry Bentley, known throughout his life as Thomas, was born in September 1853 in his parents' shop. Shortly after her confinement, Catherine and her young family were on the road.

*

The summer of 1853 brought the predictable fusion of heat, dust and savage episodes of scorching wind. Flies crawled through meat carcasses and into wet, sticky human orifices. Colonial typhus menaced the goldfields populace, just as it did Melbourne's, with its low fever and high mortality rate. Dysentery was another quiet killer, especially of babies. Rumblings of discontent vibrated beneath the seemingly solid foundations of a tent city built on gold. Christmas was almost here, bringing its celebration of birth, its hope for renewal and its inevitable focus on those who were not invited into the stable.

For the imminent Yuletide revelry, Frances Pierson decided to combat homesickness with generosity. *Frances is well and stands it here first rate*, wrote Thomas, with a touch of incredulity that his wife had managed to make such a smooth transition to a suntan in December. She had recently purchased a Yankee cooking stove from Melbourne for £8 plus £3 cartage, benefiting from the economical summer transport costs. She baked a load of apple pies, cranberry tarts and sweet cakes. Enough for her small family to enjoy, and to share with some of the many single diggers who would be celebrating the festive season devoid of mothers, sisters and home comforts. Perhaps she would even sell some of her precious wares. Lord knew they could use the extra shillings.

On Christmas Day 1853, Thomas Pierson cast a glance at his robust wife, stoking the campfire, and his teenage son, skylarking with a crew of new mates. Surprised by his own high spirits, he wrote in his diary: *Well here we are on the Ballarat diggings. The question naturally occurs: where will we all be the next Christmas of '54?*

PART 2

TRANSFORMATIONS

FIVE

THE GOLD DIGGERS OF '54

Martha Clendinning was a woman who knew her own noddle. Like Frances Pierson, she was not content to remain in Melbourne while her husband went to the diggings. When Dr George Clendinning announced his imminent departure to Ballarat in the autumn of 1853, Martha *declared her intention* to accompany him. She was thirty-one years old; George was sixteen years her senior, but Martha would not be cowed. *I had made up my mind*, she declared. She would go to Ballarat, and so would her five-year-old daughter, Margaret, and Martha's younger sister, Sarah Lloyd, despite Sarah's husband's objection that there were *no decent women there, only a few of the Vandies' wives*. Tom Lloyd repeated the judgment of men throughout the ages when they didn't want to share their self-proclaimed territory. The goldfields were *no fit place for any respectable woman*.

The husbands went to scout the fields for the most promising tent site, and Martha and Sarah got to talking. *After they had left us women*, wrote Martha in her reminiscences, *we had discussed our future life at the diggings and we at once came to the conclusion that we never could sit down in our tents there with our hands before us*. Martha was pragmatic. *Our house work (if I may use the term) would take up very little time, and there was but one child between us to attend to.* Martha was also shrewd. *Besides finding something to occupy our time, we felt we should much like some way of making a little money to help our husbands in their hard work.* The Doctor, as Martha called her husband, was intending to dig for gold, not to practise medicine. Since few people got rich overnight, he might need some help at first, even if he would not countenance the idea now. And after all, at forty-seven he was not a young man. But what could two well-bred Anglo-Irish girls, scions of the Protestant Ascendancy, do to earn a livelihood? *Teaching and needle-work, the usual womanly employments, were out of the question; they were not needed on the gold fields*, mused Martha. *At last the happy thought struck us. We would keep a store! A nice, tidy, little store! We were well pleased with the idea.*

Martha and Sarah conveyed their joyous plan to their husbands. The men greeted the proposal *with peals of laughter.* They'd be the laughing stock of the diggers, they said. What did a couple of women know of business, they said. You'll be cheated and mocked, they said. So Martha and Sarah said tosh! *We were disgusted at the reception*, remembered Martha years later. The sisters kept to their plan, even amid the derision of their husbands, who maintained *a quiet sense of our excessive folly*. What George did not realise was that moonlighting to support their husbands was commonplace among Ballarat wives. Being financially dependent on his wife was just one more way in which The Doctor was about to become an ordinary digger.

*

By January 1854, the Ballarat goldfields rattled with industry and hummed with domesticity. The public and private spheres—whose separation was such a Victorian-era ideal—were as permeable here as a candlelit tent. Summer was in full flight, taking its toll on a community that lived in, by and for the elements. A *tremendous blow of hot wind blew down to pieces a great many tents*, wrote Thomas Pierson on 5 January. Living in those flailing tents were 6650 women, 2150 children and 10,700 men—almost twenty thousand inhabitants. Though Castlemaine and Sandhurst (Bendigo) maintained greater populations in the summer of 1853 (21,225 and 26,500 respectively), Ballarat had the highest proportion of women: forty-five per cent of Ballarat's inhabitants were women and children, compared with twenty-three per cent at Castlemaine and thirty-one per cent at Bendigo. Even these latter percentages are a far cry from William Withers' depiction of the *womanless crowds* of the first year of the gold rush. Of the overall goldfields population of 80,000 in January 1854, one in every three people was a woman or child.[1] In Ballarat in 1854, gold digging was inextricable from breadwinning.

Newcomers to the diggings knew to expect that women and children would be there in numbers. You only had to open your eyes. The Ballarat correspondent to the GEELONG ADVERTISER wrote on 25 July 1854 of the romance of the old days when the *only amusement to be derived was from gazing at tall stringy-barks.* Now, he wrote, *it refreshes one to look back on a time when the black police kept watch and ward over adventurous ladies who had come to see the diggings, and whose arrival on the old Golden Point was greeted with a three times three.* These days, he sighed, the coach *brings up its hundreds of the fair sex, and not a solitary cheer greets its arrival.*

One fellow wrote home in late 1853 that *there are not less than 20,000 men gold digging, besides women and children, all of whom two months ago were in Melbourne or Geelong.* The correspondent's next comment was probably more fanciful than observational.

The diggers are *clothing their wives and children in silks and satins*, he wrote.[2] The image of heroic husbandry, as we have seen, was a central symbol in the gold rush iconography. Chivalrous benefactors were supposed to be the saviours of the day.

But when William Howitt visited the goldfields in 1854, the damsels did not appear to be distressed. *There are some hugely fat women on the diggings*, he wrote, *the life seems to suit them*. They seemed to enjoy the outdoor existence, adapting to its conditions. The women were not swathed in finery, but rather dressed in a fashion that suited a life of toil. *A wide awake hat, neat fitting jacket, handsome dress*, observed Howitt; *a costume quite made for the diggings*. It needed to be. In the mornings, Howitt saw women and girls hanging out the wash, cooking over campfires and *chopping wood with great axes which swung them*. They kept chickens and goats. These *diggeresses*, he concluded, provided *a certain stationary substratum beneath the fluctuating surface*. Women had quietly become the bedrock of the Victorian mining communities.

Englishman William Kelly, who had previously written books about the Californian goldfields before touring Australia in 1853 and 1858, noted that a remarkable feature of the Ballarat diggings was *the large proportion of women*. American research reveals that only three per cent to ten per cent of the 'forty-niners' were female, clearly a much smaller proportion than in Victoria.[3] (In California women's presence on the goldfields was greeted with hostility by men, who believed that women foretold an end to male camaraderie. There was a common axiom: when the women and Jews arrived, it spelled the end of the good old days.[4]) If the Californian diggings weren't an exclusively masculine terrain, men were certainly a more predominant force than in Victoria, and this would have important implications for the respective political destinies of the two frontier outposts.

Kelly noted the upside of this female presence in Ballarat. *The Californian digger had to roast, grind and boil his own coffee,* he wrote, *but the Victorian, who is surrounded with women, would be saved all that bother.* It's tempting to leave the quote there but the rest of the passage reveals his true opinion:

> I was on the point of writing the softer sex, but that would have been a misnomer for the most callous specimens of the female creation I ever encountered were mere green pulp in comparison with some of the granite-grained viragoes I had the honour of meeting in the 'field of cloth of gold' in the new world.

Kelly preferred the dewy maidens of the old country, with their acquiescent airs and compliant graces; his expectations of what women's presence on the fields should mean were constantly dashed. Other observers also felt compelled to mention that the average diggeress did not long retain the aspect of an English rose. Howitt commented that *lovely, blooming maidens* soon withered under the influence of the Australian climate. Their *physical elasticity* was impaired and they became *lamentably susceptible to the encroachments of agedness.* (Kelly recommended that men marry *greatly below* their age, which was common enough without his counsel.) As the bounds of their physical and interpersonal worlds stretched, as they mapped new social and economic terrain, so women's skin wizened like winter apples. If their shipboard sunburn had signalled a radical inversion for female immigrants—the exchange of safety and seclusion for earthly experience—the terms of the deal were written on their bodies. It was a trade-off that many women were pleased to make.

*

Right from the start, the idea that the goldfields would be worked by honest British yeomen and their cream-skinned wives was seared into the public imagination. James Bonwick was the ideologue-in-chief with his AUSTRALIAN GOLD DIGGER'S MONTHLY MAGAZINE AND COLONIAL FAMILY VISITOR, first published in October 1852. *This little magazine will be the connecting link between the goldfields and the cottage home*, Bonwick wrote in the inaugural edition. In stark contrast to the Californian diggings, which had no laws in place, no police force and no regulatory institutions (since California did not become a state of the Union until September 1850, after the Mexican-American war), Victoria was British to its bootstraps. *This golden region shall be a peaceful home for the gathering of nations*, promised Bonwick. Not the manifest destiny of mighty rivers and endless fertile plains, but the humble provision of an orderly abode.

The Bonwicks of the age were in no doubt about the importance of women in creating the micro households that would agglomerate to the macro colonial domicile. *No persons are so interested in the order and security of the diggings as the wives of diggers up there*, wrote Bonwick in February 1853. The prevailing notion of women as civilising agents—tamers of men's wilder passions, harbingers of righteous integrity, John Ruskin's famed 'angels of the hearth'—underpinned the acceptance, and indeed encouragement, of women on the diggings. According to this ideal, women would be agents of conservative restoration, reinstating the social mores, and helping to establish the social institutions, of a settled colonial outpost. These ministering angels of the imperial heath would sweep aside the detritus of frontier living, housetraining men in wholesome marriages, bearing children to send to nascent schools: holding up a moral universe in which charity and benevolence would smooth the jagged edges of greed and corruption. That was the idea, anyway.

But it was not just ideology that wove women into the fabric of goldfields society. In the hard-nosed way of British bureaucracy, there were structural provisions made for the reality that women would be integral to the colonial economy. The emblem of the Victorian domestic idyll could be not just a soother of furrowed brows, but a source of revenue too. From the first proclamation of the Gold Regulations for Victoria's auriferous regions in September 1851, women acquired a unique legal identity. They were able, indeed compelled, to take out a licence to work on the diggings. As such, women were technically afforded the political legitimacy that is the inalienable right of the property owner in a capitalist regime.

This is how the Gold Regulations worked. The administrative model adopted by La Trobe's government asserted the prerogative of the Crown over all minerals extracted from Crown land. A licence fee of 30 shillings per month was instituted, entitling individual miners to a claim of twelve feet by twelve and the right to take wood and water from the land. Commissioners were appointed to collect the fee, check licences and resolve disputes arising from mining claims.

From the very beginning the licence system was unpopular and unmanageable. With a few exceptions (for ministers of religion, pastoral lease holders, servants) it amounted to a capitation tax; in effect, every person resident on the diggings was required to pay the fee regardless of their success in finding gold. The licence fee was a poll tax, not an income tax—and it was as detested as any poll tax has ever been in the history of the Exchequer.

Because so many of the heads to be taxed rested on the shoulders of women and children, an exemption clause was written into the regulations. The Gold Regulations stated that

All females not mining or trading and children under fourteen years of age who shall only reside but not mine any Gold Field did not need to carry a licence nor apply to the commissioners for an 'exception ticket'. By implication, women who did mine or trade would need to take out their own licence in their own name. It is impossible to ascertain exactly how many women were issued with mining licences, for the gold commissioners' licensing registers no longer exist. The nineteenth-century laws of coverture would normally have meant that a woman's legal identity was literally cloaked by her husband's, but colonial exigencies required the government to take a flexible approach. The only miners and traders on the goldfields who do appear to have been genuinely exempt from licence holding were the Wathaurung.

In principle, then, anyone could access the mineral resource—even women and children—for a flat fee. This levelling approach had an important consequence: broadening the tax base increased the number of people with a stake in Victoria's fundamentally undemocratic and centralised system of government. Even female licence holders expected a modicum of representation for their taxation—as dramatic events would later demonstrate.

It wasn't just digging up the Crown's glittering soil that attracted a fee. *All persons resident upon the goldfields in the practice of a profession, trade or calling, of any permitted kind* were required to contribute to the public purse. Storekeepers were charged the weighty fee of £15 for a three-month licence to run their business. This charge was just as unpopular as the mining fee, for there was no infrastructure provided in exchange for the revenue, simply the right of occupation, and most stores in 1854 amounted to little more than a family tent with two chambers: one for sleeping in and one for trading out of. When Martha Clendinning purchased a licence for her store, she complained that she had to pay a standard £40 a year *quite irrespective of its size and business capacity. My little one was rated the same as the largest in the Main Road.* Just as petitions and demonstrations were mounted against the hated licence tax from 1852 onwards, so storekeepers rallied against the iniquitous conditions of their legal tenure. Hawkers, it was pointed out, did not require a licence; the fact that most itinerant salesmen were Jews did not help. For its part, the government refused to acknowledge that the licence fee for mining or storekeeping was a tax at all, arguing that *the amount of advantage to be drawn* from the privilege of occupying Crown land amply compensated for the loss.[5]

Bringing miners, shopkeepers and other professionals under the same regulatory rubric produced an interesting result. All goldfields inhabitants were effectively defined as small business people, creating a single category of commercial identity. This one-size-fits-all system would contribute to the famous egalitarianism of the goldfields where, as the balladeer Charles Thatcher sang to packed crowds in the theatres of Ballarat and Bendigo, *we're all upon a level.* And because women became central to the economy of the goldfields, so they became integrally entwined in the culture of complaint and the politics of dissent that grew in intensity like a summer storm over the tumultuous months of 1854.

*

Picking, panning, puddling and cradling required deep reserves of patience in this era of the small-claim system. Minuscule daily rewards only ever amounted to appreciable results after a long haul, if at all. But for that very reason, the process exerted a peculiar hold on the miner. One described the compulsive condition of sinking a hole like this: *not knowing what it would be like when we saw it, but fully expecting it every moment.*[6] This condition of never knowing but always expecting provided the primal force of gold mining's attraction. It is what historian Chris McConville has dubbed the 'Existential Now'.[7]

As with the poker machines of today's casinos, every push of the button—every thrust of the shovel, thwack of the pick, every flash in the pan—could mean a new destiny, right there and then. Over her five-year career as a *gold diggeress*, Mary Ann Tyler developed her own explanation of the existential rapture of mining.

> You work from day to day with anticipation, and soon the years pass...You can work for very little, and all at once you drop across a fortune. That is why it is so enchanting. You live in expectation...my very soul was lit with delight that I should one day discover more gold.[8]

European women's role in Australia's gold mining history goes back to its very beginnings. Edward Hammond Hargraves is the man credited with the first discovery of gold at Bathurst, New South Wales, in February 1851. *Tired of the cares and troubles of [married] life*, Hargraves had gone to California in 1849. He returned to the Turon Valley and noticed the topographical similarities between the two regions. He decided to go prospecting, on the sly, to test his hunch that there was gold in them thar hills. He went to see Mrs Lister, the publican at the Guyong Inn, a widow who had *seen better days*. Hargraves needed a friend. *It occurred to me that I could not prosecute my plans efficiently without assistance*, he later wrote, *and that Mrs Lister was a person in whom I could safely confide.* Mrs Lister trusted him too. She furnished Hargraves with a guide—*a black fellow*—to penetrate the dense region of forest and lent him her eighteen-year-old son as a companion. Most men had laughed at Hargraves' notions, but *she entered with a woman's heartiness into my views*. In his 1855 memoir, Hargraves fully acknowledged that he had Mrs Lister's generosity of spirit to thank for his subsequent fame. Hargraves also noted that Mrs Cruikshank, the wife of a squatter on the Turon, was the second person to pan with him (after Mrs Lister's son). Mrs Cruikshank found gold on her first outing. She quickly *expressed her intention of resuming her work; and procuring enough to make some rings.*

Victoria also had women at the genesis of one of its most significant gold finds. Following the discovery of gold in Ballarat in August 1851, Margaret Kennedy and Julia Farrell began fossicking in their own backyards. Around the Bendigo Creek, in late September, they had their eureka moment. Unlike Hargraves, these respectable wives did not pursue celebrity. They continued quietly panning in the creek, and were soon joined by twenty thousand other entrepreneurial souls in the great rush to the Bendigo Valley, 'the Winter diggings'.

There is also an even chance that Ballarat's gold was discovered by a woman, since a correspondent to the GEELONG ADVERTISER in September 1852 revealed that the pioneer of the Eureka Lead was an unidentified Aboriginal person: Wathaurung people of both sexes were known to participate in gold mining.[9]

William Kelly was one of the first commentators to note the everyday sight of women engaged in hands-on mining. Out walking around the Eureka Lead one morning in early 1854, Kelly spied *fossickers of the female sex at work, and these, too, of the diminutive degree both as to age and size*. You can sense that Kelly longed to mock these mining maids, as was his inclination, but he drew himself up.

> And here I must do the women the justice of remarking that their industry was accompanied with a decency of garb and demeanour which elicited respect and went to prove that becoming employment engenders respectability of feeling and healthy appetites.

Working-class women, of course, had always worked. The phenomenon that stopped Kelly short was the presence of 'decent' women performing acts of industry. It was just another of the transformations that women needed to effect to be successful in this strange new world.

Perhaps there was also something female-friendly about the work itself, for small-claim alluvial mining was in many ways a holdover from the pre-industrial domestic economy. The modest size of frontages discouraged the introduction of machinery, and working a claim relied on manual exertion rather than progressive technology. William Westgarth referred to the traditional mining cradle, in which gravel from a river's bed was rocked to separate large rocks and nuggets from the fine particles of silt or gold dust, as this *primitive and fatiguing implement*. The work didn't require great physical strength, though, or capital outlay: just patience, perseverance and bucket-loads of luck. Westgarth, writing in 1857, remarked on the peculiarly archaic state of mining technology in the wake of the industrial revolution. *There are few vocations*, he noted, *that can boast such freedom from indebtedness to that great modern creditor in society's progress*—referring, of course, to science.

Ballarat, observed Westgarth, resembled not so much an industrial landscape as *a great mercantile exchange*, where co-partnering and share-holding—complex forms of interpersonal rather than technological exchange—were required to tap the deep leads that criss-crossed the goldfields. (And as if to flesh out Westgarth's metaphor, many women were not just miners but active shareholders in the hundreds of mining ventures that were listed on the Ballarat Mining Exchange.[10]) Westgarth didn't comment on the implications of such retrograde commercial operations for women; however, there is no doubt that women who wanted or needed to mine for gold benefited from this freedom from science and modernity.

Once regulations enabled larger-scale mining claims later in the 1850s, technology (particularly steam-driven pumping) quickly appeared. But in 1854, the editor of the GEELONG ADVERTISER noted that in the three years since gold's discovery, little had changed in its mode of extraction. *Gold is got by chopping, churning and manual dexterity*, he wrote.[11] Is this mining or making mince pies? Alluvial mining was indeed a great equal opportunity employer. MURRAY'S GUIDE TO THE GOLD DIGGINGS advised its readers that mining was *a pursuit open to all who are strong enough...members of the learned professions [are] side by side with the refuse of the earth.* Human garbage. And women.

*

Martha Clendinning and her sister had made a pact: even if other storekeepers on the diggings winked at the authorities, they would never sell sly grog on their premises. It was unlawful to sell wine, beer or spirits on any of Victoria's goldfields, but everyone knew that practically every store, restaurant, boarding house and 'refreshment tent' could provide a nobbler on request. Though the laws to keep alcohol off the diggings had been *a complete failure*, Martha reckoned that she must hold to her own standards. She would only sell the *best quality* tea, coffee and sugar, candles, tobacco (*the most important item*), jams, bottled fruits, onions and apples and *some excellent small Cheshire cheeses.*

But Martha, the doctor's wife, Anglo-Irish daughter of a Kings County JP, was not so high and mighty that she couldn't read the democratic temper of the times. As Englishman John Capper wrote, *The equality system here would stun even a Yankee. We have all grades and classes... The outward garb forms no mark of distinction—all are mates.* Martha and Sarah determined to follow Mrs Massey's advice and exchange broadcloth for fustian, toning down their well-bred appearances in the hope that *we should not be distinguished as 'ladies'. We intended to pass as merely respectable women of business; anything more than that would, we felt, expose us to curiosity when we entered on our storekeeping life.* They didn't want to intimidate the diggers. They didn't want to lord it over the diggers' wives. They wanted to *blend in*. But it was more than the desire to be inconspicuous: *We prided ourselves on being careless of appearances.* New chums passed themselves off as old hands by the unceremonious cut of their cloth.

The Clendinnings set up their tent site at the centre of a treeless field on Commissioner's Flat, not far from where Charles and George Evans would establish their Criterion Auction Mart just a few months later. Martha volunteered to go to the Government Camp and purchase George Clendinning's mining licence for him while he muddled about in a tangle of flaccid canvas. As this was official business, she put on her *go-to-meeting clothes*: black cashmere dress with two deep flounces and velvet folds on the edges, paisley shawl and straw bonnet trimmed with white ribbon. At the Camp, she admired the commissioners' firmly tethered tent. *I gazed with envious eyes on the erection*, thinking of the *sad confusion* of her own tent. The commissioners were just as admiring of Martha's appearance, for, according to

Martha, the other women residents were *of a very rough class*. Martha declined a chair, and the licence was delivered to her promptly. Two diggers, who had been waiting half the day for the commissioners to deign to issue their licences, were astonished. *'Well Bill', said one, 'the next time I want my licence, I'll send my missus for it, instead of kicking my shins about here for hours'. 'All right', Bill replied, 'but you must get your missus first, my boy'.* Martha had a chuckle at her new-found influence.

Once George finally got it up, the Clendinnings' tent—*our first Australian home*—was also Martha and Sarah's store. Martha's trademark yellow canary sang in a cage outside the tent. Martha procured her own storekeeper's licence and opened for business. *I never forgot my first sale!* wrote Martha fifty years later: a box of matches for sixpence.

While their husbands got on with the *hard and dirty work* of mining, Martha and Sarah quickly established a loyal clientele for their humble wares. Martha bought a hen, a rare commodity on the diggings, and sold her eggs to mothers of sick children who could keep nothing else down. Soon there was more demand, for more goods, than they could supply. *We were constantly asked for clothing materials by the women*, but didn't have enough room to store large bolts of cloth. But the savvy sisters could see that there was something in the Ballarat waters that encouraged astonishing fertility as well as dysentery. They decided to *venture on a new branch of business*: baby clothes. Theirs was the first store on the diggings to sell such *dainty little garments*. The delight of the women at the sight of them was *beyond description*.

Martha had tapped into a profitable sociological trend. Most of her customers were women, who often shopped together. At home, an English country labourer's wife could only afford to clothe their babies in unbleached calico, coarse flannel and *poor, common print*. But now, those same women could *delight in Melbourne-made goods, simple, but being all of white material and tastefully made, with little knitted woollen hoods*. Such garments *elicited the warmest admiration and envy*. So while genteel women sought to downplay their class backgrounds by 'blending in' with the masses, former commoners were only too happy to distinguish themselves from the pack with dainty fripperies. Martha and Sarah soon sold out their modest supply of upmarket baby clothes and had to send to Melbourne for more stock. The business of frontier egalitarianism was clearly a matter of nuance. Anyone who could successfully negotiate its ambiguities and inconsistencies was onto a winner.

But Martha Clendinning did not just use women's social aspiration to turn a profit. She was also astute enough to realise that immersing herself in the cultural landscape of the early diggings would give her a new freedom beyond her stifling old identity as a gentlewoman. If the rural farm girls aped her bourgeois trimmings, so Martha took her lead from the *working class…to whom all species of employment for women seemed perfectly natural if they could carry it on with success*. Suddenly it was merit, not birthright and breeding, that made all the difference.

Dr Clendinning was *most anxious* about the changes that had taken place in his tight family circle. His plan—persist with gold digging until *the big find*, then retire with all *the decencies of the home life of a gentleman*—was slow in coming to fruition. This gave Martha a legitimate reason to pursue her *excessive folly*, despite her husband's concern that he *might be blamed for allowing me to continue at it*. While she was making money and George wasn't, Martha would do as she pleased.

She was certainly a trailblazer, but Martha Clendinning was not the only woman to cash in on the diggers' insatiable demand for supplies and services. Not long after Martha paved the way, twenty-eight-year-old Irishwoman Anne Diamond (née Keane) began retailing out of a large tent at Eureka, while her new husband Martin mined its lead. After meeting on the *Star of the East*, Martin and Anne had never formally married, but by the time they set up shop in Ballarat, Anne had taken Martin's name and they were living as a couple. Sometime in early 1854, they had a baby who died. Not ones for paperwork, they registered neither its birth nor its death.[12] The precise location of Anne Diamond's store would prove to have disastrous consequences in the summer of '54.

Phoebe Emerson also ran a store at Eureka. Phoebe had grown up in the coal mining regions of northern England. Her father was an engineer and the choirmaster and organist at Durham Cathedral. Phoebe married George Emerson on her twentieth birthday and the couple sailed to Victoria the following year. George suffered from a lung infection (which finally killed him in 1857) and Phoebe ran the store to provide the newlyweds with their livelihood. She kept several savage dogs for protection and a loaded gun to *deter any foolishness near her store*.[13]

Twenty-two-year-old Irish immigrant Mary Davison King also slept with a loaded pistol under her pillow when her husband Alexander was away from their store buying stock. Mary had migrated to Victoria soon after her marriage to Alexander and headed straight to the diggings, so they must have had some capital to seed their business. Like Martha Clendinning, Mary acquired hens and made a pile selling eggs to the Ballarat miners at eighteen pence per egg. Mary had her first baby, Henrietta, in her tent in 1854, the second, Emma in 1855, and nine more in the next seventeen years.[14]

Mrs Eakin also ran a store at Eureka. Henry Mundy

described her as *a tall, pleasant looking woman with very engaging manners, a real lady*. Henry's new wife, Ann, took heart from her husband's respect for Mrs Eakin. After their marriage, Ann was *anxious to make herself useful in doing something to make money*, so she began a grocery business and circulating library. After the birth of their first son, however, Henry changed his tune. It was *his responsibility* to provide for his wife and child. Ann wanted to make clothes to sell to a draper's shop, but Henry wouldn't hear of it. *What nonsense you are talking, of taking in sewing to keep the house*, he thundered. *By God I'll get a living for us!*

Older and longer married, Thomas Pierson wasn't so proud. He and Frances set up a large heavy canvas tent (nine metres by five) for a store, which Frances ran in addition to a slightly smaller tent with a *wooden carpet* for their domicile. In early 1854, Thomas and son Mason joined a party of Americans in a claim, resolved to extract reward for their sacrifice. Thomas hated Ballarat, considering it *a most miserable, disagreeable, unhealthy place unfit for a white man to live in*. It was also a place of extremes. The weather was one thing. On 27 February Thomas reported that there were squalls and rain, with the wind blowing hard and a mere fifty-six degrees Fahrenheit. The day before had been over a hundred degrees. The social temperature was equally tempestuous. There was *great wealth*, which profited Frances in her storekeeping, but according to Thomas *few other places could produce the same amount of destitution, poverty and want.*

*

It is possible to live in most cities of the world and not have a clue how the other half lives. Ghettos of the poor are geographically isolated from enclaves of the rich. But in the tent city of

Ballarat, where Jack was supposed to be as good as his neighbour, Jack could very clearly see that his neighbour was feasting on German sausages and Cheshire cheese while he and his brood ate damper and flyblown mutton—again. Advertisements for stores in Henry Seekamp's BALLARAT TIMES, which first began circulating in March 1854, reveal the astounding range of goods available for sale: red herrings, fresh salmon, Chilean flour, smoked bacon, fresh ground coffee, Normandy pippins, Cavendish tobacco, Havana and Manila cigars, fresh oysters and lobster, preserved partridge, grouse, woodcock, lark, plover and hare, preserved peaches, apricots, prunes and plums, French jams and jellies, fancy, soda and water biscuits, Cork butter, and the list goes on.

Apart from such delectable consumables, there was a vast array of merchandise on offer. Mrs Willey, who ran the Compton House store on Bakery Hill (red flag with white ball, for those who couldn't read her sign), advertised the following wares: parasols, silk, satin, glacé and muslin mantles, china crape and French cashmere shawls, Irish linen and calico, widows caps, ladies and babies underclothing and French kid boots. Refreshment tents sold ginger beer and cordials over the counter, and gin, brandy, whisky, porter and shandy-gaff under it.[15] You could get a dozen bottles of French champagne if you could afford it. *The stores were astonishingly well stocked with everything that could be wanted*, wrote Mrs Massey, with *the most conspicuous display of dresses, bonnets and quantities of china*. Jill knew exactly what she was missing out on if Jack's claim bottomed out.

You can almost see the vindictive, self-righteous spittle fly from the aggrieved lips of Thomas Pierson as he ups the ante on his family's future: *we determined sticking to it a while yet to make something out of this country if we can as we think it owes us something*. A dangerous position: to hold a grudge, to feel a sense of entitlement.

On 1 March 1854, the Piersons attended a monster meeting of similarly disgruntled storekeepers, a show of strength against the new law to tax storekeepers £50 a year or £15 for three months. There were by now three hundred stores at Ballarat. One Ballarat resident estimated that at least two-thirds of the stores on the diggings were run by the wives while their husbands mined during the day and perhaps conducted the business in the evening—generally the sly-grog portion of the business.[16] In late February, sixty storekeepers, including the Piersons, had been taken to court and fined £5 for being unlicensed. It was *extortion*, fumed Thomas. The fine was particularly unreasonable when residents were being asked to subscribe private funds to build a hospital. The problem, according to Thomas, was this: *the English nobility send out their Bastard children to make unprincipled and contradictory laws*. But what was to be done? At the meeting, the storekeepers resolved to refuse en masse to pay the licence fee. By the end of March they had all caved in. *Mark the independence of Englishmen*, wrote Pierson in his diary entry of 25 March, *then compare them with Americans* who would never *quietly submit* to illegal taxes and the unjust imposition of fines.

That night a huge thunderstorm burst over Ballarat and it rained and hailed for a week solid, turning the parched ground of summer into rivers of mud. Frances Pierson packed up her store and moved it to higher ground.

*

In his 1958 classic *The Australian Legend*, Russel Ward commented on the 'curiously unconventional yet powerful collectivist morality' that existed on the Victorian goldfields. Ward traced the origins of this ethos to the teamwork required for deep lead mining (a line of analysis that also runs strongly through the work of Bate and Blainey) and the common arrangement of one miner acting as a tent keeper and cook while the rest of the team worked the mine. This group solidarity, Ward argued, was reinforced by the uniformly despised practice of licence-hunting. Ward pointed out that Victorian diggers called their co-workers 'mates', in contrast to the Californian term 'partner', signifying a comradely rather than commercial relationship. The close affiliation of the Australian labour movement with the history of mining disputes tends to support Ward's case.

But Ward did not explore another unusual aspect of this Australian egalitarian affinity: the inclusion of women in its companionable embrace. As more women flocked to the fields, the traditional feminine activities of housekeeping, cooking and laundering increasingly fell to them. And a curious thing happened. Instead of these domestic jobs being devalued as women stepped in (a trend modern economists call the 'feminisation of labour', with concomitant loss of pay and status), the goldfields women found themselves highly prized. *I have become a sort of necessity*, remarked Irish-born Harriet, who travelled to the diggings with her brother and quickly became a pseudo-wife to his single buddies. Harriet was paid in gold nuggets for her puddings and pies and earned great respect for her conversation and companionship besides. In closing her letter home, Harriet echoed the words of many other former blue-blooded girls after a stint on the goldfields: *I almost fear to tell you, that I do not wish it to end!*[17]

Being paid for domestic work without having to enter service—no contract, no term of duty, no master—was a revelation to working-class women on the goldfields. It was like freelance domestic service. Public housekeeping. Many women found regular employment as tent keepers for single men. Some older women, often widows, set themselves up in business as boarding-house keepers or licensed victuallers. As a result, women left their bonded service in towns and on stations and headed to the diggings. They may have wound up doing the same work—cooking, child minding, wet nursing—but they did it on their own terms, informally aligned to a team rather than a single master or mistress. The going rates were good too, set by a bull labour market for domestic services. Mrs H. Fitchett, who ran the Victoria Labour Market, an employment service, regularly posted the fair price for servants in the GEELONG ADVERTISER in 1854. Housemaids could expect £26 to £30 per annum, cooks £30 to £40, laundresses £30 to £35 and nursemaids £20 to £24.

These rates were still low compared to male wages—stock riders, bullock drivers and waiters could expect double the amount—but, due to the scarcity of female servants, they were noticeably superior to English wages.[18] Moreover, in the golden age of mineral excavation, there was one paid domestic worker for every three miners.[19] Australia might have ridden into existence on the sheep's back—and was then stampeded to international prominence with a resources boom—but in the mid-nineteenth century its prosperity was underpinned by the taxable value of women's work.

And women knew it. They had only to look at the latest issue of MELBOURNE PUNCH to realise that everyone knew it. It was called 'the servant problem'. The social crisis wasn't so much that unprecedented numbers of women were being paid for their domestic labour, but that such women were calling the shots. PUNCH printed cartoons that illustrated the farcical implications of untutored young women telling urbane old masters where to go. In one, a girl leaves her master for the simple reason that he has not supplied her with copies of PUNCH to read. In another, the young servant expects her master to chop the wood.

It was what they call colonial bounce, surmised Mrs May Howell when her newly hired servant couldn't decide on a suitable starting date. *She means to come, but thinks as this is a free country she must show herself independent.* William Westgarth summed up the new-found power of domestic servants with wry regard: Victoria was the sort of place where a housemaid *agreed to a temporary trial of her new mistress.* But Westgarth's dry wit allowed him to make a more intoxicating point about the radical potential for change in a colony which exhibited *an equality of consideration for all classes, and by consequence a political and social inclusiveness.* He chose a decidedly gendered metaphor to illustrate this transformative process. In Victoria, traditional social gradations were *thrown off like a loose mantle* in an unabashed *disrobing process.* A sociological striptease.

*

Every folk tale has its wicked witch. In gold rush Victoria, the washerwoman represented the spectre of a world turned upside down. A new world where wives earned more money than their husbands, working women determined the parameters of their employment, and manual skills counted for more in the marriage and labour market than drawing-room refinement.

This world is magnificently captured in an illustration by John Leech titled 'Topsy Turvey—or our Antipodes', issued as a frontispiece to London PUNCH in 1854. Here on the Victorian diggings is a cast of larks and heroes from an imperial nightmare.

A group of ruffians play cards while a *Master of Arts* brings them beer. At the table sits a pipe-smoking woman. She is being served spirits by a genteel lass who is barefoot and sunburnt, her face blackened by exposure. Meanwhile, an *Intellectual Being* plays manservant to a bearded miner, while another gentleman takes off the muddy boots of a pistol-toting brute. Behind them, a fat, ugly old hag wearing pearls and self-satisfied smirk—here is our washerwoman—is being given piano lessons by a delicate English rose. It is a charming tableau of class, racial and gender mayhem.

William Kelly was quick to grasp the figurative dimensions of the washerwoman. His pen portrait has her *dressed for the washing tub.* Her hair is tied up in knot *and fixed with a huge gold pin with a father-o'-pearl head*. She's wearing a satin dress and an apron, *a pair of massive bracelets* clasped on her bulging wrists and a heavy watch chain around her neck, *stuffing a carved timepiece into her virtuous bosom*. Here, says Kelly, is *a colonial substitute for crochet-work, a contemptible economy*. Imagine a mere washerwoman decking herself out in satin and gold instead of her homespun. James Bonwick was positively apoplectic. The sheer muddy filth of mining meant that washing was a necessity, not a luxury. But could a man expect sympathy from a washerwoman? Apparently not. *These heartless creatures*, wrote Bonwick, *the laundresses, treat us in town with perfect disdain, and only occasionally and grudgingly favor us with a stony bosom. And what worse fates on the goldfields!* Bonwick had a remedy. He advised bachelors to *woo a wife*, then she would have *no option* but to wash his shirts. And, presumably, provide a more welcoming breast.

The real problem was not the airs and graces or the reluctant favours; it was the equal economic footing in a land that valued wealth above rank or status. MURRAY'S GUIDE TO THE

DIGGINGS pointed out that in Victoria *carpenters, blacksmiths, cooks and washerwomen make nearly as good a living as the diggers.* Most were paid in gold dust, just as an earlier band of Australian upstarts had been paid in the scarce commodity of rum. Like domestic servants, washerwomen could afford to pick and choose their clients and set boundaries on their working lives. Unlike domestic servants, washerwomen were typically older, sometimes married, deserted or widowed, or someone's mother. They were unlikely to be wooed into marriage and rejoin the ranks of unpaid domestic officers. Washerwomen thus symbolised the social and economic power of working women on the early colonial frontier. They were the allegorical 'gold-diggers' of '54, only they didn't dig or dance or sing for their supper. The source of their power was external. It was vested in a wafer-thin historical moment when women's scarcity and indispensible labour coincided with the culture of utilitarian democracy.

For all those men who didn't have a wife and couldn't afford to hire one, Sunday was washing day on the diggings.

No one expected any different.

SIX

WINNERS AND LOSERS

Spare a thought for Sarah Skinner.

By May 1854, Ballarat was under siege. The wet season had come early. The summer of 1853 had been dry, and now the heavens had opened themselves upon an impermeable earth. *Wind blowing hard for three weeks*, Thomas Pierson recorded in his diary. Charles Evans wrote of the *dull cloudy atmosphere and almost incessant rain*. Mining operations had practically ceased. John Manning, the schoolmaster at St Alipius, where Anastasia Hayes was working as a teacher, complained that few of the seventy-four children on his roll were in attendance *owing to the severity of the weather.*[1] Abandoned mine shafts used by the diggers as haphazard latrines became putrid cesspools. Miners who had slept rough during the warm months were suddenly vying for beds in the boarding-house tents that had been popping up as a result of the feminine exodus from the township. Bad weather meant good business for entrepreneurial women.

But Sarah Skinner was not one of those women. Sarah Skinner lay on her own rude cot in her own flimsy tent, listening to the wind and rain lash the useless fly as she struggled to deliver her baby into this sodden world. In a delirium, driving rain can sound like fire. For Sarah, everything burned. Her brow ran with sweat. The tender, swollen skin of her vulva stretched like taut canvas. A final push sent a searing tear through her perineum. She screamed; the baby wailed. Their tandem howl floated into the spectral blaze of the night. William Skinner stood by, frantic with worry, as ineffectual as a handkerchief in a tempest.

On Saturday 13 May 1854, Sarah Skinner gave birth to a live and healthy baby boy. The baby's lusty cries were music to the ears of midwife Jane Julian, Sarah and William's neighbour. Two weeks later, Jane testified at the inquest into Sarah's death[2] that she *was not a regular midwife but [had] attended a few females in their confinement*. She'd done her best. On the day after the birth, Sarah was well, sitting up nursing her baby and laughing with her older child. But that night, said Jane, the new mother was *seized with cold shivering*. William Skinner, twenty-seven, son of a Devon miner, sent for Dr William Wills (father of the doomed explorer). Dr Wills attributed Sarah's fever to her milk coming in.

Over the next week, Sarah continued to ail. Dr Wills now diagnosed *puerperal peritonitis*—the grimmest reaper of nineteenth-century childbirth—and ordered the standard treatment for postpartum infection: turpentine injections into the abdomen, turpentine enemas and blistering of the bowel, followed by an application of mercury to the open wounds. Opium every two hours.

A medical text from 1785 gives us an indication of how Sarah was faring as Wills attended her.

> Child-bed fever...begins, like most other fevers, with a cold or shivering fit, which is succeeded by restlessness, pain of the head, great sickness at stomach, and bilious vomiting...A great pain is usually felt in the back, hips, and region of the womb;...and the patient

> is frequently troubled with a tenesmus, or constant inclination to go to stool. The urine, which is very high-colored, is discharged in small quantity, and generally with pain. The belly sometimes swells to a considerable bulk…a bilious or putrid looseness, of an obstinate and dangerous nature, comes on, and accompanies the disease through all its future progress.[3]

Sarah's baby also began suffering bowel complaints and bloody stools. He died by the end of his first week, without a name, and was laid to rest five days later. Dr Wills gave *weakness* as the official cause of death. Sarah was too fragile herself to attend the quiet burial. She knew what it looked like, having already put two other babies in the ground.

A distraught William Skinner fetched another medical man, Dr Stewart, who considered the baby's demise to have been *caused by the mother's milk*. Dr Stewart observed Sarah's deteriorating condition and, though he continued the enemas and blistering, claimed *it was beyond human skill to save her life*. He denied her the last-ditch treatment of leeching the abdomen, though leeches were abundantly available from the many pharmacists retailing on the Ballarat goldfields. Almost two weeks after the birth, and two days after his son's funeral, William Skinner held his wife's limp, clammy hand for the last time.

At Sarah's inquest on 25 May, the coroner pronounced that the woman had died from *natural causes*. A jury of William's peers added a rider to the verdict: *We consider that if a little more attention had have been paid the deceased by the medical man her days might have been prolonged*. The now-widowed William Skinner was, in a perverse way, one of the lucky ones. Although his wife's body was a bloated, festering, bloody pulp by the time the doctors had finished 'attending' her, he had managed to secure professional services. In that, at least, he had succeeded.

Fellow miner Patrick Carey was out shooting possums for dinner when his baby son succumbed to the fever that had racked him for days. The coroner asked Patrick why he hadn't sent for medical assistance. His reply: *Because we had not a blessed sixpence in the tent.*[4]

*

The idea that the Australian gold rush produced a classless society, founded on the sort of egalitarianism that only a resources boom can buy, is one of the enduring myths of the Eureka legend. From the beginning, Ballarat was a competitive environment. How could it be otherwise, when its *raison d'être* was the lucky strike? And in competitive environments, there are bound to be winners and losers. In their classic text *The Psychology of Gambling*, Jon Halliday and Peter Fuller define gambling as 'a redistribution of wealth on the basis of chance and risk, an event that always involves loss to one party and gain to another'. The psychological and sociological bedrock of the gold rush ethos was, in fact, the antithesis of egalitarianism.

Here lies the paradox of diggings society: a world turned upside down, but not levelled. Who wanted to be a millionaire? Everyone. How many succeeded? Few. What was the difference? Chance.

For most punters on the early Victorian goldfields, successful mining required three things: diligence, stamina and a godsend. *It is said by some*, wrote Henry Mundy, *there is no such thing as luck, that every man is the architect of his own fortune. Such people had never been gold digging.* Swiss miner Charles Eberle agreed. *It is a lottery*, he concluded after a long tour of duty in Ballarat.[5] Ellen

Clacy called the diggings *the lottery fields*. In this game of chance, Mother Nature was the house.

In Ballarat, it was geology that safeguarded her stash. The lines of gold deposits were *capricious and uncertain*, as one miner put it, following the subterranean maze of buried rivers. On the surface, the creeks and gullies revealed nothing of what lay beneath. Deep lead mining was like recreational fishing, casting a line into a dark pool in the pure hope of a bite. But deep lead mining was also dangerous, costly and time-consuming work, requiring fortitude but little manual skill or technical knowledge.

You could sink a shaft not ten feet from your neighbour's claim. You could both dig; both line your shaft with split timbers to hold the loose ground, and bucket out the constant cascade of seeping water. You could both wallow in the cold and dark and wet (or, in summer, hot and foetid) earth for five, six, nine months. And he might hit the gold-infused riverbed while your hole dropped over a bend in the gutter, missing the mark. He wins. You lose. Rock bottom. Duffered out. A shicer. But still you have to pay your licence fee, month in, month out, gold or no gold.

The deep lead mining of Ballarat, wrote Geoffrey Blainey in *The Rush That Never Ended*, 'was therefore more of a gamble than any other branch of gold mining'. Like childbirth, deep lead mining was exhilarating, wildly profitable, completely ruinous, risky business.

Eberle's conclusion that mining was a lottery was tinged with disgust, not devil-may-care jouissance. He reckoned he'd been sold a pup. *The gilded imagination of European publicists has, with few exceptions*, Eberle considered, *influenced the general attitude.* Expectations of easy pickings were still high, even in late 1854 when Eberle left Lausanne. But it did not take long *for the scales to fall from our eyes.* For Eberle and so many others, it was *a bitter deception*. Still, as the experts will tell you, 'loss chasing' is an important component in the psychology of gambling, inducing players to persevere longer and raise the stakes higher in an attempt to recoup misdirected finances, time and pride.

Thomas McCombie was quick to point out that the independent diggers of the early 1850s were not the professional miners of the 1860s. The former were only in the game, he believed, *for short-term gain or failure*. Mining was not *a regular calling*, as it would become for the salaried men of the syndicalised mining companies that had already begun taking over operations by late 1854. The amateur gold diggers knew little of science, engineering, metallurgy, chemistry or geology—all subjects that would be taught at the Ballarat School of Mines from 1870. No, the early diggers, said McCombie, were purely individual speculators, *anxious about their families*, eager to make a killing and go home. That they could not earn enough to buy an egg, let alone a passage, was the hard-luck story told around countless campfires. Young Martin Mossman poured out his tale of woe in a letter to his Aunt Hetty. He went to the diggings three times, but had no success. He was poorer than when he started. *I have no good fortune*, he wrote, *I am not a lucky digger*. Martin's Uncle Charles, on the other hand, went into *a speculation* and is *now worth £40,000*. Uncle Charles was coming home, but *I am just worth what I carry on my back*, wrote Martin.[6]

What's more, 1854 represented a significant turning point in the attitude of many immigrants to rolling the dice. Antoine Fauchery, a French digger and photographer who lived at Ballarat from 1852 to 1854, reflected on the mounting disillusionment with short-term gold mining:

> In 1853 if you took ten emigrants, nine of them would have worked resolutely on the diggings, while

> the tenth would, with great regret, have gone in for business. Towards the middle of 1855, the proportions were completely reversed. Out of ten emigrants nine were speculating in something or other—tool handles or lemonade at a penny a glass, and the tenth, stripped of all resources, kept to his pick, but with what ill grace.[7]

The assumption of easy pickings had put the wind in the sails of over a quarter of a million immigrants between 1852 and 1854. By mid-1854, things were changing. And the longer people—especially family men—spent embedded in unsuccessful speculations, the deeper the hole they seemed to have dug for themselves.

The conditions of life on the goldfields were to a certain extent 'democratising': everyone was in the same leaky boat, regardless of rank, breeding, qualification, nationality or religion. There was only one place you could have a baby and that was in a tent. The rough, raw newness of it all made for a sort of temporal and material parity. But this pioneer equivalence was in itself such a wild anomaly that most everyone felt the need to comment on it. MURRAY'S GUIDE described gold digging as *a pursuit open to all who are strong enough...members of the learned profession side by side with the refuse of the earth.* Thomas McCombie commented that *the many persons of birth and education [were] rather difficult to recognize in their blue serge shirts and cord small clothes.* It's fair to say there was an obsessive focus on the ease with which clothes could disguise caste, a simple sleight of hand overturning centuries of vigilant class-consciousness.

Why did Sarah Skinner's placental site turn septic, while the other women attended by Jane Julian survived? Nothing was dependable; everything was a matter of happenstance. The straitjacket of the Old World had not been undone, simply re-laced. It felt like a bitter deception indeed. Who could be made to blame?

*

Martha Clendinning didn't need a demographer to crunch the numbers and suggest a marketing plan for her shop. She could see with her own eyes that Ballarat was experiencing a baby boom. With no hospital or midwifery services, Ballarat's tent city rang with the cries of birthing. At least one pharmacist advertised breast pumps to relieve the agony of hyper-lactating new mothers. (*Milk fever*, which we now call mastitis, was a painful and, before antibiotics, a potentially fatal infection. Dr Stewart was not unreasonable in suspecting Sarah Skinner's bursting breasts as the cause of her delirium.) It also did not take George Clendinning long to realise that he could lay his hands on more reliable sources of profit than his barren mine shaft. By 1856, Dr Clendinning had hung out his shingle as a *Coroner, Surgeon and Accoucheur* at Bakery Hill.

In 1850, one birth was registered in Ballarat. In 1851, there were five. That figured doubled to ten in 1852 and leapt to twenty-eight in 1853. Then, in 1854, 404 babies squalled their way into life. Those women not having babies were busy making them. In 1855, there were 756 registered births and in 1856 that figure almost doubled to 1242. You might expect the rate of increase to have remained constant as Ballarat grew into a fully-fledged town with schools and other institutions of progress. But that's not what happened. In 1860, there were 1652 births and by 1880, 1216. For the rest of the nineteenth century, there was never as much per capita procreation going on as there was in 1854 and

1855.[8] In mid-1850s Ballarat, there was not only a resources boom, but also a baby boom.

How to explain the demographic spike? Most obviously, the population of Victoria was—overwhelmingly—young. In 1854, sixty-two per cent of the population was between the ages of fifteen and forty-five, and the majority of these were between twenty and thirty. The trend was even more pronounced on the goldfields, where the character of the population was seen as inextricably bound to its remarkable youth. Robert Caldwell described the digger genus as *young, impulsive, generous and restless [with] amazing energy.* To James Bonwick, the demographic profile of Victoria was a metaphor for statehood. *Once we were a sheep walk,* he wrote, *now we are a gold field. So young and yet so celebrated...already the talk of the world.* Elizabeth Massey saw nothing but romance in Victoria's *young people of active energetic habits.*

Others saw danger. Excitement can mean enthusiasm, but it can also mean agitation.[9] Canadian Samuel Huyghue was employed as the chief clerk to Resident Commissioner Robert Rede at the Ballarat Camp in 1854. He doubted the government was up to the task of responding to the *mixed multitude, eager for enterprise and revelling in a sense of freedom and anticipation.* Instead of finding constructive ways to deal with *the progress of the tide,* he feared the government would do its best to *restrain these new born impulses.* So far, its chosen method of sandbagging was *an exorbitant tax enforced at the point of the bayonet.*[10] Those wielding the weapons, as well as those making the rules, were themselves young men. The average age of the soldiers of the 12th Regiment, permanently stationed at Ballarat, was 21.7 years; the average age of the 40th Regiment, later brought in as reinforcements, was 28.2 years. Huyghue described the soldiers of the 40th as *half weaned cubs of the Lion Mother.*[11] Both Huyghue and Resident Commissioner Rede were positively ancient at thirty-nine years old. Assistant Commissioner James Johnston—*dear Jamie*—was twenty-eight when he married Margaret Brown Howden in August 1854 and took her to Ballarat as his bride. By the time they arrived, twenty-three-year-old Margaret was pregnant. Her honeymoon conception would soon turn into a nightmare gestation.

The majority of the goldfields population laboured under a common illusion of youth: the idea that honest industry and good intentions would bring just rewards. They were wrong.

*

The well-being of a colony, wrote James Bonwick in 1852, *is intimately associated with marriage.* This is just what the state wanted its restive citizens to believe. The discovery of gold might have resulted in moral chaos, but it had been noted since the 1840s that the lack of women's 'civilising influence' had led to sodomy, prostitution, the sexual abuse of Aboriginal women and killing of mixed-race babies, as well as that thorny old perennial of social control, drunkenness. Governor La Trobe's vision was that social stability would result from equal numbers of the sexes. From 1852, the government's interest in importing women into the colony changed from supplying labour to rectifying the gender imbalance.[12] Boatloads of young assisted female immigrants would arrive, they hoped, to be snapped up at the wharves by the hordes of eligible bachelors. Statistically, the design worked. In 1850, there were 2668 marriages registered in Victoria. In 1853 this had skyrocketed to 6946 *recorded* nuptials. But then a curious thing happened. Despite the steady increases in population, the targeted migration programs and the hefty demographic bulge in the twenty to thirty age bracket, the marriage rate remained remarkably flat. There were only 7760 marriages in 1854, 7816 in 1855 and 8254 in 1856. This suggests that although it was a seller's market, women were choosing not to put up their wares.[13]

There's no doubt that women in Victoria felt a power in the marriage stakes that they had never experienced before. Ellen Clacy arrived in Victoria in the winter of 1852 as a single woman accompanied by her brother, and departed in April 1853 on the arm of her husband. On her return to England, she wrote an advice manual for women desiring to emigrate. *Do so by all means*, she counselled, *the worst risk you run is that of getting married and finding yourself treated with twenty times the respect and consideration you may meet in England.* The reason for this unaccustomed reverence? According to Ellen, the imbalance of the sexes meant *we may be pretty sure of having our own way.*

Englishman Henry Catchpole, who arrived in Melbourne in February 1854, wrote home to encourage his sisters to emigrate and get *a Golden Husband. Tell them that it is a first rate opportunity for them*. After six months in the colony, he was still on message. *There are many young chaps looking out in Melbourne when the ship comes in*, wrote Henry. *I shall soon begin to think about doing the same for I am really sick and tired of so much male society.* Henry expressed unease that men of thirty to forty years of age were *actually marrying girls at 15 and 16 on these diggings* due to the numerical disproportions.[14] It was a competitive market for wives. Some women talked of men as if they were prize studs, assessing their attributes with an air of studied detachment. *There is a hardiness and manliness about the colonial gentlemen which I find pleasing*, wrote Mary Bristow.

If women could pluck husbands like so many wild flowers,

why do the marriage statistics suggest they were reluctant to do so? For some daughters, life in the colonies meant the blessed chance to escape—at least for a defined period of their choosing—the cloying family obligations and small horizons of parish life. Most of them literate, with an exalted sense of entitlement, these harbingers of change no longer looked to the past (or their parents) for example. Catherine Chisholm, a thirty-three-year-old unmarried woman from rural Scotland, was constantly chided by her family for not sending more news of her comings and goings in Victoria, including her marriage in 1857, four years after her arrival. *We are greatly astonished at you for not mentioning anything concerning your husband,* scolded Catherine's brother Colin, taking up the paternal authority of her recently deceased father. *Even what is his name, is he a native of the colony, or is he a native of Britain and what is he at for his daily bread.* Away from prying eyes, some gold rush women enjoyed the anonymity of distance.[15]

The fact that women of humble birth could make discerning (and secretive) choices about their prospective partners bordered on the subversive. The imperial anxiety caused by this unexpected development is perfectly captured in another of John Leech's cartoons for London PUNCH. In 'Alarming Prospect: The Single Ladies off to the Diggings', Leach depicts the preposterous idea that instead of men choosing their brides at the wharf, the women were thumbing their noses at offers from decent, upstanding gentlemen and electing to head to the goldfields on their own. *A cottage! Fiddle de dee Sir!* exclaims one pretty bonneted lass. *Bother yer Hundred Pounds and House in the Public line*, says an imperious woman with head held high. The women help each other to debark from the ship, to the confusion and consternation of the men who thought they could prance in as shining knights and wander home with a full-time cook *gratis*.

Englishman Henry Catchpole revealed what men were forced to do when they could neither afford domestic help nor snare a wife. He wrote home to his mother, *I can now roast meat, make plum puddings, pies and tarts...I'm a first-rate washerwoman, or if the lasses like, washerman...I am also a capital chambermaid.* Instead of digging for gold, young Henry was left shovelling his own shit.

*

In the anything-goes early years of the gold rush, tying the knot became a favourite avenue for conspicuous consumption. *Fortunate diggers*, observed Jane McCracken, *would do anything to spend money and so be seen that they have it.* What better way for a young man to prove to his peers that he has thrived and prospered than to show off a trophy bride? Saturday night in Collins Street, Melbourne circa 1854 was like a weekly Brownlow Medal count: a spectacle of tarted-up horseflesh arrayed in celebration of virility.[16] Here, lucky diggers would come to town to parade their good fortune in the cultural phenomenon of the 'Digger's Wedding'. Ellen Clacy reported that diggers' weddings were *all the rage.* Thomas McCombie described the event as *an exhibition so fantastic and absurd* that it symbolised *the convulsion under which the social system of Victoria was at the time labouring.*

This is the staging. A newly cashed-up digger would pay a woman to act as a *model bride.* He would deck her out in the finest wedding couture a nugget could buy, hire carriages and coachmen in gaudy livery, and purchase half the stock of the nearest pub. Very commonly, according to McCombie, the girl was a domestic servant (not a prostitute), *a fat, stumpy girl, redolent of the most odious vulgarity*, who would delight in being plucked out of an obscure kitchen and *thrust into a situation of temporary notoriety.* A crowd of intoxicated digger mates would march alongside the carriage all the way to the bayside suburb of St Kilda, where there would be a *champagne dinner* for all. The women drank too, leading McCombie to demur that *the after-dinner orgies therefore need not be minutely detailed.*

Like the line-crossing ceremony at sea, this was Carnival. Cinderella without the sentimental ending. Performance art. The sham wedding cocked a snook at the modes and morals of conventional respectability. In a mock wedding, the prosperous gent got to flaunt his success (without actually assuming the responsibilities of marriage) and the lucky lady got to keep her gowns and jewels (with a minimum of mutual obligation). James Bonwick had placed his civilised faith in the institution of marriage, but now found that the *freedom of marriages* led to *grotesque and immoral scenes.* It was not unheard of to spend £200 in a single evening. By the next morning, the carriage had turned back into a pumpkin and the digger returned to the goldfields to chase the next windfall. In the elaborate theatre of the Digger's Wedding, the inversions and reversions happened virtually overnight. The only lasting change occurred if the ersatz bride contributed another entry to the expanding ledger of ex-nuptial pregnancies.

Remarkably, in 1854 there were seventy registered births in Victoria for which the name of the father is listed as unknown. The baby is given his or her mother's surname. For some women, the father's identity truly may have been a mystery. Others were simply unmarried. Registering the birth of a legally illegitimate chid was an extraordinary public disclosure and suggests that women were less eager to cover the tracks of ex-nuptial conception, and less likely to see another man's child as an impediment to future marriage prospects, at a time when it was a seller's market. It was also not uncommon for single mothers to apply to magistrates for maintenance orders for their children. Court reporters conveyed such cases without an overtone of scandal. This is fascinating, suggesting a lack of shame—even a sense of implied legitimacy—on the women's part. In an era when the demand for popular rights and freedoms was a mounting clamour, even a woman beyond the pale of respectability might draw public attention to her quest for justice—and expect restitution.

The moment did not last. In 1855, fifty births were registered with an unknown father and in 1856—none! (Less than half a dozen ex-nuptial births per year were recorded over the next decade.) You can bet your last Trojan that ex-nuptial conception was still happening. But women were no longer prepared to out themselves. Cue the long reign of illegal abortions, shotgun weddings and benevolent homes for fallen women.

*

In the mid-nineteenth century, few women faced childbirth free of the well-founded fear of death. They weren't just aware the odds were against them; they could feel it in their waters. In fact, women referred to their entire pregnancy as a period of *sickness*. In popular euphemism, to labour was to *be ill*. The linguistic delicacy made sense. Up until the 1940s, maternal death ranked second only to tuberculosis as a killer of Australian women aged between fifteen and forty-nine.[17] There are no official maternal or infant mortality statistics available for the early period of Victoria's history. But based on records from Melbourne's Royal Women's Hospital, historian Janet McCalman calculates that from 1856 to 1874, stillbirths fluctuated between four and eleven per cent, while maternal death rates could be as high as 4.5 per cent, or one in every 22.5 confinements.[18] As these numbers were achieved in a hospital, with midwives and obstetricians on hand, it is likely the maternal mortality rate on the goldfields was much higher. Dr Walter Richardson (father of the author Henry Handel Richardson), who practised in Ballarat in the mid-1850s, estimated that seven per cent of full-term births ended in a fatality.[19] He attributed this shameful record to the unsanitary squalor of Ballarat and the inadequate colonial laws that permitted unqualified charlatans and drunken illiterates to attend confinements on the goldfields, resulting in otherwise preventable deaths, stillbirths and deformities. International studies of maternal mortality in the nineteenth century support him: they show that the quality of obstetric care available to women was the definitive risk factor. Though malnutrition and other pre-existing health problems could contribute to childbirth complications, the single most important predictor of poor outcomes was access to an experienced accoucheur.

On the goldfields, as the diligent Dr Richardson attested, finding a good doctor was very chancy. Mothers, friends or neighbours were most likely to attend births on the diggings. Such women may or may not have had experience in delivering babies, particularly obstructed labours or high-risk deliveries such as twins or breech births. And prior to the development of antiseptic practices in 1870, post-partum infection was just as deadly following labour as maternal exhaustion and haemorrhage were during it. Henry Mundy noted that in Ballarat in 1854, a Mrs Charlton was *the most famous midwife round her quarter*. Mrs Charlton was a forty-five-year-old woman from Nottinghamshire who always had *a joke and a pleasant word for everyone*. But her patch may have been very small, limited to those in her immediate locality.

It's also not clear whether she was a trained or lay midwife. There is no evidence that there were any trained midwives practising on the early goldfields.

In all probability, Mrs Charlton provided her services cheaply. The same cannot be said for the goldfields doctors, who were largely reviled as opportunist vultures, extorting profit from a vulnerable population. The standard call-out fee for a birth was a whopping £5, the same amount as the fine for failing to show a valid mining licence.[20] Dr James Selby came to Victoria in 1852 to become a digger. It quickly became apparent to him that he would *make much more by my profession than gold seeking in the earth*. He soon found that he had as much work as he could handle and, as people continued to flood onto the fields, *the remuneration is increased tenfold. No man after practising here*, wrote Selby, *would be content to receive the London prices.* (And he only charged £1 for a birth.)[21] It didn't help the community standing of doctors that, until 1865, there was no system of registration for legally qualified medical practitioners. Medical historian Keith Bowden has claimed that the Ballarat goldfields were 'awash with quacks and imposters'.

Henry Mundy paid for two doctors and a midwife to attend the birth of his wife Ann's first child. But not even this precaution could save the baby, who was *sacrificed* to salvage the mother—this generally meant cranial crushing to remove the baby from the mother's body. Seventeen-year-old Ann suffered a long labour. All the women who busied themselves around Ann *looked gloomy and distressed*. Henry stayed out of the tent. *For God's sake…save my poor little wife's life at all hazards*, beseeched Henry, *never mind the baby*. Ann barely cheated death. Later, Henry buried the baby in a rough box on the side of a range and fenced the grave with barked saplings where *no diggings were likely to occur*. Come Ann's second delivery a year later, she was *dreading I should be as I was the last time, but thank God it was nothing this time like that*. Baby George was born healthy and whole. *I'm so thankful it is all over*, said Ann, high on hormones, relief and the brandy she was given as the only form of pain relief.

When things went wrong in childbirth, the results could be ghoulishly catastrophic: cervical tears, prolapsed uteri, pelvic damage. British women were traditionally delivered lying on their left sides, which was thought to lessen the likelihood of perineal trauma. Women still tore, though, and the result would be a mangled anal sphincter and the lifelong opprobrium of faecal incontinence. Nineteenth-century midwifery practice included packing the vagina and perineal tears with rock salt. Women may also have had their knees tied together to facilitate healing.[22] Yet recurrent infections at scar sites, exacerbated by repeated births—one child born every two years from age twenty to forty was the regular pattern—plagued women of all class, ethnic and religious origins. Childbirth was, perhaps, the only true social leveller.

Goldfields residents may have despised doctors for their extortionate fees, but doctors blamed midwives for the high rates of maternal and infant mortality. They were locked in a tussle for vocational supremacy that often went all the way to the courts. One such skirmish occurred when Mrs Katherine Hancock died eleven days after giving birth to her fourth child. Her birth attendant, Mrs Elizabeth Hazlehurst, was charged with manslaughter. Katherine was administered gin and sherry on the orders of the socially prominent Dr Wakefield. Mrs Hazlehurst testified that, in her opinion, *the baby was wrong for the world* and *she had to turn it*. (Katherine, before her death, reportedly remarked, *if that was turning a child, she would not like to go through it again*.) But the birth proceeded quickly and the baby was born *with a fine head of hair, ready for the curling irons.* Mrs Hazlehurst left, and a neighbour, Louisa Vining, stayed through the night. At the trial Mrs Hazlehurst explained *she was employed as a midwife, not as a nurse tender.* Dr Wakefield visited Katherine five days after the birth. He found her low and weak, with her uterus completely inverted and *external to her person.* She died five days later of *mortification of the uterus.* A post-mortem concluded that Katherine's uterus was hanging from her vagina and some of her small intestines had also been pulled out of her body.

The court case turned on whether the use of stimulants had caused the inverted uterus. Dr Wakefield testified that labouring women were regularly given as much as a whole bottle of brandy, even by medical men. The real problem, he charged, was the ineptitude of Mrs Hazlehurst. *I have attended thousands of women, never with a midwife in attendance*, boasted Dr Wakefield. Other doctors agreed the only cause of uterus inversion could be *gross ignorance* and *the expulsive power used for the birth of a child.* The jury found Mrs Hazlehurst guilty, but made a recommendation to mercy. Their rider, it seems, was occasioned by the lengthy statement made by Mrs Hazlehurst in her own defence at the conclusion of the trial. This is how the BALLARAT TIMES reported her mercy plea:

> She considered from her knowledge of medical terms, that she could have conducted her case better than [her defence lawyer] Mr Dunne; she attended the deceased purely from benevolence; she had been 16 year a midwife—never had a bad case, and was called, proverbially, 'The Lucky Woman'. Dr Wakefield had a spite against her, and never had a previous opportunity of venting it. She had confined Mrs Vining herself, and with perfect success.

Mrs Hazlehurst then gave an extensive account of her midwifery experience and asked the judge to treat her leniently. Despite the fact that Mrs Hazlehurst had managed to impugn the reputation of both her lawyer and a high-flying doctor, the judge was persuaded by her testimony. The Lucky Woman was fined £20 and ordered to serve one hour in prison.[23]

*

It's tempting to think that because death was a frequent and indiscriminate visitor in the nineteenth century, those touched by it were less psychologically wounded than we might be today, when science has given us more 'illusory control' than humanity has ever before enjoyed. Testimonies of goldfields mourners do not bear out this conceit. Deaths, particularly the deaths of children, were mourned with all the force of a lightning bolt to the heart. A child was considered born under a lucky star if she reached her first birthday on the goldfields.

The MINER AND WEEKLY STAR newspaper reported in January 1860 that of the sixty-one deaths in the Ballarat district in the previous two weeks, fifty-five were children, ninety per cent of whom were under eighteen months old. For the quarter ending in March 1861, in Ballarat alone there were sixty-seven deaths under six months, forty-nine under twelve months, twenty-six under two years and eleven under three years.

Dysentery was the great killer, closely shadowed by *marasmus* (an archaic medical term for wasting caused by malnutrition, or what we would now call 'failure to thrive') and common diarrhoea.[24] George Francis Train described Victoria as a place where *children die like the spring flowers.*

Mary Ann Tyler, the auspicious diggeress, lost her first

baby soon after her birth. *I cannot remember who was at the burial,* Mary Ann recalled later, *I was in such distress and kept fainting.* Scottish immigrant Jane McCracken attended the funeral of her four-year-old nephew who drowned in a creek. *It was a dreadful tryall for his Mother,* wrote Jane in a letter home to Auchencrosh, *as far as mind goes [she] has stood the bereavement much better than could be expected but she is very nervous and it has given her a great shock.* Apart from base grief, Jane also gave another explanation for the earth-shattering effect of losing a loved one in Victoria. The funeral represented *the laying of earth of the First of a Race in a New Country, the land of their adoption. An act of History in a Family, the consecrating of a sacred spot, that indissolvable [sic] link of connection to that soil.* Burying the dead in a virgin country meant the start of history and an end to forgetting. Jane herself was terrified that such a destiny might be hers. *There has been a good many died in their confinement or soon after it this season that I have heard of which made me more nervous,* she wrote to her mother soon after the birth of her second child in April 1853. *Death is making many changes among our acquaintances.*

When Willie Davis Train became pregnant in May 1854, George Francis sent her back to America to have the baby. He wasn't prepared to take the risk that this new baby would go the way of their first (who had died in America just prior to the Trains' passage, so the decision wasn't entirely rational). Men grieved for their lost babies too. Charles Evans was a young bachelor but he was a keen observer of human tragedy. Evans watched a miner suffer over the death of an infant. He noted in his diary on 8 November 1853 that *the clinging insinuating love for a child is one of the greatest happinesses which the labouring man is blessed with and it is a hard trial for him to contemplate the sorrowful gap which the loss of one occasions.*

People with strong religious convictions found a common way to bear up under their suffering. *I suppose that I must now submit to that humble position in which it has pleased Providence to place me*, wrote one woman when grappling with her fate. Divine Providence: the protective care of God. A belief in the higher wisdom and logic of Nature—the idea that there is a sovereignty or superintending power that is beyond our human control—was long the chief opium of the grieving masses. A merciful God would take away, but he could also give. *There is an overruling Providence*, wrote Jane McCracken, *who orders all things wisely and well if we would only trust in him. God alone can give us either prosperity or adversity as he sees good for us.* The flip side of the tragic was the miraculous.

But Jane was prescient in realising the dreadful temptation that stalked even the most devout believer in times of adversity. She warned, *our carnal hearts is [sic] prone to discontent when worldly things seem to go against us.*

*

A cartoon engraved by Samuel Calvert for MELBOURNE PUNCH in 1856 shows a digger sitting bolt upright in bed, rudely woken by the rain streaming through his patently un-waterproof tent. A dog cowers under the man's stretcher. A tent-mate sits huddled under a blanket, face obscured. The title of the cartoon is 'Domestic Bliss in Victoria'. But judging by contemporary accounts of tent living on the goldfields, a little precipitation was the least of your worries. A more chilling prospect was the alarming prevalence of domestic violence in Victoria.

Many female commentators noted that diggers could be rough in their manners, but seldom would they harm a woman.

Martha Clendinning recalled that she was never disturbed in her tent at night while her husband was away. One male digger, who was far from enamoured of life on the goldfields, wrote in a letter to a friend, *There is one thing, however—bad as the diggers are…I must do them the justice to admit that they prove themselves at least men where a woman is the case.*[25] Charles Rudston Read similarly noted that he never heard of any outrage or incivility towards a woman on the goldfields inflicted by a stranger. Yet, he added in ominous parentheses, *(I have heard screaming and rows, but from whom did it proceed? Invariably husband and wife).*

When a woman *got spliced*, the colonial idiom for either legal or de facto marriage, she took her chances that her new other half would not beat, rape or otherwise abuse her. Popular belief in the apocryphal 'rule of thumb'—the maximum thickness of an item that could legally be used to beat a wife for the purposes of 'correction'—was common but assault of a spouse was never in fact legally sanctioned. Rather, in the nineteenth century, wife beating was a widespread social custom, referred to by the French as *the English disease*.

The problem was that a woman had little practical recourse if she or her children were battered. The control a head of the household could exert over members of his family was paramount in western jurisprudence. A wife was construed as having the legal status of a chattel: an item of property, no better than a slave. Until the passage of the Married Women's Property Acts in the 1870s, upon marriage a woman lost all rights to ownership of property, and even the custody of her children. Before the end of the 1850s, there was no means of divorce in the Australian colonies. It was not until 1878 that Britain passed laws to allow a woman to obtain a legal separation from a husband on the grounds of cruelty. But well into the twentieth century, as legal historian Jocelynne Scutt has written in her landmark investigation into domestic violence in Australia, 'the courts continued to enshrine the position of head of family as one to be occupied by a dominant male person, with wife and children submissive adjuncts to his authority'.[26]

It is impossible to know whether women tended to suffer more at the hands of men they met and married in Victoria, or partners whom they had accompanied across the seas. What is clear, however, is the profound impression that domestic violence had on those who witnessed it on the goldfields. Perhaps this was an effect of the intimacy of living in a tent city, where everything and everyone was experienced up close. Just as you could see through canvas backlit by a candle, so too the sounds of internal struggle could not be muffled. Just as the cries of labour and birth could be heard throughout the immediate vicinity, so too the thumps and screams of a thrashing. The inescapability of family violence on the goldfields startled the largely middle-class chroniclers who had not previously lived in such close proximity to members of the 'lower orders'. It is a thoroughly discredited myth that the upper echelons of society are immune from spousal abuse; still, on the goldfields a black eye received in a domestic assault was colloquially known as a *Hobart Town coat of arms*, a reference to the convict stain of Vandemonians.[27]

Martha Clendinning witnessed the beating of a butcher's wife, *a horrid looking woman.* The woman, it was rumoured, was an old lag, transported for killing her baby. *I saw the butcher fling her out of the tent and kick her savagely till the blood streamed from her face*, wrote Martha, without evident emotion. Mrs Massey was horrified by what she saw of domestic bliss on the goldfields. *Alas! Poor human nature*, she wrote, *most of the wives in the camp exhibit on their faces the brutal marks of their husbands fists.*

Sociologists and social workers report the spikes in domestic violence in the aftermath of floods, hurricanes and other natural disasters. On the goldfields women bore the brunt of men's need to assert irrefutable physical authority at a time when all else was spiralling out of control. As the balance of gendered power shifted in women's favour, bigger, more hardened fists could be trusted to beat them back down.

Was domestic violence a crude levelling mechanism, then, or a form of blood sport for the angry and aggrieved?

Thomas Pierson attributed the Victorian phenomenon of public pugilism to rampant intemperance. *There are more taverns in Melbourne, according to the population*, he wrote, *than in any other place I ever saw and yet they are all full from the time they open until they close. It is very common here to see women fighting each other, men licking [beating up] women and women men.* A few doors up from Frances and Thomas, a whole household were drunk and fighting one night. The next day they appeared one by one *with black eyes and scratched faces.* Charles Evans also witnessed the spectacle of a drunken woman staggering along a road on the Ballarat diggings. Her husband tried to drag her home by her wrist. *She resisted*, wrote Charles, *and an interesting struggle took place much to the entertainment of a group of diggers.* Henry Mundy recalled a *wag* playing a trick on this mate by *beating an erring wife*, thumping a bag of flour *and a man's voice yelling out 'you call yourself a wife'…then an imitation of a woman's voice. 'You wretch you wretch you brute do you call yerself a man'. Thump went the blows again thick and heavy 'oh oh' in a wailing woman's voice.* The sham Punch and Judy show went on like this until a crowd rushed to the spot *to save the woman from further ill treatment, only to be laughed at.* Bare-knuckle boxing. Cock-fighting. Wife-beating. Anything for a dust-up and a wager.

Mrs Massey found the overt violence between men and women more confronting than humorous. She also came up with a plausible explanation for its origin. She too blamed the effects of drink, *to which [the diggers] are tempted by disappointment to resort, in order to drown care.* According to Mrs Massey's theory, drink was a way to alleviate despair rather than frivolously pass the time. Once under the influence, the pent-up disenchantment of some diggers then detonated in a savage show of strength against their wives. This was often credited as being part and parcel of the 'animal instinct' of the lower orders. (James Bonwick advised frustrated diggers to shoulder their burdens by reading. *Battle manfully for mental food*, he counselled. *When the intellect is starved, the moral power is weakened*—thus leading good men, let alone inferior ones, into temptation.)

Jocelynne Scutt claims, however, that violence against women is not used as an outlet or circuit-breaker for frustration and despair (or boredom), but as a way to establish authority over someone who is perceived as a legitimate subject of male domination and control. This is most likely to occur when the man feels powerless: socially, culturally or economically undermined, his prerogative to govern threatened.

*

Whether by law or circumstance, women generally felt compelled to stand by their beastly man. Yet perpetrators of domestic violence could be forced into a form of public reckoning. Ballarat court records from 1854 and 1855 are full of cases of women hauling their husbands before the magistrates on charges of assault, using abusive language and threatening their life. In some instances, it appears the woman had tried to leave her husband. Elizabeth

Johnson charged Thomas Johnson with *threatening to have her back to live with him or he would take her life.* The case was referred to the police for further investigation. John Williams was charged with beating his wife. He testified that he had not kicked her as she alleged; *he had only given her one blow because she would not stay at home.* He promised the judge *he would not strike her any more but he hoped she would stay at home.* The prosecutrix declared that her husband *was in the habit of beating her, but had not done so much lately.* Williams was bound to keep the peace for three months, with two sureties of £10.[28] Many such cases ended by being settled out of court, or by both parties failing to appear. Women may have used the justice system as a way of leveraging power they could not otherwise muster. In doing so, they took a calculated risk that the act of public disclosure would not further inflame a husband whose self-esteem was already at rock bottom.

Court cases give us rare access to the voices of women who did not have the leisure or literacy to write diaries—a sneak peak behind closed calico. Mary Ann Clay, for example, charged George Copely with violently assaulting her. Mary Ann said on oath:

> I am the wife of Elijah Clay of Ballarat. My husband had a few words with me on Thursday the 5th [of January 1854]. [Copely] began to interfere. He has one tent and we have another. I told him to mind his own business and affairs. He then called me most awful names unfit to mention. I went to sleep and he woke me by the names he was calling me. I went to his tent and asked what he meant by it and what he should interfere for in my husband's business and mine. He jumped out of his bed and kicked me violently in the head and various parts of my body and ill-treated me and struck my child. The kicks

> and blows cut my head. I had told him that he had no business to interfere between me and my husband… The assault took place in the defendant's tent. I used no bad language nor gave him any provocation. I swear positively that I was not drunk that day.

Copely pleaded not guilty. Police Magistrate John D'Ewes disagreed, and fined him £5 or one month's prison.

Mary Ann had justice on her mind. At the same court session, she charged her husband Elijah with assault.

> On Thursday night the 5th I went to a store on these diggings to pay for a dress I had bought. When I returned my husband said did you pay that pound I said yes. We had supper and afterwards we had some words. I wanted to reason with my husband but he would not hear. He beat me most dreadfully about my head and face. It was then he gave me the blow on the jaw. I forgave him for that blow.

Like Copely, Elijah Clay pleaded not guilty. But this time Mary Ann withdrew her complaint, and Elijah was ordered to find sureties of £40 to keep the peace for six months.

Because of the unprecedented economic opportunities available to women in the early gold rush, some found they could successfully leave abusive or otherwise damaging relationships. Eliza Perrin sailed to Victoria from Derbyshire in June 1853 with her daughter Fanny. Her husband John was already in the colony. The reunited family went to Ballarat. Before long, Eliza realised John was no more inclined towards gallant husbandhood than he had been in England. Her letters home are not explicit about the shame of domestic violence, but she alludes to it. *Alas the one I was tied to was far from being what he ought to have been*, she wrote to her cousin in 1859.

> I will not say much in writing but as regards behaviour from him I have had about the worst. We might have been well to do if he had been like myself persevering but he carried on as he did at home with his drink and jealousy until at last I brought him before his betters and he was bound over to keep the peace for six months.[29]

After Eliza's day in court, John left to live with his brothers. Eliza had been keeping a *Refreshment House*, but John *drank and destroyed all that I had before he went away*. John paid no maintenance for their three children and Eliza heard he was *passing as a single young man*. In the meantime, Eliza rebuilt her business, saving money and eventually building a public house for £70 on the main Melbourne to Ballarat road. Through her good relationship with Ballarat's merchants, she was able to *buy any amount of goods…all in my own name. It was only with my own endeavours that I had kept the 3 children and myself*, wrote Eliza to her cousin.

> He does not know that the house belongs to me or anything in it. The Divorce Act is not passed here yet or I would be rid of him altogether. I am determined he shall not live with me anymore. I only wish I had left him sooner and you had been out here. We should have had money in our pockets. I think of buying 2 or 3 acres of ground at the back [of the public house]…I am rearing poultry and fencing in a garden. I can hire a man for 15 shillings per week and find him meat that will pay me better than a miserable husband.

Eliza encouraged her cousin, who had a fatherless child, to come to Victoria. *But never let it be known but what your husband is dead*, Eliza advised. The women and their children could enjoy both the fruits of Eliza's hard-won independence and the frontier trend for identity fraud.

*

The early gold rush period represents a unique state of social fluidity, as hundreds of thousands of people effectively became hunter-gatherers, classic nomads following one rush after another. Whole communities could disappear literally overnight, on the back of a rumour that a glittering new lead had been unearthed in a distant gully. Like solipsistic gypsies, gold seekers carried their homes on their backs and told their own fortunes.

But in a place where housing was temporary, clothing was rudimentary and work was almost exclusively manual, what was to distinguish the civilised folk from the so-called savages? To confuse matters further, the Wathaurung were not merely spectators of the curious ways of these feverish strangers; they were speculators in their own right, accepting the risk of remaining on their traditional lands, not just in fulfilment of spiritual obligations, but in the hope of economic reward too. If you looked closely, you could see white men acting like wild beasts while black men lived on the profits of their labours.

Some observers noted the success of Indigenous people in selling cloaks and rugs, yet, almost without exception, commentators chose to focus on the gender relations they observed among Aboriginal tribes. Robert Caldwell is typical. *The natives*, he wrote in 1854, *are the most miserable beings...As among other savages, the women do all the work, while the men lie idle in the sun.* He called up every racially charged cliché in the book: uncivilised, naked, heathen. To Caldwell, talk of Aboriginal land rights, which he had evidently heard, was nothing more than *mawkish philosophy*. He believed *it was no more of an injustice to deprive the black man of his land than that of a kangaroo or cockatoo*. The Aborigine did not possess it, because he did not cultivate it. And why did the Aboriginal man squander the opportunity to work the land? Because he was content to leave *the poor squaws labouring under heavy loads, while the men burden themselves with little or nothing*. Such an appalling lack of manliness was what set the Aborigines apart from the white diggers whose steadfast labour underpinned their virtue.

What was more, the blacks beat their women! J. J. Bond observed that when Aboriginal men were drunk at night, you could hear their *loud yabbering* and *the howling of the lubras* as their menfolk beat them. Thomas McCombie extended description to judgment. *The domestic relations of the aborigines are only suitable to a race at the very bottom of the scale of refinement*, he wrote. Evidence for the prosecution? They don't marry, their women are given away against their will by male relatives, who are *mean spirited enough to desire the wages of such prostitution*, then are beaten if they won't go quietly, even speared on the spot if *very obstinate*. The Aboriginal women, conceded McCombie, are *naturally well-behaved, but are treated with cruel neglect*, regarded by their menfolk as *mere domestic slaves to obtain provisions or to drudge for them*.

The fact that so many white men on the goldfields were dependent on their wives or other women for financial support was a contradiction that, unsurprisingly, went unremarked.

*

If Aborigines were condemned for the shabby treatment of their women, the Chinese diggers were reviled for an even greater sin: they did not bring their women with them at all. The fraught relationship between Europeans and Chinese on the goldfields is a well-worked claim in Australian history. School children are typically taught about the Lambing Flat riots on the Burrangong goldfields in New South Wales in 1861. In this incident, long-held anti-Chinese animosity spilt over into a brutal massacre, with thousands of miners actively rallying against the Chinese diggers to drive them off the field and the police called in to quell the riot.

But the forces of the state were hardly impartial adjudicators. The state-sanctioned discrimination of taxing Chinese immigrants to disembark in Victoria (which began in 1855) gave the lie to the idea of a utopian brotherhood of man under the Southern Cross. Classically, the complaints made against the Chinese were that they muddied the water holes through their tendency to work over the tailings of European diggers, that they worked on the Sabbath, that they were thieves and gamblers, and that they accepted low wages and would therefore drive down the value of labour. But in 1854, the chief grievance against the Chinese was their dubious, and possibly devious, homogeneity.

This was the problem: the Chinese kept to themselves. Though they seemed harmless, they came to Victoria in great numbers—*thousands at a time*, wrote one commentator—and stuck together, walking in long files to the goldfields and then setting up separate camps. Here, they ate their own strange food and dressed in their own strange costumes: high conical hats instead of the ubiquitous cabbage hat, loose gowns that looked like women's attire and long pigtails that were similarly more suited to a schoolgirl than a working man. They practised their own medicine—acupuncture was readily available at the Chinese camps, and some Europeans availed themselves of its benefits—and they opened their own restaurants. They preferred opium to alcohol. And they diligently sent their winnings home to family members in China, where their wives were looking after the old and the young in the community in line with Confucian tradition, rather than blowing it on a spree. All this marked the Chinese out as different and peculiar.

But who might be hurt by *John Chinaman*? European women. This is what Mrs W. May Howell was warned when she went to the diggings. *Oh the diggers would not annoy you*, she was told by a friend. *It's those brutes of Chinamen; but they'd better not begin to insult white women, or they'll find it rather dangerous.* Though Mrs Howell's friend admitted he had never heard of it happening at any diggings, you had to wonder at what a man wouldn't be capable of when he had none of his own kind of woman about. And what better way to assert one's own manliness than to threaten vengeance on any cur who dared touch his womenfolk?

Early in 1855, a scandal erupted in Melbourne that brought to a head all the disparate suspicion of the Chinese diggers' masculine exclusivity. Police discovered a set of *foul and wicked prints*. The pictures, which were evidently of naked ladies (whether Chinese or European is not clear) and were said to bring *the blush of shame and indignation into the cheek* of respectable men, were being sold on the sly to Europeans. One writer, suspicious of Melburnians' tendency to lurch *from panic to panic*, wrote an article on 'The Chinese Puzzle' in the MELBOURNE MONTHLY MAGAZINE. He was a lone voice in publicly defending the Chinese, pointing out their industry and energy, their impeccable credentials as citizens, their intelligence and cleanliness. *But ask a Britoner on the street what objection they have to the Celestials*, he wrote, *and they will answer: Morals, sir, morals. Pagans, you know Pagans. No Mrs Chisholm at the Chinese Ports…no wives for the Pagans, sir, Prints, sir, improper Prints.*

Without women to keep them on the straight and narrow, no wonder they wanted to look at dirty pictures. Or so the scare-mongering tactics went. The panic reached fever pitch in 1856 when a prosperous high-class English-born prostitute called Sophia Lewis was found murdered in her bed, her neck slashed from ear to ear. Sophia was known to entertain rich Chinese merchants in her Little Bourke Street brothel; she spoke Cantonese and decorated her parlour with oriental ornaments. Two Chinese men were tracked to the Bendigo diggings and eventually tried and hanged for her murder—although there were many who doubted the competence of the police investigation.[30]

As the writer of 'The Chinese Puzzle' duly noted, the only argument against an otherwise *intelligent, educated and industrious people* was the absence of their wives. The rest was *blind prejudice. We are afraid of the Chinese, and we have not the moral courage to say so*, he wrote. *Meanwhile, Mrs Chisholm is requested to smuggle us a few China women, and, by all means, to let those she brings be young*. Failing that improbable event, the writer suggested another course of action. Miscegenation. Encouraging some of the pagans to *unite themselves to more durable British spinsters and attaching themselves to the soil of Victoria* was the crucial piece of the racial puzzle. The conundrum of division and prejudice would only be solved once the Chinese inter-married to *found a new family upon the face of the earth.*

The fate of the Chinese was sealed when the Gold Fields Commission, empowered to investigate the turbulence on the diggings in late 1854, handed down its final report in April 1855. It estimated that there were up to 3000 Chinese in Ballarat, 2000 in Bendigo, 1000 in Forest Creek and, most disturbingly, 1400 landed in Melbourne in the month of February 1855. *The question of the influx of such large numbers of a pagan and inferior race is a very serious one*, judged the commission. *Even if the Chinese were considered desirable colonists, they are unaccompanied by their wives and families, under which circumstances no immigration can prove of real advantage to any society.* According to the commission's report, the Chinese immigrants' *low scale of domestic comfort*, *incurable habit of gaming and absurd superstition* were *vicious tendencies* that were *degrading* to the morale of a civilised white society. Victoria needed rational men, graced by a woman's touch, to restore its presently deranged society to an even keel.

Within a few months of the Gold Fields Commission report, a law was passed charging the Chinese £10 per head to land in Victoria. They came in greater numbers than ever before, disembarking at Robe in South Australia and walking 400 kilometres overland to the diggings. The racialised poll tax was a gamble that never produced dividends for the Victorian Government. It was classic loss chasing; they should have learned by then.

*

Only one other minority group received as much private and public commentary as Aborigines and the Chinese. Jews. Remember the Californian digger who jibed that you knew the good old days had ended once the women and Jews arrived? In Victoria, the wisecrack never quite held up. Jewish miners were among the first on the fields, and their presence in Ballarat is indivisible from the establishment and progress of the Lucky City.

In 1851, there were 364 Jews in Victoria, two-thirds the number there were in New South Wales. The Victorian Census recorded 2903 Jews in 1861: 1857 males and 1046 females. Overall, the Jewish population of Australia trebled in the decade between 1851 and 1861, allowing Jewish congregations to become self-sufficient for the first time. While the Victorian Jewish community increased almost tenfold over this period, the New South Wales community did not quite double. By 1861, the Jewish population of Australia constituted 0.48 per cent of the total, a proportion that has not changed significantly since that time.[31] Such was the impact of gold.

The Ballarat Hebrew Congregation was established in the dining room of the Clarendon Hotel in Lydiard Street South, just a stone's throw from the Government Camp, on Yom Kippur (the Day of Atonement) 11 October 1853.[32] Henry Harris, who may have been a Cornish Jew, ran the Clarendon Hotel. Harris was also the first president of the Congregation.[33] One of the founding members was Charles Dyte, a thirty-two-year-old Londoner five feet tall, with mercantile training. He arrived in Ballarat in August 1853 and wasted no time in setting up a prominent auction house.

Many gold rush Jews came from Britain and bore anglicised names such as Harris, Franks, Marks, Isaacs, Simons, Josephs, Davis and Moss. There was also a fair share of the more distinguishable Levys, Cohens and Lazaruses. Others came from the wider Jewish Diaspora, particularly Germany and parts of Eastern Europe. Annie Silberberg was born in Poland in 1836 and educated in Paris. She arrived in Victoria in August 1853 with her parents Golda and Jacques, and siblings Esther, Eva, Meyer and Isaac. Annie married Lewis Hollander at Melbourne's Stephen Street synagogue in 1860, moved to Ballarat and bore sixteen children.

Rebecca Abrahams married Polish-born Alfred Isaacs in London in August 1853 and set out for Victoria soon after, arriving in 1854 on the *Queen of the East*. Her first son, Isaac, became

Governor-General of Australia in 1934, after serving as a member of Australia's first federal parliament, attorney general and Chief Justice of the High Court. Isaac Isaacs described his mother as *an extraordinarily gifted woman with a phenomenal faculty of absorbing and retaining knowledge* who personally supervised the education of each of her four living children. From 1859, the Isaacs family lived in the gold towns of Yackandandah and Beechworth.[34]

Though some Jews did actively mine for gold, they more commonly entered into business on the goldfields, rapidly assuming leading positions as auctioneers, storekeepers, hawkers, jewellers, tobacconists and publicans. (Alfred Isaacs was a tailor.) This follows the pattern of Jewish integration into other western communities; the Jews of Cornwall, for example, occupied the trades of silversmith, watchmaker, pawnbroker, merchant, pedlar, auctioneer and brokers, with women working as milliners, dress-makers and shopkeepers.[35] The Jews of Victoria chased a new opportunity for enterprise and endeavour, but they did not break the pattern of previous migrations.

Unlike the Chinese, Ballarat's Jews were quickly accepted as part of the vibrant, edgy, entrepreneurial flavour of the day. Being there at the genesis of a new local community, Jews were able to play leading roles in the establishment of institutions and civic ideas, rather than accommodating themselves to the scraps they were thrown by a chary host. London Jews, by contrast, had historically become pedlars and secondhand dealers because of a city ordinance prohibiting Jews entering the retail trades. Depending on the locality, similar restriction applied to the finance sector and the professions. In continental Europe the ghetto system established such occupational boundaries geographically. But in Australia, there was no such formal impediment to freedom of movement or trade.

Still, anti-Semitism was alive and well in the partisan prism of individual minds. Mrs Massey, in surveying the many nations assembled in Victoria, singled *out a dark, Jewish-looking man* for special comment. His black eyes, wrote Mrs Massey, showed *more than shrewdness; it amounted to unpleasant cunning*. She made no such remarks about the Egyptians, Syrians, Persians, Indians, Maoris and African-Americans whom she also encountered on Melbourne's streets. Henry Mundy performed a stylised rendition of a visit to *a jew's shop* in Collins Street: *you vant a pair trousers…I sell sheep, very sheep, yo get nodding so sheep in anoder shop*. Oddly, MELBOURNE PUNCH, which began publication in late 1855, ran a regular column called 'Shylock', which purported to expose Jewish converts to Christianity. It may have been a victory to convert the heathen Chinese, but successful evangelism in the Jewish community purportedly exposed the scheming duplicity of its members.

In October 1856, following the depiction of a German Jew as *naturally criminal* in Ballarat's MINER AND WEEKLY STAR newspaper, Charles Dyte wrote a letter to the editor pointing out that *Jews as Cosmopolitans [have] ever been esteemed as being most loyal, orderly and quiet*. It is significant that Dyte felt enough confidence in his own social status to stand up and defend his people publicly. He had good reason to be assertive. Though he was less than five feet tall, *Ikey Dyte* was a big man on campus. He would go on to become the chairman of the Ballarat Mining Exchange, the chairman of the first borough council of East Ballarat and a Member of the Legislative Assembly from 1864 to 1871. Dyte would later be hailed for *play[ing] his part manfully in the famous affair at Eureka*.[36]

If the Chinese were tarnished for deliberately leaving their women behind as permanent grass widows, the Jews faced a different problem. An article appearing in the LONDON JEWISH CHRONICLE in August 1852 summed up the challenge:

> The recent discoveries of gold have tempted many young men to leave the land of their birth and depart in pursuit of fortune. Among their ranks the young Hebrew has gone also to seek an independence by frugal habits, industrious pursuits, and the sweat of his brow...the steady-going English Jew will not expect to build up a fortune with such rapidity... yet, by reason of the fast increasing population of the gold colonies, he will see the acquisition of gain must of necessity become a work of time. Such being the true state of the case, the young Jewish emigrant will find that after he has become settled...the social and domestic feeling, inherited from his ancestors, will make him find that he requires affection; that he wants a home; that he craves a gentle partner, who by her assiduous love and sweetness may lighten his labour.[37]

So, the Jewish immigrant supposedly played his game according to reason, not chance. But he was, nonetheless, a man of emotion. His independence was not predicated on fleeing the cloying constraints of domesticity. Rather, he coveted a home of *love and sweetness* as just reward for industry. But where would he find such a homemaker, when there were so few Jewish girls in Australia? The CHRONICLE had a solution. It called for English rabbis to preach female emigration from the pulpit, *unless in the interim a Mrs Chisholm rises up out of Israel.* This was the only thing that would *save many a young man from marrying a Christian.* The rallying cry was heard, apparently, and by August 1853 none other than the real Caroline Chisholm came to the rescue. With the Jewish Ladies Benevolent Society of London, she corralled a contingent of twenty ready and willing single Jewish women. The precious cargo sailed on the newly built *Caroline Chisholm*, along with other Jewish families immigrating to Australia. The spectre of intermarriage was averted—for a time at least. Two generations on, few of the grandchildren of the gold rush Jews still identified themselves as Jewish.[38]

Robert Caldwell predicted that Victoria would provide the peaceful gathering place for all nations. But plenty of others mapped a social geography of division and distinction. Jews and other minority religious groups were not eligible for public aid to establish denominational schools. In 1854, there was a growing movement for a change to the relevant act of parliament, but William Westgarth favoured abolishing aid altogether and returning to pure user-pays. This, he argued, would be the only truly non-discriminatory practice, if Victoria were to live up to its reputation of *political and social inclusiveness.* Colonial liberality was a tetchy beast; it relied on visionary leaders to give constitutional rights their cultural claws. *To dream of excluding a Jew from the colonial parliament would be as foreign to the law as to the public sentiment*, wrote Westgarth in 1858, the same year that the Melbourne Club moved out of John Pascoe Fawkner's pub and into its purpose-built citadel in Collins Street. Jews were customarily barred from the elite gentlemen's club, and women were officially disqualified.

William Westgarth noted that there was *a sprinkling of all the nations of the earth* on the Ballarat goldfields—he estimated that ten per cent of the population was *foreign*—but each tended to stick to its own turf. In particular, he pointed out a locality thirty metres distant from any other tents that was inhabited by several hundred Frenchmen. Raffaello Carboni, an Italian, noted that the English, Germans and Scots diggers of Ballarat worked generally on the Gravel Pits, while the Irish *had their stronghold on the Eureka*. The Americans, he tells us in typically idiosyncratic fashion, *fraternised with all the wide-awake, ubi caro, ibi vultures.* The Latin translates roughly as 'where there is flesh, there are vultures'.

This aphorism neatly sums up the suspicion and wariness with which many British immigrants viewed the large contingent of Americans on the goldfields. Thomas Pierson, the Philadelphia freemason, noted *a general prejudice* against Americans, which he put down to envy of their *superiority in all things*. Westgarth, on the other hand, noted the American belief in *self-adjustment* rather than government regulation; their trust in human nature over vested authority. People accustomed to self-government, these commentators worried, were bound to clash with people accustomed to the rule of law. *We have no sympathy with mob law in the Queen's dominions*, said Henry Mundy ruefully. The mob was such an unruly, unpredictable ogre precisely because it was constituted by such a diverse range of human beings, all with their own codes, superstitions, values, resentments, methods of wish-fulfilment and personal histories of loss, shame and frustration.

A conciliation of such diverse pretensions and interests, realised the Swiss miner Charles Eberle, *will not be achieved without conflict.*

SEVEN

THE WINTER OF THEIR DISCONTENT

It was to be a winter of untold discontent.

By June, plummeting temperatures amplified the cruelty of the past weeks' driving rain. With the benefit of modern meteorology, we now know that the mercury dips lower in Ballarat than just about anywhere else in Victoria outside the Alpine regions. It is only 115 kilometres from metropolitan Melbourne, only 435 metres above sea level, yet it has a mean (very mean) winter maximum temperature of 10.7 degrees Celsius. And then there's the cunning wind chill factor: a southwesterly draught of cold discomfort blowing down off the escarpment. No one was immune from the surly blast. Those perched up in the Camp and those nestled down on the Flat all shivered in their tents, imagining what family and friends at home were doing in the northern summer sunshine.

Jones' Circus might have been emblematic of gold rush illusions, but its tent was exceptional for its size and solidity. It was like a citadel compared with the simple pitched-roof tents of most miners and shopkeepers and their families. Many diggers slept on the bare ground, noted Thomas McCombie, with a canvas fly for protection from the rain and wind. According to McCombie, a great number of single men lived under the eucalypt branches they made into *miams or wigwams*. Frances Pierson, on the other hand, had made a cosy tent home for herself, Thomas and Mason. She had transported feather beds, bedsteads and a mountain of covers to the diggings. The Piersons had been warned that you could use as many blankets in Ballarat on a spring or autumn night as you would in a frozen American winter. Thomas was thankful for the advice, and felt nothing but sympathy for the *99 out of 100 people who had but two blankets to sleep on under and over*. Those who were lucky enough to tap a vein that winter went straight to the waiting Wathaurung and bought a possum skin cloak.

Charles Evans, never one to whinge, was compelled to note the frigid conditions. He woke each morning *half perished with cold* and was amazed to find ice crusting the drinking water in his buckets. Once that was thawed, mobility provided the next test of physical and mental endurance. To pass from one part of the diggings to another, wrote the Ballarat correspondent to the GEELONG ADVERTISER,

> requires the combined characteristics of a water rat and a steam engine; for when the gullies and flats are not actually covered with water, they are so deep with mud as to require more than ordinary strength to make across them in safety.[1]

Thomas Pierson, who seemed never to stop whingeing, recorded in his diary that 25 June 1854 was the grimmest day since his family of three had arrived eighteen months ago. *A strong, damp wind and cold as could be without freezing*, wrote Thomas. He had just cause for his crabbiness. *Incessant rains*, Police Magistrate John D'Ewes later recalled of Ballarat's winter of '54, *a raw cold atmosphere and unfathomable mud.*

The fair-weather campers left. Forty-four-year-old Ellen

Young, ensconced on Golden Point since the spring of 1852, burrowed in for another cold season. She burned what wood she and her husband Frederick could cut and carry back from Black Hill. Woodcutting was a daily chore now that they were committing it in such large quantities to the sod chimney built into the rear of their tent. And it was harder to come by than when the Youngs first arrived on the fields. So many more people, and still arriving daily, fresh off the boats, despite the ugly conditions and dire predictions that Ballarat had lost its golden sheen. But the Youngs' labour was made bearable by the remarkable fact that timber collection was an entitlement of Frederick's mining licence. This, thought Ellen, was an enlightened idea of the commons. It was just a shame the monthly renewal fee was so high, and the penalty for non-compliance so harsh. Ellen could see the frightened, dejected look in the eyes of the men who had to choose between the thirty shillings for a valid licence (and lawful timber collection) and a loaf for their hungry children.

And this winter, Ellen was bound to concede, the whole town appeared out of sorts. Fragmented. Undone. Still manically busy, but with a haunted feeling about it. Yes, by mid-1854 *everything seemed out of joint*, as one journalist put it.[2] Even Mother Nature appeared to have turned the tables. The rainy season was supposed to be the *harvest of diggers*, as James Bonwick had said in the April 1853 edition of the GOLD DIGGERS MONTHLY MAGAZINE, furnishing plenty of the water you needed for puddling and washing. But by 1854 that wasn't the sort of operation most miners were undertaking. It was all deep lead sinking now, great long shafts yawning into the ground, and the water was a terrible menace. More than that, every miner, and every miner's poor anxious wife, knew the water could be deadly. A shaft could fill with water faster than you could say Joe, loosening the timbers that held back the great weight of earth, engorging the hole, ruining months of backbreaking labour. Or worse, drowning the poor wretch whose turn it was to bucket. If eight men were in the digging party and each of those men had three children, that was two dozen bairns who would go hungry. Hence the endless bucketing, day and night, night and day, to keep the shafts clear.

Water was supposed to be the key, not the lock. *The water, after all*, wrote Bonwick, *is the true philosopher's stone; for by its touch the gold is brought to view.* But Ellen Young was a perceptive woman, as well as an educated one, and she knew if there was a real alchemical substance, an elixir of life that could turn base survival into blissful perfection, it was not water or gold, but bread.

*

Ellen Young is the closest thing Australia has to a Madame de Staël. Like the literary matriarch of the French Revolution, Ellen was a woman of keen intellect who used the power of her pen to rally popular forces in a period of upheaval. Her influence was local, not international like de Staël's, yet she played a crucial role in an event that has come to hold national significance as a key political turning point.

Ellen Francis Warboys was born in Hampshire in 1810. In 1837, she married Frederick Young, probably in St James Anglican Church on the Clerkenwell Green. At twenty-seven, Ellen was two years older than her new husband, who was a chemist by trade. We know little about the Youngs' early life together, beyond their marriage in Clerkenwell. This was an area of central London famous for its long association with radicalism, from the anticlerical Lollards of the English Reformation to the mid-nineteenth-century Chartists—and beyond, to the Marxists of the early twentieth century. (We can possibly infer from their choice of parish church that the Youngs were politically progressive, as we might deduce about someone who lives in Newtown or Fitzroy in modern Australia.)

Census data for 1841 shows Ellen and Frederick living in Shoreditch, another central London location, where an extensive network of Warboys kin also resided. The Youngs lived with Frederick's mother and sister. Frederick arrived in Victoria on 3 April 1851, prior to the discovery of gold, and Ellen followed two years later, debarking at Geelong on 11 July 1853. The reunited couple travelled in February 1854 to Ballarat, where Frederick became a digger. Many years later he returned to his vocation as a chemist and became the first mayor of Ballarat East.

Ellen was a prolific poet who transcribed her lifetime's works (she wrote the first poem aged thirteen) into a 175-page hardbound volume with marbled endpapers in May 1870, two years before her death in Ballarat at the age of sixty-two. The book was donated to the Ballarat Library in 1911 and remains there today, in excellent condition, neither treasured nor forgotten.

The body of work reveals many things: Ellen was classically tutored in literature, history and theology; she was pious, fashionably hyper-sentimental and proud of her English heritage; she was deeply in love with her husband, whom she variously refers to as *my lover* or *my mentor*. She was passionately connected to both the inner world of the heart and the exterior world of public affairs. And she once had a beloved son named Arthur. In the volume's first poem, 'Smiles and Tears', Ellen writes: *My heart oppress'd, smoking with grief/For pleasing Poesy sought relief.* An Arthur Young died in St Pancras, just round the corner from

Clerkenwell, in 1850. *Like digger on his long rough road/I cannot cast my useless load*, wrote Ellen many years later. It seems Ellen put an ocean between herself and her misfortune, but could never escape this anguish.[3]

Ellen Young's earliest published poem appeared in the GEELONG ADVERTISER on the first day of the winter of 1854. She had written it the previous week, caught in the maelstrom of a flood. At the height of the storm, Ellen later recalled, she secured her mattress from danger and then her *spleen evaporated* into her first truly political poem. Published as 'Ballarat' (but transcribed into her volume as 'A Digger's Lament'), the poem is a sixteen-stanza commentary on the miserable living conditions and depressed emotions of a community crushed under the weight of high expectations and disappointment. It begins ominously:

> If you've not been to Ballarat
> Then stay away from there;
> I would not have my worst foe's cat
> To have such sorry fare.

Ellen described the poor state of the roads, the lack of fresh food, the famine prices, the infinite mud, the futility of complaining to the resident commissioners, the apocryphal gold and the burdensome memories of times and places past. She was trapped, they were all trapped, caught between the distant rock of 'home' and a hard place of ceaseless toil. *The gold I promised still is hid; The past is all a sham*, wrote Ellen of the dark corner of hopelessness into which the diggers were wedged. (Raffaello Carboni would later come up with his own version of this truth, much quoted by historians since. *This Ballarat*, he wrote, a *Nugety Eldorado for the few, a ruinous field of hard labour for many, a profound ditch of Perdition for Body and Soul to all.*) There they are, *'mid crowds from many climes* (said Ellen), bogged in a culvert, stuck in a rut, the wheels desperately spinning.

Mid-stream, Ellen's 'Ballarat' begins to take on a more righteous air, throwing off the soppiness of *mem'ries craved* and how her heart heaves in her breast. It's indignation she summons now, taking offence at the insult of the situation:

The floods were out, the mail-man drunk,
What matter the delay?
That though the hearts of many sunk—
They're diggers! Who are they?...
They're men—high tax'd, ill log'd, worse fed
Of strong and stalwart frame
Better was ne'er by hero led
Or earn'd a hero's name.

Suddenly, Ellen has introduced a new element into public discourse about the diggings. A sense of grievance. An air of affront. A polarising of the forces of good and evil through the positioning of heroes against villains.

It was a position that would increasingly be taken up by other organs of public opinion in the spring of '54. The GEELONG ADVERTISER did not begin to echo Ellen's sentiments until 27 September, when it represented the diggers as *hard-working, taxed, unrepresented members of the body politic*, hamstrung by *absurd, insulting regulations*. Ellen Young was at the crest of an inexorable wave of grievance. Or perhaps, to use another watery metaphor, she had unplugged the dyke that held back public fury.

Forty-four years old, Ellen was a senior citizen, a community elder. All of the leaders who would later emerge in the popular uprising were younger: in 1854, Peter Lalor was twenty-seven, Raffaello Carboni—the acclaimed scribe of Eureka, whose work did not appear until December 1855—was thirty-seven, and John Basson Humffray, who would later sit in parliament with Lalor, was thirty. Timothy Hayes, Anastasia's husband, was thirty-four. Like the counter-culture revolution of more than a century later, the mounting wave of protest on the Ballarat diggings was a youth movement.[4]

In Ballarat, Ellen adopted the tone of a civic Mother Lion, defending the integrity of her valiant cubs. No one disputed her authority or right to become the mouthpiece for the people of Ballarat. In fact she was actively encouraged by Henry Seekamp, the twenty-five-year-old editor of the new BALLARAT TIMES, which first went to print in March 1854. Henry published Ellen's increasingly political poems and strident letters to the editor in the spring of 1854. Unlike later Australian female writers with a critical edge and a finger on the public pulse, Ellen didn't write anonymously.[5] Rather, she flamboyantly ruffled her feathers and published as *Ellen F Young, the Ballarat Poetess*.[6]

Henry Seekamp may have been encouraged to publish Ellen's work by his common-law wife, Clara Du Val Seekamp, who was herself something of a firebrand. As we have seen, Irish-born Clara arrived in Victoria in May 1853 on the *Marco Polo*, with two of her three young children. By early 1854 she had hooked up with German-born Henry Seekamp, ten years her junior, and taken his name, though there is no record of their marriage. It appears to have been a meeting of minds between Clara and the passionate young journalist. Years later she said of her young husband: *if he's sinned, it was with the single-minded aim of bettering the people*.[7]

The BALLARAT TIMES—a voice for the beleaguered people—was run out of the Seekamps' home on Bakery Hill. It was a financial success: within a year the Seekamps would buy all the land surrounding their little timber shack, including the houses and tents upon it, to establish a veritable compound. One house was used for the printing office, and there was a separate residence, a kitchen, a coach house, stables and a detached office. Though the relationship would not be as successful as the business enterprise, Clara would defend her (estranged) husband's role in Ballarat's history for the rest of her long life. She had good reason to perpetuate the BALLARAT TIMES's legacy. By New Year's Day 1855, she would be its editor.

*

In the winter of 1854, a profound movement of communal disaffection mushroomed in the damp, putrid fields of Ballarat. Under Ellen Young's matriarchal tutelage, distrust of authority and collective grievance started to generate broader political debate about the big-ticket items of poverty, land reform, health and economic management—not to mention the whole damned notion of British justice.

Chief among the complaints of the goldfields polity was poverty: crushing, irrefutable, seemingly irredeemable poverty. Thomas Pierson wrote that in Ballarat he had seen examples of *great wealth but few other places could produce the same amount of destitution poverty and want.* Thomas Mundy, who carted illegal alcohol to the diggings rather than dig himself, saw it every day. People arrived at the goldfields with a few shillings or no money at all. They pitched their eight foot by six calico tent *thinking to pick up gold as soon as they land.* The result for forty-nine out of fifty of them? *What privations the most of them had to go through*, Mundy wrote, *hard living, hard lodging, bad drinking water [which] often brings on Colonial fever or dysentery.* Average weekly earnings on the Ballarat goldfield in 1854 were £1-13-9 (not quite thirty-four shillings). When a bag of flour cost £14, a loaf of bread 4 shillings, rice 1s per pound, sugar 9s, butter 4s, and brandy or gin 8s per pint—not to mention the monthly licence fee of 30s—there was clearly no fat (or fibre) in a family's weekly rations.[8]

Jane McCracken wrote home to her mother that for every family that did well in the colony, two or three did not. *I have felt more truly sorry for people here than ever I did at home*, confessed Jane. Poverty has always been a women's issue. In the French uprising of 1871, wrote historian Edith Thomas, *les petroleuses*, the incendiary women, literally torched Paris in rage and despair at their devastating penury and the exorbitant price of bread.

Jane McCracken's personal sympathy highlights another problem: the lack of help for those in need. *No one seems to care for the poor immigrant, good or bad, body or soul*, echoed Crown Land Commissioner C. Rudston Read. The goldfields were still a frontier: no hospitals, no benevolent institutions funded by the state or friendly societies. Everything was still too new and raw and mobile and undone for that. There was not even an almshouse. Martha Clendinning would help establish the Ballarat Female Refuge in 1867, but in 1854, welfare was a matter of individual goodwill extended by kin if you had any, friends if you had made some or shipmates if you could track them down.

In this unfinished part of the world, wrote twenty-two-year-old Noah Dalway in a letter home to his mother in Ireland, *it is now that I feel the loss of you all and of a home where, had I been what was required of a son, I might now be happy in that home without any care anxiety or laborious work, all of which are now my only companions.*[9] Wasn't the El Dorado of the South meant to put an end to care, anxiety and unrewarding toil? *This Australia, dear mother, is most falsely represented*, Noah declared in 1854, after months on the goldfields. *So many thousands, what are they doing, barely making a living.* According to Noah, only men of capital who could start their own line of business had any guarantee of raising themselves out of destitution. *I often grieve*, he said, *to think that I have not as much as a £5 note to call my own and to send you some.*

Harry Hastings Pearce's grandmother lived on the Creswick Creek diggings, twenty miles from Ballarat, in the 1850s. Later she would tell her family that the number one cause of all the trouble in the summer of '54 was poverty. William Howitt reckoned that the diggers were primarily aggrieved by false accounts of the richness of the diggings and the ease of procuring gold, followed closely by the exorbitant price of food. But the arbitrary nature of gold mining, and Ballarat's particular palaeo-geology, meant that not everyone was starving. A quick glance at the advertisements in the BALLARAT TIMES would still show that while some families couldn't afford bread, others were dining on potted pheasant and imported jellies. If my neighbour could eat like a king, why not I?

Those who made their fortunes often packed their bags and went home triumphant. But for the majority who had failed, there was not even enough loose change for a coach ride to Geelong, let alone a passage to Britain. To many, there seemed an obvious solution. If gold digging was so futile, why not farm the millions of acres of Crown land that surrounded the goldfields? Till the virgin soil. On the land, people imagined, there could be an end to the restless pursuit of fortune and an acceptance of a modest livelihood of rural toil. It's where many immigrants had started their journeys, after all.

The idea was especially attractive to family men, who longed for a home base where they could leave their wives and children while they continued to follow the rushes, chasing new leads to golden success. Gypsy life was initially fun and adventurous, but uprooting a large family time and time again became tiresome and humiliating. Set up on a farm, the missus could grow a garden and feed the kids wholesome food; perhaps even send them to school. It was not just the starving diggers who envisaged this redemptive possibility. Prosperous diggers who felt an affinity with the Australian landscape and social outlook (not to mention the speculative potential of all that fertile pasture) also fancied themselves as landed gentlemen. For this emergent middle class, access to land was not about subsistence but accelerating social status. Here was the yeoman ideal of independence and mastery combined with the launching pad to upward mobility of a land boom.

There was one big hitch. 1n 1851, when the Port Phillip District was granted political separation from New South Wales, the new colony was divided into about one thousand unfenced and unsurveyed sheep runs. The squatters who controlled these runs produced the wool that accounted for more than ninety per cent of Victoria's exports. Only some 400,000 acres had been sold—in the towns of Melbourne, Geelong and Portland and in the 'settled' areas near them, tiny agricultural outposts such as Bacchus Marsh and Kilmore.[10] The 'land question' was both 'bewilderingly complex', as Geoffrey Serle has ably demonstrated, and crystal clear. Through a tangled legal web of long leases and pre-emptive buying rights to the squatters—many of whom sat in the Legislative Council—the lands were effectively 'locked'. The land question was an A-grade political battleground, contested by urban radicals, cautious moderates and extremist aristocrats alike. And this was *before* the land-hungry gold rush immigrants began clamouring for a piece of the pie.

In late 1852, Governor La Trobe began making promises

that town allotments and agricultural plots near the diggings would be sold. A deputation representing the wishes of over seven thousand people, recruited in part by James Bonwick, had convinced him that the *bulk of the working population and most of the married men wish to become landholders*. La Trobe made good his pledge, and for eighteen months from early 1853 more than half a million acres were sold. But there was another snag: as squatters and wealthy speculators outbid each other to gobble up the new allotments, the price of land skyrocketed. In 1850 the average price of rural land was 25s per acre. By 1853 the price had more than trebled, to £4. The immigrant married men and workers who thought to exchange shovel for scythe had been dudded. It didn't help matters that much of the land sold around the goldfields was bought by employees of the government camps—the gold commissioners, police inspectors and magistrates—with money borrowed from prosperous local publicans and merchants. James Johnston, Margaret's Jamie, on a salary of £400 a year, started buying up land almost as soon as the two of them arrived in Ballarat in the winter of 1854.

The capitalist land-grabbers did nothing to improve the lands, let alone cultivate them, so there was still no agricultural produce flowing to the goldfields, and diggers were no closer to their pastoral idylls. Food prices remained high, especially in winter when the roads became impassable. Unskilled workers could find no alternative employment at a time when public expenditure on roads, docks or other infrastructure was negligible. Thus most miners, concluded Harry Hastings Pearce via his grandmother's tales, *were condemned to the hopeless search for gold*.

Land reform. The concept became a pernicious irritant precisely because it was also a palpable remedy. Three little words formed a potent mantra. Unlock the lands. Unlock the lands!

UNLOCK THE LANDS. Public debate was on the side of the diggers, and even conservative merchants like Robert Caldwell, who was still touting the myth that there was no such thing as poverty in Australia, advocated land reform as an antidote to intemperance. *Cannot the government come into competition with the publican, and, instead of presenting the means of a debauch, put before the eyes of the returned digger a sweet little corner of fifty acres,* he wrote. *How many a wife longs for this bait to be hung out!*

Certain diggers agreed. Locked lands meant spare money was spent in pubs rather than on homesteads. American Seth Rudolphus Clark thought it was *sheer bad management on the part of the government...to encourage low dissipation and drunkenness* when family farms might be built, and fruit and vegetables grown. Creating a means for miners to buy small plots of agricultural land *had long been the subject of anxious attention*, as one goldfields official put it, but the issue increased in urgency as the proportion of women and children on the diggings increased.[11] This fundamental shift from pure industry to entrenched domesticity had reached its undeniable zenith by the winter of 1854.

*

It's not that there wasn't a record of disaffection before Ellen Young arrived on the scene. In February 1854 two English Chartists, George Black and H. R. Nicholls, began publishing the GOLD DIGGER'S ADVOCATE from their HQ in Melbourne. The ADVOCATE drew on arguments and emotions that had been in circulation at least since the Bendigo anti-licence protests of mid-1853. Its self-proclaimed charter was to please *all true lovers of liberty of conscience and freedom of action.* (At one shilling and sixpence it was more expensive, as well as more political, than

Bonwick's journal and lasted about as long; the ADVOCATE folded in September 1854.) Like Chartist newspapers in England, the ADVOCATE advanced a number of causes with a broadly democratic agenda. It argued for an amendment to Victoria's Constitution to extend electoral representation to (male) diggers, and railed against the petty tyranny of the goldfields officials over the disenfranchised diggers. The ADVOCATE commented at an urban remove for all diggers on all diggings. It predicted *dire consequences* if the diggers were forced to submit to political slavery.

What Ellen Young did was different. Ellen spoke for the people, as one of the people, about what it was like to be among the people. Her husband was a digger. She was a digger's wife who had decided to toil with a pen instead of a pick. But this was no drawing room dirge: there was no drawing room, just a leaky tent. Ellen, you could say, was an early fan of the notion that the personal is political; that personal grievance can and should amount to political utterance.

Given her association with Clerkenwell and the sophisticated references to democratic traditions in her poetry and letters, she may well have been an activist in Chartist struggles in England, the popular democratic movement that drew in many radicalised women, particularly in the early 1840s. Certainly, Ellen's poetry bears all the hallmarks of classic Chartist melodrama: a redemptive narrative based around a golden age of autonomy, present misery and oppression, an enemy outsider, liberation by heroic Chartist manhood, and a radiant future based on citizenship, chivalry and domestic harmony.[12] Ellen may even have come to Victoria with hopes of fulfilling the early Chartist promise of political equality for men and women, a platform that by the 1850s had been pragmatically dumped in favour of manhood suffrage, perceived as a more achievable goal.

Ellen would have found like minds in some of the other women steeped in Chartist heritage who also found their way to Ballarat. Twenty-nine-year-old Cornish-born Jane Cuming (née Sweet) arrived in Victoria in 1852 with her husband Stephen and their first two children. The Cumings were deeply influenced by Chartist and liberal philosophy. Their daughter Martineau, born in the revolutionary year of 1848, was named after the English feminist writer, political economist and abolitionist Harriet Martineau. Jane Fryer was another active Chartist who went to Ballarat with her husband in 1854. At twenty-two years old, Jane was buzzing with the reformist zeal of the young. She was one of the first to marry in a British registry office, eschewing a church wedding in favour of what she saw as the more equitable vows of a civil ceremony. Jane went on to become a prominent socialist, co-founding the Australian Secular Society and working tirelessly for the Eight Hour Movement, the women's suffrage movement and anti-conscription and peace campaigns.

Ballarat was overflowing with budding political radicals and religious nonconformists in the winter of '54. Hunched over in their tents, warmed by brandy and outrage as they watched their children sleep, couples like the Cumings and the Fryers applied careworn dreams of liberty and justice to their beleaguered lot. Victoria promised a tabula rasa for their utopian visions.

Ellen Young spoke directly to these people. In her poem 'Ballarat', she offered an explanation for her protesting the plight of the diggers. *Emblem of hope the poets sing*, she writes, *And I've the fancy caught*. She makes it sound almost light-hearted—impulsive—but as Ellen would have known, a form of 'militant domesticity' was part of the Chartist tradition, with some women writing themselves into the melodramatic narrative as crusading heroines. They were champions for the right to suitable housing, decent food and companionable marriages. Such crusaders argued the need for women to be independent, not subservient to men, slaves to neither the workhouse nor their husband's dominion. Educated women from Britain to France to Germany took a leading role in the revolutionary movements that swept across Europe in 1848, raising awareness that the struggle for political sex equality was also an economic and social struggle for a better standard of living for working people.[13] Participatory democracy started at home.

There was also home-grown Australian precedent for the political evangelism of Ellen Young's poetry. Adelaide Ironside is best known as the first Australian woman artist to study overseas; however, she also did a smashing line in political poetry and published at least twenty of her fiery, patriotic poems in the pro-republican PEOPLE'S ADVOCATE in 1853 and 1854. Other members of the Australian League, the circle of young radicals in which she moved, encouraged Adelaide in her actions. It's quite feasible that copies of the PEOPLE'S ADVOCATE were in circulation on the Ballarat goldfields. George Lang, the twenty-two-year-old son of the group's spiritual leader, Reverend John Dunmore Lang, was in Ballarat in 1854. He was working as the manager of the local branch of the Bank of New South Wales and also wrote for the BALLARAT TIMES. Adelaide had worked as a governess to the younger Lang children and George would have known her. He may even have drawn attention to Adelaide's rousing poems; possibly he encouraged Henry Seekamp, who shared Lang's republican fervour, to publish Ellen Young's work. Seekamp was certainly prepared to accord Ellen a prominent space in which to forge her own identity as an intellectual leader in the local struggle for democratic reform.

Together, Ellen Young and Henry Seekamp became the

mouthpiece for the people of Ballarat in late 1854. He was the hothead; she was the calm but deadly serious moral conscience of the community. Good cop, bad cop: tag-team political advocacy.

*

Ellen's cadence was remarkably upbeat in early months of that glacial winter. She saw reason for hope. She rallied the flagging troops. Her optimism was pinned on the new governor, due to arrive in Victoria at any moment. She published a new poem in the GEELONG ADVERTISER on 1 June 1854:

> For much I hope a change is near;
> New brooms, they say, sweep clean;
> We soon shall have Sir Hotham here,
> He'll make a change, I ween.[14]

Ellen felt her literary role was to raise the spirits, to find a way out of the emotional morass that had settled upon Ballarat's diggers like a moorland fog. She employed homespun images—cats, brooms, fancies—to convey ideas of historically mutinous significance. She entreated the diggers to *each one join in joyous song/The song of liberty.*[15] She wished *good luck to every man*. She blessed the Queen, *our Queen*, and all who *nobly toil.* In the last line of the poem she added an unconventional but apposite flourish: *God bless their babes and wives.* Ellen's words were intended to unify: to strengthen the bonds of a collective spirit in crisis. To find a common enemy.

The diggers may not have had a representative in parliament, but they had a free press and a maverick poet to call their own.

*

British and *Justice* were the two words on everyone's lips in the winter of 1854. The words generally carried a question mark. This? You call *this* British justice? There were many ways to illustrate the hypocrisy. Thomas Mundy winced every time he saw the soldiers pass by. It wasn't because he was afraid they'd find the illegal alcohol stashed in his cart (he knew sly grog was tacitly approved) but because of the aristocratic pretensions of *lords and duke's sons, friends of La Trobe, mincing around with their gold epaulettes and lace on their coats who knew nothing of the people or the country*. The indignity of educated professional men being lorded over by a pack of exiled nincompoops stuck in Mundy's craw, and he knew he wasn't alone. *Things will not remain long as they are*, he predicted. *The British are a loyal law abiding people but they expect, what they have been accustomed to, British justice.*

English journalist William Howitt also noticed how incensed the diggers were by heavy-handed, arrogant treatment from the police. *The arbitrary, Russian sort of way in which they were visited by the authorities*, he wrote, was especially galling for gentlemen. Weren't the British at the very moment fighting a war against the Czar in the Crimea for failing to honour enlightened standards of diplomacy?

Examples of injustice and incivility occurred day after day, burgeoning on the grapevine of community outrage. Prisoners could be left manacled to tree logs if the tiny lockup was full or if the turnkey took a set against them. Honest but poor licence defaulters were chained together with hardened thieves and assorted ex-cons from Van Diemen's Land. Women were incarcerated with men, nothing but a flimsy partition between them. Other inmates were forced to draw water and hew wood for the camp. After a sick man died in the Ballarat lockup because there was no hospital in which to receive proper care, Thomas

Pierson cried *Oh! How humane is Brittish [sic] law and Brittish freedom*. Since he was an American, Pierson's lament took on an even more divisive bent. His condemnation of seemingly local offences spiralled out into critique of transnational significance. Thomas and Frances went to the Ballarat Magistrates Court one Saturday morning and witnessed several *licence cases*. One man had borrowed another's licence. He was gaoled for two months in Geelong. *A still more heathenish part of the matter*, Thomas later reflected in his diary, *is that the man had a wife and six children in his tent in Ballarat*. The poor woman had *just been confined* with the sixth. *The English conduct in governing is a disgrace to any civilised nation*, concluded Thomas. Government oppression and negligence were beginning to be a factor in the struggle for survival. Another word was added to the lexicon of complaint: tyranny.

Ballarat society was mired in complaint. To add to the administrative quagmire, Ballarat was dealing with a new top dog. Robert Rede was appointed resident commissioner of the Ballarat goldfields on the eve of the winter deluge. Whether he was sent as a punishment or a peace offering is unclear. English-born Rede was the son of a Royal Navy man, but pursued a career in medicine before tossing in his studies and sailing to Victoria in November 1851. He soon entered the public service and, with his excitable nature, quickly came to the attention of the Gold Fields Commission. Promoted to resident commissioner on a salary of £700 a year plus accommodation and rations, the thirty-nine-year-old bachelor immediately realised the Eureka diggings was the place to be. *At Eureka more activity is to be seen at present both amongst Miners and Storekeepers than on any other portion of these Fields*, Rede's benign predecessor reported to his superiors in the Melbourne HQ of the commission. *It now forms the most important section and contains a larger population than anywhere else*. In the first of his weekly reports, Robert Rede described Eureka as the *most populated and unruly part of the district*.[16] His reports tend to be loquacious and colourful, perhaps the better to show up his immediate junior, James Johnston, whom the colonial secretary had previously dressed down for being *very curt* with his reports, so deficient in information that *he might as well have sent none*. (The colonial secretary expected Johnston *to be more communicative* in future, but Rede took over the filing of weekly returns altogether.[17]) Rede used his reports to give an appearance of peace and order at his new post. When a prisoner was rescued from the lockup by his mates, Rede reported the incident but assured HQ the incident *arose from drink and not from any ill feeling against the authorities*. Johnston had probably been smart. Sometimes no news is the best news.

Some members of the goldfields administration could see that the subterranean civic impulses would not be kept down. On 3 July 1854, magistrate John D'Ewes wrote to the colonial secretary in Melbourne to warn about the lack of basic services available to the diggers and townsfolk at Ballarat:

> The painful impossibility that at present exists of affording relief to sick aging and destitute persons here at this inclement season of the year, and of which I am sorry to say a large number exists in this daily increasing population, owing to the non-existence of any hospital or asylum, except the small one belonging to the Camp and restricted to Government servants.

The people were taking matters into their own hands, he reported. A meeting at the Ballarat Hotel on 1 July took subscriptions for a new hospital. The *well know liberality of the diggers* when it came to public subscriptions meant that £270 was donated by twenty-four persons that night. D'Ewes thought it ill-judged for the government not to be seen to be contributing in some way to this fund. He came up with the canny idea of auctioning confiscated sly grog and donating the proceeds to the hospital, instead of 'destroying' the cache, a thinly veiled euphemism for handing it out to police. While Ellen Young was rallying the forces of cohesion among the diggers, D'Ewes was trying to ameliorate the toxic sense of 'us and them' that was ever creeping into the Ballarat populace.

Destitution, lack of access to land and inadequate public services made a formidable backdrop, but the focal point of daily complaints was the method of checking licences. *Nothing*, wrote William Howitt, *could exceed the avidity, the rigidity and arbitrary spirit with which the licence fees were enforced on the diggings*. The police, charged with the task of enforcing compliance with the monthly renewal process, were uniformly despised. If the military presence was made up of the simpering sons of insolvent gentry, the police were drawn largely from the flotsam of ex-Vandemonians and other layabouts.

The Victorian Government paid peanuts and got the inevitable monkeys. The police force was young, ill trained, inexperienced and frequently shickered. A *more proud, lazy, ignorant, tyrannical set of vagabonds could not easily be found*, was Thomas Pierson's summation of the 'traps' who gave Frances 'a call' in her store on St Patrick's Day, a sure sign she was selling sly grog.

The Ballarat community expressed outrage that their licence fees were used to support a police force that did nothing to check crime, but was more likely to be embroiled in corruption. Storekeepers who sold grog paid the police. (Frances Pierson didn't sustain a conviction, so she may have been one of the many paying hush money.) Meanwhile, many miners disappeared down shafts in the black of night, either through mishap or misdeed, never to be seen again. Claim jumping was rife, and more often sorted out by fists and bowie knives than police investigation and arbitration. If a policeman deigned to turn up when a digger was killed in a mining accident, reported Thomas Mundy, *Yes he would say he's dead right enough* before thrusting his hand into the dead man's pocket and extracting what money or valuables he had. Chained dogs and pistols under pillows were the preferred means of safeguarding against crime. No one had a shred of confidence in Victoria's finest.

The arbitrary and heavy-handed method of licence hunting was intimately connected in the hearts and minds of the more educated, politicised diggers with the affront of destitution. *Very few like to have their poverty exposed*, assessed the GEELONG ADVERTISER. Public disclosure was precisely what the practice of indiscriminate licence checking achieved: *the licence law makes poverty a crime*. Exposure led to imprisonment, which turned a loyal subject into *a broken-spirited man*. The crowning insult was for an unlicensed digger to be arrested in front of his wife and children and dragged away at the point of a bayonet. James Johnston was singled out by the Ballarat correspondent to the GEELONG ADVERTISER as being *on a crusade* against unlicensed miners, a mission that *exceeded the limits of his office*. Margaret Brown Howden could have no idea how profoundly her *dear Jamie* was despised in her new home town.

Foremost among the howling gale of protest against the authorities was that the police lorded it over a population that was more highly educated and civilised than the supposed guardians of decency and order. *Beardless boys just pitched-forked into assistant commissionerships*, wrote digger John Bastin, *would not leave the camp unless arrayed in uniform and gold lace.*[18] Thomas Mundy pointed out the diversity of the digging community, *as fine a class of men as anyone could wish to see; many of them well educated, doctors, lawyers, merchants sons; in fact all trades and professions.* The problem was that the rag-tag police were *continually taunting the diggers with their mule like subjugation.* The insult stung. *These were men of pluck and spirit and intolerant of injustice*, wrote Mundy, *indignant at the impervious and corrupt administration of the law.*

Different nationalities saw the problem of governance from a different point of view, but the landscape was the same. The Irish knew all about the cant of British justice; the atavistic pulse of harassment and discrimination at the hands of the British throbbed in their veins. To Raffaello Carboni, *it was the hated Austrian rule, which was now attempted, in defiance of God and man, to be transplanted into this colony.* American George Francis Train had no argument with the licence fee; he thought it a perfectly reasonable trade for wood, water, a gold escort, police protection and the privilege of driving a spade into the earth. What Train deplored was the Legislative Council, an institution he called a *burlesque on free representation.* It was *absurd* that the miners had no representation. Citizen George, who would later run for the US presidency as an independent, could patently see *there is a strong Australian feeling growing up*, rooted in the principle that *taxation without representation is tyranny.*

It was never a long-term option to bully those who had themselves been at the top of the literate, entitled, bullying professions at home. Penury was shame enough. Being antagonised by stroppy British boy scouts was salt in the wounds.

*

Towards the end of June, Ellen Young's beacon of hope appeared on the horizon. Sailing on the *Queen of the South*, Sir Charles Hotham and Lady Jane Sarah Hotham arrived in Victoria on 21 June 1854. Their advent was greeted with rapturous relief. The colony had been in a state of leadership limbo for eighteen months since Governor La Trobe's resignation on the last day of 1852. More than that, a black cloud shrouded his departure, which did not eventuate until May 1854. While La Trobe waited for his replacement, his beloved Swiss wife, Sophie, died in her home town of Neufchatel. She had left prior to La Trobe with their two daughters, anticipating his speedy return. La Trobe was broken-hearted, and though his body remained in Victoria through to the autumn of '54, his heart and soul were long gone.

William Kelly witnessed La Trobe's physical departure. *I saw the man in deep mourning*, wrote Kelly, *attended by a small cortege of attached friends, endeavouring to hide his sadness and dejection as he returned the parting salutes of those who at least esteemed him as a man if they could not extol him as a viceroy.* Whatever La Trobe's achievements—he had seen Victoria progress from a political satellite of Sydney to a prosperous gold-driven self-governing colony—all hint of success had been subsumed in a general public reproach for his perceived economic mismanagement and political ineptitude. On 28 June the GEELONG ADVERTISER reported on the quiet departure of La Trobe: *the lonely, bereaved man... the yells and hootings of his savage persecutors salute him as he goes.* It would be cold comfort to learn that, unlike his successor, La Trobe at least got away with his life.

Victoria Welcomes Victoria's Choice read the banner strung across Princes Bridge for the grand procession to lead Governor Hotham and his lady from Sandridge Pier to Flagstaff Gardens. Sir Charles proceeded on horseback. Lady Hotham and Mrs

Kaye, wife of the new colonial secretary who had arrived on the same ship, followed in a carriage and four. They were greeted by the flags of all nations and sects, miles of bunting, brass bands and wild cheers for the official welcome parade through the streets of Melbourne. An installation ceremony was held at the government offices. Hotham swore his oaths before the Bishop of Melbourne, Church of England clergy, the Rabbi of the Melbourne congregation and the heads of other denominations. A proclamation was read. The Union Jack was hoisted. Artillery fire sounded from Flagstaff Hill. Hotham made an impromptu speech to the rejoicing crowd, promising to *do his duty as an honest, straightforward man should do.*[19] Such *frank, liberal speeches*, as Charles Evans noted, won Hotham the goodwill of the people.

The press were sympathetic towards the herculean task ahead. The GEELONG ADVERTISER recognised that Hotham had to bring to heel *a whole army of lazy and incompetent hangers-on, indolent, careless, incorrigible*; men given jobs on the goldfields *simply because they could not be kept sober in town*. There was also the matter of the massive public debt accrued by La Trobe's administration. Hotham was a slightly built man, with a long nose and mutton chops stretching down his thin face, but he wore his burden gallantly. Born into nobility, the eldest son in a family of eleven children, with a distinguished naval and diplomatic career behind him, Hotham had been expecting to command a ship in the Crimea. He took his gubernatorial appointment to Victoria as an unwarranted slap. Imperial duty alone fuelled his passage.

But there was some cause for exuberance, for Sir Charles Hotham, at forty-eight years of age, had recently married for the first time. As for so many other gold rush immigrants, the Hothams' voyage would be their honeymoon. And Sir Charles's new wife was a formidable consolation prize. Jane Sarah Hood was the daughter of Samuel Hood, the 2nd Baron Bridport and a Tory MP, and Charlotte Nelson, Duchesa di Bronte, niece of Horatio Nelson. The third of seven children, Jane moved between court commitments at Windsor and her family's lands in Somerset. Petite, beautiful and accomplished, she had married for the first time in 1838. Her husband, Hugh Holbech, died eleven years later; they had no children.[20] On 10 December 1853, aged thirty-six, and four years a widow, she married Sir Charles Hotham, who had been appointed lieutenant governor of Victoria just four days earlier.

She knew what she was signing up for. Lady Hotham's new life would take her far away from Somerset garden parties and court appearances routinely noted in THE TIMES. In April, the Hothams sailed for Victoria, accompanied by three servants, Mr and Mrs Kaye and a cargo of furniture to fit out the newly acquired Government House at Toorak. The ARGUS reported that when the new first lady of Victoria arrived at the dock, her sweet face was illuminated by a huge smile of genuine excitement. *She has a very amiable countenance*, sketched the ARGUS journalist, *her complexion is fair, with light, soft blue eyes...unaffected in her manner and very prepossessing*. The journalist was impressed that, at Hotham's induction ceremony, Lady Hotham showed *evident satisfaction in so cordial a reception, her pleasure beamed in every glance. She showed plainly that she enjoyed the whole affair and went through a rather protracted ceremony with nerve, cheerfulness and unmistakable gratification.*[21]

You've got to admire the buoyancy of the people too. All their great expectations smashed to smithereens, and now reassembled by faith in a viceregal second coming: a human mosaic of optimism, with child-like trust as the glue. *The people of Melbourne are looking for the arrival of Sir Charles Hotham as religious enthusiasts might look forward to the millennium*, wrote the editor of the GEELONG ADVERTISER on 8 June. The Messiah. Father Christmas. Any old patriarch would do. But the editor was guarded in his praise. It would not be wise for Hotham to remain *on the poop*; he must acquaint himself with *the poor devils of the third class* and the sooner he went *tween decks* the better. George Francis Train was similarly cautious. *I hope [Hotham] is equal to the times in which he lives,* wrote Train in his weekly despatch to the BOSTON GLOBE on 23 July, *for if he is not, depend upon it his official reign will be painfully brief, for our people have begun to think.* Train conjured a sticky prophecy: *Our politics are in their infancy, but their manhood will be reached ere they touch their youth. They'll burst out in all their glory when it will be least suspected.* Which sounds, at the very least, messy.

But in those early days of Hotham's period in office, more people shared Ellen Young's confidence than Train's doubts. Hotham was expected to be all things to all people. Shopkeepers thought their trade would increase. Landowners thought the value of their property would rise. Diggers thought their licence fees would be reduced and their grievances sympathetically heard. *He is certain to arrive with inflated notions of his importance and ability*, warned the GEELONG ADVERTISER, but the people wanted to believe in this *new* new beginning, this *fresh* fresh start. It seemed a good sign when Hotham began reducing the wages of public servants and sacking others outright. The icing on the cake of such fiscal discipline was Lady Hotham's decision to cultivate her own garden at Toorak, reducing the need for groundsmen. She would be *a gratuitous labourer*, the DIGGERS' ADVOCATE reported with satisfaction.

The decision to house the new governor in the lofty hills of Toorak (La Trobe had lived in a modest home by the river in Richmond) and to undertake an expensive renovation and furnishing of the home, rented from a prosperous merchant, was not without controversy. La Trobe had been hounded for the stupendous amount of public debt he had accumulated, despite his own personal frugality. And these were anti-aristocratic times. The Hothams would soon encounter the perverse collective psychology of their new home town. 'Downstairs' thought it right that everyone should live as one. As Martha Clendinning had realised to the benefit of her business, it was politic to dress down. Yet those who had managed to climb to higher social ground were affronted to find muslin where they expected silk. When the Hothams threw a viceregal ball, the press had a field day with the penny-pinching in the drinks department. Hotham served colonial beer instead of champagne and was forever after known as the *Small Beer Governor*. When one of the guests later got sick, supposedly from the toxic alcohol, and Hotham sacked the public servant who ordered the beer, there was an uproar. What a despot! The fine line between viceregal authority and populism was proving difficult to identify.

So when Sir Charles announced that he and his wife would leave the comfortable confines of their Toorak mansion to visit the goldfields and personally take the temperature of the restive people, the news was taken as a sure sign that restitution was imminent. Ellen wrote another poem, the first of her offerings to be published in the BALLARAT TIMES. Henry Seekamp also had ten copies of the poem printed on a pale pink silk, one of which Ellen later pasted into the front of her poetry volume. The title: *Visit of Sir Charles Hotham, K.C.B., Lieut. Gov. of Victoria, To Ballarat*. The by-line: *by Ellen F. Young, the Ballarat Poetess.* The gist:

The man of upright heart and daring deed,

Comes to relieve us in our urgent need…
Our future guide to happiness and peace,
To us securing all true wealth's increase.

Ever mindful of purist Chartism's aims—companionate marriage, equality of purpose and valour between the sexes—Ellen also includes Lady Jane Hotham in her salutation.

For the great good Victoria will gain—
Let us all honor on Sir Hotham rain,
And let his fair, accomplish'd, gentle bride,
Her equal due, —share in his fame, world-wide.
To her we'll give an equal meed of praise
(As one Heav'n-sent, our moral worth to raise)…
And soon may Ballarat, Victoria's pride,
Be honor'd with Sir Hotham and his bride.

Despite Ellen's tribute, Sir Charles's bride has been anything but honoured with an equal measure of history's attention. Whole biographies have been written about Governor Hotham, but there is not one extant image of Lady Hotham to place beside the official portraits of His Excellency. No photos, paintings or sketches exist. Lady Hotham did keep a diary of her time in Victoria, but only snippets survive. However, there is enough information in other fragmentary sources to know that Lady Jane Hotham was no puffed-up princess.

*

Of the two Hothams, it was 'her ladyship' who proved more adaptable to the new circumstances. Journalists noted that she was gracious and open, perpetually cheerful and appeared to greet every new situation with wide-eyed enthusiasm. She intuited the need to shed aristocratic pretension when mixing with the hoi polloi, but to stroke the plumes of the nouveau riche who flocked to Toorak in their finery. She threw dinner parties every week, and invited both *all the best people in the colony*, as William Kelly described the squattocracy, as well as those who, before striking gold, *never trod on a carpeted floor.* Such *stalwart dames and strapping girls* wore *low evening costume* for morning engagements, but were always accepted graciously by the lady of the house. When Mrs Massey attended her first ball at Toorak—which she describes as *a large handsome place, which the winding Yarra almost surrounds by her silver girdle*—there were so many guests it took two hours to get the carriages up the drive to the front entrance. Lady Hotham's *affability* was often contrasted to the *unbending* nature of her husband.

She also took to the streets. Before leaving for their tour of the diggings, Sir Charles and Lady Hotham attended a tradesman's ball at the Criterion Hotel. There, described Kelly, they met an *assemblage of hard-brushed, shiny-haired operatives, publicans, corporations and small shopkeepers, with their wives and daughters, girthed in silk or satin, and moist with mock eau-de-cologne.* It was a tough crowd: common, aspirational, monied, star struck. Lady Hotham, with the *consummate tact of her sex*, merrily drank a low-rent brandy cocktail at the urging of one of the guests. Charles bristled. Lady Hotham was the belle of the ball.

Lady Hotham took her tact, her joie de vivre, her kindly yin to Charles's dour yang—whatever it was she possessed that her husband didn't—all the way to the diggings. Their goldfields tour took them to Bendigo, Ballarat and Castlemaine, bumping along in a Yankee Telegraph carriage, *a grotesque article*, according to William Westgarth, built for strength not comfort. First stop: Ballarat. They arrived at 5pm on Saturday 26 August, Sir Charles on horseback, her ladyship in the carriage. It had been raining steadily all afternoon. Their appearance elicited little fanfare. In fact, they saw the advantage in entering the stage unannounced and unrecognised, the better to take in an undoctored scene. The couple slipped quietly into the Government Camp, where they were staying in Police Inspector Robert Evans' quarters (*into which we managed to convey almost every piece of furniture to be found in the Camp*, griped Police Magistrate D'Ewes). On Sunday they walked together through the diggings, stopping to ask questions of the diggers.

In a despatch to Lord Grey in London, Hotham later wrote that *for some time I was enabled to walk undiscovered amongst them, and thus I gathered their real feeling towards the Government, and obtained an insight into some minor causes on which they desired redress.* He concluded that the digging population was generally orderly, loyal and *having among them a large proportion of women and children...there was an appearance of tranquillity and confidence.* He concluded that it was through the influence of women that *this restless population must be restrained.* Hotham predicted that where a militia would fail to tame the more restive diggers, the wives would succeed. *I would rather see an army of ten thousand women arrive, than an equal number of soldiers*, he ended his despatch.[22]

On Monday, Lady Hotham went without her husband to Black Hill to view the mining operations there. She made a distinct impression. All were pleased with the governor, the GEELONG ADVERTISER later reported, *but Lady Hotham ranks still higher. The diggers considered her a perfect darling and no more frightened of the mud than ourselves.* It was considered a stroke of policy genius to conduct a private tour, an unobtrusive, inconspicuous visit rather than the *tinsel, formality and studied effect* of a public tour, which the diggers would have despised. Was this judicious decision made by Lady Hotham? She certainly seemed to enjoy the unorthodox viceregal outing. *It was indeed a grand and gratifying sight*, wrote the DIGGERS' ADVOCATE, *to see her Ladyship shaking hands and exchanging civilities with the clay-besmeared but generous-hearted diggers...scattering to the winds the almost blinding cloud of aristocratic prejudice.* A miner wrote to the BALLARAT TIMES to express the same appreciation of Lady Hotham's egalitarian inclinations. C.G.D. (Constantly Growling Digger) expected the Hothams *to come up here as aristocratic novelties to have a look at us cattle [and] shrug their shoulders in horror.* But he was delighted to observe her ladyship *breaking and examining bits of clay in her white, delicate little hand and talking and smiling to the people about her all the while...why, bless your soul, she hasn't half the airs and graces of your innkeeper's or storekeeper's wives.*[23] That was the diggings: the common slags getting all uppity, while the governor's wife got down in the dirt.

It is thanks to the no-longer-growling digger that we have the best eyewitness pen portrait of the governor's wife available:

> There is Lady Hotham on his arm, her shoes and stockings all over mud, she doesn't care a straw—she is joyous, and evidently happy. She is a tall young woman of six and twenty [actually she was thirty and seven][24] fine symmetrical figure, very active, no mock delicacy about her, blond complexion, fine liquid ox-eyes, fair hair, teeth white and regular, as a greyhound's, and affable and conciliating manner—none of all that *hauteur* in her manner you might expect in her high position—cheerfulness and goodness are impressed upon her countenance. But dear me, how plain she dresses; plaid dress, red stripe, very plain bonnet...A gold watch, suspended by a massive gold chain, and hanging carelessly from her neck is the only ornament she wears.

The passage is descriptive, but sounds a cautionary note. All those women whose behaviour and attitude in the colonies has become uncomfortably defiant, ambitious or demanding, beware.

> Now, if all the diggers, storekeepers and publicans wives would throw by their silks and satins, and appear like Lady Hotham, *simplex in munditiis*, they would confer a great boon upon their indulgent husbands; and be more respected, the closer they would follow Lady Hotham's example.[25]

Less pressure to perform, more yielding to the simplicity of their surroundings—that's what the miners of Ballarat wanted from their wives.

But Lady Hotham was not merely a walking mannequin of feminine decency. When the people threw up a hearty three cheers for Hotham and his lady, Jane turned around to face the crowd, *her eyes beaming with delight and face suffused with gladness. She smiled, not with the cold dignity of a high born dame but with holiday glee.* She said plainly, *'Well, I declare, these diggers are, after all, fine hearty fellows; I'll speak to Charles to be kind to the poor fellows, when we get back to town again'.*

There is a more celebrated image of Lady Hotham at the Ballarat diggings: the moment when she was swept up in the arms of a hefty digger, who transported her safely over a muddy ditch. Either Lady Hotham was an independent spirit by nature, or her adaptable nature adjusted readily to the sense of freedom from convention that many women experienced on the diggings.

There's a moment in Bendigo on their goldfields tour when we see the Hothams in an arresting snapshot of marital dissonance. In Bendigo Hotham was invited to a public dinner at the Criterion Hotel. Earlier that day, in front of a crowd of nine thousand, he promised to throw open the lands, and encouraged the people to pursue agricultural activities and *make beautiful homes for themselves on the rich lands of the colony.* He was presented with a petition to abolish the licence tax. He could not promise, he said, to do away with so large a portion of public revenue. *All must pay for liberty and freedom in some shape or another*, he consoled. To show his man-of-the-people stripes, he confided that he paid ten per cent tax on his property in England—*and I can assure you, I dislike it most infernally, but I still must pay it.* He agreed to give the subject his full attention but warned, *having made up my mind as to what is right, I am just the boy to stick to it.*

At the dinner that night, the boy prophesied that although Victoria was in its *infancy*, it would soon reach its *manhood* and live happily into *old age.* Though no individual would be threatened, Hotham was certain that the introduction of machinery to the goldfields would be an essential part of its *rigorous manhood.*

Now it was time to get on with the toasts. The chairman proposed a toast to Lady Hotham, who was present. Perhaps she wanted to answer the toast herself, to use the voice that Ballarat's diggers had found so refreshing and open. But Sir Charles rose and spoke for her.

> As you know, it is not in the power of a lady to take part in politics, and it is certainly not my wish that Lady Hotham should do so. In her name, I thank you for the toast that has been given. It is her part, and I believe I may add, her study, to take part in all those charities, and other works of a social character, which women are best suited for. (Cheers) If she adhere to this part of her duty, she can be as useful in that way to the people of this country, as I, with God's blessing, can be in mine. (Great cheering.)[26]

What an odd speech. Who is it really for? The audience who met his uncontroversial ideas about women's place with applause? Or Lady Hotham, who must have sat in silence, as she absorbed the subtle sting of rebuke from her husband of just nine months? It is possible that Hotham's backhander was intended partly for Ellen Young, whose overtly political incursions may well have been brought to his attention in Ballarat. But later events cast it in the most personal light.

Fifty years after the Hothams' goldfields tour, an old Ballarat pioneer added a piece to the Jane Hotham jigsaw. One day in the winter of '54, the digger recalled in a letter to the Ballarat Council on 3 December 1904, he had sheltered a fugitive from a licence hunt, hiding the man in his tent. The next day the digger encountered a gentleman and his wife, asking directions to Bath's Hotel. He walked them to their destination, and was surprised to find them asking him many questions about the conditions on the goldfields. Happy for an audience, he denounced the impudence and cruelty of the authorities, giving the events of the previous day as example. The gentleman halted, stood in front of the digger and said *I am surprised Sir, that you, an Englishman, should give sanctuary to a rebel against your Queen. Do you know who I am?* Yes, the governor. The digger protested: *I simply did my duty as an Englishman should do to try and free a fellow man from oppression*. An animated discussion then ensued, in which fifteen minutes was spent *arguing the point of justification for my action, in which her Ladyship very energetically joined*. Sir Charles retorted that he would *not stand for insubordination*—whether from the digger or his wife is unclear.[27]

Of course, the pugnacious digger could have been gilding the historical lily, half a century on—showcasing his courage in taking on the new governor. But then why bring Lady Hotham into the reminiscence of what he described as *a triangular debate*? Why draw a woman into the ring? Lady Hotham's actions that day must have made a lasting impression on him, either from the sheer force of her energy or the unorthodox nature of her involvement in the discussion. Was her ladyship always so lippy, or was there something in the colonial air that made her feel suddenly reckless? It may have been this indiscretion, this challenge to his authority, that led Hotham to rein his wife in publicly at the Bendigo dinner. How could the governor rule with an iron fist if he could not control his lady? The governor certainly would not *look* like the sort of boy who stuck to his guns if even his outspoken young wife was prepared to take him on.

After the goldfields tour, the Hothams returned to Toorak, where Lady Hotham tended her unchaperoned garden and sold off all the gaudy, glittering ottomans and easy chairs that came with the house, while Sir Charles got on with the business of firing public servants and answering his mail.

*

In one of the *frank, liberal speeches* Hotham delivered on arrival, he encouraged the people to contact him directly should they wish to discuss a problem. *Whenever a suggestion can be made or a hint given*, he said magnanimously, *let the author come to me, and he will always find me ready to attend to his wants. At all events he will find in me a friend who is willing to give a patient and attentive hearing.*[28]

Be careful what you wish for. Raising and signing petitions had long been a way for individuals and groups to register protest and call attention to their causes. These days, we sign mass petitions on the internet or at stalls outside shopping centres with no real belief that we will have an effect. It is a gesture, a way of registering support for a cause, rather than a conscious act of participatory democracy. But in the nineteenth century petitions were a direct link between people and their leaders; the word 'petitioner' was, in some real sense, a synonym for 'citizen'. Petitioning also performed an adhesive function, rallying support for local issues that gave people a sense of belonging to a moral, political or geographic community. (Internet petitions do have the effect of rallying what Benedict Anderson famously called 'imagined communities'.)

In the early to mid-nineteenth-century, it was not uncommon for women to act as organisers for mass petitions in their towns, villages or neighbourhoods, although these petitions were customarily signed by men only. The British Anti-Corn Law League made masterful use of middle-class women to mobilise public opinion in its 1840s campaigns against government economic policy. The TIMES sneered at such women as *the petticoat politicians of Manchester*.[29] Individual women also produced their own petitions supporting the rights of their husbands, dependents, local freedom fighters, victims of persecution or others for whom they pleaded for amnesty or mercy.

There are also several celebrated petitions, signed by thousands of women, to represent the interests of women as a group against a perceived social evil. Examples include the *Women's Petition Against Coffee Representing to Publick Consideration the Grand Inconveniencies accruing to their Sex from the Excessive Use of that Drying Enfeebling Liquor* (1674)[30] and the Women's Petition to the National Assembly, presented in Versailles in 1789 by the women of France, demanding an *equality of rights for all individuals*, including *the sweetest and most interesting half among you.* Some historians claim that women's petitioning efforts in Britain contributed substantively to parliament's decision to end slavery.

It should come as no surprise, then, to find women involved in the petitioning activity that was one of the dominant forms for non-representative democracy on the early goldfields. Five thousand diggers, including two hardy women, Florence Foley and Sarah Williamson, signed the Bendigo Goldfields Petition, presented to Governor La Trobe in August 1853 in protest over the licence fee. At least one of the major petitions written by Ballarat miners pertaining to the licence fee or judicial proceedings in the final months of 1854 contains women's names. With their husbands down a shaft, diggers' wives probably did much of the footwork to collect signatures.

But goldfields women found other ways of making their presence felt at Toorak. Many eagerly accepted Hotham's kind offer to be a friend when in need. Their individual petitions are peppered through the dusty piles of inward correspondence to the Colonial Office, tied with ragged string, secure in the vaults of the Public Record Office of Victoria.

The brittle blue pages make compulsive reading. In them we find women who were otherwise voiceless and undistinguished sending out distress signals that can still be heard today. Mary Sullivan of Bendigo began her campaign for compassion in May 1853, and was still fighting it with serial petitions up to January 1855. Mary's husband had been sentenced to five years hard labour for *stealing in a tent £5*. She begged for remittance of the sentence, as she and her eighteen-month-old child were *entirely without the means of living in an honest manner*. In one of her petitions, Mary explained that her husband *was only a few weeks in bad Company* and promised to *use all of my influence to lead him to the path of honesty*. She hinted at her fate should her husband not be restored to her: *I am Young and in a Town abounding in Vice, already I have been insulted*. Mary was finally told that not enough of her husband's sentence had been served; she should try again in October 1855.[31] That Mary did not furnish this final petition suggests a poor outcome for her efforts to remain respectable.

Ann Middleton of Buninyong petitioned the governor on behalf of her husband, Charles, a butcher by trade, who had been convicted of sheep stealing and sentenced to five years hard labour on the roads. Ann pleaded for the welfare of her five children, aged between eight years and two weeks. She maintained that this was a first offence, and in any case Charles was not guilty; his partner claimed to have purchased the sheep and her husband paid half the purchase price. Please, begged Ann, *restore him to his distressed and unhappy wife and by doing so enable him to provide the necessities of his now distressed family*. Some forty signatures were attached to the petition, plus testimonials from former employees. Hotham scrawled his reply on the bottom corner of the petition. *Cannot interfere with the course of the law*. The law, as administered by the local judiciary, was so clearly regarded as an ass that such dismissive responses could only have fuelled the tension that was mounting in the second half of 1854.[32]

There are multiple petitions written by women—or, if a woman could only sign with her mark, by a literate friend—seeking to commute their husbands' gaol sentences or have them freed from lunatic asylums. Some petitions are written in French and Italian. Mrs Grant collected 117 signatures in her petition to remit the gaol sentence of her husband, James Grant, who was nicked for *shewing another person's licence*. Mrs Grant's appeal was poignant.

Zealous diggers: mining as a family affair. S. T. Gill, 1852.

A 'refreshment tent' on the diggings. S. T. Gill, 1852–3.

Sarah Hanmer,
probably c. 1860.

Interior of Adelphi Theatre, with Sarah Hanmer on the right, 1854.

A store on the diggings, like the one Martha Clendinning would have kept. Thomas Ham, 1854.

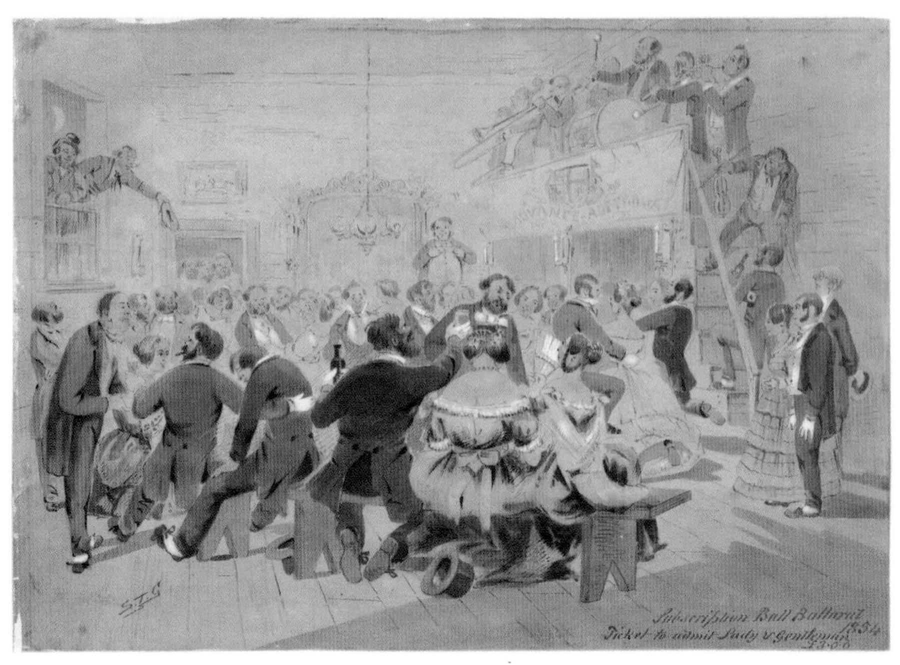

Subscription Ball Ballarat 1854
Ticket to admit Lady & Gentleman

Subscription ball in Ballarat. S. T. Gill, 1854.

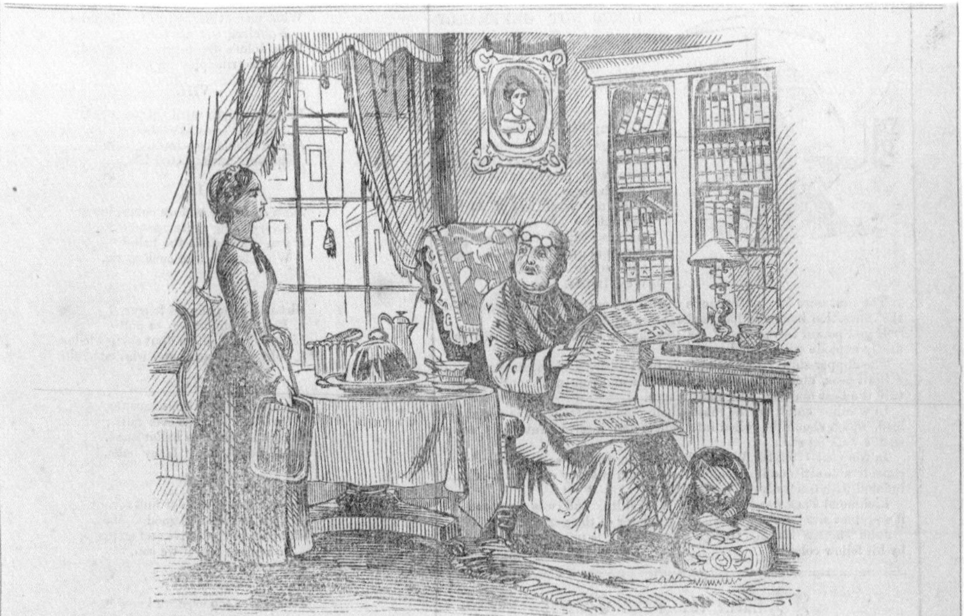

A VERY JUST COMPLAINT.
OLD GENTLEMAN: You want to leave Mary! What for? I should have thought you had a comfortable place.
MARY: Well, sir, mostly things is very comfortable here indeed; but there aint no "Punch" took in, and one must 'ave somethink to compingsate one for the climate.

'The servant problem' as seen by *Melbourne Punch*, 1856.

> Your Petitioner is at the present time in abject poverty and not able to procure the means of livelihood having just been confined, she wrote. Your Petitioner has also other children who are looking to her for the means of subsistence and what will become of herself and them during her husband's imprisonment Petitioner knoweth not.

These heartfelt pleas fell on deaf ears, terminating with Governor Hotham's standard and abrupt response: *Cannot entertain. Not granted. Put away.* To Mrs Grant's appeal, the governor appended an extra chastisement: *Never interfere with sentences. Culprit knew the law and risked being found out.*[33]

Hotham tossed formal petitions bearing hundreds of signatures in the same bin as the many barely decipherable notes, which he marked *begging letters*, received from impoverished widows in search of pecuniary aid or frantic wives seeking work for their unemployed husbands. These women's letters, along with their formal petitions, are immensely significant. Historian R. D. Walshe has claimed that the Eureka clash was inevitable due to Hotham's 'absolute intransigence' in his mission to revamp the colony's economy no matter the consequences.

Hotham's resulting policy—of small government, smaller heart—was put under intense pressure by the constant barrage of earnest missives from desperate and deserving women. Some women even travelled down from the goldfields to seek a personal audience with the governor. Honoria Anna Bayley came from Ballarat to request employment for her husband. *I trust that as one of her Majesty's subjects you will not consider my request an intrusion*, she wrote to Hotham.[34] Others cast aside the usual petitioners' attitude of fawning humility and came out all guns blazing. Eliza Dixon wrote to Hotham on behalf of her husband, who was awaiting his death sentence in jail. *Should the sentence be carried into effect*, she pleaded, *you will leave a Wife and Mother of 4 children utterly destitute neither of them being able to support themselves one being at the breast and the rest all under 5 years of age*. Eliza attributed personal responsibility to Hotham for this potential outcome, and she was remarkably forthright in her solution: *Your Excellency's mercy is a great attribute. Extend it to a poor unfortunate man who now cannot help himself and the Great Judge (should you ever require it) will do the same by you.*[35] Eliza's letter was put away with all the others, and we can only guess what she thought when Hotham met his maker just over a year later.

Suspicious of what their governor's friendship meant, people formed a new strategy. Lady Hotham began receiving her own cache of begging letters. Mrs O'Neill, supporting herself and her three children by *needle work and selling mostly everything I had*, requested assistance in finding a position for her two boys. *Hoping your Ladyship will not think me too impolite*, she wrote, *perhaps you would have the goodness to speak to Sir Charles Hotham.*[36] Twenty-three-year-old Esther McKenzie petitioned Lady Hotham the same week. Owing to her husband being *indisposed* and her sixteen-month-old baby *dangerously ill by Dentition and Colonial Fever and is not expected to live*, she was *very distressed* and *without the necessities of life*. Money for rent, medicine, medical attendance and even *the very sixpence with which I post this petition was borrowed*. Lady Hotham had developed a reputation for benevolence; her largesse seemed to exist in inverse proportion to her husband's. Esther was *fully convinced of your Ladyship's kindness to the distressed*, and wrote that *she is filled with hopes... in bestowing her a trifle to purchase some bread for her disabled family*. Lady Hotham was not without pity. She instructed her clerk to acknowledge receipt of Esther's petition, and ask her to *forward testimonials from respectable persons who are acquainted with you.* There is no further notation on the file. We can assume it too was *put away*. By coincidence, Lady Hotham did send £5 to another Mrs O'Neil in October 1854, after receiving her plea for assistance. Gold Commissioner Wright had appended a note to Mrs O'Neil's letter explaining that her husband was a lieutenant in the 4th Regiment before he became ill and died. Mrs O'Neil argued that her husband's military service entitled her to a grant of land in the colony, but £5 was all she got.[37]

What did men think of women's petitioning efforts? Did they put their wives up to it, thinking that women's appeals would fire a more penetrating arrow into the steely breast of the administration?

It seems not. The women's letters were neither a ruse nor a joint strategy. The GEELONG ADVERTISER reported on the exacerbated humiliation of imprisoned diggers, knowing their wives were peddling for their release. When one man was inhumanely punished for his poverty with a gaol term for being unlicensed, the paper editorialised that what was worse than the injustice was the indignity.

> These men in gold and silver lace, armed from head to heel, have taken the aged and sick from their tents. The spectacle is presented to us of a wife taking round, for signature, a petition for the release of her husband from gaol, by reason of his poverty and ill health.[38]

A spectacle. A debacle. A disgrace.

*

Can the writing of begging letters and petitions by women be considered a form of political activism? Clearly, they contribute to no formal political agenda or structural goal. They do not constitute part of an organised push for reform; there is no association or lobby group. No League of Extraordinary Gentlewomen. But when they are read as a block—and there are countless numbers of these petitions and begging letters—there's no doubt that the ill-spelled, scribbled tales of deprivation, suffering and despair represented a significant rebuke to Hotham's administration, and particularly to the moral legitimacy of his rule.

This wasn't mob violence. There were no barricades or stone-throwing; no burning of effigies. But the message was the same. By constitutional means, these humble petitioners contributed to the growing murmur of public opprobrium inspired by Hotham's obstinate refusal to listen to the people's grievances. Unlike La Trobe, he openly promised to give a *patient and attentive hearing* to the hungry, homeless people. Instead, the men and women of Ballarat found their life-or-death pleas hastily *put away*.

EIGHT

PARTING WITH MY SEX

Everyone had the blues that winter. But there was jazz, too, plenty of it. The rhythm of life on the Ballarat diggings was syncopated, improvised, dissonant, ecstatic. The circus was in town. There were late-night card games, wandering minstrels, beer and skittles. *Many potent, grave, rich citizens look back at the '50s as the happiest and best days of their lives*, wrote pioneer digger John Deegan in his memoirs. Amid the doom and gloom, perhaps as an antidote to it—a delirious subculture of leisure and entertainment. Balls, plays, music, dancing, drinking and sex flourished. Central to the provision of such amusements and diversions were, of course, women, laying it on and lapping it up. At the end of another hard day's digging there was another long, cold, dark night to face. Women not only offered a welcome diversion—they also profited from the exchange.

At the head of the queue, handing out pleasure for a price, was Sarah Hanmer. Trading under the respectable title of Mrs Leicester Hanmer, Sarah was among the first women to capitalise on the golden potential above ground. She had arrived in Victoria with her twelve-year-old daughter, Julia, and her brother William McCullough in August 1853. By early 1854, mother and daughter were working as actresses in Stephen Clarke's Queen's

Theatre, the first to open at Eureka, and the only competition to Coleman's tent theatre at Red Hill, where Clara Du Val, prior to her union with Henry Seekamp, was treading the boards. In May, the ARGUS reported that Sarah Hanmer had become *the chief, if not sole attraction of the Queen's Theatre.*[1] But by this time, Sarah already had her sights set on an even grander entrance.

On 7 May 1854, she placed an advertisement in the GEELONG ADVERTISER for her new establishment, the Adelphi Theatre. The advertisement, which ran daily for three weeks, announced that:

> Mrs Leicester Hanmer has the honor to announce to her friends, the public, that she is about opening at the above place, on or about the 15th instant, in a style worthy of herself and the colonies.

She took out another ad the following week to declare, without false modesty, that *an engagement is open to a leading man and light comedian. Applications from ladies will be unnecessary, as the Press have declared, without hesitation, she possesses the best female talent in the country.*[2] The troupe included Sarah's daughter Julia and several other American actors and actresses, including Mary Stevens, who would soon have a leading role to play in Ballarat's political life. By early June, the Ballarat correspondent to the GEELONG ADVERTISER could confidently file his glowing report that Mrs Hanmer's Adelphi had become the resort of all old playgoers. The BALLARAT TIMES would have promoted the venue with equal vigour. Former actress Clara Du Val had by this time retired from acting, having accepted the part of Mrs Seekamp.

The State Library of Victoria holds a magnificent contemporary watercolour, by an unknown artist, simply entitled *Interior Adelphi Theatre, Ballarat 1855*. Nothing is known of its provenance. The painting shows a large, high-pitched canvas tent. Wooden benches are arranged in neat rows before a timber stage. The stage holds several sections of painted sets, depicting European scenes (a Grecian temple? a Roman villa?). Five men congregate in the tent, performing various menial tasks: fixing a set, washing down the benches. At the right, a woman stands proudly overseeing her terrain. She is tall and solidly built, her hair swept up in a bun. She stands straight-backed in her striking blue gown, with her hands clasped in front of her abdomen: regal, haughty. The painting is incomplete; a man sitting at the front gesticulates with an arm that has no hand. Perhaps it was meant to be a preliminary sketch for a larger artwork. The artist captured Sarah Hanmer at a moment when her notoriety was at its apex: after her theatre had become the venue for show-stopping political rallies that would change the course of Australian history.

American miner and restaurateur Charles Ferguson first encountered Sarah Hanmer in early 1854 when her aim was more modest. She wanted out of the Queen's and into her own theatre. The upward social mobility of actresses, according to English theatre historian Michael Booth, is 'an interesting phenomenon of the Victorian [era] stage'. Ferguson had built a large (tent) concert hall where the Empire minstrels played to packed houses. He received a curious offer. *One Mrs Hanmer* offered to move the hall to Red Hill *and lease it for a theatre, which we accepted, moved it and re-christened it the Adelphi Theatre.* Here is Ferguson with the rest of his story.

> But somehow Mrs Hanmer and I could not get along happily together, and disagreed respecting the rent. She wished to pay in promises and smiles, which I did not consider legal tender, so I closed the theatre. Now there was a young man, Mr Smith, one of the firm of Moody, Nichols and Smith [American

> merchants] who differed from me respecting the value of Mrs Hanmer's promises and smiles. He seemed to consider them as way above par and reproached me for declining the lady's terms, and said he would have accepted her circulating medium.

Ferguson sold the theatre to Smith for US$3500. Smith ran it for one month when, according to Ferguson,

> in the last scene of this eventful history, the lady appeared, sans promises, sans smiles, sans money, sans everything but a horsewhip, which she laid over the head of poor Smith with the spirit and vigor of a McDuff, and that closed his theatrical partnership with Mrs Hanmer.[3]

Sarah Hanmer now had the Adelphi on her own terms, and soon advertised its imminent opening with herself as its *lessee and directress*. She had learnt to use shrewdly the femininity expected of her, schooled in that compelling mix of personal history and cultural expectation.

The theatre was the semi-respectable guiding light of Victorian-era culture. People were mad for it. Everyone from the highest-ranking official to the street sweepers flocked to see the latest production of Shakespeare, or classic melodramas like the *Hunchback* or *The Lady of Lyons*. And now Ballarat finally had a first-rate theatre company, the Adelphi Players. *Mrs Hanmer's Adelphi has become the resort of all old play-goers*, reported the Ballarat correspondent to the GEELONG ADVERTISER in the first week of winter. *The Adelphi, under this lady's superintendence, has achieved a position hardly, if anything, inferior to any theatre in Victoria.*[4] The handbills for the Adelphi Theatre were printed at Charles Evans' Criterion Printing Office, located across the road in Main Street. *We have all the business for the theatre*, noted Charles in his diary, a sign of his own effective management.

Once established as its indisputable boss, and pulling in rapturous, loyal crowds, Sarah Hanmer regularly volunteered her theatre for holding charity events, such as benefits for the Miners' Hospital. These gestures were noted in the press as expressive of Mrs Hanmer's *great generosity and the energy and ability of her management*. The acclaim continued. *Mrs Hanmer is deserving the utmost praise for her kindness*, gushed the editor of the Melbourne-based SPIRIT OF THE AGE. She was the darling of the BALLARAT TIMES; homilies such as this one appeared regularly:

> Mrs Hanmer and her daughter are immense favourites on the diggings, and we do not wonder at it, for there are none here who have more earnestly strove to gain the good-will of the digging community… her endeavours to please deserve every success.

A crowd-pleaser plus an eager crowd: it was a recipe for financial success.

Sarah wasn't afraid, however, to risk her bankable reputation for feminine benevolence by publicly contesting behaviours that she found repugnant. At the end of winter, she wrote a letter to the editor of the BALLARAT TIMES, defending herself against a slight that must have been doing the rounds on the streets, for it was not aired in the papers. Signing herself off as *the Public's Obedient Servant*, Sarah took the fight up to her accuser, a former employee called Bartlett:

> Mr Bartlett is a sillier little gentleman than even I suppose him if he imagines the public feel at all interested about him. And I should not have done a person of his very moderate pretensions, the honor of noticing him, but that he has been *cowardly* enough

> to insinuate what he dares not speak out openly about—my character.

Showing no such spinelessness herself, Sarah continued:

> I here challenge him to say I am other than an honest, virtuous woman, in the strictest sense of the words...And as to my being a weak-minded woman, that should excite his pity, though weak-minded as I am, I was too much for him...the Theatre is carried on in a systematic manner...and Mr Bartlett not being consulted on the matter, was most decidedly and distinctly because he was not of sufficient consequence.

Mrs Hanmer went public with her moral indignation, daring Bartlett to be man enough to do the same. In a final flourish, she also showcased her superior education, paraphrasing Shakespeare: *For this Hanmer has borne herself so honestly in her great office, that her virtues will speak trumpet-tongued against the deep damnation of her slanderers.*[5] If anyone was concerned that Sarah Hanmer was playing the gender card—bending the rules to suit her own maverick ends—you don't get a whiff of it in the local press or at the licensing bench. Official records show she was never denied a theatrical licence, despite allegations from her male rivals that she was not of fit character to hold one.[6] Instead of bureaucratic obstruction, there was only gratitude that her theatrical offerings, and suitably feminine inclination to philanthropy, had raised Ballarat's intellectual and moral standard.

The theatre, pointed out actress and writer Olive Logan in 1869, was *the single avenue in those days where women could expect to receive equal pay for equal work.*[7] For centuries in England, France, Italy and Spain, the only acceptable role for women in the theatre was as wife, daughter or mother of a male performer. But the international gold rushes of the 1850s changed all that. Isolated, exhausted, predominantly male crowds were eager for any amusement, all the more so if they could see women. With the general atmosphere of freedom on the frontier, entrepreneurial women eschewed theatrical traditions and stepped into the void, advertising their companies as providing more refined entertainment than the usual drinking, gambling and whoring.

Female theatre managers hired, trained, paid, supervised and disciplined the men in their company: actors, set builders, roadies and promoters. It was the theatre manager's task to administer a stock company, own or lease a theatre, hire actors or other personnel, select plays for production, direct rehearsals and organise publicity. In addition, many female managers also acted in leading roles, or performed in benefit performances, where the house takings were donated to a worthy local cause, chosen by the manager. It was unusual, radical even, for women to be in such a position of power in any other professional field. But, argues historian Jane Kathleen Curry in her book on nineteenth-century American female theatre managers, 'while their mere existence could be read as a threat to the social order, most women managers were careful not to disturb the status quo more than necessary'. That is, a woman had to be careful that by taking on the powerful, traditionally male position of manager, she did not undermine her public persona as a model of femininity: honest, charitable and chaste. It was a fine balancing act, and not all theatrical women walked the line.

Just over a year after Sarah Hanmer opened her locally celebrated theatre, the world-famous Lola Montez demonstrated what could happen when female performers disturbed the status quo more than necessary. Lola Montez, born Maria Eliza Delores Rosanna Gilbert in Limerick, Ireland in 1818, lived in

England, India, Germany, France, Russia and Switzerland before travelling to California in 1852. By then she was thrice married and twice widowed and had been exiled from her politically influential position as the consort of King Ludwig of Prussia. Lola had smoked cigars with the cross-dressing George Sand in Paris. She had bought her own gold mine in California. She arrived in Melbourne in August 1855 but not before a warrant was issued for her arrest for unpaid debts in Sydney. Reviewing the Melbourne performance of *Lola Montez in Bavaria*, an autobiographical pantomime recalling Lola's days spent routing the Jesuit-controlled monarchy from Prussia, PUNCH derided Lola for wearing her hair in short curls *like a barrister's wig. She can talk politics like a book*, continued the review, *and teach kings how to govern their people more easily than you and I could conjugate a French verb.*[8] This was faint praise, and Lola was damned too for her blatant self-promotion and delusions of grandeur, unchecked by charitable gestures or community-minded benefits.

Lola toured the Ballarat diggings in March 1856, where she found the crowds as generous with their nuggets as the critics were with their vituperation. There had been no such difficulty for her predecessor, Sarah Hanmer, who, in that muddy winter of 1854, kept her purse open and her politics to herself. In a matter of months she had converted herself from an actress and single mother into a respectable businesswoman and civic identity. That was enough—for now.

*

The Victorian-era theatre was fascinated by metamorphic themes, and thus perfectly in tune with the unruly, unstable nature of gold rush society. Audiences loved to follow the miraculous transformations of characters, revelling in the subversive power of the act of concealing or switching identities. Apart from theatrical players, there was also a surfeit of blackface minstrels, magicians, gymnasts, ventriloquists, puppeteers and mesmerists on the diggings, cashing in on the fixation with modification and makeovers.

In particular, audiences were enthralled by acts of cross-dressing. The Ballarat diggers may have beaten their bumptious wives but they didn't mind a bit of role reversal on stage. According to Henry Mundy, they were especially fond of the actress Margaret Catchpole, *a big masculine looking woman [who] often played men's parts and parts in which a woman disguises herself as a man*. She was renowned for her roles as Hamlet and Romeo, *playing to the satisfaction of all beholders*. Indeed, wrote Mundy, *many experienced playgoers declared her Romeo to be the best they had ever seen.* Transvestism has been a part of the theatrical tradition since the classical Greek period, but it typically sees a resurgence in times of critical social flux. At such moments, argues theatre historian Jean Howard, extreme social mobility and rapid economic change are paralleled by instability in the gender system and this is no better, no more safely, reflected than in theatre.[9]

Many plays were intensely preoccupied with threats or disruptions to the sex-gender system, as portrayed by cross-dressing characters, narratives of mistaken identity, women masquerading as soldiers and men taking refuge in feminine disguise. Theatre played a role in managing anxieties about women on top, women not in their rightful places as well as the fragility of male authority. The transvestite waif was a favourite character; wearing lower-class, working man's clothes licensed her to be insolent, cheeky, independent and free of the constraints of her bourgeois upbringing. For men to play women required them to become the other: subservient, restricted, dependant. For women to play men required them to be domineering, confident and mobile. This was no great feat for actors; all in a night's work. It is precisely the protean nature of actors' bodies and personas that has dictated their customary status as outsiders. Neither was it such a stretch of the imagination for Ballarat audiences. It was a relief. The stage, argues theatre-studies expert Laurence Senelick, 'offers licence and liberty, not anxiety and crisis'.

There is a rare extant playbill for the 1854 farce *The Stage-Struck Digger*, written by a Mrs Hetherington. Numerous acting families and troupes toured the goldfields—as well as the permanent players like Mrs Hanmer's crew at the Adelphi—and Mr and Mrs Hetherington were one such couple. Mr ran the company, and Mrs, apart from writing, did the acting. No script survives that would give an inkling of *The Stage-Struck Digger*'s content but it's likely to have been topical. Theatre had long been a forum for discussion of what we would now call 'current affairs'. Pantomimes, in particular, had an emphasis on contemporary jokes about local personalities, places and newsworthy events of the preceding twelve months.

In 1854, William Akhurst, an English-born journalist with a flair for topical themes, penned a farce called *Rights of Woman*. Characters in the play included *a strong-minded lady who is a Pupil of the New Age and a firm supporter of the Rights of Woman*, a barrister and a waitress.[10] Another early colonial entertainer with an eye for contemporary relevance, Charles Thatcher, wrote many songs about how girls in Australia *gave themselves airs*. In 'London and the Diggings', included in his popular *Colonial Songster* of 1857, Thatcher crooned that *The gals that come out to Australia to roam/Have much higher notions than when they're at home.*[11] In 1854, Akhurst and the Nelson family also teamed up to perform *Colonial Experience*, whose well-worn theme was the difficulty of engaging and managing domestic servants. As we've seen, MELBOURNE PUNCH also regularly published illustrations depicting maids defying their masters and haughty, self-important young women displaying uncommon recalcitrance in the colonial marriage market.[12] In the mid-1850s, the creative arts reflected widespread disquiet about women's new-found social, economic and cultural authority.

You certainly didn't have to look far to find creative inspiration for tales of inversion. Miska Hauser was a Jewish Viennese violinist, a child prodigy who had travelled the world, and made a killing in California. He arrived in Australia in late 1854 and was struck by the *feverish enthusiasm* with which audiences attended concerts, operas and plays. Here, songstresses such as Catherine Hayes and Madame Carandini were *literally showered with gold.* But it was the scenes on the streets, not on the stage, that most piqued Hauser's fascination. In Melbourne, wrote Hauser to his brother in May 1855, *emancipated wenches in unbecoming riding habits, and with smoking cigars in their mouths, appear on horseback, and crazy gentlemen…career madly after them and laugh delightedly if a flirtatious equestrienne in a spicy mood aims a mock smack at them with her riding crop.* Why, it was just like a bawdy farce. When would the tables turn and the wenches get their ritual comeuppance? Not, it appeared to Hauser, in the foreseeable future. He was incensed to find that he couldn't book a theatre to demonstrate his virtuosity. *A veritable army of songstresses, virtuosi, ropedancers, danseuses, and other such birds of paradise,* he wrote, *all wanting to shake the fruit from the tree simultaneously, had taken or bespoken all the concert halls, or hired them for weeks again.* This man, who had lived his life on the stage, could not believe his eyes.

> Life here is like a Venetian carnival!...Nowhere in the world do husbands get as short shrift from their wives as here...You see all the dykes of civil order torn down...Women who have long since forsaken the joys of family life and despised all regard for respectability are here hoisted to rank and wealth. Even young ladies who nevertheless claim to be well-reared and cultured, sit all day at the latter-day gambling tables, where every decent impulse disintegrates...no one seems to want to develop a solid middle-class society.[13]

For a time in the mid-1850s, everyone was simply having too much fun.

Hauser attended one meeting in Melbourne to determine how the ever-worsening fickleness of women could be most quickly and safely remedied. One suggestion, which Hauser didn't dismiss, was a house of correction for *undutiful and flighty wives*. Following the meeting, he marched to the theatre where Lola Montez was performing *Lola Montez in Bavaria*. Hauser denounced her as *a wicked specimen of a female Satan*. Art imitating life, or vice versa? In the grand colonial masquerade, who could tell?

*

Gold rush Victoria was a colony of shape-shifters. The stage was not the only place where women got to wear the pants. Harriet, the Irish orphan girl who accompanied her brother Frank to the diggings and soon became *something of a necessity*, in fact travelled as a man. Donning male attire, she reckoned, was her best chance at the blissful anonymity she craved. Here's how she did it.

> I was resolved to accompany my brother and his friends to the diggings, and I felt that to do so in my own proper costume and character would be to run an unnecessary hazard. Hence my change. I cut my hair into a very masculine fashion; I purchased a broad felt hat, a sort of tunic or smock of coarse blue cloth, trousers to conform, boots of a miner, and thus parting with my sex for a season (I hoped a better one), behold me an accomplished candidate for mining operations, and all the perils and inconveniences they might be supposed to bring.

Harriet was reconfigured as *Mr Harry.* All the diggings was a stage, and all the men and women merely players. Harriet exited her proper costume and character, and entered as a young man. *All this transmutation took place with Frank's sanction*, Harriet tells us, as they both believed she would be safer in male attire. Safer, it's presumed, from predatory male admirers on the road to the goldfields. Harriet was not the only woman to protect herself from the dangers of the road, real or imagined, in this fashion.

But once at the diggings, Harriet's cover was blown. *Of course, my sex is generally known*, she laughed. She had suitors—*I have them in plenty*—but preferred the *merry company* of brotherly diggers who gathered together each night in her tent. And she maintained the external trappings of the gender subterfuge. The short hair, the coarse smock, the nom de guerre. 'Parting with her sex' meant more to Harriet than a quick costume change backstage. And 'safety' was merely an acceptable rationale for gender bending. Cross-dressing allowed a mobility and freedom that subverted the customary expectations of domesticity and romance. Harriet could cook and wash and mend for her 'fellow' diggers, but she could also play in their company without risk to her sexual reputation. Did Frank's mates enjoy a homoerotic charge in her presence? Was it exciting to be in the presence of a sweet young companion with whom, should 'he' consent to disrobe, you could have legitimate heterosexual sex?

Cultural historian Lucy Chesser, who has thoroughly analysed the many instances of gender ambiguity in colonial Australia—from the Kelly Gang to encounters between European and Aboriginal people—argues that cross-dressing is an indicator of 'category crisis', a process of 'working-through, or managing pre-existing contradictions or confusions'.[14] Gender bending does not create but rather reflects the inconsistencies and ambiguities of a time of intense social flux.

And it was perversely comforting to the players, all this gender gymnastics. It's possible John Capper chose to include Harriet/Mr Harry's tale in his phenomenally successful guidebook to the goldfields precisely to illustrate the ease with which the radical transmutations occurring within women on the diggings could revert back to 'normal', to the Victorian-era gender status quo of public (political) men and private (domestic) women. (He may even have invented Harriet and Frank as cultural archetypes, much like Hansel and Gretel or Jack and Jill.) Independence and self-rule for women becomes a glitch: a wardrobe malfunction.

But there were plenty of flesh-and-bone women on the goldfields who adopted male attire for pragmatic, not symbolic, reasons. Women readily abandoned the most restrictive elements of their daily dress in deference to the practical conditions of colonial life. Emma Macpherson, who arrived in Victoria at the beginning of 1854, wrote in her published travel reminiscences that men had high boots to counter the scandalous condition of the roads, but for women:

> the condition presented by their long flowing dresses was pitiable in the extreme; I really think they will eventually adopt the Bloomer costume, which, if allowable under any circumstances, would certainly be so there, for traversing these terrible quagmires.

Some gold rush immigrants didn't wait to see whether fashion or social mores permitted them to reject conventional feminine attire. Henrietta Dugdale, who arrived in Victoria in 1852 and would go on to found Australia's first women's suffrage society in 1884, wore a long bifurcated skirt to match her defiant gaze.[15]

Others were traumatised out of their corsetry. Eliza Lucus's teenage sister, Fanny, died *through the cursed crinolines*. It was a horrific accident. Fanny was dishing up dinner when her voluminous dress caught alight from the open fireplace. She lived for five hours in excruciating pain. *It was nearly the death of poor mother*, recalled Eliza, *her grief was great*. Eliza's mother never wore crinolines again. For goldfields women, corsets and crinolines made even less sense in the stifling heat or noxious mud, especially if there was manual work to be done. For gentlewomen, 'dressing down' also made a potent statement of solidarity with the democratic ethos of goldfields life.

But as Lucy Chesser documents, and contrary to John Capper's reassurances, many cross-dressing colonial women did not reconstitute themselves as outwardly female, instead choosing to live out their days as 'men', some with wives. Others had a bet each way. As late as 1879, you could still find women working alongside male miners during the week, dressed as men, then stepping out in satin and lace to a Saturday night dance on the arm of their husband.[16]

If some women were dressing down, there was also an upswing in conspicuous consumption by successful digging families. Genteel Mrs Massey lampooned the material girls of the goldfields: newly married, newly rich, spending up on luxury items such as parasols and lace, with which they had no previous acquaintance. She dismissed them as *the most absurd caricature of a digger's wife*: gaudy, ostentatious, laughable. Numerous commentators remarked with snobbish surprise on the superior quality and taste of Victoria's fashions. William Westgarth is typical. *The ladies are attired with an elegance and costliness that would scarcely be looked for in the miscellaneous gathering of so young a society*, he wrote. Robert Caldwell missed the elegance: *every extravagance and peculiarity of costume*, he marvelled, *is indulged in at pleasure.*

Men, too, trialled new looks and fashion statements. By day, you couldn't distinguish a gentleman from an ex-convict because of the unofficial diggings uniform of blue flannel shirt, gray neckerchief, straw hat, knee-high boots and beard and moustache, which was worn by miners, labourers and draymen alike. But at night, some men cast off their utilitarian duds and slipped into evening clothes: black pants, white shirt, a red sash, patent leather boots and black plush hat. John Deegan describes such men as *swells* or *mashers*, and says they took their sartorial cues from the Californians in their midst. The outmoded term *masher* is a real gem. It derives from the Romani gypsy word *masha*, meaning to entice, allure, delude or fascinate, and was originally used in the theatre, although it is unclear who these diggers were setting out to delude.

Men were caught cross-dressing too, but as an entirely different form of escape. Fugitives fleeing from the hands of justice regularly disguised themselves as women. Charles Evans was returning to Ballarat from a trip to Melbourne when he *met a man in woman's clothes, handcuffed and guarded by an armed policeman*. Evans later learned that the man had shot dead another man a short distance up the road.

So while some women and men dressed down, either for political or practical purposes, others played dress-ups, experimenting with new-found wealth or social flexibility. Just as a girl in her mother's wardrobe will try on new identities—imagining herself as twice the woman she knows herself to be—so the early gold rush generation experimented with wearing the breeches of alluring power and prosperity, whether they permanently achieved it or not. Could anybody blame them for playing the game?

*

Thousands of men from every corner of the globe, all living in tents, *en plein air*, manually labouring, in holiday mode, young and free. The La Trobe government took one look at the social landscape of the goldfields and came to the speedy realisation that the only way to prevent complete carnage was to regulate the sale of alcohol. Publicans licences would only be granted in the surrounding townships. No alcohol was to be sold on the diggings. It was a cunning plan bound to fail.

Every storekeeper sold sly-grog, Police Magistrate John D'Ewes wrote in his 1857 memoir of Ballarat in 1854. A first offence for unlicensed selling elicited a £50 fine or four months in prison for non-payment. Police officers received a portion of the fine if they recorded a conviction. A second offence received six to twelve months gaol, with hard labour. The local magistrates had no power to commute; only the governor could interfere with statutory sentences. The cards were stacked in favour of the police, and they either pursued known sly groggers relentlessly or extracted sufficient hush money—and no doubt other 'favours'—to stay on the right side of the cut. Samuel Huyghue, from his view inside the Camp, believed the system of rewards for sly-grog seizures was to blame for the demoralisation of the police force.

Every traveller to or resident on the diggings remarked on the presence of sly-grog sellers. There were an estimated seven hundred sly-grog outlets in Ballarat.[17] That means approximately one venue for every thirty adult residents. Ellen Clacy theorised that *the privacy and risk gives the obtaining it an excitement which the diggers enjoy as much as the spirit itself.* It helped that women ran most of the 'refreshment tents' on the diggings. Mrs Massey called sly grog *this most hateful traffic*. But since she knew the sale of alcohol was the most lucrative activity on the goldfields, she took its presence for granted, along with everybody else.

Apart from the grog that was sold from the stores, there were what Henry Mundy called *regular grog shanties*. These were conspicuous by having a large square shutter hung on hinges at the top of one gable of the tent, facing the road. Inside, a rough counter with five- to ten-gallon kegs of hops beer, ginger beer, lemonade and cider was retailed out at sixpence a pannikin. Jugs could be filled up and taken home, to be shared among friends and family. Such shanties were similarly the domain of women, and have been immortalised in S. T. Gill's famous watercolours. Charles Thatcher also made a legend of Big Poll the Grog Seller, who epitomised youthful colonial pluck and bounce, dodging and weaving authorities while *turning in plenty of tin people say/ for she knows what she's about.*[18] Even artful young women were making an ass of the law.

Not only were women selling the grog, but they were consuming it too. Some women delighted in having a nobbler or a shandy gaff—pale ale mixed with ginger beer—telling *racy jokes, which were none of the choicest as far as language was concerned.* This is Henry Mundy's assessment of a Mrs Charlton who saw no reason *to be squeamish. She could see no harm in her talk nor cared if others did.* Charles Evans noted a similar tendency for women to feel liberated from more polite behaviour on the goldfields where drinking was concerned. *It is painful to contemplate,* he wrote in his diary,

> the horrible havoc which drunkenness makes on the diggings, even women feeling themselves relieved from the salutary checks which society in civilised life lays on them fall into a view bad enough in men, but disgusting and repulsive beyond expression in women.

Some women were dead-set alcoholics, either before they arrived at the diggings or due to its harsh realities, but others were merely joining in the carnival. Some, buoyed by the mood of entitlement, may even have felt a drink at the end of the day was their own just reward for ceaseless toil.

Certainly, women expected to be included in the effervescent social life of Ballarat. Mrs Massey attended a ball on the diggings and described the scene in detail. The event occurred in a large tent, with smaller refreshment tents and ladies dressing-room tents scattered about like satellites. Gentlemen diggers and their wives, and Camp officials and their wives, attended the evening. The 'ball-room' walls were covered with pink and white calico, the pillars supporting the roof were adorned with garlands intermixed of pink and white. There were lighted Chinese lamps, carpets, divans and sofas. The band was excellent and there was dancing until sun-up. The effect, thought Mrs Massey, was *charming*.

The sober Englishwoman also noted a feature of the event

that young artist S. T. Gill failed to capture in his well-known sketch, *Subscription Ball, Ballarat 1854*. Women were hired to care for the babies, aged from newborns to toddlers. Mrs Massey explained that the mothers were *not able to leave them at home, and wishing to join in the evening's amusement*, brought them along and put them to sleep on beds and sofas, popping in to visit between dances. *During the evening*, she said, *I saw several ladies walking about, in full ball dress of course, nursing and hushing their dearly beloved infants*. So here was another goldfields innovation: paid childcare at social functions so the hard-working, bread-winning mothers of Ballarat weren't left holding the baby.

By the winter of 1854, it was clear that the licensing laws would have to change. Police magistrates such as John D'Ewes were begging the government to review its policies. The diggings were awash with sly grog, and the police were drunk on their power to either overlook infringements (for a price) or shut down an operation with brutal force. *Rum, gin, brandy, beer and stout have been known to run down Camp Hill from Lydiard Street in streams*, attested Henry Mundy. He was speaking literally: the police poured away rivers of contraband alcohol, draining it into the dirt.

The waste of so valued a commodity was seen as flagrant baiting of the impoverished community by a bloody-minded police force. Poor shanty keepers, often widows, were used as scapegoats of caution; *they paid the penalty of the pretended vigilance of the police*, observed Henry Mundy. Too poor to pay bribes, the sly-grog seller would be bailed up by a commissioner and six troopers who would proceed *to set fire to the frail tenement over the owner's head and burn it to the ground and everything combustible in it*. It was a show trial. The members of the open-air court would stand by helplessly as judge and jury dispensed their justice, and the now homeless woman in the dock wept piteously.

Legitimate access to liquor was a major source of grievance for a population that had both the original hard-earned thirst and a libertarian taste for self-rule. Meanwhile, legitimate publicans in the township rued the competition of the sly groggers. The authorities deemed that the new breed of publicans, only a piece of paper away from their illicit origins, could be used to help dob in sly-grog sellers. It was considered truly bad form to lag on a sly-grog seller if you couldn't pay the bill, but desperate diggers were known to do it. Spies were *the blackest of Satan's crew*, according to Henry Mundy: if found out, an informer's life was in danger. Publicans and sly groggers—former comrades in crime—were now to be set against each other in a risky strategy of divide and conquer.

The new law was proclaimed on 1 June, in the administrative black hole between La Trobe's departure and Hotham's arrival. Publicans licences would now be granted on the goldfields, but exclusively to *owners of substantial houses only on sold lands or within half a mile of such*. It was a licence not just to sell booze but to print money, and the government knew it. The annual fee to sell spirits was set at £100, with an extra £50 to occupy Crown Lands for the purpose.

The good news for the government was that opening the floodgates to legal liquor sales would generate much-needed revenue. But the legislators had sowed the seeds of the policy's own demise. *In other localities good tents may be licensed at the discretion of the Bench of Magistrates*, read one clause of the new legislation. So discretionary power was back in the hands of local warlords. And what on earth did *good tents* mean? Good structure? Good conduct? Good connections? The scene was set for a tragic turf war between the owners of licensed public houses (which, by law, had to provide accommodation and meals), licensed tents (which merely had to be *good*), the residual sly groggers (selling out of their coffee houses, refreshment tents and stores), and the already abhorred local authorities who were entrusted to act as umpire.

But there was a startling twist. In July, a further qualification was introduced. Applicants for a publicans licence had to show their marriage certificates. No single men would be eligible for a licence. One Melbourne journalist drew a long bow between this novel constraint on men's commercial freedom and the palpable zeitgeist of autonomy (and votes) for women. *Good news for the ladies*, he wrote, *this will, most probably, cause an increase in the marriage returns.* The mocking continued.

> Why should we not go the whole hog and recommend the ladies get up an agitation for a universal marriage act, which should disqualify bachelors from voting at elections, entering the public service etc?[19]

The new licensing law made its own kind of sense: it had been designed to control the distribution of alcohol, based on the logic that women were more likely to regulate men's behaviour and run establishments that were more domesticated, offering food and accommodation, rather than exclusively devoted to drinking. This was a principle that had been applied in Australia since the granting of licences in the penal settlement of Sydney in the 1790s. But this journalist's curious, slightly paranoid response managed to see the legislative change as part of goldfields women's collusion to restrict male liberties. Perhaps this suggests that women's wider 'agitations' were having an influence on the public domain. At any rate, the law had the undisputed effect of catapulting women into the epicentre of social and economic life: the pub.

Enter Catherine Bentley, stage right.

*

In July 1854 James and Catherine Bentley were in pole position when the goldfields authorities reversed the ban on issuing liquor licences on the diggings. They had come prepared to capitalise on this new opportunity to mine for liquid gold. James had sureties from leading bankers and merchants in Melbourne. He had the sufficient confidence of creditors to build an extravagant landmark of a hotel on the profitable Eureka Lead. He had a bona fide wife to satisfy the marriage requirements. And he had the pre-emptive right to a section of Crown land, secured and signed for in Catherine's name on 13 June that year.[20]

Ballarat was still a tent city, to be sure. But with a population of twenty thousand, the occasional whopping nugget still being pulled from the ground, a host of shops selling everything from fresh ground coffee to preserved hare to Havana cigars, a cultural life infused with theatres, circuses and concert halls, and even a racing carnival planned for December, it was a canvas community well on its way to becoming a rip-roaring town.

The Bentleys intended to be in on the ground floor, staking their claim to the economic and social heart of a new mercantile class of affluent, influential publicans and traders. Thomas Bath's hotel in Lydiard Street might play host to the Camp officials and professional men of the district, but Bentley's Hotel would soon provide a worthy competitor at Eureka, the bustling heartland of East Ballarat. Just to mark his territory further, James Bentley became president of the fledgling Licensed Victuallers Association of Ballarat. His network of local associates included leading merchants, auctioneers and bankers.

On 15 July, the BALLARAT TIMES announced the opening of Bentley's Eureka Hotel:

> Placards had been circulated and by ten o'clock the place was crowded with men eager to join in the jollification. Paltzer's fine brass band kept things lively and as champagne was served with the sumptuous free breakfast for all visitors, the greatest hilarity prevailed which was kept up all day. So happy a house warming has seldom been seen in these parts.

The hotel's main bar was *tastefully arranged in the style of San Francisco*, and the newspaper praised the barman for understanding the finer points of gin slings and mint juleps. A confident prediction was made:

> It is expected that the next good lead opened up in the vicinity will be called Bently [sic] Flat as some acknowledgment for the energy displayed by Mr Bently in providing the miners with such a respectable and comfortable house of accommodation.[21]

Bentley may have been an ex-con with a limp, but he had hit the ground running.

By August, the Bentleys' stock orders included twenty-five dozen bottles of champagne, forty dozen bottles of sherry and port, twenty-five gallons of whisky and two thousand cigars. Catherine purchased electroplated silver cutlery. A chandelier bathed the hotel in a dreamy light of candlelit opulence. The main public bar had a sixty-foot frontage and three entrances. Inside the double-storey weatherboard structure were three parlours, three bars, a dining room, concert room, billiard room and bagatelle room. Upstairs were seven bedrooms, with an equal amount of additional space, still in the process of construction, earmarked for use as a superior concert room. Adjacent to the hotel was a ninety-foot bowling alley, with its own bar, 120 feet of stabling and a large storehouse. These facilities surrounded a vast auction yard, let for an annual sum of £500. Two water closets and a kitchen with brick oven completed the minor metropolis that was Bentley's Eureka Hotel. The whole edifice was painted gold, green and vermillion.

The venue was such a landmark that other traders advertised their whereabouts in relation to the hotel: just across from, one mile east of. The prominent Jewish merchants and auctioneers Henry Harris and Charles Dyte stored their goods at the hotel. Jacques Paltzer's band got a regular gig, and the musicians took up residence in the upstairs bedrooms. James was on good terms with Ballarat's mercantile and administrative elite. And Catherine was pregnant with their second child. The Bentleys' self-assurance was such that they named the rising land on which their premises stood 'Bentley's Hill'. A beacon. A signal of success. A very tall poppy.

*

The move to grant licences on the diggings caused an immediate onslaught of applications. No sooner was the law proclaimed than the licensing bench was besieged with applicants. *Every individual who had the means, seemed desirous of setting up a public house as a certain method of making a fortune*, recalled magistrate John D'Ewes, who was on the bench. Over a hundred applications were received overnight. At Eureka, licences were granted to the Free Trade run by Alfred Lester, the London run by Benden Hassell and Robert Monkton, the Star run by William McRae, the Turf Inn run by William Tait, and the Victoria Hotel run by Germans Brandt and Hirschler. Other diggings hotels included the Alhambra on Esmond Street, and the Arcade on York Street, just up from Main Road. The Duchess of Kent Hotel, on Main Road, was licensed to Mrs Spanhake, the twenty-five-year-old wife of a German miner. Raffaello Carboni lodged here for some period in 1854. There was the Eagle on Scotchman's Hill and the Prince Albert on Bakery Hill. Carboni said the publican at the Prince Albert was *as wealthy and proud as a merchant-prince of the City of London.* Hotels were licensed to Englishmen, Germans, Jews, the Irish and Scots. New publicans vied for the custom that had previously been monopolised by the town hotels, Bath's, the Clarendon and the George.

Women like Mrs Spanhake seized the opportunity to enter into the liberalised market, joining the ranks of female publicans who had long been legends in the district. Mother Jamieson had run the hotel at Buninyong, eight miles from Ballarat, since 1845. John D'Ewes described Mrs Jamieson as:

> an extraordinary specimen of a Scotch landlady, whose colonial independence of character (except when she took a liking) always verged upon insolence, and very often abuse; woe to be the mistaken individual who tried to oppose her when in these moods as he had little chance of either food or lodging at her hands.

D'Ewes felt fortunate to *fall in her good graces*, suggesting the power of such landladies to call the shots.

Catherine Bentley had now joined the ranks of women who were legally empowered to say who was in and who was out.

*

Prostitution is notoriously hard to research. Reconstructing the lives of prostitutes on the mining frontier—a history that has been either suppressed by Victorian-era prudery or distorted by modernity's obsession with the salacious—is a research project all of its own. American historian Marion S. Goldman has completed the rare undertaking brilliantly.[22] Her 1981 book *Gold Diggers and Silver Miners* examines the history of prostitution on the Comstock Lode in Nevada circa 1860–80. Goldman set out to gracefully bury the legend of the frontier prostitute as the 'harlot heroine', whose beauty, wealth, luxurious surroundings, adoring male companions, envious female rivals and eventual mobility into respectable affluence has been the mainstay of novels, films and other popular historical representations. The legend of the whore with a heart of gold, argues Goldman, rests on a primordial male ambivalence towards women's sexual power, which has the capacity simultaneously to comfort, manipulate and destroy. The idealised frontier prostitute also appealed to women, suggests Goldman, as 'she epitomised feminine strivings for adventure and autonomy at a time when most women were constricted by economic discrimination and custom'. Over the course of her book, Goldman demolishes the myth of the good-time girl and replaces it with the reality that most frontier prostitutes led miserable lives of poverty, degradation, disease and violence.

Goldman was lucky. Nevada is the only American state where prostitution, along with gambling, is legally tolerated. Organised sexual commerce, as she calls it, was thus a visible and documented part of everyday life, and she found 'information about it everywhere'. Ballarat is another story.

Ballarat's red-light district centred around Brown Hill, Specimen Hill, Esmond and Arcade streets and Main Road. Prostitution enterprises were female-run small businesses that, unlike shopkeeping, could always continue to operate on a small scale—well after businesses with greater access to capital had muscled out smaller competitors.[23] *The clandestine diversions and opportunities for orgies were not lacking*, Charles Eberle wrote in his diary. *It could not be otherwise in a populous environment composed of men with often very loose morals.*

Now, an orgy can mean simple drunken revelry, but its more common connotation of excessive sexual indulgence is apparent in Eberle's account. There was certainly nothing clandestine about a standard piss-up on the diggings. He goes further.

> The thirst for gold led to that for pleasure and there were always traders ready to promote this leaning, by means of establishments, more or less dubious, where the diverse passions of this still undisciplined population found satisfaction.

Pleasure. Passion. Satisfaction. Eberle talks openly about hotels and sly-grog shops; the nature of the establishments he politely alludes to is obvious.

It's also possible to identify some of Ballarat's more notorious prostitutes. Mary Clarke alias Margaret Clarke alias Margaret Allen was known to all and sundry as the *Bull Pup*. On 20 January 1854, she was charged with being *an idle and disorderly person*, a quaint legal euphemism for a street hooker. Poor Margaret got herself nicked by coming to the Camp in her cups to press charges against another woman. Margaret was drunk at the time, and Sergeant Major Milne remembered seeing her previously on the side of the road with *her clothes above her head*. In 1854, the Bull Pup spent two stints in the Ballarat lockup, the first time for two months, the second for six months, for being idle and disorderly.[24] She later moved to the Brown Hill diggings, east of Eureka, where Henry Mundy spotted her. *All the pleasures and amusements common in Ballarat were to be found*, wrote Mundy, *a theatre, dancing saloons, bowling alleys, gymnasiums, concert rooms, Hobart Town Poll with her bevy of girls, Bones, the Bull Pup, Cross-Eyed Luke etc and grog shanties galore.*

Hobart Town Poll is the most easily identifiable madam on the 1850s goldfields. Henry Mundy first came to know of her operations, which were corralled into *an isolated little township of tents snugly ensconced among the trees* by the roadside near Ballarat. He asked a passer-by what went on in that discreet camp, and was informed it was *Hobart Town Poll's establishment where the aristocratic ladies hang out.* Mundy, who was married to Ann Gillingham by this time, appears to have made an objective study.

> Scenes of revelry were going on by day; the laughing and screeching of men and women was uproarious. If I had been a single man I should probably have passed through the excited crowd, to see what the fun was about but being a married man and father of a family I thought of the proprieties and passed by like a serious Benedict.

What a spectacle, viewed from the roadside! Nothing discreet about it. But madams like Hobart Town Poll garnered a considerable amount of esteem, within the Victorian underworld at least, for their management skills and business nous. In a social microcosm that valued entrepreneurship, economic success and the ability to stay afloat in the fast lane, top brothel madams were both respected and traduced.

But Ballarat's prostitutes knew they need not be too prudent where the authorities were concerned. Gentlemen of the Government Camp were among their best customers. For soldiers, the purchase of sex while on campaign or in barracks was an open connivance. It was British army policy until 1885 that soldiers should not marry, and a quota system of permissible marriages was enforced: one wife per seven cavalrymen and one per twelve infantrymen. There was no quota for officers' wives. If that wasn't restrictive enough, only a small number of those registered wives were permitted to follow their husbands on any given overseas campaign. Selection was made by drawing lots or throwing dice.

'Large garrisons inevitably attracted prostitutes,' writes military historian Richard Holmes. Women lived among the army camps in makeshift huts, and were known as 'wrens', flocking to the morsels thrown to them by sexually deprived soldiers. A subculture of survival prevailed among the camp followers. Older women minded children while younger women set off for trysts with soldiers. The fact that up to twenty-five per cent of a camp would be infected with venereal disease in any given year led the British army to establish 'lock hospitals' or regimental brothels, where women's sexual health could be monitored. Such 'licensed sin' or 'mercenary love', as Holmes calls it, was seen as vastly preferable to the consequences of 'forced repression of physiological natural instincts'.[25] Meanwhile, officers kept 'their own girls', mistresses whom they could afford to set up in quasi-brothels for the duration of a campaign. These women often held day jobs as serving girls and laundresses.

It was not until the late nineteenth century that the British army decided that it was only by increasing the allowable quota of regimental wives that homosexual acts and rates of venereal disease would decline. Hobart Town Poll's enclave, with its *aristocratic ladies*, may well have been the brothel for the top end of town. Ballarat's hated police, who were already in cahoots with the sly-grog sellers, were more likely to patronise than shut down the services that such houses of pleasure provided on the side, forcing up prices while they were at it.

There's little evidence to suggest that Ballarat's prostitutes either suffered under conditions of a punitive and discriminatory criminal justice system or experienced everyday social stigma. Court records show that most women who came before the law were brought up on charges of theft or drunkenness. On 8 February 1855, a man called Burroughs was sentenced to four months hard labour for *keeping a disorderly tent* at Ballarat. The judge found his brothel—for this is clearly what it was—*utterly subversive of order and decency.*[26] There is no mention of the women who worked in his tent. In February 1858, Mary Johnson pleaded not guilty in the Ballarat Circuit Court to *keeping and maintaining a certain common ill governed and disorderly house, and in the said house for the lucre and gain etc etc.* Richard Ireland, for the prosecution, said the superintendent of police had entered the house in Arcade Street on a Sunday morning and found seventeen men and Mary Johnson *drinking, kicking up a row and using obscene language.* In another room he saw a man and woman in bed together *who he did not disturb.* Mary admitted to being the tenant of one Wilson, who had built a number of similar establishments, but said she had given back the key and *virtually vacated the premises.* Mary Johnson was found guilty and sentenced to one month in prison.[27]

Such reports of convictions for prostitution are remarkable for their scarcity and are limited to brothel keepers. When Mary Ann Harvey appealed against her conviction for vagrancy in Ballarat in 1858 (being *without lawful means of support* was another euphemism for sex work), the judge did not accept the police constable's evidence that he heard at least five women and two men in the house using *most filthy language.* The judge concluded *it was not known how those unfortunate girls obtained their living, it might be by dress-making or anything else.*[28] Though the house was an infamous resort of thieves and prostitutes, the judge preferred the local form of arbitration: turning a blind eye.

*

Ballarat was just the place to let it all hang out. Love mightn't have come free, but it was not hard to find. There's no such thing as a back alley in a tent city. John Deegan remembered arriving at Ballarat as a young lad in late 1854. Sitting atop a dray, rolling through the honeycombed streets, he was gobsmacked by the sight of the inhabitants, *[men] lounging about saloon fronts, loud in voice and laughter, bandying free jests with buxom, red-cheeked wenches, who boldly smirked at them from the open doorways.* Were these women working for themselves, or the proprietors of the 'saloons' to which they attracted custom?

Deegan gives us an idea of how the system might have worked. The dancing saloon, Deegan explained, was the place of *base, common, popular* entertainment for the mass of diggers, those *wild spirits* who found music and drama too slow. Most concert rooms and theatres were cleared of seats following an evening's performance and turned over to bacchanalian dancing after 9pm. *What wild, whirling, reckless carnivals of unrestrained frolic these bal masques were!* recalled Deegan in his 1889 lecture to the Australian Natives Association (so let's allow for the rosy tint of memory and concede that the female dancers mightn't have been as deliriously happy as their partners). *Scenes of orgie*, beside which scenes of Paris would be *chaste*. Central to the frenzy were the dancers, women who were *mostly retainers, or camp followers, maintained by the landlord.* By day, these women worked as barmaids, waitresses, housemaids or servants. *But their chief business duty was to dance at night with the gay and festive miners,* said Deegan, *and to cajole their partners into a lavish outlay.* Young and handsome, the women were brightly and richly dressed in fashionable crinolines, revealing high-heeled boots and a show of ankle when spinning around in a dance. According to Deegan, they were not ones to show *maidenly modesty or high-bred manners, but some of them were intensely fascinating.* No doubt paid sex was on the dance card at these establishments; whether the payment went directly to the 'dancer' or whether she was merely on wages is impossible to tell.

Since the beginning of European occupation of Australia, white men had formed sexual relationships with Aboriginal women. The terms of their liaisons could range from rape to consensual casual sex to paid prostitution to long-term unions.[29] There is no direct evidence of Aboriginal women working in Ballarat's brothels, but sanctimonious white men like Thomas McCombie did accuse black men of selling their *lubras* into sex slavery instead of working honourably themselves. Aboriginal women, he lamented, *were forced to consent to the improper advances of Europeans* for money or provisions that their men were *too lazy* to procure.

Historian Richard Broome has shown that after European occupation, Aboriginal women frequently offered themselves for sexual service to white men, or were 'gifted' by their husbands, because they saw this as their best chance for gaining food, tobacco or alcohol for themselves, their children and extended kin networks. Broome argues that they did not interpret such social transactions as prostitution, even if that's how Europeans perceived it, and cultural misunderstanding over sex often led to violence. Genuine and longstanding sexual unions between non-Indigenous miners and Aboriginal women were also common, with many mixed-ethnicity relationships occurring on the Ballarat goldfields.[30]

The question of how to define prostitution applies to relationships between white people too. Is a prostitute strictly someone who exchanges sex for a negotiated or set fee? What about women who enter into de facto living arrangements with men, not for love but survival? According to Lord Cecil, a former digger informed him *that when he was in Bendigo a lady had offered to 'be his wife' for the moderate charge of 1/6.* The number of registered ex-nuptial births in Victoria in 1854 and 1855 suggests that many single women who immigrated to Australia found themselves in sexual liaisons that, although not sanctioned by church or state, were not officially illegal either. Providing sexual and domestic services in exchange for a dry roof and warm bed in a temporary capacity is not technically prostitution, but neither is it necessarily born of romance. That 1/6 might come in the form of housekeeping, for as long as the woman wished to keep house.

Of course, there are those critics who would say that the whole institution of marriage is nothing but legalised prostitution, and not just modern-day radical feminists. American women's rights campaigners in the 1850s saw their movement as the natural legacy of the pioneer tradition, arguing that women had crossed continents, fought Indians, tilled the soil and established homesteads, thus proving themselves to be *more than playthings of men, whose only pleasure was to breed and serve.*[31] Elizabeth Cady Stanton and Amelia Bloomer, both married in 1840, omitted the word 'obey' from their marriage vows. In 1883 Henrietta Dugdale wrote a utopian novella about women's emancipation called *A Few Hours in a Far Off Age* and predicted that *the marriage of the future* would be based solely on *fidelity and lasting affection which can only spring from the mutual respect of one equal for another in that life-long bond.* For living a life of shame and indignity brought on by their oppression of women, Dugdale called men *the real prostitutes.*

In gold rush Ballarat, not all men were happy about the easy availability of women for a price. A letter published in the GOLD DIGGERS' ADVOCATE on 19 August 1854 conflated the autocratic rule of the goldfields administration with the domination of heartless women who sold grog and then, perhaps, a more lucrative chaser. First, wrote the miner, the diggers were fleeced through *the wanton and petty tyranny of public officers.*

> Next, for the digger's plunder, are a long roll of harpies, who toil not, neither do they spin; but I will not say they do not rob; for they are, in general, wealthy. But how have they become so? Even young women, with large anguishing eyes, seem to derive a large revenue for their use from the digger.

These predatory women ran *pop-shops*, wrote the disgruntled digger, where they served up grog with a *soft and tender glance in the administration of the dose.*

Alexander Dick, who came to Victoria from Scotland with the Christian and Temperance Emigration Society, frequented a grog shanty that was run by a highlander named Shaw. Shaw *had a wife whose price was not above rubies*, tutted Dick. He was also partial to another shanty run by a Geordie chap called Lal Matt; he too had a female partner *who did not pretend to be his wife.* Dick was often invited to spend an evening under their hospitable canvas, but he resolved to stay clear of *such demoralising temptations.* By the by, Dick tells us that both Shaw and Lal Matt worked gold claims. It's likely, then, that the grog shanties were run by the ersatz wives, who might have served other wares during the day while their men were out digging. The rules of sexual engagement were clearly played fast and loose. Whether the women who ended up in such situations had foreseen that this was where their antipodean journey would lead them is simply impossible to determine. If there were high-class courtesans on the Victorian goldfields, as there were in Nevada, they have resisted disclosure. There are no names that stand out, unless you count Lola Montez, who was married to her manager Noel Follin only for the duration of her Australian tour, or the former French courtesan, Céleste de Chabrillan, now married to the French consul to Victoria.

In all likelihood, however, there was a ranking system, as has been documented on the American mining frontier, from high- to low-status prostitutes. The higher the grade, the more clandestine in soliciting custom, subtle about obtaining payment, likely to offer skills or talents besides just sex, and be involved with fewer and richer men. This sort of stratification also fits with what we know of the Ballarat goldfields, where competition for precious resources led to status rewards. Lucky men could afford to drink champagne, smoke cigars and hire attractive, gracious whores on a more or less permanent basis. Unlucky diggers were left to line up for the coarse, foul-mouthed tarts that hung about in the doorways of hotels and shanties. And some men couldn't even scrape together the two bits required to lay their burden down.

*

By the end of the winter of 1854, Ballarat was transformed. It was no longer a frontier outpost predicated on yanking nuggets of gold from the ground, but a fledgling town boasting *all the appliances of civilised life...the comforts and conveniences of high civilisation*, as Thomas McCombie put it. The hotel. The store. The theatre. The printing press. McCombie crossed them off his list of heralds of progress. And they were institutions, McCombie failed to note, with women at the helm. Catherine Bentley and Mother Jamieson at the hotel. Tick. Martha Clendinning and Anne Diamond at the store. Tick. Sarah Hanmer at the theatre. Tick. Clara du Val Seekamp at the printing press with Ellen Young feeding her the copy. Tick.

The town was settling down. So why did no one feel at ease? Samuel Huyghue, high up on the hill, could see only a population *in a constant state of chronic irritation*. There they all were, scratching at an itch that would not subside, further inflaming the exquisite pain with every scrape of the flesh.

If, as Governor Hotham and James Bonwick believed, women were the ground order of society, and if they now controlled the instruments of civilisation in Ballarat, then the town should have been on the fast track to stability and regulation. But it wasn't. It was heading for a train wreck. And the women weren't hauling on the brake. They were stoking the coals.

PART 3

TRANSGRESSIONS

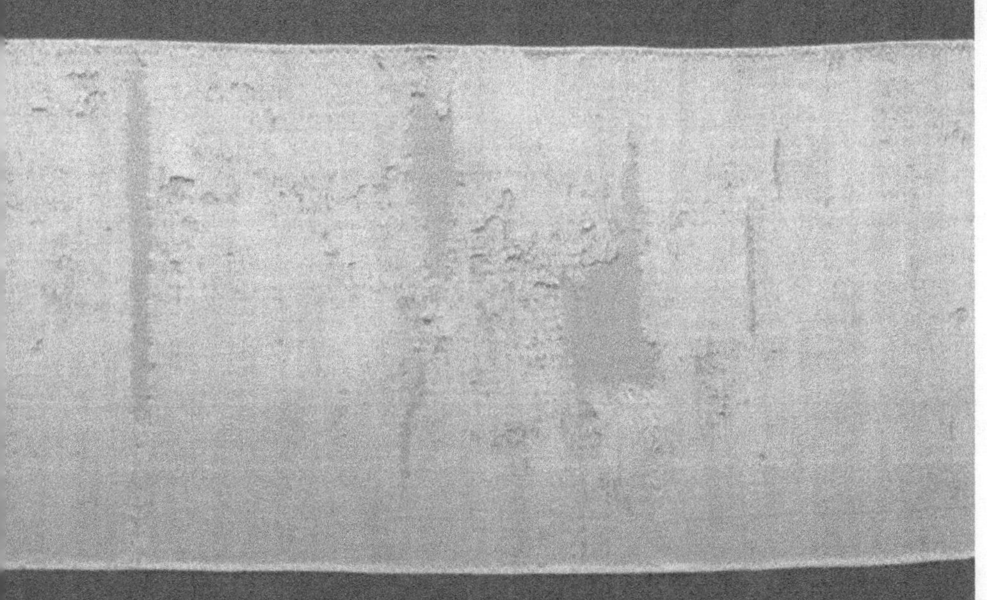

NINE

BURNING DOWN THE HOUSE

Spring.

verb move rapidly or suddenly from a constrained position.

noun **1** the season after winter and before summer, in which vegetation begins to appear, in the northern hemisphere from March to May and in the southern hemisphere from September to November.

2 a resilient device, typically a helical metal coil, that can be pressed or pulled but returns to its former shape when released, used chiefly to exert constant tension or absorb movement.

*

They didn't call this Bentley's Hill for nothing. Catherine Bentley had a commanding view of the Ballarat diggings from the second-storey bedroom of her hotel. To the south, the vast sea of honeycombed earth stretching towards Red Hill and the Canadian Lead. To the northwest, the tent hamlet of Bakery Hill, where Clara Seekamp and her husband were churning out their newspaper. Stretched out along the Yarrowee River to the north, the golden gutters of the Gravel Pits Lead, and over the river, the old alluvial flats of Black Hill. To the east loomed Mt

Warrenheip: grave, solid, like a conscience. To the southwest, she could see Golden Point. In one of those tents over there sat Ellen Young, scribbling the letters and poems that kept appearing in the TIMES.

This vast landscape of endeavour was now dry and thirsty. Spring had only just arrived and already the ground looked parched. A month ago, Catherine's lad Thomas was chipping ice from the water pail in the morning; now she would have to chase him to put his bonnet on. Come summer, she would have a new baby to shelter from Ballarat's inscrutable climate. A week of rain would put a stop to digging—a busy week at the bar—then a week of hot winds would blow up clouds of dust. What a country, where things could turn around so just like that.

Beyond Bakery Hill, Catherine could see clear through to the Camp. The government men still did their drinking at Bath's Hotel, but by September 1854 she and James were raking in so much (£350 on their first night alone) that the toffs could go to hell anyway. She didn't need them in her front bar; they'd only scare off the locals. In any case, she and James would be in demand to attend to the next Subscription Ball; all the leading townsfolk were invited, especially if they had deep pockets. Even men like the Jews—auctioneer Henry Harris and his mate Charles Dyte—were always on the subscription list.[1] And now Harris and Ikey Dyte were storing their goods at her hotel. The merchant George Smith also entrusted over £300 worth of his wares to her care, including two dozen black satin neckties, five dozen fine linen shirts, three double-barrelled Dean and Adams revolvers, fifty-three gold signet rings, forty-four gold pencil cases and four dozen electroplated dessert spoons and forks. Smith even asked them to guard his Masonic certificate and apron.[2] Jacques Paltzer had been quick to sign up his band as the regular entertainment at

Bentley's Eureka Hotel, especially since the band members could live upstairs. They were the most sought-after concert band on the goldfields and would no doubt be asked to play at the next ball. People might talk in envious whispers about what went on inside the big red house on the hill, but they wanted what the Bentleys had to offer regardless. Not just grog and cash, but the structure itself: the sense of permanence.

Now that the weather had fined up, the last stage of the hotel's construction could gather pace. The bowling alley was finally operational but there were still seven bedrooms upstairs to be finished and the new concert rooms out the back. And of course there were bills to pay: £230 for paint—white, gold, green and vermillion; 150 squares of glass; cornices, wallpaper and ceiling paper; £320 to five contractors for the stables and concert room; £96 to the sawyer; £190 to Thomas Bath for ten casks of his porter and ten cases of his gin; Rutherford and Tingman, the wine and spirit merchants, would get £596 for twenty-five dozen bottles of champagne, sherry, and port, two thousand cigars, 124 dozen bottles of ale, porter and twenty-two gallons of whisky. Fifty single beds, ten double beds and one hundred pillows also had to be paid for. A massive bill, but it all paled in comparison to the £4540 owed to F. E. Beaver for cartage since May.[3] (This was the opportunity cost of building in winter, when the roads turned to something resembling Irish stew.) Some people might call the Eureka Hotel the *slaughterhouse*, but many believed that James Bentley was a fair dealer, upright, well mannered and in thriving circumstances. They needed no inducement to give him credit.

But the Eureka Hotel was not just a business, it was also home—to Catherine and James and wee Thomas, and the new baby quickening inside her. Just an ex-con and a Sligo girl—she was only twenty-two—but they had built themselves a fine home.

Practically a palace. The hotel was also home to Catherine's sister Mary, and Mary's husband, Everard Gadd, to Duncan the barman and the nursemaid, Agnes Sinclair. Two other servants as well, Mrs Gill and Mary Haines. Michael Walsh, the waiter. Sam in the stables and George in the bowling alley. Isaac Rigby, the carpenter working on the adjoining concert rooms. Charles Smith, the cook and baker. The musicians: Augustus Neill, Edward West and Jacques Paltzer. And Farrell and Hance, the watchmen and rouseabouts.

Nineteen residents in all. It was quite a compound. Those who lived in a hotel were, by Victorian law, called *inmates.* So what did that make the hundreds of people who flocked to drink and gamble and bowl and dance there each night? Outsiders? Hardly. It was Catherine and James's job to make everyone feel welcome: offer hospitality. They did it well.

*

The change of season brought a flurry of activity, as if a clutch of baby spiders had burst from a taut maternal egg-sac and scattered into the warm spring air. *Business of all kinds has looked up amazingly,* noted the DIGGERS' ADVOCATE.[4] A ball was held on 2 September in the new Lydiard Street Arcade in aid of the Hospital Fund. *The sexes were nearly equal in number*, noted the correspondent, *some of the ladies did complain, but not much, that there was too little variety in the dances.* Resident Gold Commissioner Robert Rede, Magistrate John D'Ewes, Police Inspector Gordon Evans and *many leading storekeepers were there.* Down on the Eureka, the stores that had cleared out over winter were now returning. A glee club started up at Bath's Hotel. A lending library opened on the diggings, with copies of Dickens, Thackeray and Ida Pfeiffer, the popular writers of the day. Messrs Robinson and Cole opened their chemist at Ballarat Flat. Their inventory included:

> Robinson's Dysentery Mixture, a never-failing remedy; Robinson's Carmative and Preservative for infants, Robinson's Patent Groats, Robinson's Amboyna Tincture for the teeth and gums; and surgical instruments of all kinds, trusses, cupping apparatus, enema apparatus, breast pumps, nipple shields, feeding bottles, puff boxes, etc.[5]

Ellen Young's husband, Frederick, was a chemist but lacked Robinson's entrepreneurial flair.

New enterprises caught the waft of rejuvenation on the clement breeze. It was announced that a bathing house was to be erected near the Gravel Pits, at an investment of £900, offering hot and cold shower baths. *By making the luxury of bathing available to all, rich and poor alike, the proprietors will not only invite a large concourse of eager customers but also monopolise the business*, heralded the advertorial in the TIMES.[6] A time to plant, a time to reap.

Seeds that were furtively sown in the desperate clutch of winter would now begin to swell. Sixteen-year-old Anne Duke discovered she was pregnant with her first child. So was Margaret Johnston. She and James had married in August; theirs was a honeymoon baby, conceived along the road to Maggie's new home in Ballarat's Government Camp. Bridget Nolan would also be in her first trimester this Christmas. Realising her situation, Bridget was to marry her travelling companion Thomas Hynes on 2 October at St Alipius Church on the Eureka, with Father Patrick Smyth officiating and old shipmate Paddy Gittens as best man. Eight weeks later the young blacksmith Gittens would be beaten to death by redcoats amid a hail of bullets and the acrid smoke of a hundred fires. A time to be born, a time to die.

*

On Sundays, diggers washed their clothes. Then, enjoying the blue skies and balmy air, they joined in hunting parties in the bush. Storekeepers continued to inflame the Sabbath Alliance by openly trading, vending and carting on the Lord's Day. It was the only day that diggers were not mining, so of course they needed to buy and sell, argued the shopkeepers. Members of the alliance trudged through the diggings, remonstrating with the violators of *the Pearl of Days*. A pulpit-thumping meeting was held at the Wesleyan Tent Chapel in the second week of September, attended by Resident Commissioner Robert Rede, who offered his full support. The DIGGERS' ADVOCATE, reporting the meeting, referred to Rede as *our strutting, swellish, little head commissioner, our little handsome functionary.*[7] George Evans attended the Wesleyan Chapel but was *not much pleased* by the tone of the minister. His brother Charles had forsaken religious observance for the time being; he was busy working at the Criterion Printing Office in partnership with a twenty-five-year-old Yorkshire man named Thomas Fletcher.

The Ballarat court held its General Sessions. Most cases pertained to horse theft; *the real blame for this deeply rooted crime*, wrote the court reporter, should lie with the auctioneers, a commercial *gentry* who were too liberally licensed. Horses were even stolen from the Government Camp, *as if to hold up the vigilance of our guardians to public scorn*. (Most of Ballarat's auctioneers were Jewish but the reporter's dog whistle largely fell on deaf ears, on this uniquely level playing field.) As the weather became more benign, thefts increased noticeably. Armed gangs and *flash mobs* skulked around tents, day and night. The chained dogs went ballistic.

Spring, it seemed, unleashed all the passions.

On 23 September, an assault and battery charge was heard in front of Robert Rede. The BALLARAT TIMES reported:

> It was proved that John Doyle and John Doyle's wife threatened to rip open John Bidsil and John Bidsil's wife, and John Doyle and John Doyle's wife being unable to prove to the contrary, John Doyle and not John Doyle's wife was bound to keep the peace towards John Bidsil and John Bidsil's wife, and all within the realm of Victoria, for the term of six months, himself in the sum of £100 and two sureties of £50 each.[8]

Slapped with such a ruinous fine, no doubt John Doyle wished he had been party to a recent milestone. On 8 September, a nugget weighing ninety-eight pounds was extracted from the Canadian Lead, the second most valuable lump yet extracted from Victoria's underbelly. It was named the Lady Hotham Nugget, in honour of Her Excellency's recent visit. Along with the gold from the washing stuff drawn from the same claim, the shaft produced over two thousand pounds of gold. Most claims around the area, reminded the GEELONG ADVERTISER, *won't pay the cost of sinking*.[9] But such finds always caused a fresh burst of enthusiasm and a new influx of cocksure diggers.

Down at the Adelphi Theatre, Sheridan Knowles played the Hunchback to rapturous applause. *It was the most intellectual treat we have had on the diggings*, said the DIGGERS' ADVOCATE reporter. *We congratulate Mrs Hanmer on the energy and ability of her management*. There was acclaim for fourteen-year-old Julia Hanmer too: *To see one so young as Miss Hanmer capable, not only of understanding but appreciating, and finely personating so delicate and difficult part as Julia demands our highest praise*.[10] Charles

Evans was often in the crowd to watch Sarah Hanmer and her remarkable daughter perform. A time to laugh, a time to weep.

In mid-September, a new detachment of the 40th Regiment arrived to relieve the old pensioners who had held the fort through the long winter. The departure scene was one of great amusement, reported the DIGGERS' ADVOCATE: *nearly all of them were so drunk as to be scarcely able to stand, much less walk, in their proper order*. The publicans will lose their *staunch supporters*, scoffed the paper. Captain Russell, who had been in charge of the Pensioners, was placed in the Camp hospital. He was so drunk he'd become *deranged*.[11]

In the commissioners' weekly reports to the Melbourne Goldfields Office HQ, new father-to-be James Johnston noted at the end of September that on the diggings *the workings are progressing favourably but the want of good water is already felt at Eureka*.[12] Ballarat's population would increase by nine thousand people between September and December. As new hopefuls continued to stream in, the tide of nature's bounty was on its way out.

The weather here is remarkably fine and bids fair to continue, predicted the DIGGERS' ADVOCATE on 16 September. Could the rhythm of life have continued to play out like this, under the clear, blue skies of a wide, brown, gold-laced land? An arrest here. A ball there. A death here. A new restaurant there. A nugget here. A play there. An intermittent changing of the guard. Good news. Bad news. Turn, turn, turn.

Perhaps Ballarat was coiled like a spring, clenched from winter's deep freeze of disappointment, frustration and grinding poverty. *Like the eternal sting of insects*, as German digger Frederick Vern put it, the petty tyranny and insolence of the administrators *maddened the people*.[13] Among the traders, victuallers and entertainers, the competition for custom was intense. The people of Ballarat were not ready to thaw; they were ready to pounce. *Everybody was ripe for anything*, reckoned Vern. Primed. Wired. *It only wanted the spark to explode.*

*

The night of 6 October was crowned by a full moon. James Scobie, a young Scottish miner, was encouraged by the bright evening to prolong his drunken revelries. Scobie bumped into his mate, Peter Martin, and the two proceeded to the Eureka Hotel. The day had been hot and the air was even now stagnant, sultry. It was well after midnight, but in Ballarat every businessman had his price. Surely they could get a nightcap from Bentley.

The hotel was shut up when they arrived. Scobie knocked loudly on the door. Catherine and James had retired for the night, but Michael Walsh, the waiter, was still in the bar. He told Scobie and Martin to go away. Scobie continued to make his presence felt, kicking at the door, and smashing a pane of glass. Catherine came downstairs to the bar and told him to go away. Scobie, as Walsh testified at James and Catherine's subsequent murder trial, called the landlady a whore. William Hance, the watchman who had now joined the posse in the bar, said *that was not language to use to any woman*. James Bentley now entered the bar in his trousers and shirtsleeves, as did Farrell, and Duncan the barman. Scobie and Martin scampered away towards a cluster of nearby tents, about seventy metres from the hotel.

What happened next has been told and retold in history books, literature, song and dance, an indissoluble amalgam of speculation, hearsay, sworn testimony and myth. The following version is synthesised from the primary sources only. Even then, there are multiple layers to the onion and trying to peel them apart is a fiddly exercise in perseverance, if not tears.

After their property was damaged and Catherine insulted, the Bentleys, Hance and Farrell pursued Scobie. A violent altercation occurred once the party caught up to the drunken, staggering Scobie. Eleven-year-old Barnard Welch was asleep in his family's tent when he was woken by voices outside. He peeped through a flap to see Mr and Mrs Bentley, and three or four men. One of them picked up a spade from the corner of the Welches' tent. Barnard couldn't say, when he was later required to give a sworn testimony, which of the party picked it up. Barnard's mother Mary Ann also awoke and heard the voices. She thought they might belong to Mr and Mrs Bentley *but could not be sure*. The party moved on. Barnard heard a scuffle and a blow struck. Peter Martin later testified that he was struck down by a group of men and one woman, but he could not identify them. Scobie received a blow to the head. Martin ran to fetch help. He returned with the local butcher, Archibald Carmichael, and Dr Carr. Carr could detect no signs of life. Carr and Carmichael took the body to the Eureka Hotel. (The Victorian licensing law required that hotels also serve as morgues and sites of coronial enquiries.) According to William Duncan, no one from the hotel left the premises from the time the drunken men tottered off to the time Dr Carr arrived with Scobie's dead body.

According to Catherine Bentley, in the note she scrawled almost forty years later, the dead body dragged into her hotel that night did not belong to Scobie at all, but another young miner. Scobie, she argued, was transported surreptitiously to Melbourne by another Irish miner, Peter Lalor, and secreted in the Abbotsford Convent. Catherine believed that James Scobie had gone on to marry and live a fruitful life in Dowling Forest. Remarkably, there is no death certificate for James Scobie to prove her wrong.[14]

*

It was now past 2am. At the Eureka Hotel, Dr Alfred Carr conducted a post-mortem on the deceased. *The stomach*, he found, *was filled with a large quantity of partially digested food and when opened the odour of spirits was very perceptible.* Carr believed the cause of death to be the rupture of one or more vessels within the substance of the brain *caused in all probability by a blow.* He determined that *the state of the stomach from food and spirituous liquor would render a blow more dangerous and more likely to cause a rupture of the blood vessels.* His final conclusion was crucial: *I think the injury was inflicted by a kick and not by the spade now produced.*[15]

All these details came to the fore at the coronial inquest held the following day, Saturday 7 October. Many more particulars—potential fact and scurrilous fiction—emerged at the subsequent Ballarat and Melbourne trials of the Bentleys and two of their employees.[16] That James Bentley was still in his slippers when he left the hotel. That Catherine and James were not really married. That James Bentley boasted he had taken over £200 on the day of the inquest. That Mary Ann Welch heard Mrs Bentley say *how dare you break my windows* before the fatal blow was struck. That Mrs Bentley was heard laughing in the dining room shortly before Scobie's body was dragged to her front door. When the waiter asked why the landlady was laughing, the barman said *Oh, that fellow has got a clip what was at the door.* One witness said Scobie did not call out *you whore* or use any bad language. Another said he heard Mrs Bentley say *that is the sweeps what broke my windows.* Yet another witness said he heard a woman say *that serves you right* after the blow was struck but swore that woman was not Mrs Bentley. The watchman, Thomas Mooney, who turned Crown witness against his former boss, said there was no foul language used by Scobie—but also conceded [I] *cannot swear I am in my right mind.*

At the coronial inquest on the morning of 7 October, no one mentioned the alleged slur to Mrs Bentley's good name that became the centrepiece of the subsequent murder trial in Melbourne. Carr's autopsy conclusion ruled the day: that the death was occasioned by a blow to the head from a scuffle, most likely from a fist or kick, not a spade. But that day was short lived.

Word soon spread that a poor, young Irish miner had been murdered by a rich, well-connected English publican. And not just any publican but the most successful liquor distributor on the diggings. Magistrate John D'Ewes himself later said that Bentley had made *the enmity of a large class in the diggings, the sly grog sellers, whose trade had been ruined by the licensed houses, of which Bentley's was the largest.* The fact that Bentley was the president of the Licensed Victuallers Association only *added venom to their gall.*[17] On the 8th, a deputation of miners visited the Camp. On the 9th, Bentley, Farrell and Hance were arrested and bailed (at £200 each), and the case was remanded for three days. During this time, the accused and their supporters, including the numerous residents at the hotel, were able to get their stories straight, a fact that was not lost on the grieving relatives and aggrieved countrymen of Scobie, particularly his older brother George. Bentley was also spotted at the Camp, where it was assumed he was communicating with Police Magistrate John D'Ewes. There had long been a rumour that D'Ewes was financially indebted to Bentley. On Thursday 12 October, an enquiry into Scobie's murder was held before D'Ewes, Robert Rede and James Johnston.

The decision of the bench that day saw a family's dreams go up in smoke.

*

Summer set in in ernest, recorded Thomas Pierson, though it was only early October. North winds. Dust. Oppressive heat. In the three days between Bentley's arrest and his appearance before the bench, another inflammatory incident occurred. It had nothing to do with James, or Catherine, or the hotel, or even alcohol, but it would start a devastating domino effect on the Bentleys' future.

On Tuesday 10 October, a crippled Armenian servant named Johannes Gregorius was visiting a sick man in his tent on the Gravel Pits. Gregorius had limped from his residence, a flimsy vestibule attached to the cavernous tent that served as the Catholic church. Gregorius was the servant of Father Patrick Smyth, the young Irish priest who had recently been transferred to minister to Ballarat's nine thousand (predominantly Irish) Catholics. Gregorius had no reason to fear being spotted at large among the diggers; ministers of religion and their live-in servants were not required to hold a licence. On this day, however, a callow mounted policeman stopped Gregorius and demanded to see his licence. In faltering English, Gregorius attempted to explain his exemption. But the trooper was in no mood to listen. *Damn you and your priest*, the trooper spat,[18] and dismounted to assault the lame man. Horrified onlookers watched as the horse, unrestrained by his master, proceeded to trample Gregorius.

As luck would have it, James Johnston was in the vicinity. The crowd expected their assistant commissioner would discipline the policeman, who was so clearly overstepping the line. Johnston, however, drew his own arbitrary limits: regardless of any alleged assault, there was the assumed issue of the outstanding licence to deal with. Gregorius would have to attend court the following day. Father Smyth arrived on the scene and offered Johnston £5 bail to take his injured servant home.

What began as a tragedy ended as a farce. In court the next day, in front of John D'Ewes with James Johnston as witness, the battered Armenian was fined £5 for being unlicensed, despite his legal exemption. As Smyth had already paid that sum, the slate should have been cleared—however unjustly the offense was accrued. But Johnston decided to up the ante. He charged that it was the cripple Gregorius who had in fact assaulted the mounted policeman. D'Ewes found this new indictment proved and fined Gregorius another £5.

The Catholics of Ballarat were ropable. Autocratic and illogical miscarriages of justice had become commonplace in Ballarat that winter, but the Catholic community took this one as a direct insult to its priest. A petition was raised on behalf of *the aggregate Catholic body at Ballarat*. The petition, nominally headed up by Timothy Hayes, was undoubtedly the project of his wife Anastasia, who was working as a teacher at the Catholic school. Anastasia, as later events would prove, was a born litigant: quick to assert her rights and defend the rights of those she cared for. In 1854 (though not later) Anastasia Hayes cared most about the Catholics of Ballarat.

The petition wanted *the feelings of an offended people recognised*, and these people held James Johnston personally responsible for the slight. Johnston had never been popular, but now he was in complete disgrace. The petition called for the immediate removal of Johnston from Ballarat and an enquiry into his *ungentlemanly and overbearing* character. (Frederick Vern later called Johnston the most *insolent and unscrupulous* of all the government officers.) As if pre-empting an accusation that the victimised petitioners were but a bunch of Irish ratbags, the petition stated: *The Catholics of Ballarat are a large and influential body comprising inhabitants of every recognised country under heaven.* This corpus begged leave *to observe that the constitutional means taken to obtain a redress of the wrong here complained of evinces our respect for the law.*[19] Not just Irish. Not a mob either. Constitutional. Lawful. Legitimate.

Governor Hotham, alerted to the sectarian crisis brewing at his most populous goldfield, momentarily considered transferring Johnston to another district, but decided it would be *impolitic* to do so. Robert Rede made clear his intention to stand by his right-hand man. It would not be in the best interests of the Camp for its leader to undermine his deputy. Johnston stayed. Margaret Brown Howden Johnston bought a cradle for her gestating baby, noting the purchase in her diary. The Irish of Ballarat considered sewing a large flag to make their point; a *Monster national banner*, reported the ARGUS, to fly over *the disputed ground of the Eureka.*[20]

Another turn of the screw. The coil tightens.

*

The court was crammed to suffocation on the morning of the judicial enquiry into the murder of James Scobie. It was 12 October. James and Catherine Bentley and their servants, Farrell and Hance, were in the dock. D'Ewes, Rede and Johnston presided over an agitated crowd. There was no jury. The BALLARAT TIMES had been fulminating about the case for days. James Bentley was characterised as exhibiting *all the wiles and blandishments of a wealthy publican.* Scobie's death was described as *melancholy.* The newspaper detailed inconsistencies and irregularities of the coronial inquest, and proffered 'facts' counter to the ones given at the inquest.

Yet a letter to the BALLARAT TIMES published on 14 October shows that the Bentleys did have the support of certain sections of Ballarat society. The letter was addressed to James and signed by more than a hundred of Ballarat's *storekeepers, diggers and inhabitants*. It stated that the signatories

> duly appreciating the conduct and manner you have evinced in carrying on the Eureka Hotel, and feeling that you could not either directly or indirectly, in the late lamentable occurrence, have been in any way accessary [sic]...are assured that your urbanity and manly behaviour will still continue to guarantee to so well a conducted house, its full share of public patronage.

A portion of the Ballarat population was confident of the Bentleys' innocence.

Over two nail-biting days, the witnesses took the stand. All the residents of the hotel testified that Mr and Mrs Bentley had not left that evening, that they remained in their bedroom together until Dr Carr arrived. Mary Gadd, Catherine's sister, swore that she could *hear every thing that passes in [their] room*. A butcher residing opposite the hotel swore that Bentley was not one of the men he saw fighting. *It was moonlight* so he could see clearly and *[I] would know him by his general appearance and being lame*. Mary Ann Welch and her son Barnard were called last. It was now that Mary Ann testified that she heard Catherine Bentley say 'How dare you break my window'. *The voice, to the best of my belief, was Mrs Bentley's*, said Mary Ann. *I live within a few yards at the back of the hotel, and often heard Mrs Bentley's voice before*. Barnard Welch told again what he'd seen through his peephole. The TIMES thought him *a very intelligent boy*.

The magistrates retired to an adjoining room for half

an hour to make their decision. Before a hushed crowed, John D'Ewes declared that after assessing all the evidence, *not a shadow of an imputation remained on Mr Bentley's character*. Robert Rede followed suit. James Johnston dissented, unpredictable as ever. The prisoners were free to go.

*

Thomas Pierson made a tally of the grievances under which Ballarat was now groaning. The governor's actions didn't match his promises. Hotham's hypocrisy had *created quite a dislike for him*. There was no representation of the miners in the legislature. Digger hunts had increased to five days per week. Sixteen bullies on horseback, their muskets loaded and swords drawn, would descend on the diggings. Fifty foot soldiers with clubs would *vomit themselves forth* from the Camp. The diggers felt under siege, with no benevolent governor to shield them and no elected leader to represent them. Constitutionally, there was nowhere to run and nowhere to hide.

*

The residents of Ballarat were not the only ones to sense danger in the air that October of 1854. Back in March, Britain had declared war on Russia. The Crimean War, fought by an alliance of the British Empire, France and the Ottoman Empire against the Russian Empire, played like a backbeat against the local pulse of dissonance and discord in Victoria over the winter and spring of that watershed year. The war (so far as any military conflict can be reduced to a sentence) was fought over Russian imperialist expansion into territories in Turkey, the Baltic and the Middle

East. There was also a minor naval skirmish in the Far East in September 1854. News from the various fronts, culled from the British press months after the reports were written, flooded the Victorian newspapers. Victoria followed Britain's lead in observing a day of fasting on 4 August, to commemorate lives lost in the war. Subscriptions were collected to send to the Widows' Fund in Britain.

Then, in a bizarre twist of reason, the inhabitants of Melbourne managed to convince themselves that their humble port town was under threat from Russian invasion. There was no strategic logic in the panic, only wartime paranoia and, perhaps, projected fear of mutiny from the unruly goldfields. In Geelong, a rifle corps was organised and a weekly half-holiday proclaimed to give citizens time to practise rifle shooting, lest their town come under attack. The holiday was quickly abandoned and the corps reduced to a few gung-ho Germans, but the sense of lingering peril remained.[21]

Céleste de Chabrillan, wife of the French consul to Victoria, Lionel de Chabrillan, was in Melbourne in October 1854 when anxiety about an imminent attack came to a head. Her diary entry:

> Cannon fire has again just signalled the arrival of a ship. Tomorrow we shall have news from France. The cannon rumbled all night. All the inhabitants stayed on their feet, either in the streets or at their windows. Since the Crimean War, which is always on their minds, and because there is not a single warship in the Melbourne harbour, they are always imagining that the Russians are going to attempt an invasion to pillage the gold of the whole of Australia. They walk about in large groups, prepared for battle.

> The governor has been informed and he arrives from Toorack [sic], situated six leagues from Melbourne. They follow him; they run towards the harbour. Lionel does likewise. The sky is red and all the ships in port seem to be on fire. They think they hear cries of distress.

Mrs Massey was at a ball when reports of the invasion struck. Pandemonium! Scottish-born Robert Anderson joined the thousands of people flocking to the harbour *in a state of great excitement. Shots were thundering away, rockets, shells and everything else to make the colonials believe the Russians had arrived*, Anderson recalled in his memoir. *The whole town was roused up, all was uproar, the soldiers called out and armed, all the policemen we could muster.*

It was not until daylight that the hoax was revealed. The Battle of Melbourne, as it became known, was an elaborate practical joke played by the captain of the *Great Britain*, as revenge for having his ship put in quarantine. Hotham, who longed to command a naval battalion in the real war, was not amused. PUNCH had a field day. A farcical play called *The Battle of Melbourne* was quickly written and performed. The *scaremongers and alarmists*, as Céleste de Chabrillan called them, were forced to lick their wounded pride. One commentator later noted that Melburnians were prone *to lurch from panic to panic.*[22]

The Russians were not coming, but the communal adrenaline had barely subsided when news of a genuine breach of the peace hit the presses.

*

What is a land of opportunity if not an invitation to opportunism? On 16 October, at 2pm, four felons seized the day. Wearing black crepe veils tied around their faces, cord trousers, blue shirts and sou'westers, the thieves marched into the Ballarat branch of the Bank of Victoria and marched straight back out again bearing £15,000 in gold and cash. *It was a clever robbery and well carried out*, remembered Charles Ferguson, *and had it not been for the extravagant and dashing Madam Quin, it probably would not have been exposed.*

Mrs Ann Quin was the wife of one of the thieves, and the Ballarat, Geelong and Melbourne newspapers followed her and the other scoundrels' movements with tremulous interest (not least because of the £500 reward offered for information leading to an arrest). The robbery, reported in the Tasmanian press as a daring escapade, emblematic of the anarchic, ungovernable diggings, was a cause célèbre: a brazen theft of the golden goose and her eggs, carried out virtually under the nose of the sleeping giants at the Camp.

For weeks the robbery was a complete mystery to the police. Police Inspector Gordon Evans reported to his Melbourne superiors that four men had forcibly entered the bank, bound and gagged the manager and clerk and then emptied the safe, leaving behind them their hats, veils and shirts. The criminals had simply melted back into the landscape of uniform canvas tents and rabbit holes as slickly as they had emerged. No identification could be made and there was no clue to the road taken. For two weeks, it looked like the perfect crime. Since the robbery, the police are *all alive*, reported the GEELONG ADVERTISER; the handsome reward had made the force suddenly alert to the slightest innuendo.[23]

But in Victoria, money didn't whisper, it roared, and such prodigious booty could not long be muffled. Quin—of the Ballarat grocery firm of Garret, Marriet and Quin—was captured on 18 November at the Sir Charles Hotham Hotel in Flinders Street in the company of Mrs Quin and their three children. Ann Quin had been sighted in Geelong where *she was cutting a rather wide swath and spending money left and right.* Quin had been caught out buying a £50 diamond ring with the stolen Bank of Victoria notes.

Mrs Quin entered the dock with a babe in arms. The ARGUS reported:

> she is a plump, rosy-cheeked, country-looking, young woman, about twenty-two years of age, and certainly does not seem very largely endowed with either intelligence, cunning or daring to mark her as the helpmeet for a first class burglar.[24]

Ann Quin was refused bail. Marriet was caught the next day in bed with a prostitute in a Spring Street *house of ill-fame.* Garret was spied on his way to Adelaide but some time later fled to London. His *fancy woman* (a Ballarat actress) had already left for England on the *Calcutta.* The Quin family had also booked a passage on the ship prior to their arrest. Mr Quin later turned *state approver* and *peached* on his former business associates. He confessed that the robbery had been planned a week prior to its execution, that their guns were loaded with paper, not powder or shot, and that they had made a prior agreement that no violence was to be done.

But what of the fourth man? It was three more weeks before 'he' was brought in, and over 150 years before it became readily apparent that the fourth felon was in all likelihood a woman. At the front of the relevant files in the Public Record Office of Victoria, the name Elijah Smith is listed with the others. Yet inside, in the court testimonies themselves, the name Eliza Smith appears repeatedly.[25] The fourth robber, Elijah, was in fact Eliza, disguised beneath a veil drawn by gender-blind bureaucrats.

Eliza Smith was arrested at the Turf Hotel on the Eureka Lead. Like Mrs Quin, she was spending freely in local stores and showing off her ample cleavage to every miner who took an interest. Tucked in her bodice was a roll of £10 notes, fresh from the Bank of Victoria. She was also eager to flash another roll of notes secreted in her stockings. Robert Tait, the landlord of the hotel, was witness to one of Eliza's displays (*she called me on one side and pulled a number of notes from her bosom…she stooped down and produced a parcel of notes from her stockings*) and called the police. When the traps came to arrest her, along with a man who was also passing stolen notes, Eliza fought like fury. *I had great difficulty taking them*, said the arresting officer in court,

> I had great difficulty with the woman, I asked her what money she had on her person, she produced twenty two pound notes six shillings…she then handed me a roll of notes, which she took from one of her stockings, saying take that you 'Bugger'.

After she'd unburdened her smalls of their booty, Eliza Smith was found to have been carrying £262 on her person.

Eliza was brought to Melbourne to be tried, and was convicted of receiving: a lesser crime than that for which her companions were sentenced to seven years. It was Eliza who persuaded Quin to turn Queen's witness, urging him to do so *for the sake of [his] wife and children*. But not even Eliza's defence counsel, Adam Loftus Lynn, thought her a saint. He described her to the jury *as not being constant as Penelope to her dear lord*, of whom she *took French leave*. The implication was that Eliza was in need of fast money to fund an escape from her husband, a mitigating rationale for her crime.

The BALLARAT TIMES was utterly uninterested in the morals or motives of the offenders. There was only one victim in this crime, and that was the careworn community of Ballarat. In a stinging editorial on 4 November, Henry Seekamp accused the town fathers of sowing the seeds of disaster with their own ineptitude.

> Had it been originally the intention of the managers in town to have their property stolen, they could not have selected a site more favourable to the exercise of the distinguished art, or science, of 'sticking up'.

Seekamp was not the only one to point out that the Bank's position behind the township, practically in the bush, was not conducive to public faith in the building as a financial institution. Of the bank's site, the ARGUS said *it really almost speaks out, and says, come and rob me, as much as a big nugget lying on the road-side would invite a traveller.*[26] To add insult, the building was a flimsy box, *resembling as much as possible the zinc lining of some packing-case, with a hole knocked through the bottom to serve as a door.* It was the people, as usual, who had lost their savings due to the dim-witted authorities.

The Bank of Victoria robbery had demonstrated that gold was not safe as houses, or at least not safe *in* houses. But nor, it seemed, was it secure in men's hands. On 3 October, George Dunmore Lang, son of Reverend John Dunmore Lang of Sydney, resigned his position as the manager of the Ballarat branch of the Bank of New South Wales. He was given a farewell dinner by Ballarat's leading merchants and storekeepers, who presented him with a gold cup and their best wishes. In August, George had written a letter to his mother in Sydney. He proudly reported that the bank was in *a most flourishing state.* He then confided that he was arranging to start a private bank with five others. The Bank of New South Wales may have been bursting with deposits, but it did not amply reward its employees. But George could dream of opening his own bank only because he had in fact been amply rewarding himself; two months after his resignation George was convicted of embezzling more than £10,000. The press left Lang alone, perhaps out of courtesy for his well-respected father, or perhaps there wasn't much column space to spare in October.

But it soon became known that under Lang the Bank of New South Wales had allowed James Bentley to overdraw his account by £2000. The bank did not generally trade in loans—only deposits and gold purchases—but made an exception for Bentley because of his *flourishing circumstances* and superior collateral.[27] It was also discovered that Lang had recently purchased a gold-broking business from one James Burchall, who had suddenly fled after his name was raised in relation to the Bank of Victoria robbery. Burchall had also tried to cash promissory notes in favour of John D'Ewes, signed by a local hotel landlord, presumably Bentley. As Eureka historian Ian MacFarlane has written, 'like ripples from a stone thrown into a pond, the murky financial dealing of the Ballarat officials seemed to extend everywhere'.[28]

*

Commissioner Rede read the verdict into the Scobie enquiry on Saturday 14 October. The court and its verandah were filled to overflowing. Hot winds from the arid north whipped up clouds of dust. People choked on their own breath, just as they gagged over the greatest miscarriage of justice yet witnessed in a town that thought matters could get no worse. A wealthy and influential man, allowed to walk away scot-free from a crime that he had patently committed. *Herculean though the task may appear*, roared the TIMES in its edition that evening, *we intend to cleanse the Augean Stable of the Ballarat Camp, and purify its fetid atmosphere of those putrescent particles which offend the senses, by a rigid but wholesome exposure before the bar of public opinion*. Thomas Pierson feared for the publican's safety. Such was the hostility towards not only the magistrates and commissioners but Bentley himself that *I should not wonder if his whole house was razed to the ground*, Pierson wrote in his diary that night.

Bentley's exoneration was a scandal. A public demonstration was called for the following Tuesday, 17 October. Notices were posted. The grapevine sent out its tendrils of insinuation. The meeting would be held within spitting distance of the Eureka Hotel, on the site of Scobie's murder. Thomas Pierson was there, and twenty-seven-year-old Catholic woman Elizabeth Rowlands, cradling her six-month-old baby Mary Ann. They were joined by thousands of others.[29] Pierson says 10,000 in his diary; a subsequent parliamentary enquiry reckoned 5000.[30] A few mounted troopers hung back warily. Speakers came before the crowd to decry the outrage of Bentley's acquittal and the incompetence—nay, impudence—of the Camp.

The decision was a perversion of justice resulting from entrenched venality. The Eureka Hotel was a safe house for murderers and thieves, *connived at by the authorities*. Bentley kept his clientele drunk, all the better for pickpockets to rob them. D'Ewes interfered with all aspects of the goldfields management, from licensing to land sales. Johnston had a share in Brandt's Victoria Hotel. Most of the Camp's higher officials were nothing more than land speculators. Rede was a puppet, a fool. The bench had no impartiality, no transparency. The Camp was a kind of legal store, *where justice was bought and sold*. Where was British liberty? Were the diggers slaves or serfs? Why, the Russians treated their people better than the diggers of Ballarat. On the accusations went, constricting the emotional helix of a blustery spring morning.[31]

At 10am, Police Inspector Gordon Evans sent a garrison of his men to the Eureka Hotel. Led by Maurice Ximines, the men snuck into the hotel, unseen by the crowd. Bentley had asked the police to watch over his property. He had received threats that the people intended to *hang him by the lamp post*. Bentley also had a pregnant young wife, a toddler and a hotel full of employees and guests, not to mention a mountain of private property, to protect. By this stage, the crowd had begun to bay for his blood. *The cries of the mob were for Bentley*, Ximines later testified.

At some point, the mood of the crowd changed. The sun was beating down. The wind was gusting strong. A peaceful public assembly began to turn ugly. *Symptoms of riot began to show themselves*, wrote Thomas Pierson back in his tent that night. He left, and watched the rest of the calamitous proceedings from a safe vantage point at a distance from the crowd. The multitude became a mob, moving with a vicious urgency towards the hotel.

James Bentley, convinced he was going to be lynched, fled on horseback to the Camp. On the way, he passed Charles Evans. *I think I never saw such a look of terror on a man's face*, Evans wrote in his diary. Ellen Young saw him too, *without hat or coat his white shirt sleeves tucked up, a trooper closely following*. Ellen thought it was *a race in fun*. She turned to her next-door neighbour and said *white shirt will win*. But this was no game. Was Bentley on a mission to call for more protection? Was he saving his own neck? Or trying to create a diversion, thinking that the mob might change course and follow him, like a swarm of angry bees?

But it was not only his scalp the crowd wanted: a miner named John Westoby stepped in front of the hotel. *I propose that this house belong to the diggers*, he proclaimed, to wild cheering.

It's a telling line. Here was the first instance during this watershed spring when Ballarat's digging community overtly defined itself as a collective. Now it took Ellen Young's literary lead: *we (the people) demand*... The time had come for the body politic of Ballarat to take matters of justice into its own hands.

'Public punishment', writes British historian Bernard Capp (in his study of the way that aggrieved communities in the English Revolution of the seventeenth century wielded shaming rituals against perceived enemies), 'symbolised the community's collective repudiation of the offence and its reassertion of traditional values'. Jeering, hooting, burning effigies and smashing windows were all activities that could be ritually performed by the whole community, including women and children, as a way to maintain a moral order. This is sometimes called charivari or 'rough music': a terrifying dirge tuned to righteous mob indignation, intended to punish transgression. It was all about loss of face in a society predicated on face-to-face contact.

The rough music accompanying James Bentley in his flight to the Camp from his overrun hotel underscores a central paradox in Ballarat's looming political crisis. Those who immigrated in their thousands to the Victorian goldfields aspired to something different from what they knew, and particularly from the hierarchies of Home. Yet they also expected that the substructure—the traditional values and social assurance of law, order and justice—would stay the same.

Westoby's proposition tapped directly into one of the chief moral concerns of the diggers: the dignity of providing a permanent and prosperous home for their families. How better to cut a man down to size than to invade his castle? Shame him in front of his wife and child. Show him to be no better than the rest of the dispossessed, disempowered crowd outside his painted door.

They would seize the high ground, both morally and literally. Bentley's Hill would be no more. Let his house belong to the diggers. Not an egalitarian gesture of sharing property, but a cutthroat ritual of exclusion.

The same people who had only moments before decried the arbitrary flouting of due process and the flagrant cruelty of its custodians now turned itself to retributive justice. And so, in the words of Samuel Huyghue, *the match was applied to the train of long gathering discontent.*

*

Riots are the kissing cousin of charivari. Add alcohol and soaring temperatures to a public display of disaffection, and it doesn't take much for things to get perilously out of hand. The mob was a feature of pre-modern societies; authorities held a traditional fear and loathing for irate crowds as riots waiting to happen: embryonic uprisings. 'Neither mindless nor revolutionary', writes Bernard Capp, 'riots were an attempt by the disenfranchised to connect with the political and administrative structures of the state'.

Once the crowd had surrounded the Eureka Hotel and its half-acre of funhouses, stables and storage facilities, Robert Rede was called from the Camp. Rede attempted to quell the mob's fury. He stood up on a window ledge. He called for order. He was hooted and jeered, pelted with bottles, bricks, stones and eggs. Someone threw a rock at a window. One report says a little girl cast the first stone; another says it was a teenage lad. It is of no consequence. Once the glass shattered, so did the last of the crowd's equilibrium. That very morning, the final touches to the hotel's major construction works had been completed. Within minutes, the crowd had set upon the process of disassembling all the Bentleys had taken months to build: ripping at boards, smashing windows, throwing stones at lamps. The edifice of Bentley's success was demolished.

*

Imagine Catherine Bentley's terror. As the hotel rocked with the force of the crowd's fury, Ximines' men, holed up inside the hotel, scattered. Catherine and the other residents were left to fend for themselves. Climbing through shattered windows and splintered doors, people began to infiltrate the building. Kegs of liquor were dragged out of storage rooms and eagerly tapped. Furniture was hurled from windows. Someone found Catherine's bedroom and began throwing her jewellery to the people below, stretching their arms up like a pack of savage bridesmaids.

A cry of *Fire!* went up. Someone had set light to the canvas of the bowling alley. The wind had been blowing hot all day, recalled Raffaello Carboni, and at *this fatal precise hour... [it was] blowing a hurricane.* And that was it. The fire in the bowling alley leaped to the main building. Flames consumed the hotel before the glistening, vengeful eyes of the crowd. *It burnt like paper*, said Robert Rede. *A few hours before*, said D'Ewes, *had stood by far the most extensive building in the diggings, painted and decked out in gay and gaudy colours, with a long row of stables and outhouses, erected at an expense of £30,000, and totally uninsured.* Minutes after the blaze was started, Charles Evans arrived. He saw only *a black heap of smoking ashes.*

Ellen Young could clearly see the rioters and the fire from her vantage point outside her tent at Golden Point. She saw clothes and linen being thrown from upstairs windows. She watched a bonfire *made of the contents of the house of every description.* As goods rained down from the hotel windows, people tossed them into the inferno. One person threw Catherine Bentley's jewellery box on the bonfire, quickly fished it out again, studied it, then *threw it with great force into the flames.* Finally a handsome gig was backed onto the fire, turning status to cinders.

James Bentley, having fled to the Camp on horseback, spent the night in Inspector Gordon Evans' tent. But what happened to Catherine as her home combusted around her? Emily Eliza Boyce, twelve years old in October 1854, was present at the burning of Bentley's Hotel. She saw *Mrs Bentley and her child landed safely from one of the windows.*[32] Kenneth McLeod, a wine and spirit merchant, had rushed to the hotel when it was engulfed. He entered the building and found Catherine. With the assistance of a man named Robert McLaren, and *at the risk of my own life*, he tossed Catherine and little Thomas from the second storey, into the arms of the crowd.[33] As in a chivalrous mosh pit, Catherine was caught and released.

Did she join James at the Camp? Ellen Young says *the inmates fled in terror.* It's not clear whether Catherine was among them. But Catherine did find someone to take her in. One of her later petitions for compensation for the financial loss of her property states that she was *dependent on the kindness of a few friends for her daily bread.*[34]

*

Perhaps the Bentleys, Catherine and James alike, had been too cocky in parading their success before an increasingly alienated and aggrieved mining community. Not only were they close to the seat of parochial power, but their ostentatious demeanour reflected the growing social cleavages in Ballarat at precisely the time when democratic sentiment was reaching its apex. Martha Clendinning knew that 'dressing down' was the key to her business success. Lady Hotham had been praised for her willingness to get hands dirty among the people, crumbling chunks of mullock. Remember one digger's remark: *she hasn't half the airs of your innkeeper's and storekeeper's wives.*[35]

That Catherine Bentley may have 'had airs' is alluded to in the evidence of Mary Ann Welch. In testifying that it was definitely Mrs Bentley she had overheard saying 'how dare you break my window', Mary Ann stated that *Mrs Bentley was a stranger to her; had never spoken to her but had often heard her speak.* Given that the Welches' tent was not ten yards from Bentley's Hotel, it is odd that Catherine had never made the acquaintance of a neighbour with eight children, including one boy of similar age to Thomas. Perhaps the thirty-nine-year-old miner's wife was affronted that the twenty-two-year-old publican's wife had not been more solicitous of her friendship, quarantining her precious child from the rabble. The struggling English mother might also have been less than sympathetic herself towards a bejewelled Irish mother who employed a small army of live-in servants and regularly entertained the cream of the Jewish merchants. After all, Mary Ann was herself high born, the daughter of a barrister. In choosing a farmer's son she had married down. *Envy, hatred, malice and all uncharitableness* was how Ellen Young summed up the burning of Bentley's Hotel in a letter to the editor of the BALLARAT TIMES on 4 November.[36]

In late 1854, Catherine would attest to how thoroughly the destruction of her hotel had levelled her circumstances. In one of many petitions to Charles Hotham outlining her situation, the former publican claimed *she was blameless in the above lamentable affair and in no way connected with the assault on the deceased.* In consequence of being blamed, Catherine had *been reduced from comparative affluence to absolute poverty*. And in the note penned in 1892, scrawled on the back of a petition written by the citizens of Ballarat attesting to James Bentley's innocence, Catherine went further. She offered an alternative version of what happened on the night of Scobie's apparent murder. *The man Scoby mentioned in the printed form as killed, was hid in the Abbotsford Convent during the riots, under the influence of Peter Lalor.*[37] Catherine went to her grave believing that her family had been intentionally robbed of their fortune, reputation and status in the Ballarat community.

Fire is not as discerning as friendship, and the Bentleys were not the only ones to suffer losses that day. Twenty-six people later submitted claims for compensation, either for the material destruction of property or as creditors to the now-bankrupt Bentleys. Alexander West lost all his musical instruments and was thus forced to *relinquish his profession*. James Waldock had conducted a livery and licensed auctioneer's business from the stables at the hotel; he lost his large stock of cattle, drays, bridles, saddles, hay and oats to the tune of £2,000 and was *reduced to beggary*. All of these claims were subsequently denied.

Michael Walsh's rejected compensation case was the most poignant. Walsh had a tent close to the hotel. It was also consumed by the wayward flames, burning down around the ears of his family. Mrs Walsh was in labour at the time, striving to deliver her first child. Assistant Commissioner Amos assisted in getting Mrs Walsh away from the blazing tent. He carried her to safety. *I thought she was dying at the time*, Amos later told the select committee, *[but] she was in the pains of labour*. Mrs Walsh delivered a stillborn baby. In 1857, Michael Walsh considered that his *actual pecuniary loss* was insubstantial when *compared with the long illness of my wife...consequent upon the Great Excitement, the effects of which she nor I have never been able to overcome.* The Walshes went on to have eleven children, never registering the death of the first baby on that tempestuous October day.

It was obvious to all that no attempt had been made to control the crowd or protect life and property. *One thing is certain*, a select committee later determined, *the destruction of Bentley's Hotel was not confined to a few, but thousands of men and women too were engaged in the work of destruction.* Why hadn't Commissioner Rede read the Riot Act, the parliamentary enquiry asked. Rede blamed Police Inspector Gordon Evans, who had authority over the police, for not clearing the crowd or defending the hotel despite the fact that Ximines and his men had occupied the hotel all morning. Rede also claimed he had no power over the military, who were despatched only after the fire began. Other police testified that Evans had *lacked determination* to stop the rioting. Had his instructions been more direct, the hotel would have been saved. Evans defended himself against the charges of inaction. *My hands were completely tied*, he said, *I must obey my orders.* Only the resident commissioner could read the Riot Act. What a shambles. Who exactly was in charge of Ballarat?

It was only after the Eureka Hotel riot that Rede was given a letter of *absolute power*. He now stood at the apex of a chain of command that included the police and military. But many believed that the damage had been done. The people had carried the day. They had sensed their own power. Samuel Huyghue assessed the disposition of the police and government on the afternoon of the riot. A silent hush had settled over the Camp. Troopers and traps spoke in low mutters in their tents. There was *angry humiliation* that Rede had tried to make conciliatory speeches rather than take swift action. There had been a *loss of prestige*. How could it be regained?

A huge downpour came in the night, settling dust and tempers. For now.

*

There was something in the air that spring. No doubt about it. Back in 1853, James Bonwick had read the mood of the people and predicted that *a sudden excitement, a sudden revolution, a sudden political change may take place*. But Bonwick feared that a society oddly composed of the ill educated and newly rich might have been democratic but it was also *unmistakeably given up to selfishness, and often to impure indulgence*. Now, his dystopian vision seemed to be coming true. 'Excitement' was the word used by most commentators to describe Ballarat's heady mix of anxiety, restlessness, disaffection and disregard for authority. It was contagious, and while Bendigo was undoubtedly the locus of unrest in 1853, there was no more exciting place to be in late 1854 than Ballarat.

Henry Seekamp could not contain his sense of a unique destiny rolling, like an electrical storm, towards his adopted town. On 19 October, the Bentleys, Hance and Farrell were rearrested to stand trial in Melbourne for James Scobie's murder. On 21 October, two miners, twenty-four-year-old Scot Andrew McIntyre and Charles Evans' business partner Thomas Fletcher, were named arbitrarily out of the thousands of rioters and charged with the arson of the Eureka Hotel (a third, John Westoby, would later be added). Here is Henry Seekamp's editorial on 21 October:

> In all the history of Australia—from its earliest discovery to the present time—from the days the soil

> first bore the impression of the white man's foot—during all the different phases of convictism—of commercial failures—of the discovery of the different gold fields—of the agitation for the repeal of that incubus of industry, the miner's licence—of the feting and rejoicing on the arrival and visiting of a new chum Governor—of the expected invasion of the Russians, never has there been a more eventful period than the present of Ballarat. Public feeling is so great that no rumour, however absurd, but what gains credence—everything is believed and everything is expected. The people have, for once…begun to feel their own strength…the first taste of liberty and self-government.

Seekamp could only view the cascade of October's events as an inevitable step towards liberty, *a child beginning to walk, in a little time the child will be able to stand alone.* But twenty-six-year-old Henry had no offspring of his own; he was stepfather to Clara's children. He may not have been in the best position to wield metaphors of infant development. Children also discover their narcissistic will. Separating from their psychically overbearing parents requires a monstrous act of defiance—something approximating Bonwick's prophecy of *selfishness* and *indulgence.*

Surely some malignant spell, surmised the ARGUS, *must blind the Captain, that he cannot see the rocks ahead.*[38]

*

The fine weather was a boon to government surveillance of the diggings. From late September, licence hunting stepped up with a new vigour now the winter mud was gone. Suddenly, large, armed military forces were sent out from the Camp to patrol the diggings. Foot police carried batons. Soldiers wielded carbines, swords and holster pistols. Some were mounted, parading frisky horses through tents and holes in search of unlicensed miners. *A new chum*, wrote An Englishman to the GEELONG ADVERTISER on 10 October, might think the show of force was to intimidate criminals against the dog poisoning, horse stealing and tent breaking that had become endemic this spring. But no, it was merely digger hunting, pursued with an *unusual degree of severity* since Hotham's visit to the goldfields. The Englishman attributed the new regime to the resident commissioner *proving his utility*.

Others could see that the new governor had pledged to remedy the colony's ailing economy and was going about the task with obdurate zeal. The public service was being whittled to a shoestring to reduce expenditure. On the income side of the ledger there were only liquor excises and mining licences to lift the bottom line. The diggers would conveniently drink to their hearts' content, but showed increasing reluctance to produce a valid licence. What was a governor to do, other than order his minions to carry out more licence hunts? If once a week was not enough to demonstrate that this government meant business, then make it twice. Or every day bar the Sabbath. *Is it to be endured*, wrote the Englishman, *in a possession of the British Crown, that an armed police force may 'bail up' and require the production of your badge in all places at all times? Does this happen in London?* He finished by calling for some *more influential pen* to take up the cause of the unrepresented digger. Ellen Young patriotically obliged.

On 4 November, following Scobie's murder, the Eureka Hotel riot and the fire, the arrests, the trials and the public meetings, Ellen captured the mood of her clan in a long letter to the BALLARAT TIMES.

> I can but remark on the sad picture of humanity your last Saturday's paper presents...Alas for the poor diggers, over whose spoil the whole tribe are squabbling. Alas for the honest of each party that he should be sacrificed to the dishonest. Alas, alas for us all that we cannot get a snap of land to keep a pig live pretty, and grow cabbages on; and *three times* alas; let it *three times* be for us (the people) poor dupes... following in high hopes the jack o' lantern dancing over the land, his false light blinding all.

Here we have the diggers as fools and their governor as the will-o'-the-wisp trickster figure of English folklore who draws innocent travellers down the garden path with devilish false promises. Hotham had betrayed Ellen's early trust. She would now place her faith in another organ of authority, the fourth estate. Her letter continued: *We ought to congratulate ourselves in possessing so admirable a vent as your paper for the spleen. How amiable shall we become in time...I am but a simple dreamer at the foot of the mount.*

*

While Ellen Young waxed lyrical at her literary base camp, a host of nameless sherpas did the grunt work to spread the word of mutiny on the streets. Gossip and rumour, writes Bernard Capp, were 'a powerful coercive weapon, defining and reasserting the social values of the community'. Traditionally, he says, women have wielded gossip as a form of 'quasi-public power'. Through informal networks and collective pressure, women were able to play a role as active citizens, turning private grievances into public issues and refashioning themselves as the persecutors rather than the persecuted. Capp argues that this 'informal political world based on female networks' was vital in shaping public opinion in pre-industrial communities, particularly in times of crisis. Gossip and rumour could be malicious and judgmental or simply informative about comings and goings central to the community's wellbeing. Gossip was a powerful tool for otherwise disenfranchised people, but its central importance is not reflected in the public/historical record, for the simple fact that by its very nature rumour is spread discreetly, in whispers—often Chinese whispers—at the marketplace or at work in the fields. Gossip is the backdrop to what survives in hard copy, such as Ellen Young's letters to the editor.

The public record of Ballarat's rumour-mongers is surprisingly resilient. Ellen Clacy described the interior of your average shop on the diggings: *pork and currants, saddles and frocks, baby linen and tallow, all are heaped indiscriminately together...added to which, there are children bawling, men swearing, store-keeper sulky, and last, not least, women's tongues going nineteen to the dozen.* Raffaello Carboni begins his account of the Catholic servant affair like so: *The following story was going the rounds of the Eureka.* The TIMES revealed that prior to the destruction of the Eureka Hotel, rumours had been flying thick and fast. Police Magistrate D'Ewes was a partner in the business. Bentley had paid thousands of pounds for exoneration. The licensing bench was bribed. And the paramount tall story: Catherine Bentley was in fact Scobie's wife!

On 24 October, the AGE reported *an eventful week at Ballarat*: Monday, the bank robbery; Tuesday, rioting; Wednesday and Thursday *taken up guessing at what might be next looked for*, including brazen anecdotes that Avoca, Maryborough and Creswick Creek *had on the same or following day as ourselves set the authorities at defiance*; Friday, arrest of the manager of the Bank of New South Wales; and Sunday, a meeting of the Irish regarding the Father Smyth and Johnston incident. The AGE's Ballarat correspondent revealed rumours that the Avoca Camp had been burned down, that the Maryborough Camp was under siege by diggers, that the unemployed of Melbourne had risen up at the news of the Ballarat riot, and that the Bank of Victoria was broke. *Added to the talk about such matters*, wrote the correspondent, *was an interminable controversy as to the pros and cons of Bentley's case.* You didn't need a soapbox to be heard in Ballarat. A person couldn't blow her nose *without drawing around them a crowd of sympathisers.*

As the ARGUS correspondent wrote, *The growth of revolutionary opinion* is predicated on such tittle-tattle.[39]

*

When James Bentley fled from the flames of his ruined empire to the protection of the commissioners, an insidious rumour started doing the rounds. The government compound was going to be attacked! The diggers were going to come that night. Vengeful miners were going to prise Bentley from his refuge and drag him back to his smoking lair. Justice would be done, even if Judge Lynch had to do the reckoning.

Spies brought the news from the Flat to the Camp. The garrison was put under arms. No one was allowed to enter or leave. The night, according to Camp resident Samuel Huyghue, *passed alert in expectation* of an attack. The next day, 18 October, *the females were ordered to leave the Camp, as it was considered that at such a time they would be safer anywhere than with us.* Families split up. Anxious wives abandoned their husbands to the patent fury of the mob. Did pregnant Margaret Brown Howden Johnston leave? Where did she go? Her diary is mute. *Some poor souls*, said Huyghue, *were ultimately permitted to remain on the plea that they had no home or protectors elsewhere.* These women and children took refuge in the commissariat store *whenever there was an alarm.* The walls of the store were partly bullet proof, being formed of roughly hewn slabs. *But you could still insert a finger between them*, worried Huyghue.

And rumours could slide under doors like shape-shifting vapours in the night. They could waft between slabs. Seep beneath skin. Penetrate the soundest of minds. Gossip and rumour could fuel a fire as well as any kindling and flame.

Shaken to its core by the power of an idea, the Camp would never recover.

TEN

HIGH CAMP

On the ship of the Victorian goldfields, the resident commissioner was captain. His first mates were the assistant commissioners, magistrates and other senior civil servants; the coroner was the ship's surgeon-superintendent. The police were the ordinary seamen, poorly paid henchmen who did the hard slog. A submission to a commission of enquiry into the Victorian police force, held in late 1854, described the boys in blue like this:

> The service generally is so unpopular, that, with few exceptions, only those who are either too idle to do any thing else, or who having failed in all their other attempts to gain a livelihood as a last resource enlist into the Police, the latter, after having accumulated a little money become disgusted with the Service, and either desert or commit some fault in the hope of being discharged. This is more particularly applicable to the Police on the Gold Fields.[1]

On the Victorian goldfields there was also a military presence, a royal barge with its own hierarchies of power and customs of privilege. There was, of course, no ship's matron to regulate the behaviour or check the welfare of the goldfields women.

In Ballarat, this whole clamorous crew was housed at the

Government Camp. To the diggers and storekeepers, the Camp was a hive of treachery and deceit, a bastion of vested interests and autocratic inconsistency. But what of the Camp's inhabitants? Were they sitting pretty up in their topographical tower? Enjoying a room with an enchanting view? Living the high life? Alas no. Long before the exoneration of James Bentley made the government's compound a target of enmity, its residents were anything but happy campers.

*

When Assistant Commissioner James Johnston's young bride arrived at her new home on 5 September, this is what she found. A high picket fence bound a two-acre parcel of land on the north-eastern edge of the township escarpment. (Today it is bounded by Lydiard, Mair, Camp and Sturt streets.) A second fence divided off a sloping portion of the hill near its eastern border. Parallel with this fence was a row of tents with sod chimneys. These tents were for the employees of the Gold Fields Department, such as the assistant civil commissioner, Samuel Huyghue. Behind these, more central to the picketed perimeter, were more rows of tents—mess rooms and gold commission offices—flanked by a few wooden buildings that had only recently been erected at substantial cost.

One of these housed the now-pregnant Margaret and her dear Jamie. Another was the domicile of Resident Commissioner Robert Rede. Police Inspector Gordon Evans, a twenty-nine-year-old native of Montreal, Canada, occupied another. At the rear of the Camp stretched a long line of commissariat stores. The military and police quarters—more tents—were on the northern face of the hill. There was a courthouse with a deep verandah and a prison built of logs. This ill-planned, makeshift arrangement of lodgings accommodated the civil force stationed at Ballarat, their families and servants (tent keepers, drivers, packhorse keepers) as well as the police force and military forces, including some wives and children. In total, over one hundred people were crammed into the government ghetto.[2] *The architects of the camp may have a method in their madness*, wrote the GEELONG ADVERTISER in February 1854, *but it is not easily seen.* There was little evident cause for pride; nevertheless, a flagstaff ascended from beside the courthouse, its rippling Union Jack marking territory.

Margaret wrote about none of this in her diary. *Took possession of our house in camp and was busy getting things put right*, she recorded on 8 September.

September 9 Saturday
Still unpacking

September 10 Sunday
Made our first appearance at the church.

September 11 Monday
Received callers.

Then all goes quiet on the Johnston front. Margaret didn't write in her diary again until 22 November. Two and a half months of blank pages. Why? Did she have nothing to say? Not even *Jamie dined at the mess. Had a walk. Took tea with Mrs Lane*—all activities she recorded prior to 9/11. Did she have debilitating morning sickness late in her pregnancy? Was she too busy keeping house? Or, on the contrary, was she depressingly bored? Her ship diary reveals a cheerful personality able to revel in the smallest detail of daily living. *Had breakfast. Cool breeze. A wet day. A long chat after dinner.* As we have seen, spring in Ballarat brought a riot of colourful events. Given the dramas she could have reported, Maggie Johnston's silence is curiously golden.

But she could have been forgiven for finding her surroundings shamefully lacking. Her fellow inmates had been writing letters to Melbourne complaining about the conditions at the Camp for the best part of a year. In June 1854, the assistant colonial surgeon, Dr Heisse, had stepped down from his position after an enquiry into his conduct. (He had billed a digger after treating him for a gunshot wound in the Camp hospital.) *I have much pleasure in resigning a situation which has been one of the greatest discomfort to my family and a personal pecuniary sacrifice*, he wrote to the colonial secretary.[3]

A series of letters from the top dogs of the Ballarat Camp to their Melbourne superiors from February to October reveals the sort of discomfort that the Heisse family may have experienced: overcrowding, poor sanitation, substandard tents, provisional offices. Even the post office was a dark and dirty tent open at both ends to the elements. The mail was sorted on a stretcher. On a blustery day, noted the GEELONG ADVERTISER, letters were distributed on the wind *to a grateful public*.[4] The irony is that one of the letters, penned in March, complained of the *great want of proper accommodation at this Hospital owing to nearly the entire building being occupied by the Assistant Colonial Surgeon and his family, which leaves only one ward for the reception of all classes of Patients*.[5] Perhaps the only way to evict Heisse was to accuse him of financial impropriety.

Each of the Camp's three independent power blocs—the Gold Fields Department, the police, and the military—had its own chain of command and own internal codes of conduct. One of the chief gripes of Camp officials was that certain factions had more access to amenities than others. It was, after all, a very small pie, and every division wanted a more generous slice of it.

The bickering was fierce and incessant. The Gold Commission occupied the lion's share of the camp grounds. Its reserve was twice as large as that of the police. Most of the police grounds were taken up by the married non-commissioned officers' tents. There was not enough room for the foot and mounted constables—mostly young, poorly paid single men—to be accommodated. Apart from overcrowding, the lower-ranked police tents were shoddy and ill kept. The tents of the foot police were *unfit for the men to reside in*, wrote Sub-Inspector Taylor to his Melbourne superiors in August. The canvas tents were *for the most part perfectly rotten*, proof against neither rain nor sun, as they had been in use for over two years. Taylor was inspired to alert HQ to the situation after the tents were torn to shreds in a fierce storm. *The rain of last night completely saturated the beds and blankets*, he wrote in July, *so much so that the men were all huddled together in one tent*. Just as the diggers on the Flat clung to their accusations of injustice through the frigid gales of a Ballarat winter, so the soldiers anchored their despair with the weight of grievance. *There have been frequent complaints of late from the men in consequence of the very great discomfort in their tents*, wrote Taylor, *and there does not appear any prospect of the Police Barracks being erected*. Here was the nub of the problem: over eighteen months of occupation and still no sign of the promised barracks. And now Hotham was in Victoria, cutting a swathe through the colony's £2 million deficit with razor-edged determination. Taylor knew the best he could do was request some new tents. A roof over his force's collective sore heads was clearly too much to ask for.

*

An uninhabitable tent is one thing, but derelict pants are quite another. Yet on 13 July, Police Inspector Gordon Evans had the honour to inform his superiors in Melbourne that *much dissatisfaction has arisen on the part of the Foot Police in this District in consequence of the high prices charged for the trousers.* The problem was this: *they are charged at the same rate as the mounted men whose trousers are made of fine cloth with white stripes whilst those of the Foot Police are made of a very inferior coarse pilot cloth.*

Rank and file police were required to purchase their own uniforms, but they couldn't select a supplier: they were compelled to purchase from the government stores. The snag was that coarse pilot cloth trousers exported from England could be purchased from any shopkeeper on the diggings for half the price of the colonial-made trousers supplied on contract to the government. Hence the foot police either paid a fortune for inferior itchy pants, or wore their old pair till the arse fell out of them. Not an enviable choice, especially in a Ballarat winter with the wind whistling through every crack.

It was not only the human members of the government contingent who suffered. The Camp's stables were *all falling to pieces owing to the damage done to them by the horses.* Captive horses kicked at their stabling the world over, but in Hotham's Victoria the splintered stalls were simply not repaired.

In September 1854, Police Magistrate John D'Ewes (who despite his misleading title was not actually a member of the Victoria Police but of the Gold Commission) and Robert Rede jointly wrote to Melbourne to protest that the original reserved area of the Ballarat Camp was insufficient. More land was needed. In the meantime, they applied to take over a piece of land hitherto earmarked for the police. The land, adjoining the married officers' tents, was being used as a vegetable garden. The Camp had been unable to persuade Melbourne to appoint a gardener to raise much-needed fresh produce for its inhabitants, so an improvised cottage garden was established. In all likelihood the Camp wives cultivated the unofficial garden, just as women generally tended the home vegetable plots on the diggings. D'Ewes wanted to use the land for his own residence.

Of all the senior officials, D'Ewes was the one who complained the loudest about the inadequacy and injustice of his domestic circumstances. He had missed out on one of the newly erected wooden homes. Robert Rede's house, completed in September, cost £1,200. Inspector Evans' house cost £1000. Even the colonial architect had a handsome new cottage. D'Ewes, by stark contrast, was living in the small walled-in verandah attached to the court building, a space that was also used as a jury room for nine weeks of the year. When he couldn't sleep on the verandah, he had to share someone's tent.

The affront and the material deprivation of this situation stuck in D'Ewes' craw like a fish bone. On 3 August he wrote to the colonial secretary that

> the accommodation for the Police Magistrate at this most important gold field is decidedly worse than that of any other officer stationed at this place...Good houses are built or in the process of being built at large costs for the heads of all other departments.

He stressed the importance of his position. He complained that he could not offer the hospitality to *passing strangers* that was expected from one of his station. He offered to pay a portion of the expense of building a residence. The colonial secretary was unmoved. The issue was held over until the spring. When the matter had not been dealt with by late September, D'Ewes tried again, twice, but this time he gave an indication that his distress did not merely relate to his unaccommodated ego: *I have sent upwards of £500 of property to Ballarat as well as my wife and family. No house is in process of erection for the Police Magistrate*, he wrote, *I am totally without quarters for myself and family and an exception to all the officers on the Camp.* By now it was 28 September—about a week before Scobie's murder—and Hotham himself responded to this latest letter. In shirty tones the governor asked, *Does Mr Dews [sic] suppose the request forgotten? Can he not imagine that some good cause may exist for the delay?*[6] But by this stage D'Ewes was simply pleading for a tent of his own, forget a building, so that he could move his wife and child from their expensive hotel into the Camp. As fate would have it, D'Ewes did not get to stay in Ballarat long enough to see even so much as a bivouac come his way. On 4 November, he was dismissed as a magistrate, the first formal victim of the Eureka Hotel affair. The non-commissioned officers' wives would get to keep their vegie patch.

It is tempting to think that at least the married officers were content, but no. On 14 June, Evans reported to Melbourne on the inadequacy of the married non-commissioned officers quarters being located next to the unmarried commissioned officers quarters. Those tents, he advised, were supposed to be used for the non-commissioned officers' servants. That they were instead occupied by the unmarried officers led to *inconvenience and unpleasantness.* There were three grounds for rectifying the untenable situation, argued Evans. 1. *The proximity of this building to the officers' quarters admits of every word that is spoken in one being heard in the other.* 2. The servants were too far away. 3. The non-commissioned officers quarters were too small and *not at all adapted to accommodate married non-commissioned officers.* Married people could not be expected to do what married people do with all the world watching and listening. And then have to stomp all the way across the Camp to fetch a servant to wash the sheets!

It wasn't just the superior ranks of police who were disgruntled by the conditions of their employment. Some in the lower echelons of police were going completely off the deep end in the *Black Hole of Calcutta,* which is how Samuel Huyghue described the Camp. In July, Sub-Inspector Taylor had cause to write to his immediate Ballarat superior, Inspector Gordon Evans, about the meltdown of Constable Patrick Hopkins. Hopkins, while searching for unlicensed miners, *was getting under the influence of liquor*. Taylor cautioned him:

> A short time after I saw him go into a public house and call for drink. I prevented his being served with any, about a half an hour after this two respectable women came to me saying that he had been into their tents and insulted them, one of the women was crying. I perceived that he was then very drunk I immediately ordered him under arrest, he flourished his baton and flung it from him.

Hopkins then struck another officer and shouted that he wanted to be discharged from the police. *The exhibition he made on the Gold Fields*, worried Taylor, *was calculated to bring disgrace on the force.*

It wouldn't have taken much. The police cohort at Ballarat did not exactly float on a tide of public esteem. Reports from Inspector Gordon Evans to Melbourne throughout 1854 attest to either the low standard of recruits or the effects of the conditions on formerly upstanding fellows. Police constable John Reagan was suspended for being *not shaved, dirty, and having all the appearance of an habitual drunkard.* Daniel Wright was *discharged with bad character as he was frequently under the influence of liquor*. Trooper James Butler was transferred to the foot police due to being a *very slovenly man who knows nothing of horses.* Arthur Shirvington was imprisoned in the Camp lockup for two days after he went absent without leave all night and *returned home drunk and fighting in public houses.* Acting Sergeant John Dougherty was found in Canadian Gully *lying in a state of stupidity from the effects of drink.* Thomas Milne was sentenced to three days' imprisonment for being drunk on guard. In August the lockup keeper requested the sub-inspector to accompany him to the prison *to see the state of the Sentry posted there…the sentry was lying on his face and hands insensibly drunk, his arms were placed by the side of the door…the man was in such a state that he was obliged to be carried away on the shoulders of another man.* Constable John Regan was given three days' imprisonment for *making use of abusive and highly obscene language to Sgt Rutter while in the execution of his duty.* The bench sentenced Constable William Thompson to three months' imprisonment for habitual drunkenness. Thompson was *presently labouring under a very severe attack of Delirium tremens.*

There is a theme emerging.

By late August, Evans was asked to explain what he intended to do about his force's appalling behaviour and morale. He responded that he couldn't discharge all the men whom he rightfully should due to their *inveterate habitual drunkenness.* If he took such drastic action, he wouldn't have enough men to do the job. The number of commissioned officers was already much below its authorised number and those who were in the Camp *frequently complain of their duties being rendered more arduous in consequence of this insufficiency.* Guards on night shift were forced to perform on the following day various backbreaking tasks (including carting wood and water, which should have been the job of a paid labourer) *and frequently that of searching for unlicensed miners.* He also wished to point out:

> the great discomfort and hardships endured by the men during the past winter owing to the want of proper accommodation and which no doubt of itself tended to make them unhappy and discontented, there being no Barracks and on many occasions no stretchers or blankets for them in the miserable tents they were compelled to live in.

Many men had either applied for discharges, committed some heinous act in the hope of being discharged or simply deserted. In July, one brave and uncommonly literate constable, L. H. Webb, had written directly to the chief commissioner of police requesting a discharge. He knew the proper procedure was to go through Ballarat's inspector, but he was loath to do so because of Evans' past form in taunting and bullying his men. *I am not a drunken soldier*, wrote Webb,

> I can pluck up spirit to complain of oppression… petty tyranny should be restrained and the advantages of position should not be a vantage ground wherein the officer may insult and wound the feelings of an inferior with impunity.

Was this a trap or a digger? The language employed by those on the hill and those on the flats to express grievance was eerily similar.

The third sibling squabbling over its puny share of the pie of the civil service and the police was the military. By the winter of 1854, the members of the 40th Regiment stationed at Ballarat were still housed in leaky, breezy tents. The garrison included some army wives. Corporal John Neill, an Irishman, lived in the Camp with his wife, Ellen, and their baby, Fanny, who had been born in Waterford shortly before her parents' departure for Australia. Neill kept a diary that speaks poignantly of the conflict between his family duties and his military role. He wrote of having to coax his daughter to sleep in her cot on the hill, *only to have her awaken screaming* as gun shots rang out on the flats each night.[7] Ellen Neill was certainly not the only military wife in the Camp, but since the army didn't keep records of its wives, there is no information about any others.

There was, however, a surfeit of correspondence regarding all other matters of daily intercourse. From June to December, the military leadership waged a campaign of paper warfare on the Colonial Office, with the strategic aim of securing a new barracks for the soldiers stationed at Ballarat. A barrage of letters flew between Ballarat and Melbourne. As the Camp was so overcrowded, the military proposed constructing a new building *adjacent to but not within the present limits* of the Camp. The Colonial Office prevaricated, suggesting it planned to sell the present Camp site and build a *far more commodious* Camp of stone buildings on a site one hundred yards from the present one. It was clear to all, however, that this could not happen. Town allotments had already been sold all around the Camp, which was now boxed in by private property. There was simply no room to expand. *It was a great error in the first instance not to have made a larger Reserve for the Government Establishments*, wrote Assistant Engineer Henry Lane—if for no other reason than that the Camp's congested tangle of wood and canvas structures was a perfect firetrap. One spark and the whole place would go up in flames.

Meanwhile, once the police command got wind of the military's intention to station its contingent outside the Camp's perimeter, it made a rearguard pitch to secure any new barracks for itself. Who would get the improved quarters, should they ever be built, was now in dispute. Robert Rede conceded *the impossibility of ever making the Ballarat Camp a good one*.[8]

*

If it was tense and uncomfortable on the inside, there was no relief to be had outside the Camp. Relations between the mining community and the police, soldiers and government officials had been on the nose for months. *There are no Standing Orders for the guidance of the Force,* one man wrote anonymously to the Police Commission of Enquiry, *consequently the men are very often led unwittingly into the committal of acts of harshness which inflames the Public Mind against the Government and its employees.*[9] The informant suggested that issuing a rulebook to every officer would be a good start to rebuilding trust. But it would take more than an etiquette manual to restore public confidence. After the Eureka Hotel riot, the serfs began to smell fear in their masters. On 22 October, Thomas Pierson recorded in his diary that the soldiers and police *don't dare leave the Camp*. People would *hoot* at them in the street, jeer as they rode high in their saddles, shout *Joe! Joe! Joe!*—a snappy goldfields pejorative for the pigs, the filth.

And there was precedent for what could happen when local outrage against the British imperial ruling class, and its blatant disregard for citizens' aspirations to democratic rights and freedoms, boiled over. In Canada in 1837, eight hundred followers of a popular reformist movement marched on Toronto armed with pitchforks, staves and guns, in an attempt to overthrow the oligarchic administration and establish self-government. Local militias mercilessly put down the uprising. But the Upper Canada rebellions of 1838 ultimately led to the introduction of responsible government and the end of authoritarian rule in Canada. Gordon Evans' father was a general in the British army stationed in Canada and may have been stationed in Quebec—a witness to the carnage.

On 27 October, the day after Andrew McIntyre and Thomas Fletcher were arbitrarily arrested for their alleged role in the Eureka Hotel arson, a plan was hatched to defend the indefensible Camp.

*

There was more pissing on posts happening in the Ballarat Camp than all the chained guard dogs of the diggings could manage in a month of Sundays. As chief of the civil force, Resident Commissioner Robert Rede was theoretically entitled to choose his post. Or was he? In-fighting about accommodation was just the acquisitive tip of a looming iceberg of power struggles within the Camp.

The foremost clash was between Rede (aged thirty-nine) and Police Inspector Gordon Evans (aged twenty-nine). Evans was appointed to Ballarat in February 1854, Rede in May. They were both on a salary of £700 a year. As we have seen from the parliamentary fallout over the Eureka Hotel fire, both manipulated the curious power vacuum when it suited them to avoid ultimate responsibility. But the fact is that these men were engaged in a dispute that began in June over the Camp's hierarchy and demarcation. The conflict started when Evans wrote to the chief commissioner of police in Melbourne regarding Rede's requests to station more police at Creswick Creek. Was Evans in charge of his men's movements or not? Why was Rede involving himself in matters of policing? By late September, the dispute was putatively resolved when a circular was sent from Melbourne stating that at all times Rede was to have paramount authority.[10] Evans was clearly still smarting about this when he blamed Rede for the riot outside Bentley's Hotel.

The riot was the unanticipated turning point in Rede's one-upmanship with Evans. He now had to back up his dominant position: prove that the powers-that-be in Melbourne had shown faith in the right fellow. He wasn't just demonstrating to the irritated and unruly digging community that insubordination would not be tolerated. He was performing for his own troops as well. And not all in Melbourne were in one mind about Rede's fitness to command a sinking ship. A week after the hotel riot, the chief commissioner of police publicly recorded his opinion that *in consequence of the still excited state of this Gold Field [Ballarat]... it is probable that we may not be able to avoid a collision*. In the face of *a powerful mob*—in particular *the Tipperary Mob, one of the most powerful and troublesome to contend with and who seem bent on mischief*—the chief commissioner called for a reinforcement of police numbers. The Camp, he believed, was *impossible to defend*.[11] Did Rede take it as a personal slight or a judgment on the architectural and geographic insecurity of the site? It was Rede who ordered the arrest of Fletcher and McIntyre *to give a fearful lesson*.[12] But a lesson to whom?

*

What Ballarat's resident commissioner needed was an ally. Instead, he had Gordon Evans.

When Evans was appointed as police inspector of Ballarat in February 1854, his appointment met with *great dissatisfaction* from both residents and the force he was to command. On first hearing the news, police officers piled their arms and refused to serve under Evans, while the GEELONG ADVERTISER labelled his appointment *a decided insult* to the inhabitants of Ballarat. At twenty-nine, Evans had already made a lifetime's worth of enemies. In March, the diggers and storekeepers of Ballarat got up a petition against the appointment, outlining instances of his past abuses of power and insisting that *no self-respecting man will submit to the control of a tyrannical Inspector*. The GEELONG ADVERTISER, reporting the signing of the petition, warned of the *rapidly increasing dangerous position of disorder* under Evans.[13] This was all before Evans and Rede began their cutthroat pas de deux. Frederick Vern later wrote that *it was the sneering conduct of Captain Evans* during the meeting to protest Scobie's murder *that was the direct cause of the burning down of the Eureka Hotel.* Evans drew heated criticism from many quarters, but the most open challenge to his fitness for office, the loudest call for the redress of wrongs inflicted by his hand came from a woman. The stone was cast by one of those troublesome non-commissioned officers' wives.

On 27 October—just eleven days after the Eureka Hotel riot and the same day that the Camp drew up plans for its defence—Mrs Catherine McLister served a written complaint to the chief commissioner of police, Captain McMahon. Catherine was the wife of Sergeant Robert McLister, who was based at the Ballarat Camp. Catherine was a twenty-eight-year-old Irish woman from County Donegal, newly married to Robert, then a clerk. Marrying down, she had arrived in Victoria in late 1853. This is what she wrote in her explosive letter to McMahon:

> I beg to state that about two months ago Capt Evans grossly insulted me a non-commissioned officer's wife by indecently expressing his person in his own room and also by his frequent visits to my tent in the absence of my husband.[14]

Catherine was clearly literate and unfazed by the bureaucracy of sin. As the second daughter of William Fenton, a member of the Northern Irish Protestant gentry and the governor at the jail in Lifford, a British army garrison, she had been raised on a diet of discipline and punishment.

Captain McMahon took Catherine's complaint with due gravity. He investigated her claim and found that *the explanation forwarded by the Inspector of Police was insufficient.* McMahon came to Ballarat and assembled a board to hear evidence from both parties. The board was comprised of Police Magistrate Charles Hackett, a Protestant Irish barrister with a splendid set of blond whiskers, Police Magistrate Evelyn Pitfield Shirley Sturt, the East India man who took over from D'Ewes after his dishonourable discharge, and Robert Rede. Hackett and Sturt had both served on the board of enquiry into the burning of the Eureka Hotel. Sturt would go on to serve as a member of the royal commission on the ill-fated Burke and Wills expedition. The three men made for a formidable inquisition.

The board of enquiry sat on 28 October. Catherine's original letter was read aloud. Then Gordon Evans came out swinging. He wholly disputed Catherine's claim of impropriety. He did craftily admit *that a certain degree of familiarity has existed between us* but said that he had *always considered that that familiarity was sought for by her.* But Catherine was not intimidated by the suggestion of her implied consent to Evans' familiarities. Before the board, with Evans present, Catherine gave this extraordinary testimony:

> I was working at my tent. Mr Evans came down and asked me to sew a few buttons on his shirt. I told him to send them by his servant. He said the servant was busy and asked me to go for them. He said if he was not there I should find them on the table. I said if my husband will allow me, I will go. I asked my husband who had no objection—this was in

> the evening not dark about 4. I went to Mr Evans and he shut the door and locked it—I did not know it was locked until it had occasion to be opened. He pointed out the shirts...Mr Evans came behind me and put his arm round my waist. He was dressed, the front of his pantaloons were open and his person exposed...Mr Evans did not use any violence when he put his arm round my waist. He said 'look at this' and then I saw his trousers were undone.

Catherine was not finished. *I was always suspicious of Mr Evans, from the way he looked at me*, she said, *he was very often down at my tent. I often would not answer him. He came when he knew my husband was off the camp as he had given him leave.* She distrusted his motives, she said, but never thought he would accost her.

The offence had taken place two months earlier. Catherine had not told anybody, including her husband. She was coming forward now, she said, because her husband had recently been arrested and mistreated by Evans, which, she believed, was because she had not *complied with Mr Evans desire.*

Perhaps Catherine was also inspired to action by a meeting of fifteen thousand members of the digging community who had gathered on 22 October—five days before the date of her complaint—at Bakery Hill to raise funds for the defence of McIntyre and Fletcher. At the meeting, the people had passed a resolution condemning the *daily violation of the personal liberty of the subject.* Did Catherine see a parallel between the scape-goating of McIntyre and Fletcher and her husband's susceptibility to Evans' wrath? Did she equate the violation of her own body with the liberal agenda of the mass body politic? Did she liken male predation and female vulnerability to the autocratic misrule that was clearly occurring on both sides of the Camp's white picketed perimeter? Perhaps she was simply a wrathful woman responding to the anger in the air. Perhaps Evans was simply a letch, and Ballarat's culture of complaint gave Catherine licence to warn him off for good.

Next Evans cross-examined Catherine. She acknowledged that she had been in Evans' room several times, in order to do small jobs for him, with her husband's permission. Evans had never before *insulted* her. He had *joked but was tartly answered.* Nothing a girl who had grown up in a garrison town could not handle. Evans had often been to her tent, but was never admitted. *I positively deny that any improper familiarity existed between myself and Mr Evans*, she told the board firmly.

Mrs Elizabeth Crowther, another officer's wife, came forward as a witness. Mrs Crowther was often in Mrs McLister's tent because *it was more comfortable than mine* and *for the sake of company.* She testified that *[Catherine] never told me that Mr Evans had taken any liberties with her, but she seemed to be afraid of being with Mr Evans alone.* Robert Kane, servant to Evans, swore that Mrs McLister had previously been to the captain's room to put buttons on his shirts but *I never saw her look excited* when she left. Would 'looking excited' be a good thing or a bad thing, though? A sign of guilty pleasure or of furious indignation?

Catherine herself cross-examined the witnesses, who could not fault her character. Only one witness, Sergeant Major Robert Milne, hinted at a motivation for Catherine to make a false claim: that Evans had put her husband under arrest and that he had overheard Captain McLister say that *somebody would have to pay for it.* Evans swooped on this logic, claiming that the *vindictive motives of the prosecution were self evident.*

The board deliberated briefly before declaring that Catherine's charge could not be supported. The decision was unanimous. Rede might have made use of the occasion in the war against his rival; he chose not to. The board's reasoning was that Catherine had not told anyone about the incident at the time, not even her *intimate friend* Mrs Crowther. Surely an offended woman would admit the source of her shock to another woman. Further, the board found it improbable that such *a gross insult*—Evans flashing his John Thomas—would not occasion a woman to cry for help.

> That the impulse of the moment would naturally have led to exclamation on the part of Mrs McLister, which must have been heard, on the contrary the shirts alluded to were taken away by Mrs McLister for the purpose required.

So, if Catherine had made a more womanly scene—throwing the shirts up in the air and running from the room shrieking—she might have been believed. But having calmly instigated an official enquiry, she found her claim dismissed as vexatious.

The McLister incident was not quietly dismissed as a quaint colonial bedroom farce. The board's decision was forwarded to Governor Hotham in Melbourne. In the context of other recent acts of rebelliousness in Ballarat, Catherine's stand might have been viewed as yet more evidence of the mounting tension, antagonism and complex web of deceit of which His Excellency needed to be kept abreast. A woman taking senior officials to task—the inspector of police, no less—was further proof that the entire Ballarat population was disorderly and ungovernable and thus required a firm hand.

On 6 November, Hotham appended a note to the McLister file with his characteristic brevity: *The Report of the Board is conclusive*. That the complainant was a woman may have been another factor in keeping close tabs on the intra-Camp skirmish. Men who made a fuss in the Camp could be dealt with by their immediate hierarchical superiors. But wives like Catherine McLister were not servants of the state; only their husbands could discipline them. And if their husbands could not?

Trouble.

*

There are few traces of Mrs Catherine McLister other than the transcripts of her day in court and her death certificate, which reveals that she died during the birth of her first child, James, in March 1858 in Geelong. By this time, Robert McLister's profession was listed as *gold digger*, indicating that his wife's principled action may have cost him his job.[15] Catherine had suffered from consumption for over four years and the official cause of her death was *phthisis larengis*, throat lesions caused by acute tuberculosis. Baby James died of *debility* eleven days later. It's unclear why Catherine and Robert chose to migrate to Victoria (her health? his career? the recent deaths of her father and sister?), whether her upbringing in County Donegal nurtured an insubordinate spirit or how a well-heeled woman felt about living in a wind-blown tent at the arse-end of the colonial world. But there is no doubt that Catherine's official complaint was a radical act of disclosure: her way of saying *look at this*.

There are many unanswered questions around Catherine's courageous decision to haul a police inspector before a judicial board. But the case clearly demonstrates two important points. First, her vocal opposition to being manhandled by Evans shows that while the Camp may have been a bastion of power and privilege—male privilege—it was not an exclusively male domain. It was a civil base camp-cum-garrison that housed women alongside their partners. They walked its muddy corridors, slept under its canvas ceilings, serviced its masters and provided corporeal fodder for the fantasies and responsibilities of men. Catherine's presence lends another perspective to the mood and motivation of the Camp when faced with threats of attack from the rebellious digging population. Yes, the Camp represented an *ancien regime* sandbagging itself against the tides of democratic change: the Camp was 'The Man', and the diggers and storekeepers believed it was time to stick it to The Man. But the Camp was also an isolated and physically vulnerable outpost of imperial authority, in which husbands daily feared for the safety of their wives and children. Both from enemies without, and, it appears, from within. The presence of women at the Camp restores some of the humanity to the men on the offensive side of the Stockade, even crude bullies like Evans.[16]

Second, in witnessing the power struggles in a gendered world, we come to realise that the Camp was not a unified, harmonious entity—as its cosily inclusive label might suggest. The battles being fought on the Ballarat diggings were not so black and white as the conventional 'miners versus military' line-up implies. Rather, tensions around ethnicity, rank and sex fuelled internal resentments, even while, as Samuel Huyghue described, the commissioners maintained an *aristocratic and exclusive front, tricked out in scraps of braid and gold lace…and often redolent of perfume…faithful to the prescriptions of caste.* Once the crack appears—and Catherine McLister's public defiance of abusive relationships of authority constitutes such a fissure—we can begin to prise open the surprisingly brittle front of goldfields officialdom.

*

If Chief Commissioner McMahon in Melbourne could see the writing on the tatty canvas walls, he should have paid heed to just one line in the barrage of correspondence issuing from the Camp. On 25 September, Captain Evans warned *I have not accommodation beyond my own complement of men for any emergency that may arise.* Three weeks later Bentley's Hotel was a pile of cinders and the whole miserable, maudlin, mutinous Camp was under siege. Or, more precisely, it was in the grip of a siege mentality, as not a single stone had yet been hurled in the Camp's direction. But the mere scent of a digger revolt rising up from the Flat, compounded by internal chaos, was enough to frighten the horses.

On 24 October, a company of twenty-eight mounted troops from the 40th Regiment arrived in Ballarat, led by the veteran warrior Captain Thomas. Four days later, two more companies, one from the 40th, one from the 12th Regiment, marched from Melbourne to the already swollen Camp. Defending the Camp meant strengthening its numbers. By the month's end, there were over 260 members of the military concertinaed into a few rows of ragged tents. The population of the Camp had tripled in a matter of weeks.

As the pre-summer temperature began to climb, so the pressure of living cheek by jowl intensified. The whole situation is reminiscent of that classic scene from the Marx Brothers movie *A Night at the Opera*, when the stowaway Groucho is hiding in a tiny ship's bolthole. People keep knocking on his door—a porter, a maid, another Marx brother—and he stuffs them into his cabin like sardines. *Make that two, no, make that three hard boiled eggs*, he says to the waiter outside the door, trying to keep up with the swelling numbers. Critical mass is finally reached, and when a newcomer opens the door, the whole heaving contingent spews out in a flume of cascading bodies and luggage and lunch.

High camp.

ELEVEN

CROSSING THE LINE (REPRISE)

November. There is no turning back the clock of 1854. Whatever aspirations you might have had for this bright year either have been happily realised or are about to become history in the headlong rush towards Yuletide. It's still hard to fathom that your Christmas dinner will be consumed under the blaze of the southern sun, with these desiccated trees shedding their lizard-skin bark and the green of mistletoe replaced by dung-brown grasses that spit and fizz if they catch a wayward ember. You know bushfire is a steadfast threat. An inferno sped through this time last year, leaving its wake of black char here. And then, just like that, so soon, new green shoots like a graveyard of insolent asparagus. There are clouds of dust in place of the snowy blanket that enveloped your childhood Christmases.

Perhaps, like young Scotsman Alexander Dick, you have just travelled the road to Ballarat and arrived at this place, with its electric crackle of anticipation and agitation. *A very mutinous and excited spirit prevalent*, wrote Alexander in his diary after walking from Geelong and pitching his tent on the Eureka Lead, *ripe for an explosion.* It makes you tingle with a delicious shiver of hope and dread.

Or perhaps you thought you'd be long gone by now, sailed

back over the seas, back home, transformed, triumphant. It would make you cry, then, to think of another long year of fruitless toil and bottomless yearning, earning not even enough for a ticket home. Or perhaps you are one of the many who found a mate this spring and *got spliced*; the new year will bring your first child.

One thing is certain. The time has passed to wait submissively, to wait and see whether the intimations and pleas and petitions and letters and now, since Bentley's, the explosive grass fires of public protest will nudge a mulish government over the line of reform. The time has come to take command of events. The time has come to harness the energies of an agitated and anxious multitude and steer them towards an early resolution.

In a poem called 'The Wise Resolve' that Ellen Young published in the BALLARAT TIMES, she put words in the mouth of a hypothetically redeemed Governor Hotham:

> Those lubberly boys—vagabond diggers—
> Toil all day, like so many niggers;
> Like niggers I'll drive them, and force them to do
> Whatever I choose, or have mind to do…[But]
> As there's among them doctors and tailors,
> Parsons and clerks, there's sure to be sailors
> Tell them to pipe hands and choose their own crew,
> Their rights to protect, as freemen should do.[1]

Time to choose your own crew. Time for the Pollywogs to take over the ship. Time to cross the line.

*

If you're going to draw a line the question will inevitably arise: which side are you on?

Sarah Hanmer was among the first of Ballarat's prominent citizens to nail her colours to the mast. After the arrests of Andrew McIntyre and Thomas Fletcher for the burning of the Bentleys' hotel, a 'monster meeting' was called for 22 October. Over ten thousand people gathered at Bakery Hill to hear thirty-year-old John Basson Humffray, twenty-four-year-old Henry Holyoake and twenty-seven-year-old Thomas Kennedy—all men with Chartist connections—deliver rousing speeches about the infringement of rights daily occurring at Ballarat. *We are worse off than either Russian serf or American slave!!* was how the BALLARAT TIMES framed the problem. Nothing short of the removal of the Camp officials who so flagrantly abused their offices would resolve the matter. The speakers called on the government to muck out their own stables before the people of Ballarat were forced to make a clean sweep themselves.

The ashes of the Eureka Hotel fire lay as unadorned proof of the might of the people if justice was denied them. But still, at this stage, the TIMES predicted that the collective angst would settle down into *a quiet constitutional agitation*, argued with moral not physical force, and fought on the twin issues of taxation and representation.[2] A Diggers Rights Society was thereby established to keep the Camp honest, and Holyoake called for subscriptions to help pay for the legal defence of McIntyre and Fletcher.

It was behind this cause, the Diggers Defence Fund, that Sarah Hanmer threw her considerable energies. She announced a benefit to be held at the Adelphi Theatre on 26 October. At the end of the monster meeting three cheers were raised for the recently defunct GOLD DIGGERS' ADVOCATE to be re-established; three groans were given for the turncoat ARGUS; and *three cheers and one more for the kindness of Mrs Hanmer* for her benefit at the Adelphi.[3] Sarah's theatre had earned the status of the Fifth

Estate. The printing presses at Clara Seekamp's home might be giving voice to the people, but Sarah Hanmer's business was providing the stage for action as well as filling the war chest.

Apart from natural justice, there was another reason to give financial succour to those arbitrarily fingered for the Eureka Hotel fire. McIntyre's twenty-six-year-old wife, Christina, was heavily pregnant with their second child. This fact has never before been revealed, yet it is an important piece of evidence in that McIntyre's family situation would have been germane to the communal outrage over his arrest. It was common practice—almost a point of honour—for diggers to rally around the impoverished wife of a fellow miner after he was gaoled for being unlicensed.

Andrew McIntyre and Christina (née Winton) arrived in Victoria from their native Scotland on the *Success* in 1852. Their first child, James, was born at sea. By October 1854, Christina was seven months pregnant with their son Thomas, who would be born on 15 February. With her twenty-five-year-old husband committed for trial on 6 November in Geelong, Christina was left alone with her troubles. To add insult to injury, many people believed Andrew McIntyre was one of the few present at the riot who was actually trying to save the hotel property and its inhabitants. Even Assistant Commissioner Amos, who was stationed at Eureka and knew its diggers better than anyone, testified in McIntyre's defence.

Thomas Kennedy, who spoke at the monster meeting, was himself married with four children. And John 'Yorkey' Westoby, tried along with McIntyre and Fletcher, would be married to his sweetheart Margaret Stewart in 1855. Thomas Fletcher, twenty-five, was a single man, but he was intimately connected with the social and commercial world of Ballarat. By late 1854, Fletcher had, with Charles and George Evans, established the Criterion

Printing Office located opposite the Adelphi Theatre. As well as printing all Sarah Hanmer's playbills, the Criterion was also responsible for producing the posters for the monster meetings on Bakery Hill. Significantly, these posters rallied together *the diggers, storekeepers and inhabitants of Ballarat generally.* We, the people.

Fletcher, wrote Charles Evans in his diary, *is about the last man I should have thought likely to take part in such a proceeding and besides this I knew from several circumstances that he was like myself nothing more than a passive spectator.* The arbitrary nature of the arrests left the thousands of bystanders with a there-but-for-the-grace-of-god shudder.

The Eureka population was starting to coalesce around its sense of grievance and Sarah Hanmer had the capital, resources and heart to mobilise the community. Christina McIntyre reaped the advantage of this unwritten social contract in a way that Catherine Bentley, who was also pregnant with a toddler, and now homeless to boot, would not. Catherine had, according to popular assumption, crossed the line to the dark side: to bureaucratic corruption and its attendent privileges. In the moral economy of gold seeking, this would not do. It was acceptable to get rich through hard work and luck, but not through graft and influence.

At the Adelphi, Sarah hung out her star-spangled flag for the disenfranchised miners. Her benefit for the Diggers Defence Fund was a corker. The event was *of literally great benefit to the fund*, reported the GEELONG ADVERTISER, *Mrs Hanmer's liberality and characteristic style of acting in the piece of the evening (*The Stranger*) which she had made her own, were fully appreciated.*[4] On a hot and sultry night, the same night that reinforcements from the 40th Regiment rolled into town, Sarah and her troupe played to *a respectable and crowded house*. Charles Evans was present and noted the animating effect the event had on the community. *Mrs Hanmer*, Charles wrote,

> gave up her theatre for their benefit and *The Stranger* was performed to a crowded house, and in fact throughout the diggings there seemed to be but one feeling, a warm sympathy for Fletcher & McIntyre and deep indignation at the conduct of the Authorities.

Sarah's benefit raised over £70. The success of the event, and no doubt the amount of press it garnered, prompted other theatre managers—Mr Hetherington at the Royal and Mr Clarke at the Queen's—to quickly follow suit. Sarah Hanmer held several more benefits for the diggers' cause during November. By the time it was all over, she had contributed more money to the popular rights movement than any other citizen.

*

If the crew up at the Camp had been on their game instead of worrying over the cut of their trousers, they would have been keeping a close eye on the Adelphi and its high-flying prima donna. Back in August, a seemingly routine event occurred that would have a lasting effect on the future of Ballarat's power dynamics. Frank Carey, a twenty-four-year-old boarding-house keeper from Orange County, New York, was arrested on a sly-grog charge. Carey was tried at the Ballarat Petty Sessions court on 25 August for *selling spirituous liquors without a licence* at his Excelsior Boarding House, and fined £50. Nothing unusual there. Then Carey was charged again on 18 September. Rumour had it that Carey had been framed by the roundly detested Police Sergeant Major Robert Milne. For his second offence, Carey received a sentence of six months in the vermin-infested Ballarat lockup.

Now there was outrage. Seventeen hundred people signed a petition praying for executive clemency in the case, on the grounds that there had been no violation in the second instance. The petition was signed by all of the ten boarders at the Excelsior, including Henry Holyoake, Robert Burnett and A. W. Arnold. The petitioners claimed that Carey was an upstanding, law-abiding fellow *whose house had never been the scene of any disorderly or riotous conduct whatsoever.*[5] Why, the only thing out of the ordinary at Mr Carey's house was his *nigger cook*. And even that wasn't so exceptional. Charles and George Evans also employed a white-haired old Aboriginal fellow to prepare their meals

What is noteworthy about the petition, apart from the huge number of signatories, is the fact that it was almost certainly written by a woman—Mary Stevens. Again, this is information that has never before come to light, though it's not difficult to deduce, since Mary's careful handwriting tops the list of signatures. But who was Mary Stevens? Both she and A. W. Arnold were employed at the Adelphi Theatre: they were actors, noted for their fine performances in Sarah Hanmer's productions. Arnold was also a witness to the burning of Bentley's Hotel, and Robert Burnett, a fellow American working as a barber, has been credited as the man who fired the first shot in the 'Ballarat War'.[6] It's unclear whether Mary Stevens and the incarcerated Frank Carey were in a romantic relationship when Mary took it upon herself to orchestrate his liberation. If they were, it didn't last. Frank Carey married nineteen-year-old German-born immigrant Dorette Hahn in 1855. Their only child, Francis, was born in September 1856, by which stage Carey was a fully licensed hotelkeeper.

Any government spy worth his salt would have realised that the Adelphi Theatre had become the primary nucleus of radicalism over the winter of 1854. Digger activists could gripe and moan and rally and plot and plan in the open air, around their shafts or the campfire at night, but rabble-rousing was warmer, drier and less susceptible to pricked ears within the confines of a spacious tent-cum-theatre guarded by a trustworthy collaborator. The Adelphi was a safe house, presided over by Mrs Hanmer, a respectable widow and acclaimed theatrical manager. She provided a refuge for the disaffected, with whose cause she clearly sympathised. After Carey was arrested the second time, Mrs Hanmer gave a benefit to raise funds for his release. While the Jews of Ballarat kvetched and prayed at the Clarendon Hotel (it was there they formed a minyan prior to the erection of the first synagogue in 1861), the Germans drank and caroused at the Wiesenhavern Brothers' Prince Albert Hotel on Bakery Hill and the Irish centred their activities at Father Smyth's St Alipius tent church, Mrs Hanmer presented the Americans with a velvet-curtained front. Another of Sarah's actors, Frank D'Amari, later attested that *most of the principal players in bringing justice to Bentley* were Americans.[7] It was the Americans, he said, who called for Bentley's lynching.

But here was the crucial rub. The American community of Victoria formed a large and prosperous class of merchants and entrepreneurs. In January 1854, Freeman Cobb, John Murray Peck, John Lamber and James Swanton established the American Telegraph Line of Coaches, later to be known as Cobb and Co. The company ran coaches that linked all the major goldfields with Melbourne and with each other. This transport network was crucial to pastoral and commercial expansion in Victoria. In Melbourne, George Francis Train, Henry Nicholls and others were presiding over prosperous mercantile businesses with links to large international financiers. Train was the major backer of Cobb and Co. as well as the Australian correspondent to the BOSTON GLOBE. A goldfields fracas involving an American citizen, then, was a tricky affair: a delicate balancing act of diplomacy between local affairs and the bigger picture of American influence. And it was for this reason that twenty-one-year-old Mary Stevens' petition, with its lengthy trail of signatures, went straight to the top of the government's in-tray.

Chief Commissioner McMahon wrote to Robert Rede on 3 October, enclosing a copy of the petition and requesting immediate clarification from the magistrates as to whether any grounds existed for His Excellency's clemency. This was definitely not standard operating procedure. Matters became still more peculiar when the American consul in Melbourne, James Tarleton, made representations to Governor Hotham on behalf of the Ballarat boarding-house keeper Carey. He vouched that the Americans at Ballarat were *law loving and law abiding citizens.*[8] On 29 October, Frank Carey's sentence was remitted. Mrs Hanmer's players: take a bow. Your encore is yet to come.

*

Governor Hotham made two deft moves in response to the burning of Bentley's Hotel. With the right hand, he empowered a select committee to investigate the matter, taking evidence from any person who wished to speak up. E. P. S. Sturt was to head it up, fresh from presiding over Catherine McLister's sexual harassment hearing. With the left hand, Hotham ordered the extra companies of the 12th and 40th regiments to fill the Camp with redcoats. It seemed an ingenious plan. Give the people the chance to vent their collective spleen while making it obvious that Ballarat was now awash with a military presence. Not everyone was convinced, however, that Hotham had Ballarat's best interests at heart. *We ask for bread and we get a stone*, wrote the Ballarat correspondent to the GEELONG ADVERTISER. *We demand some attention be paid to our miserable conditions and get sent an army.*[9]

The committee took evidence at Bath's Hotel from 2 November to 10 November. The weather was oppressively hot during this week, and hundreds of diggers availed themselves of the opportunity to sit for a while in the lounge bar and tell the commissioners about what ailed them. Women gave evidence too, including Mrs Joanna Bath, though their testimony didn't make it into the published report that was tabled in parliament on 21 November. The commissioners' job was to establish whether there were any grounds for supposing that *improper motives* influenced the magistrates in their exoneration of James Bentley for Scobie's murder, and also whether the conduct of the officers of the Camp generally had been such *as to inspire respect and confidence amongst the population*. When the enquiry was completed, the answers were no and yes. This would not be popular news.

But there was a concession. Both James and Catherine Bentley, along with their servants Hance and Farrell, had been rearrested in the middle of October and sent to Melbourne for trial. And now, as another sop to the offended diggers, John D'Ewes and Robert Milne were relieved of their duties. Still this did not satisfy the irate residents of Ballarat. Many believed the wrong men had copped it. *This affair will make Ballarat too hot for Mr Johnstone in a short time*, wrote the GEELONG ADVERTISER; *the sooner he is shifted the better.*[10] James Johnston continued to receive threats to his life and liberty after the commission cleared him. (Maggie's diary reveals nothing of the pressure-cooker tensions of November.) Robert Rede and Gordon Evans were also absolved of any wrongdoing. Meanwhile, John D'Ewes refused to go quietly. He protested his honesty and integrity until the last, all the while claiming that every other senior official in the Camp was nothing more than a money-grubbing land speculator tricked out in brass buttons and government-issue bayonets.

At least D'Ewes no longer had to fret about his accommodation. That was left to those remaining in Camp. The second half of Hotham's plan was about as efficacious as the first. The arrival of the extra troops meant squashing more stinky little fish into an already overpacked tin. *Every corner of the Camp is taken up in attempting to accommodate the men and horses now poured in on us*, wrote the Ballarat correspondent to the GEELONG ADVERTISER, *the men are stored away anywhere under cover and the horses are tied to a fence. Neither the men nor the officers pull well together.*[11] The fear of attack, underpinned by Captain Thomas's new plan of defence, meant that soldiers and police were on twenty-four-hour patrols. From the outside, it seemed like the tightrope was about to snap.

On 2 November, a fight broke out in the Camp between the police and the military. Without this skirmish, the BALLARAT TIMES reported facetiously, *we should have little to talk about*. The rumour spread that a group of soldiers had assaulted some police and the affair had been quickly hushed up. Nine days later, a soldier resident at the Camp wrote an anonymous letter to the editor of the BALLARAT TIMES. He complained of the conditions endured by his company on their recent march from Melbourne to Ballarat. (This means the letter's author arrived with either the 40th Regiment on 24 October or the 12th on 28 October.) His detachment was on short rations, receiving only a pound of bread and a pound of meat daily. They were forced to spend two nights on the road without a tent or any bedding *as if to inure us to the anticipated campaign with the diggers*. With the *inadequate remuneration* of only two shillings a day, *the soldier is unjustly dealt with*, complained the man.[12] Who did he think might read the paper and champion the soldiers' cause? The military leadership? The diggers, who were so intent on their own just treatment and might extend some brotherly love? His fellow soldiers, who might unite in a little rebellion of their own?

*

While the Camp was busy chewing off its own leg, the diggers were getting organised. *A few minutes are quite sufficient at any time to get a crowd together*, noted the GEELONG ADVERTISER of the particular mood of urgency and apprehension that now gripped Ballarat. On 1 November, five thousand people gathered on the Gravel Pits and passed a resolution to form a league with diggers from other goldfields. The object of the league would be the *attainment of the moral and social rights of the diggers*. Around the speakers platform were placed English, Scots, Irish, French and United States national flags. A German band played. Henry Holyoake, Thomas Kennedy and George Black spoke for over four hours. The Camp was under arms this whole time, with sentries posted from dusk to dawn. American consul James Tarleton was in town, at the behest of Ballarat's American community, who put on *an American dinner* in his honour at the Adelphi. Tarleton asked to address the meeting about the Carey affair. This odd gesture was, perhaps, a pre-emptive move to ward off a growing insinuation of favouritism towards the Americans, especially after charges of arson were dropped against young Yankee digger Albert Hurd, who had also been arrested after the Eureka

Hotel fire. It was rumoured that Hurd's release was influenced by back-room deals that were *half American, half Masonic.*[13]

The Gravel Pits meeting proved to be a warm-up for the events that would now tumble like dominoes towards their catastrophic resolution.

On 11 November 1854, a scorching hot Saturday, ten thousand people met at Bakery Hill to witness the foundation of the Ballarat Reform League. Canadian miner-turned-carrier Alpheus Boynton was there and noted in his diary the *talented men* who put down picks and pans and *took their stand upon the platform, not to fire the people with a rebellious spirit but a spirit of resistance to oppression, to claim their rights as men.* The Ballarat Reform League united the proto-societies that had been popping up over the previous weeks, an Irish union here, a German *bund* there.

The reform league elected its office bearers: English Chartists John Basson Humffray as president and George Black as secretary. Irishman Timothy Hayes, husband of the Catholic teacher Anastasia, was appointed as chairman. Humffray, Kennedy and the Hanoverian miner Frederick Vern addressed the meeting. They drafted a document—the Ballarat Reform League Charter—that committed to ink the chief grievances and goals of the league. A manifesto of democratic principles, its primary tenets were: free and fair representation in parliament; manhood suffrage; the removal of property qualifications for members of the Legislative Council; salaries for members of parliament; and fixed parliamentary terms. Thus the aim of moral rights for the disenfranchised goldfields population (dignity, equity, justice) was codified into a standard template of Chartist-inspired political rights.

The Bakery Hill meeting of 11 November is now widely

touted as the first formal step on the march to Australian parliamentary democracy. In 2006, the 'Diggers Charter' was inducted into the UNESCO Memory of the World register of significant historical documents. Yet oddly enough, the BALLARAT TIMES makes only brief—if bombastic—mention of this monster meeting. *It must never be forgotten in the future of this great country,* wrote Henry Seekamp, *that on Saturday, November 11 1854, on Bakery Hill, and in the presence of about ten thousand men, was first proposed and unanimously adopted, the draft prospectus of Australian Independence.* A lengthy letter to the editor from Ellen Young takes up the rest of the edition.

The ten thousand who witnessed the formation of the league that day were not, of course, all men. Women and children were among the crowd, and it was Ellen Young who once again chose to represent the voice of the whole people in Ballarat's only newspaper. In her letter Ellen highlighted the collective nature of popular disaffection on the goldfields. This is what she had to say:

> However we may lament great misdeeds in high places, justice must be awarded to the universal demand of an indignant people—the diseased limbs of the law must be lopped off or mortification will ensue the whole body. Thus would I speak to our Governor…Oh Sir Charles, we had better hopes of you! We, the people, demand cheap land, just magistrates, to be represented in the Legislative Council, in fact treated as the free subjects of a great nation.

Not 'request'. Not 'humbly pray'. *Demand.* And it is not Kennedy, not Black, not Holyoake, Humffray, nor Vern who committed their name to a declaration so inflammatory, so presumptuous, but Ellen Frances Young. No pseudonym. No anonymity. Others had publicly spoken of *cleaning out* but none had gone so far as *lopping off*. The irony of the gender inversion was not lost on Ellen herself. *Is there not one man, Mr Editor, to insist on the above demands?* she provoked. *And if refused, let us demand them of England.*

Ellen's indictment of masculine courage and foresight was printed on 18 November, the first edition of the TIMES to be published after the Bakery Hill monster meeting. It is likely that this edition was in fact edited and published by Clara Seekamp, who used her editorial influence to propel Ellen's equally radical departure from feminine rectitude into the public eye. When Clara's common-law husband was subsequently tried for sedition, the editions in question were those printed on 18 and 25 November, and 2 December. Henry Seekamp argued in his defence that he was not responsible for the management of the paper at that time. Later scholars have speculated that John Manning, a teacher who worked at St Alipius with Anastasia Hayes, or George Dunmore Lang, the embezzling bank manager, may have been the true authors of the seditious articles. It is more probable that the highly literate and intelligent Clara had her finger on the pulse and the pen of the newspaper that was issued from her house. As we shall see, it was widely acknowledged that she took over editing the paper following Henry Seekamp's arrest in early December.

Clara and Ellen may have had good reason to feel hostile towards their fellow freedom fighters. The Ballarat Reform League was constituted as a membership organisation, with a one-shilling entrance fee and a sixpence per week subscription. Significantly, the membership was to be gender exclusive. It's not clear exactly who wrote the association's rules, but the effect was to turn Ellen's *people* into Boynton's *men*. This is in line with the trajectory of British Chartism that saw the early goals of political equality sacrificed to a trade union model based on a male head of household supporting a dependent wife. It was a retrograde move that the unbiddable women of Ballarat strenuously resisted.

Raffaello Carboni alerts us to this drama playing out in the wings of Bakery Hill's centre stage in one of his typically obtuse asides: *Bakery reformers leagued together on its hill [No admission for the ladies at present]*. Why would Carboni specifically, if parenthetically, note the omission of women from the Ballarat Reform League's membership? In 1854, would we not assume that women were to be excluded from the formal body politic? And what to make of the qualifying phrase *at present*? So for now women cannot get a 2s ticket to the league, but, Carboni seems to imply, it is not out of the question that they will be eligible in the future.

Is this because certain women were requesting, maybe even demanding, inclusion? Was it only a matter of time before women would wear down the formalities of political convention and find themselves on an equal footing with their male co-conspirators? They were, after all, writing op-eds, topping subscription lists, starting businesses, buying property, financially supporting families, working beside their husbands on the fields, owning shares in mining ventures, speaking their minds freely, making ample use of the judicial system to assert their sovereign rights, throwing off the mantle of restrictive clothing, drinking, fornicating and otherwise behaving like perfect men.

It is the line of Latin that directly follows Carboni's reference to 'the ladies' that gives the crucial clue: *Durum sed levius fit patientia*. The reference is from Horace, *Odes* 1.24. The entire line is: *Durum: Sed levius fit patientia/Quicquid corrigere est nefas*. 'It is hard: but whatever is impossible to set right, becomes lighter by endurance.'[14]

Which ladies fought for, lost and were forced to 'endure' their struggle for political inclusion? Ellen Young? Anastasia Hayes, who later took on the Catholic Church over the issue of fair wages? Mrs Rowlands, who attended the monster meetings? Sarah Hanmer, who was contributing more coin to the Diggers Defence Fund than anyone else in Ballarat? Jane Cuming, who named her daughter Martineau after the renowned liberal philosopher and feminist? Thomas Kennedy's wife? Christina McIntyre, whose wrongfully accused husband was up on charges of arson? Fanny Smith, who in 1856 would agitate for universal municipal representation on behalf of *myself and many other ladies ambitious of a seat in the Local Legislature of Ballarat*?[15] Dorette Welge and Ellen Flemming, who in 1855 would marry Adolph Wiesenhavern and William McCrae, proprietors of the Prince Albert and Star hotels, where members of the reform league held their meetings? The wives of other nonconformist British and European radicals who had, in partnership with their husbands, travelled to Victoria to seek political refuge from the sort of conservative atavism that that would see the French revolutionary universality of *liberté, égalité, fraternité* reduced to the chauvinist dogma of the Paris Commune?[16]

It is clear that something more than manhood suffrage was envisioned by at least a vocal minority of goldfields possum-stirrers. During the Bendigo Red Ribbon Rebellion of August 1853, William Dexter took the stage to argue for *women having votes as well as men*. It was William's wife, Caroline, who would bring her bloomer costume and lectures on women's rights to Australia in January 1855. William Howitt, who witnessed William Dexter's inflammatory speech, dismissed the French-educated man's *cosmopolitan doctrines* as the *peculiarly revolting* cant of *ultra-republicans, those maniacs of revolution*.[17] But

Dexter was no raving lunatic. He would stand for the Victorian Parliament on a platform of universal suffrage in the elections of 1856, with his wife in campaign mode.

So too would a young man named Thomas Loader, who stood against John Basson Humffray in the 1856 elections for the seat of North Grant, covering East Ballarat and the Eureka Lead. Loader styled himself as a *Liberal Australian Reformer* and pledged, if elected, to introduce such reforms as are *peculiarly requisite in Australia, arranged upon liberal and progressive principles.* Loader's policies included *rights of women* but he hedged his bets about suffrage.[18] He was trounced anyway.

But such concerted public action by women, or on behalf of women by sympathetic men, constituted what the historian June Philipp has called 'both a plea and a threat'. Raising the spectre of women's political enfranchisement—their constitutional entitlement to civic rights, their elevation in status from moral compass to helmsman—cast doubt on the power and status of deeply entrenched norms of social and political behaviour. This was truly revolutionary, and the Australian people would have to wait another forty-eight years before the passage of the *Commonwealth Franchise Act* in 1902 made their nation the most democratic in the world. The internationally unprecedented legislation gave (white) women full political equality with men: the right to vote and to stand for election to parliament. America would not pass the constitutional amendment that ensured these liberties until 1920 and British women would not enjoy such rights until 1928. Aboriginal women (and men) would not be fully enfranchised until the 1960s.

*

Catherine Bentley was one woman who was definitely not clamouring for membership of the Ballarat Reform League in mid-November. The only acceptance she needed was from a jury of her peers. On 19 October, Catherine had been arrested after her former employee, Thomas Mooney, turned Queen's evidence and claimed the reward of £300 for information leading to a conviction in the Scobie murder. On 1 November Catherine was transported to Melbourne, where her husband had been apprehended.

Not everyone was thrilled by this development. There were those who, like Ellen Young, believed that the Bentleys were being unduly scapegoated for wider feelings of *envy, hatred and malice* towards the corrupt Camp officials and those they winked at. Certain merchants, storekeepers, diggers and residents of Ballarat and Melbourne got up petitions to proclaim James Bentley's good character and innocence of any crime. One of the jurors at the original inquest signed a petition to the effect that *there has been heaped on Bentley's head a greater amount of odium than he at all deserves.*[19]

But none of this could avert a show trial to demonstrate the Crown's impartiality. Catherine would have to take her starring role in the cast. Even so, a journalist for the ARGUS reported with alarm that when Catherine was conveyed by steamer from Geelong Prison to Melbourne to stand her trial, she was handcuffed all the way. Her keeper, Detective Cummings, refused *even to allow her to get dinner* regardless of the fact that she was by now seven months pregnant with her second child. *Mrs Bentley has been moving in a respectable line of life*, chided the journalist. *She is not convicted of any offence, and it is not likely that she will be.* The only cause to justify *such harsh treatment* and *cowardly brutality*, argued the journalist, was *the supposition that it was in accordance with the public feeling to heap insults on a defenceless woman.* Cummings' behaviour was *an insult to the community*, especially as the public sentiment aroused by the case evinced *not so much a virulent hatred of the alleged offenders as a mark that the people of the colony will not stand for the abuse of power and privilege by judicial authorities.*[20] Others similarly came forward to declare that 'the Bentley affair' was simply the last straw in a long line of baleful examples of disregard for the rule of law by the Ballarat authorities.

It was Justice Redmond Barry who would preside over this morality play. On 20 November there was a solar eclipse. Commentators attributed the freakishly mercurial weather—hot one minute, storms the next—to this astrological phenomenon. The packed public gallery at the Supreme Court didn't need to look into the sun to be dazzled by the strange alignment of events. Only two days before, Ann Quin had been arrested in Melbourne in connection with the Bank of Victoria robbery, Eliza Smith was brought in for all those stolen notes stuffed into her stockings and now here was another of Ballarat's daughters in the dock. And that night, another Irish Protestant Catherine, the internationally acclaimed chanteuse Catherine Hayes, would make her final appearance at the Queen's Theatre just down the road from the courts. *The lady was as rapturously encored as ever*, reported the ARGUS, *greeted with a shower of bouquets and with volleys of cheers and other manifestations of delight from the audience.*[21] Catherine Hayes was reputed to have cleared over £10,000 from her two-month tour of Sydney, Melbourne and the diggings. The only volley Catherine Bentley would receive was of jeers as she entered the court.

Three hundred diggers came to Melbourne for the Bentleys' trial, but it proved anti-climactic. The most scintillating drama occurred when Catherine was given a chair during her cross-examination in order to rest her swollen body. Dr Carr, who was there to give evidence, assessed the exhausted woman's condition and Justice Barry called an adjournment for Catherine *to have proper attention* from the doctor. (No newspaper reported that she was pregnant.) Apart from that, there were no shocks, scandals or bombshells to entertain the crowds. The circumstantial evidence was piled up against the Bentleys. The best Richard Ireland could do for the defence was to ask Mary Ann Welch whether she had any ill feeling towards Mrs Bentley that might have motivated her testimony. No, said Mary Ann. In the end, Ireland could only plead that his clients had already *suffered enough* in losing all their property and being held up to *public execration*. And he subtly pointed out that, if anything, the bulk of the evidence was ranged against Catherine Bentley. *If found guilty of this most serious charge*, Ireland told the jury, *they must expiate this accidental calamity by death, involving too the life of a woman.*

Would Catherine Bentley be the first woman to hang in Victoria? Attorney General Stawell had no qualms about such an outcome. Though the reasonable man might be *unwilling to believe that a woman had gone out to commit murder*, Stawell thundered, *the jury should lay aside all such considerations... She also seems to have rejoiced as much as anyone at the way in which the men were got rid of.*[22]

Justice Barry addressed the jury for over an hour. The jury deliberated for forty-five minutes. At 9pm on Saturday evening, as Catherine Hayes was singing her last aria, the foreman delivered the verdict. James Bentley, Farrell and Hance, guilty of manslaughter. Catherine Bentley, not guilty. (*Scot free* was how Carboni put it.) On Monday, as the sun slipped behind the moon, the men were sentenced to three years' hard labour on the roads. Catherine was released to her own version of the retributive wilderness. She would not swing, but in February she would give birth alone, to her baby Louisa. Catherine was a mother of two with no lawful means of support, and by Christmas 1855, she would be brought up on charges of illegally selling alcohol from her Maryborough refreshment tent. What a spectacular fall: from licensed victualler and owner of the largest building on the most prosperous goldfield in the world to sly grogger at an outlying diggings. The Bentley family's brief flirtation with the world of chandeliers and champagne would never be reprised. It was all downhill from here.

*

It was a busy week for Redmond Barry and Richard Ireland. On the same day that Bentley and his co-convicted were sentenced, Thomas Fletcher, Andrew McIntyre and John Westoby had their hour upon the stage. It was another show trial of sorts. The government desperately needed to save face after the Eureka Hotel riot. In the mind of the diggers' leadership, the conviction of James Bentley justified the incendiary action of the mob. The grievances at Ballarat had quickly gone from begging letters about poverty and iniquitous taxation to calls for self-government and even secession from the Crown. The ARGUS had reported Thomas Kennedy as saying in his Bakery Hill address that if the diggers did not get justice, they would *Go to the Queen of England, a simple-minded mother, far away from these her children, and ask if the child suck too long it will not injure both one and the other.*[23] (Kennedy knew what an over-sucked mother looked like: he had four small children and an enervated wife in his own tent.)

Hotham did not want to be responsible for any premature

weaning of the infant colony. But neither could he close the nursery door on the screaming baby. The howls of protest were now coming from all quarters. Even that doyenne of imperial respectability, Caroline Chisholm, was weighing in on political affairs. Mrs Chisholm had toured the diggings in November. On her return to Melbourne she made a lengthy speech to a large crowd on 17 November, the eve of the Bentley trial. She represented the miners as a fine body of men, the vast majority of whom *emphatically* possessed *heads on their shoulders, not just hands for digging*. Echoing Ellen Young, Mrs Chisholm advocated unlocking the lands to encourage more wives and families to the goldfields, and warned: *If something is not done to remove the difficulties under which these men are placed, the consequences will be terribly felt.*[24] Her lengthy speech was reprinted verbatim in the Melbourne papers.

Hotham was now eager to claw back some control of the good ship Victoria, which was veering dangerously off course. Added to the public pressure was the fact that the military reinforcement of Ballarat was costing him a fortune, precisely when London was looking for him to balance the budget: Cobb and Co. and George Francis Train alone had charged thousands of pounds to transport the extra troops to Ballarat.

In the trial of McIntyre, Fletcher and Westoby, the jury deliberated for over five hours. A defence of provocation had been mounted, citing the wrongful conduct of the Ballarat officials; Mr Justice Barry rejected it. Was it really any surprise when all three accused were found guilty of *assembling together unlawfully, riotously and tumultuously*? But the jury added a rider to the verdict: if the government at Ballarat had done *its* duty properly, the jury would never have had to perform the painful duty it had just been called upon to execute. The hushed courtroom exploded in cheering. But Barry was unmoved. He expressed particular disgust with respect to the horses that had been incinerated in the hotel blaze and sentenced Andrew McIntyre to three months in Melbourne Gaol, Fletcher to four and Westoby to six. Richard Ireland had seen six clients incarcerated in the space of two days. He would get the chance to redeem himself sooner than he knew.

*

When news reached the diggings that the Ballarat Three had been convicted, the executive of the reform league met to decide how to respond. Black and Kennedy were dispatched to Melbourne, where they met up with Humffray and made an appointment to see the governor himself. This delegation would present the concerns of the Ballarat diggers directly, including a copy of the Diggers Charter. It is a measure of the small-town intimacy of the colony, despite its recent population explosion, that the men could get an audience with His Excellency, the colonial secretary and the attorney general on Monday 27 November. (Whether Lady Hotham was party to the discussions the notaries did not record.) It was the same familiarity that had inspired Ellen Young to write to Hotham back in September, offering him her detailed ideas for an alternative licensing system.[25] It was also the source of her resentment when Hotham reneged on his promise to listen to the people. Ellen's fury is not a sign of womanly temper but a reaction to the tantalising proximity of colonial power: it was personal.

Nor did Black, Kennedy and Humffray come to the great man shaking at the knees; in fact, Hotham might have been a darned sight more amenable if they had fawned a little more.

Instead, the reform league's representatives followed Ellen Young's lead and presented Hotham with their *demands*. Black *demanded* that Fletcher, McIntyre and Westoby be released. Hotham bristled. He reminded the delegation that the Americans of Ballarat had successfully *petitioned* him for executive clemency in Carey's case. Then: *I must take my stand on the word 'demand'*, said a defensive Hotham. *I am sorry for it, but that is the position you place me in.*

The delegation did not apologise, but tried another tack. Kennedy implored Hotham to act on the diggers' grievances before blood was spilt. Black played to one of Hotham's pet concerns: bringing women to the diggings. *I am desired by the married men of Ballarat to make a request of your Excellency*, Black began.

> It is this—that every possible facility may be afforded by your Excellency to enable them to settle and have their wives and families there. They are all anxious to settle upon the land, but at present the difficulties of their so doing are too great, and I am requested to bring that subject especially before your Excellency's notice.

Hotham softened. *That is a point which presses very much*, he conceded. But he could not give an answer to take back to the married men of Ballarat, except to say that he agreed *in the necessity of some provisions being made.*

Ten days earlier Hotham had announced a commission of enquiry into the administration of the goldfields. It was to this decree that he now returned.

> Tell the Diggers from me and tell them carefully that this Commission will enquire into everything and every body, high and low, rich and poor, and you have

> only to come forward and state your grievances, and, in what relates to me they shall be redressed. I can say no more, we are all in a false position altogether.[26]

As the delegates left with pockets full of empty promises, how could they fail to notice that Hotham was *in a false position* in a mansion in leafy Toorak, while they returned to threadbare tents on a dusty goldfield.

*

The road to and from Ballarat was taking a beating in those last weeks of November. There were all the witnesses summoned to the two trials: Mary Ann and Barnard Welch, Dr Carr, the turncoat Mooney, Agnes Sinclair the nursemaid, and a slew of police happy for a night or two away from the gloom and tension at the Camp. There was the reform league's deputation, Diggers Charter in hand. There were the five hundred men and five hundred women and children still arriving each week to try their luck on the Ballarat goldfields. There was another batch of one hundred and fifty military reinforcements from the 40th Regiment sent to the Camp on 27 November, the same day Hotham took tea with the delegates.

And there were the Camp's wives and families, on the move again. Back in October, after the hotel riot, the women had been sent from Camp for their own safety. After Captain Thomas's defence plan, they returned. Following the conviction of Fletcher, McIntyre and Westoby, it was deemed prudent they leave again.

Maggie Johnston chose this occasion to resume her diary entries.

> November 22 Wednesday
>
> Went to Buninyong to the Allens. Mrs Lane and

> I—our first flight from camp.
>
> November 23 Thursday
> Spent an anxious day. Nothing happened to our beloveds.
>
> November 24 Friday
> Passed much in the same way. Still anxious. Had a letter from dear Jamie.
>
> November 25 Saturday
> My dearie came for us and we got safely back. Found everything alright.
>
> November 26 Sunday
> Was poorly, in bed. Dear Jamie went to church alone.
>
> November 27 Monday to December 2 Saturday
> Every day this week most anxious as the diggers threatened all sorts of horrid things. All the ladies out of camp—out myself.

*

Elizabeth Massey was at the Queen's Theatre to see Catherine Hayes' final performance. She concurs that the singer was indeed showered with nuggets, sovereigns and bouquets; it was said Hayes took £800 that night. But the festivities were rudely interrupted.

> Our gaieties were rather suddenly put a stop to by our friends' anxiety to return home in consequence of the frightful and exaggerated reports which were daily arriving in rapid succession from the country, of an outbreak at Ballarat.

That night, a rumour spread that the Camp had been burnt down. Another report said the whole 40th Regiment was going up. The gossip was exaggerated, but a deployment was certainly on the move. They would first sail to Geelong, gather reinforcements and head up to Ballarat from there. Mrs Massey and her friends went to see off the troops. At the docks, she expected to find doleful faces, but was flabbergasted at the celebratory atmosphere.

> I think I never saw a more joyous party. They reminded me of happy schoolboys bound for some party of pleasure, yet kept in unwilling restraint by the eye of the master...many were bestriding the guns, and otherwise testifying their satisfaction at the prospect of a fight.

Happy schoolboys. Unwilling restraint. The prospect of a fight.

Arriving at the barracks, Mrs Massey found an altogether different scene.

> The women and children, who had turned out to see the departure of their husbands and fathers, were weeping and bewailing their sad lot in not being allowed to follow them, and kind people were doing their best to console, seemingly to no purpose, these disconsolate ones.

The only solace, surmised Mrs Massey, was that the regimental wives didn't have *poverty to bear as well as loneliness*. But for some in the embrace of Her Majesty's service, there would never be compensation for the eternal grief about to descend.

*

Thursday 28 November was Thanksgiving. Turkey Day. Always keen to celebrate their nation's holidays, the American community on the diggings prepared to feast. Expat Yankees drank bourbon and sang patriotic songs, in each other's tents or at a grand ball. A lavish dinner was staged at Brandt and Hirschler's Victoria Hotel at Red Hill. The proprietors had *gone the whole hog*, providing *a perfect legion of delicacies* for the seventy men who dined from 8pm to 2am.[27] A band played 'The Star Spangled Banner', 'God Save the Queen' and 'La Marseillaise'. James Tarleton accepted an invitation to attend. So did Robert Rede, who welcomed the occasion to cement good relations with Ballarat's most prominent Americans.

Popular discontent was at its apex. In every quarter—the pub, the field, the store, the campfire, the theatre, the church—people stopped *to discuss the theory of political relationships*, as the GEELONG ADVERTISER put it. Thomas Pierson was more specific. At the daily stump meetings being held, people *speak openly in unmeasured terms against that old scamp the Governor and nearly all in office. [They] urge people to declare Independence.* One speaker Pierson heard said if all the people would just assert their rights and claim *a Republican Government*, then we could *stand here as Proud as any of the sons of America.* The agitators, noted Pierson, *seem determined to make Australia free.*

To Rede and his fellow upholders of Australia's peculiar ancien régime of squattocracy and imperial monarchy, such talk did not come cheap. Another monster meeting at Bakery Hill had been placarded for tomorrow, the 29th, and it was rumoured that a formal declaration of independence would be made. On the goldfields, Yankee-style freedom signalled frontier lawlessness: Lynch Law, the law of the bowie knife.

A recent incident in Ballarat had confirmed what a Yankee

justice system might look like. In August, American digger Robert Clarke was playing cards at the Albion Hotel with three cronies. They were playing for 'nobblers' (shots of spirits). Clarke refused to follow suit in one trick, causing a dispute with a digger called Van Winkler, who accused Clarke of cheating. Clarke backed down, but in the following hand threatened to blow out the brains of any man who disrupted the play. Van Winkler told Clarke that *a man that sat down to play on his friends and could not play without cheating was no man at all.* Clarke pulled out his pistol and fired. The bullet missed Van Winkler, whistled through a canvas wall and killed Kosman Berand, who was asleep in a cot. Mrs O'Kell, the landlady, whipped out her own pistol, while the diggers and musicians in the hotel wrestled Clarke to the ground.

On 28 October, Clarke was found guilty of manslaughter and sentenced to seven years on the road.[28] If it had happened on the American frontier, Clarke would have wiped the blood from the cards and continued his hand as the musicians picked up the tune and Berand was dragged out to the pigs. The American frontier was Robert Rede's idea of hell.

Lone ranger vigilance committees were one thing, but republican yearnings were quite another. There had always been a concern among some British bystanders at how quickly Victoria was becoming *Americanized.* It was a love–hate relationship. In George Francis Train's assessment, the colonial government admired the indomitable energy, entrepreneurial ingenuity, *can-do spirit* and brash confidence of the American immigrants, but was less comfortable with the fact that Americans had *no truck with 'the word'.* The American disrespect for constituted authority seemed to be rubbing off on the digging body as a whole, especially as the authorities did nothing to win back the people's regard. After the Eureka Hotel blaze, George Francis

Train wrote in his BOSTON GLOBE column, *Give the colonists their own way, and they will remain loyal—cross their path and they will have a flag of their own.*

*

George Francis Train predicted an inexorable flourishing of republican sentiment in the months ahead, a colonial rite of passage that he expressed in particularly gendered terms:

> Grant all the diggers ask, and they will not be satisfied. Abolish the licence fee, unlock the lands, give them universal suffrage, retrench government expenses, and it will not save the ultimate independence of the colony…Victoria's history is quickly written. The girl is hardly marriageable, yet her freedom is close at hand.

Witnesses revealed that there had been speakers at the Eureka Hotel riot urging the people *to drive off all the Government officers, send the Government home and to declare their Independence*, as Thomas Pierson recorded after he left the fracas. W. H. Foster, a civil servant on the diggings and a cousin of Charles La Trobe, wrote home in a letter to his parents in December 1854 that the licence tax issue was simply a convenient smokescreen for the Americans who were *here in great numbers…with a view to institute independence.*[29] Hotham himself admitted to Sir George Grey that Victoria *possesses wealth, strength and competency to hold its position unaided by the Mother Country.*[30] Are we to run the risk of the colony *walking alone?* he asked. Fewer than eighty years had passed since the American Revolution. In collective memory, the thought of colonists defeating redcoats was anything but ancient history.

Rede knew that his attendance at the Americans' Thanksgiving dinner was politic to say the least. He needed to curtail, not strengthen, the influence of the Americans over Ballarat's public culture. But he also needed to be respectful of Yankee traditions and of their consul, James Tarleton. James and his wife had lived with George Francis and Winnie Davis Train when they first arrived in Melbourne. Train was Melbourne's leading merchant and transport magnate, and a foreign correspondent. It required an adroit act of diplomacy to negotiate this thorny terrain.

Rede's first act—although obeisance was not his favourite pastime—was to bow graciously to Tarleton, who was, after all, the guest of honour. Tarleton, for his part, used the occasion to proclaim the loyalty of the Americans to the laws of their adopted land. He urged his countrymen to refrain from entering into the present agitations. Such entreaties were heartily welcomed by the crowd, who represented the upper echelons of Ballarat society, men like Dr Charles Kenworthy and Dr William Otway, who both ran successful medical practices in town and on the diggings. Following Hotham's instructions, Rede had sent government spies onto the diggings. One spy had delivered him a long list of names of people who had *pledged themselves to attack the camp and drive the officials off the Gold Field.*[31] One of the spies was said to be Dr Kenworthy.[32] There was a reason this dinner was being held at Brandt and Hirschler's, and not at the Adelphi.

*

If Rede and Kenworthy were planning a little reconnoitre over whiskey and rye, their liaison was cut short. During the toasts,

Rede was suddenly called away. There had been a skirmish on the Melbourne Road and troops from the Camp were being dispatched to respond.

A company of the 12th Regiment was marching into town, part of Hotham's next wave of fortification for the Camp. This particular small contingent was essentially a guard detail for several wagons full of ammunition and baggage: the real manpower would come later that night, with the arrival of the regimental units waved off by Mrs Massey. By the first day of summer, there would be a total of 546 officers and soldiers stationed at Ballarat, almost five times more than had been on the ground over winter.

As the ammunition-bearing battalion crossed Eureka, it was ambushed by a group of diggers lurking in the shadows. Incoming soldiers had become used to hostile welcoming committees of men, women and children hooting, jeering and throwing stones at them as they hup-two'd their way to the Camp. But this time a violent scuffle broke out in which the wagons were overturned, a drummer boy was shot in the thigh, an old American carrier was severely injured and several horses were wounded. Onlookers predicted fatalities. Resident Commissioner Robert Rede never got the chance to make his toast to the Queen. He left the Americans to their yankee doodle dandying, not quite convinced that Tarleton's righteous words would be mirrored in noble action.

*

While the Americans gave thanks and Rede tried to unpick the tangled web of Ballarat's allegiances, preparations were being made on the Flat for another monster meeting. Relations between the Camp and the diggers had broken down completely after the reform league's unsuccessful attempt to intercede on behalf of Fletcher, McIntyre and Westoby. Some diggers had started to burn their licences as a symbolic protest against the constituted authorities. Tent and store robberies were now occurring nightly. Horse stealing had become so common that horses without stabling were considered useless. A fierce dog was worth a king's ransom. Security measures were directed exclusively towards the Camp, and the police were now vastly outnumbered by the military, further eroding any skerrick of prestige they may have enjoyed with the community.

Scandalous anecdotes were flying every which way, gossip spinning out after every new or imagined bunfight or scuffle. *The second Ballarat revolution is in everyone's mouth,* wrote the ARGUS on the morning on 29 November. *Rumour with her many tongues is blabbing all sorts of stories.* The gold commissioner had been taken hostage. The Camp was burned to the ground. The fifteen-year-old drummer boy had been killed in the ambush of the 12th Regiment. Fletcher had *thoroughly broken down* and was a risk of suicide. James Johnston had purchased five town allotments at the Ballarat land sales that week. (This one was true.)

And yet…most miners remained buried down their holes, trapped in the daily rigour of digging. There had been some handsome finds on Eureka and the Gravel Pits these past weeks. There was not a single salary man outside the Camp, but thousands of little mouths to feed. All was work.

Bakery Hill would once again be the venue for the next monster meeting, placarded for 29 November at midday. (*Bakery Hill is obtaining creditable notoriety as the rallying ground for Australian freedom,* wrote the TIMES.[33]) Ten thousand people downed tools, shut up stores, gathered up children and headed towards Bakery Hill. It was a hot day, with clouds of dust swirling in the gusty wind. In Victoria, you know when a change is about to come. The low clouds build. The air temperature can roast chickens. You take the washing off the line before the sou'westerly front rips through. You arrive at your destination with one eye on the main game, one hand on your hat and an ear out for the roar of wildfire.

The meeting brought the usual catalogue of goldfields public protest: lengthy speeches, heartfelt resolutions—one of which was that the reform league would meet at the Adelphi Theatre at 2pm on Sunday 3 December to elect a central committee—fiery threats, troopers circling on horseback and the steady sale of sly grog on the fringes of the crowd. But three wholly new things happened on 29 November.

The first was that the next morning's papers referred to those present as *the rebels*.[34]

The second was that the diggers lined up to throw their licences upon a bonfire—an act of communal defiance of the law. The Ballarat Reform League had voted by a majority of three that its members should burn their mining and storekeeping licences. When committing their licences to the flames, the diggers swore to defend any unlicensed digger from arrest, with armed force if necessary. Those miners who did not become members of the reform league could not expect the same protection. Thus the Ballarat diggings became a closed shop.

The third was that a flag was hoisted. Not a national flag, but a purpose-made flag, a flag the GEELONG ADVERTISER dubbed *the Australian flag*.[35] This was the only flag hoisted that day.

This is the flag that we now know as the Eureka Flag. But on 29 November it was briefly raised not at Eureka but above the crowd at Bakery Hill. Its purpose was *to attract attention*: like the band that roamed the diggings playing 'La Marseillaise', it was an attempt to charm democratic tempers away from their toil, rallying them on a cloud of righteous anger towards Bakery Hill.[36]

The flag they called the Australian Flag took its design inspiration from the one thing that united each and every resident of Ballarat: the constellation of the Southern Cross. Those five bright stars in the shape of a kite were the first thing that had alerted immigrants to the existential transformation that occurred when they crossed the line into the southern hemisphere. Those five stars connected the paths of travellers from other antipodean colonies long before a constitution federated their political bodies. Those stars were the only firmament for currency lads and lasses, who knew no other heaven. Five shimmering white stars against a clear blue field, hoisted, as Frederick Vern put it, *under Australia's matchless sky*.

Raffaello Carboni gave his tribute to the idea behind the flag when he took the stage before fifteen thousand people at Bakery Hill that morning. *I called on all my fellow-diggers*, he later recalled, *irrespective of nationality, religion, and colour, to salute the 'Southern Cross' as the refuge of all the oppressed from all the countries on earth.* Carboni was well satisfied with the crowd's response: *The applause was universal.* The Ballarat Flat now had a single ensign to rival the huge Union Jack fluttering above the Camp.

Henry Seekamp was also on the spot to witness the hoisting of the new flag on its eighty-foot flagstaff at eleven o'clock on the morning of the 29th. In the issue of the TIMES printed on Sunday 3 December, he (or perhaps Clara, as this is one of the 'seditious' editions for which he disclaimed responsibility) wrote:

> Its maiden appearance was a fascinating object to behold. There is no flag in Europe, or in the civilised world, half so beautiful and Bakery Hill as being

> the first place where the Australian ensign was first hoisted will be recorded in the deathless and indelible pages of history. The flag is silk, blue ground with a large silver cross; no device or arms, but all exceedingly chaste and natural.

Thomas Pierson saw the flag too. He sketched a little replica in his diary, labelling it *the flag of the southern hemisphere... made of silk and quite neat*. Indeed the design was very different from the flag commercial artist and republican William Dexter designed for the Bendigo miners during the Red Ribbon Rebellion in August 1853. Dexter's ensign showed a pick, shovel and cradle to represent labour, scales to signal justice, the fasces (a Roman bundle of sticks) to suggest union, and a kangaroo and emu to emote Australia. To Dexter's mind, this smorgasbord of iconography was the ultimate liberation narrative. On raising it at a Bendigo rally, *he made an onslaught on the British flag. 'What had it done for liberty?'*[37] Ballarat's rebel flag, by contrast, was remarkably pure. It said simply, 'We are here'.

✶

There has always been controversy about the provenance of the 'Eureka' flag. The current orthodoxy is that it was designed by Canadian miner Henry (sometimes called Charles) Ross, who then recruited three diggers' wives to sew a standard measuring 3400 millimetres by 2580 millimetres. Ross was friendly with fellow Canadian Charles Alphonse Doudiet, who has left the clearest pictorial representation of the flag that was unfurled on Bakery Hill that day. Some have speculated that the blue flag with its white cross takes its design lead from the official ensign of Quebec (from where Doudiet, not Ross, hailed). But there is no evidence that Ross designed the flag. There is a clue, however, as to how the Chinese whisper might have started. The original cover of Raffaello Carboni's 1855 account of the Eureka Stockade bears a sketch of the flag above the words, *When Ballarat unfurled the Southern Cross the bearer was Toronto's Captain Ross*. Elsewhere in the book, Carboni refers to Ross as the *bridegroom* of the flag, a reference that is probably more literal than is sometimes supposed. Ross was the standard-bearer; he hoisted it up the flagpole.

There is also speculation about who made the flag. The most overt documentary clue is provided by Frederick Vern, who described the flag *as a banner made and wrought by English ladies*. Carboni later confirmed this version in his 1855 account, quoting Vern directly. Was Vern referring to Anastasia Hayes, Anastasia Withers and Anne Duke, the three women now generally credited by oral tradition as the clandestine seamstresses? It is certainly possible, though historian Anne Beggs-Sunter has suggested that the prominence of these names is simply 'an example of the way oral history becomes fact' when secondary accounts take descendants' theories as gospel.[38]

Beggs-Sunter gives equal weight to what she terms the 'men's flag story', first told by J. W. Wilson in 1885. Wilson quoted *a reliable eye-witness*, who told him in 1893 that Henry Ross *gave the order for the insurgents' flag* to a local tent-and tarpaulin-making firm, Darton and Walker. According to Wilson's version, Ross gave his order at 11pm on Thursday 23th and the flag was first raised thirty-nine hours later, at 2pm on Saturday the 25th. This flag was made of *bunting*.

There is another possible explanation of the flag's genesis, one that draws on many plausible strands of evidence. We know from the report in the ARGUS on 9 November that bills had been posted around the diggings for a meeting of Ballarat's Irish; the purpose was to raise a subscription for *a monster national banner* to fly over *the once disputed ground of the Eureka*. The impetus was apparently the insult directed at Father Smyth in arresting his servant. But by 24 November—the next time a new flag was reported in the papers—the BALLARAT TIMES was advertising fervidly a meeting to be held on Wednesday 29 November at which the *Australian Flag shall triumphantly wave, a symbol of Liberty. Forward! People! Forward!* There is no suggestion that the Irish flag was ever stitched. But clearly the Seekamps knew that an important standard was being raised.

A Eugene von Guérard sketch, made on the spot in January 1854, gives us a strong intimation of where that flag might have been constructed. *Katholisch Kapelle aus den Gravel Pit Lunis 3u Ballarat Januav 1854* is von Guérard's rendering of Father Smyth's Catholic church, St Alipius. It shows a large tent, timber-lined with a canvas roof, and beside it the small school hut where Anastasia Hayes was the teacher. Soaring high above the church is a flag. The sepia tones of the sketch don't show the flag's colours, but the graphic is clear: a cross on a solid background. The conventional Christian chaplain's flag is a dark blue flag with a white Latin cross. It is still used today by the chaplain corps in army units around the world. In Ballarat in 1854, Father Smyth would hoist his flag half an hour before mass commenced, to alert his largely Irish Catholic flock to put aside their worldly activities and come together in ritual communion. The flag was taken down when mass commenced.[39]

Eliza Darcy was a member of that congregation, as was Patrick Howard. They would marry at St Alipius in August 1855. Eliza and Patrick's twelfth and last child, Alicia, born in 1879, would later tell her granddaughter, Ella Hancock, that it was Patrick who designed the Eureka Flag and that Eliza helped to sew it. Did Patrick Howard, a member of the Ballarat Reform League and a proud Irishman, look up at the mass flag, then cast his gaze further to the sky above—to a constellation that united not only his offended Catholic brethren but the whole aggrieved digging community? Did he simply affix the stars of the Crux Australis to the Latin cross?[40]

Then there is the question of who really did craft the flag, and how. As the press pre-emptively observed, the diggers' flag was a monster. Kristin Phillips, the Eureka Flag's most recent conservator (and the one with the highest level of professional qualification), has argued that it was the construction of the flag that dictated its size. She believes that the seamstresses were not working to a plan; rather the size of the available fabric determined its dimensions. For it was not bunting but ordinary 'clothing fabric bought off the roll' and cut 'economically' that was used to make the flag: a full piece width, selvedge to selvedge, used in the centre with a half width affixed to the top and the bottom.[41] A dark blue ground of plain-weave cotton warp and wool weft. A cream cross of twill-weave cotton warp and wool weft. And five cream-coloured, one hundred per cent wool stars.

Phillips disavows the popular theory that the stars were made out of women's petticoats. Nineteenth-century petticoats, she assures us, were rarely made of wool. Furthermore, the stars are cut from clean pieces of fabric, without visible seams; grain changes in the stars suggest they were cut, 'economically' again, from a single piece of fabric. From a technical point of view, Phillips finds it implausible that such large stars could be taken from a single petticoat. It's a myth that might have added a touch of sexual allure to the Eureka story, but not one that the material evidence bears out.

Yet size does matter. Where to construct surreptitiously a

huge rebel flag on a camping ground like the diggings? There were few places in which a four-metre roll of fabric could be unfurled on the ground, with room around it for a team of seamstresses. The Adelphi Theatre would have been big enough, but Sarah Hanmer was sheltering the activities of the American community, not the Irish. Was the flag sewn in the Catholic church where Anastasia Hayes, the doyenne of the Catholic community, was employed? It was certainly one of the few tents large enough to lay out such an expanse of fabric. And it was already common knowledge that the Irish were making themselves a protest flag.

There is little doubt that it was women who sewed the flag. Kristin Phillips has confirmed that the flag was made using traditional women's sewing skills: flat felled seams done by hand.[42] Val D'Angri, the Ballarat craftswoman employed in 1973 to restore the flag for presentation at the Art Gallery of Ballarat, found original pins in the seams that were a common component of a mid-nineteenth-century woman's sewing kit. The 'men's flag story', as relayed by J. W. Wilson, is crucially undermined by two factors: the flag is not made of bunting, and it could not have been made in less than forty-eight hours. Kristin Phillips reckons that it would have taken many hands, gathered around the perimeter of the flag, to construct the flag with any haste. (It took Val D'Angri seventy-five hours to hand sew a reproduction flag.)

Anastasia and her compatriots were probably the *English ladies* that the German Frederick Vern refers to. Vern certainly had no political motivation to attribute the Australian Flag's origin to women. Yet whether the seamstresses were *English* is debatable. Did the Hanoverian consider that white women from the British Isles all looked the same? Anastasia Hayes, as we know, was Irish, born in Kilkenny and reared through a famine, although she and Timothy had lived in England prior to emigrating. Their daughter Anastasia was baptised in Stafford in 1850. As the wife of the chairman of the Ballarat Reform League, Anastasia Sr was certainly close to the action. Sixteen-year-old Anne Duke, heavily pregnant with her first child in the summer of 1854, was also Irish, but she had arrived in Victoria with her family when she was four years old and her accent may have receded. Anastasia Withers, née Splain, was the only ethnic *Englishwoman* among the group widely accepted as the flag's makers. Born in Bristol in 1825, she was transported to Tasmania for the theft of five shawls in 1843. There she married Samuel Withers in 1849 and had two children. The couple was one of the earliest arrivals on the Victorian goldfields. By the time they were digging at Ballarat in November 1854, Anastasia Withers had three children under five and another on the way. There is every reason to think that Eliza Darcy was also part of the team of workers, as her ninety-seven-year-old granddaughter, Ella Hancock, will tell you today.

Between the women who probably came together under cover of darkness to sew the rebel flag, there were at least nine children and two pregnancies. There is no faulting their dedication. Or maybe, if you are going to be up half the night with sleepless infants, you might as well do something that will be recorded in the pages of history.

*

On the evening of 29 November, Captain Pasley, one of the military commanders now stationed at Ballarat, wrote to Hotham. The meeting at Bakery Hill had *passed off very quietly*, he reported, with speeches less inflammatory than previous public demonstrations. *It is therefore, I think, clearly necessary*, Pasley wrote,

> that some steps should be taken to bring the matter

> to a crisis, and to teach those persons (forming, no doubt, the great majority of the mining population) who are not seditiously disposed, that it is in their interest to give practical proofs of their allegiance.[43]

Such persons, he hoped, would not only discourage the rebellious portion of the community but also actively interfere to prevent their further activities. With the appearance of the Australian Flag, community unrest had suddenly been branded seditious.

It was somewhat disingenuous for Pasley to suggest that the rebels were in the minority. Up to fifteen thousand people had assembled at Bakery Hill that day. By the end of November there were 32,000 people at Ballarat: 23,000 men, 4200 women and 4300 children. Almost half of the total population was prepared to walk off the job and attend a protest meeting. Just imagine if that sort of percentage of citizens—say half of Melbourne's current population of five million—turned up to any public meeting on climate change, maternity leave, nuclear disarmament, Aboriginal land rights, bank fees, the trains not running on time—anything. It would be political chaos.

Faced with this sort of numerical opposition, the authorities of Ballarat were now itching for the simplicity of a violent collision in order to assert their supremacy. Their power and legitimacy were being questioned daily by everyone from Ellen Young, the BALLARAT TIMES and the conscientiously objecting unlicensed diggers on the outside, to Catherine McLister and the grumbling foot police on the inside. A rebellion would sort the loyal wheat from the mutinous chaff, and the Camp would be the omnipotent threshing machine. The line would be nothing more or less than the law. Which side are you on?

*

Each man felt something would happen before the day was over. So wrote Alexander Dick on the morning of Thursday 30 November, as he sat on a hill overlooking the Gravel Pits. The heat was intense; the day overcast, windy, foul. The young Scotsman looked down on the usual comings and goings of a busy working goldfield. The noise and clamour. The shouts from holes and the creak of turning windlasses. Tents and flags flapping, children darting about. Shops trading. The workplace and the home fused in a perfect pre-industrial spectacle of manual labour.

And then, a torrent of foot and mounted police suddenly descended from the Camp to the Gravel Pits. A massive licence hunt began, led by James Johnston, on the very morning after so many diggers had burned their licences in the flames of communal resistance. It was a test of the rebellious miners' pledge to defend the unlicensed among them. It was a demonstration of strength from the Camp to put to rights the power inversion that had followed the burning of Bentley's Hotel. It was an arm-wrestle to see who, when push came to shove, would gain the upper hand; a mighty rout of deliberately unlicensed diggers by an unprecedented show of force.

There was *a tremendous uproar*. All the inhabitants of the Gravel Pits scattered among the mounds of earth and tents. *Joe! Joe! Joe!* The cry went down the line. It was mayhem, as the mounted police began to gallop among the tents. The soldiers made a sweep of the flat, with cavalry on both flanks and in the centre, clearing off all the occupants of claims to the high road beyond the lead, below Bakery Hill. Police fired shots into a crowded area, *among tents where women and children were congregated in large numbers.*[44]

The confused crowd scattered like tumbleweeds in the hot wind, seeking shelter in the lee of neighbouring tents. Troopers were dragged down from their horses *like mere stuffed effigies of men*. Police were pelted with mud, stones and broken bottles. Robert Rede stampeded in and hurriedly mouthed the Riot Act. He had been criticised for not taking such action at the Eureka Hotel riot. Now he read the Act so quickly—*with telegraphic speed*—that in one journalist's opinion *the consequent proceedings were illegal*.[45]

Elizabeth Rowlands looked on. *I was present*, she later wrote, *when the proclamation was read when the soldiers dropped on their knee and presented guns at us and told the crowd to disperse and my word they did disperse*.[46] Miners jumped down holes. Women and children melted into tents. A bugle sounded. The military marched down the hill, forming a line on the grass under the southward plateau of the Camp. *A very picturesque array*, thought Samuel Huyghue, the line of cavalry in their bright red uniforms, their brass buttons flashing in the sunlight, set against the *verdure of the grass* which had not yet lost its *winter hue*. Eight men were arrested for riotous behaviour but there were no serious injuries. First honours to the Camp.

*

No one at the Gravel Pits went back to work that day. As news of the chaos and random firing on the crowd, including turning weapons on women and children, spread to other parts of the field, sympathetic diggers downed tools to seek information and digest rumours. *Work is knocked off*, wrote one official to Hotham,

> and the whole population is talking over events of the morning...The opinions of most disinterested

> persons here is [the actions of the Camp] are alike unwise and indicative of a wish on the part of the authorities here to hurry on a collision.[47]

Even upright Martha Clendinning, a self-appointed member *of the peace portion of the residents*, thought that ordering licence hunts after the Bakery Hill meeting was *an incredible act of folly*. If James Johnston was going to step up digger hunts, which had already become an almost daily humiliation, and diggers were continuing to burn their licences in solidarity with the cause of freedom from the oppressive goldfields regime, then what were the *interested* persons to do?

From all directions on the diggings, people started in the direction of Bakery Hill. The Australian Flag was once again flying there. The people turned their eyes to the five shimmering stars, guiding their footsteps towards a just course. This would be an unplacarded meeting—no notice, no agenda, no stage, no prepared speeches. Whatever grievances had caused those assembled to lose faith in the government—hunger, grief, shame, disappointment, harassment, indignity, humiliation, powerlessness—the object now was self-defence. The leaders of Ballarat had shown they would fire upon a civilian crowd. If the people's call was sticks and stones, the Camp's response would be lead and steel. This was not a tune to which Australia's home-grown sons and daughters, or its ambitious immigrants, had ever expected to dance. This was the way masters treated servants, dogs and blacks—not free-born Britons and self-governing Yankees.

Gathered now at Bakery Hill, under the starry banner, the people looked for direction. Who would guide this exodus, deliver them from tyranny, lead them out of slavery? From the crowd stepped a twenty-seven-year-old Irishman. Peter Lalor was raised in a political family. His eldest brother had fought in the Young Irish movement in that fiery year of 1848. The Lalors had known the oppression and hypocrisy of the Union Jack. They believed in home rule. As landed gentry, the family had used its political nous to stand up for the rights of Irish peasants. Patrick Lalor, Peter's father, was an MP representing Queens County. Trained as a civil engineer and excited by the prospect of a golden frontier, Peter Lalor came to Victoria with his brother Richard, sister-in-law Margaret and sister Maria in 1852. At Ballarat, he became Timothy Hayes' mining partner. With his fiancée Alicia Dunne working as a teacher in Geelong, Lalor looked to Anastasia Hayes and her brood of children for his de facto domestic life.

On 30 November this tall, charismatic, sandy-haired, blue-eyed man stepped out of the crowd and said one word. He said it with feeling. *Liberty!* Mrs Ann Shann, twenty-four-year-old wife of digger John Shann, was there. She later vividly remembered the moment when Lalor *was chosen leader of the diggers, and it was decided to drill and oppose the police and military by force.*[48] Mrs Shann joined with other diggers, their wives and children as the assembled group of a thousand marched en masse from Bakery Hill to Eureka. The Eureka was further from the Camp, and, as a flat, not a rise, more protected. They took the flag with them.

*

At Eureka, the self-appointed leadership of the young solidarity movement met in the home-cum-store of Anne and Martin Diamond. A veritable United Nations of malcontents: Lalor, Carboni (who was needed to translate orders to the non-English-speaking rebels), Irishmen Patrick Curtain, John Manning, Patrick Howard and Timothy Hayes, Englishman George Black, Scotsman Thomas Kennedy, Frederick Vern the Hanoverian,

Canadian Henry Ross, American James McGill, who was a close friend of Sarah Hanmer, and Edward Thonen, a thirty-year-old Jewish 'lemonade seller' from Prussia. John Basson Humffray abstained from the group, citing his infinite preference for moral force over physical force, and watched his former shipmates, Anne and Martin, give shelter to the rebels. Charles Evans sided with Humffray, the man with whom he'd walked to Ballarat, over Hayes, the man with whom he'd sailed to Victoria. By temperament, Evans was a cautious observer. Kennedy, by contrast, had told a cheering crowd at Bakery Hill monster meeting that *mere persuasion is all a humbug; nothing succeeds like a lick in the lug*.[49]

The new group who met at the Diamonds' store constituted themselves as a 'council of war for the defence', though there was, at present, no territory to defend. Lalor was elected 'commander-in-chief' and began to organise drilling squads to protect the unlicensed diggers. For here was the root of the problem: the thousands of miners who had burned their licences in the fires of protest were now, technically, unauthorised to be on the diggings and could be fined or arrested for breach of the law. The Gravel Pits incident that morning had shown that the government would pursue its prerogative without mercy. Lalor concluded that the miners must *resist force by force*. But how to symbolise that resistance? A flag was one thing. It could stir hearts, but it could not shelter bodies.

When French revolutionaries proclaimed their democratic rights, they blockaded the streets of Paris. They set up rough barriers, cordoned off territory: drew a line. Men and women stationed themselves behind those barricades in a show of communal militancy. 'The barricade', writes historian David Barry, 'emerged on a large scale as a weapon of rebellion…in July 1830, creating a new mode of defensive neighbourhood action in which women, with their strong involvement in community networks, could profitably participate.'

French revolutionaries carried pikes, waved banners and shouted slogans. Their activities were confrontational and highly visible, like a frilled-neck lizard throwing out a collar of spines to shock enemies with its potency: an animal act of defensiveness. But it was a primal knee-jerk with a very human twist. As Barry tells us, men of Paris welcomed women behind the barricades because 'their presence was seen as a means of deterring the authorities from reacting with force'. There might not be safety in numbers, the freedom fighters reasoned, but there was surely safety in the company of women. No civilised government would deliberately fire on civilian women and children.

In the Diamonds' store that afternoon, the war chiefs decided to throw up a hasty barricade. There needed to be a neighbourhood refuge, an unassailable place of shelter, to *defend and protect* from arrest those diggers who had burned their licences—but how to cordon off such a zone? There were no European-style streets to speak of on the diggings, only rough transport thoroughfares lined by tent dwellings, stores and shanties. The streets were porous. A crowd (or an army) could leak out into the gaps between the canvas shelters. There was no physical structure to contain them, no wall of buildings. This being Australia, and the frontier, there was simply too much space. So the barricade would have to be self-contained, would have to close in on itself. The line would have to be a circle.

Thus an area around the Diamonds' store was immediately barricaded. It was all hands on deck, with any form of timber serving to construct a crude fortification: overturned carts, empty barrels and crates, felled trees, the thick slabs used to line shafts. Made in haste and with scavenged resources, the barrier was brutally uneven, only waist high in some sections, over six feet in others. Some sections were held together with ropes, some fixed into the ground; some slabs were given picket-like points, other links in the chain were the mounds of earth disgorged from a deep sinking.

The territory it marked was at the southern end of the Eureka line, on a gentle slope running up to the Melbourne Road, only a few hundred yards from the charred remains of Bentley's Hotel. The ground in this area was studded with tents and sinking holes. In all, about an acre of ground was enclosed. The barricade surrounded at least ten tents, the Diamonds' immediate neighbours. These tents were the homes and businesses of diggers and their families; men and women randomly, fatally, thrust centre stage. As Anne Diamond would later testify, her tent was *half in and half out* of the ramshackle cordon.[50] The ring was not even closed. It was a broken circle from the start, more of a wobbly parallelogram really, with its rear wall comprising the scrub of Brown Hill. At the heart of the enclosed turf, a flagpole was erected and the Australian Flag hoisted to stake the claim. The Eureka Stockade, as it would come to be known, made a mighty fine amphitheatre but a lousy bulwark.[51] The cornered lizard bared its frills.

*

With teams of diggers drilling on the flat ground beside their new stringybark citadel, Lalor led his war council back up to Bakery Hill. The Southern Cross was once more unfurled. Though the new stronghold at Eureka could be glimpsed from the Camp, this rise was more prominent. It would attract the attention of potential recruits as well as the wide-eyed glare of the Camp.

A division of Americans, calling themselves the Independent Californian Rangers, fell in behind Captain Ross. Vern rallied a troop of continental freedom fighters. There is no evidence of any Chinese being recruited into the stoush, but it is not impossible that someone like John Aloo, who ran a popular restaurant on the diggings, acted as an interpreter, just as Carboni did for the Italians, French and Prussians. Local Indigenous inhabitants were present at the Bendigo Red Ribbon Rebellion, public meetings; they may have been at Bakery Hill too.

This was the pointy end of a momentous day, and those still standing beneath the flag that was flapping wildly in the hot late afternoon wind were here to pledge allegiance to a cause that had turned abruptly. What had started as a lawful outpouring of communal grievance was now a calculated show of armed resistance. The stage was set, a director appointed, the actors assembled, and now the players must speak. Lalor kneeled. He removed his hat and raised his hand towards the flag: *We swear by the Southern Cross to stand truly by each other, and fight to defend our rights and liberties.*[52] A chorus of five hundred true believers chanted *Amen*.

The curtain now falls on Bakery Hill, and the players move back down to Eureka. They bring the flag with them. This time, it will not return.

*

As the storm clouds built on that afternoon of Thursday 30 November, Police Constable Henry Goodenough, a government spy, relayed a rumour that the Camp would be attacked at 4am. Henry's twenty-six-year-old wife Elizabeth and their six-month-old baby Mary Anne had no doubt been sent away from the Camp with Maggie Johnston and the other government wives as part of Captain Thomas's defence plan. Goodenough prowled the diggers' meetings dressed in miners garb, shouting oaths and pretending to be drunk. Either he was a bad actor or he really was intoxicated. At one gathering Raffaello Carboni gave the blathering oaf a sturdy kick in the privates to silence him. When *Judas Iscariot Goodenough*, as Carboni later called him, planted the story of the Camp's imminent attack, there was every reason to storm the citadel. The eight men arrested at the Gravel Pits that morning were considered political prisoners, just as Fletcher, McIntyre and Westoby had been. *We shall be ready to receive them*, wrote Captain Pasley. *I am more convinced than ever that…sedition must be put down by force…before many days have passed, it will be necessary for us to sweep the whole goldfield.*[53] Had somebody instructed Goodenough to orchestrate a crisis, if none truly existed?

That evening the barometric pressure finally plummeted. A violent thunderstorm shook the night sky. It rained for three hours solid, great lashings of fat summer rain. During the whole night, the *police troopers were exposed to the downpour*, waiting beside their horses, saddled and ready for action. Fortifications had been made to the mess house, Dr David Williams' house, the Camp hospital, Rede and Johnston's quarters (*a particularly exposed locality*) and the military barracks. It was the job of the police to guard these vulnerable targets. So the exhausted and no doubt frightened young men *lay wrapped in their cloaks on the saturated ground* or crouching under their horses for shelter. To kill time, recounted Samuel Huyghue, the lads sat *spinning yarns of former service in the field*. For some, there would have been an element of truth to their tales. For most, the one-upmanship was pure bravado.

Meanwhile, Robert Rede, dry and fortified in his quarters, scratched out a letter to Melbourne by candlelight. *The absolute necessity of putting down all meetings Public/Private I think should now be apparent*, he wrote, *for the abolition of the Licence Fee is merely a watchword.* Rede had a plan—that the whole of the goldfield be put under martial law and Hotham issue a proclamation to the effect that he would stop the agitation at all costs—but the former medical student showed less bluster than the boy soldiers. Like the diggers being magnetically drawn to Bakery Hill, Rede turned to Hotham for leadership. It would have cost his pride to write, *I must also earnestly require some instructions for my future guidance.*[54]

*

Lalor gave Rede an out. Late that night, with the dust settled by hours of soaking rain, Lalor decided to send a deputation to speak to Rede in a gentlemanly manner. The go-betweens would negotiate for the release of the prisoners. He chose George Black, who so recently had been on a similar mission to see Hotham, Raffaello Carboni, and the Catholic priest Father Smyth. When the trio reached the Yarrowee River below the Camp, the police stopped them. Only Smyth was allowed to proceed. He was taken directly to Rede. Flanked by his deputies, Rede accompanied Smyth back to where Black and Carboni waited in the company of the police.

Black immediately repeated the mistake he had made with Hotham. He *demanded* the release of the prisoners, and for good measure added his opinion that the soldiers were bullies and that Britons would not stand for such brutal treatment. The situation was hopeless. Rede expected the obedience and submission with which his office vested him. Black represented diggers who would no longer submit to tyranny; men who were desperate to assert their legitimacy after months of humiliation. The new codes smacked up against the old like waves against a cliff face.

Rede knew the licensing system was a scourge and must be replaced by something more prudent and acceptable to the people. He himself had written to Hotham on 7 November, suggesting alternative methods of raising revenue and stating baldly: *I look at all direct taxation now as impolitic.*[55] He must also have known that ordering a full-scale licence hunt on the morning after the impulsive burning of licences at Bakery Hill was sure to exacerbate the already inflamed passions of the movement's vanguard. But he was not prepared to appear anything but complete master of his senses and his forces.

Black now offered him a perfect bridge over the troubled waters that raged between them. Stop the licence hunts until the people had had the opportunity to put their case against the licensing system before Hotham once more. In return for such consideration, the people would lay down their weapons and pick up their shovels. They would cease their armed resistance if assured that they would not need to defend themselves and their families against actions such as the morning's digger hunt.

But Rede smelled a rat, or at least the acrid stench of his own reputation going up in smoke. Was this a trick? He already believed that the protest against the licence tax was merely the thin end of a deeper revolutionary wedge. Nothing short of self-government would appease the leaders of this agitation. Was he to be the man who rolled out the red carpet for their entrance to Spring Street?

No, he could not afford to be the one who stepped cautiously back from the brink. He would have to stand firm. Dig his heels in, keep from wavering and eventually emerge triumphant. He could not promise that there would be no more digger hunts, he told the deputation. Then he dismissed them.

I can only say that things look as bad as they almost possibly can, lamented the GEELONG ADVERTISER after the deputation's second failed attempt to broker a truce. *Is there no peacemaker?*[56] Martha Clendinning, alone in her store, her sister having fled back to Melbourne, wondered the same thing. *Things must come to a violent ending*, she predicted, *and that very soon.*

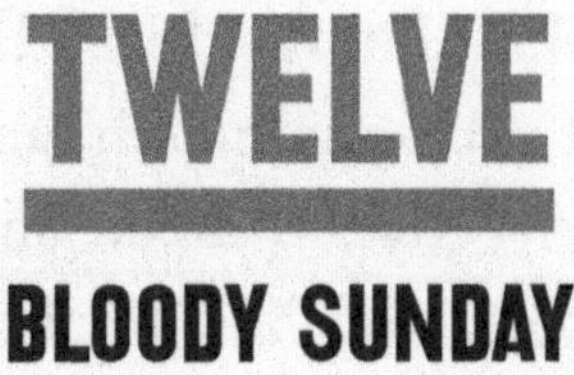

TWELVE

BLOODY SUNDAY

So it came to pass that the Ballarat diggings ground to an eerie halt on the first day of summer, 1854. If men were machines you would say that that a screw had shaken itself loose and the whole steely apparatus needed urgent maintenance. But human beings are made of flesh and bone and heart and mind, and on Friday 1 December the people of Ballarat stopped work of their own conscious accord. Miners downed tools. Storekeepers closed their doors. Families regrouped. Mates gathered in furtive clumps, like cows under a shade tree. Blacksmiths began fashioning pikes, the traditional weapon of peasant rebellion. Teams of diggers swept through the city, first requesting, then insisting, that the occupants hand over their guns and ammunition. (All requisitioned arms, it was promised, would be returned when they were no longer needed.) The hotels and shanties were humming with rumour, but there was a surprising lack of drunkenness.[1] Battening down the hatches was a serious business. An uneasy hush fell over the festive season, as a community held its collective breath.

*

That night at the Adelphi Theatre, Sarah Hanmer held a benefit performance. It was a tribute to herself, under the patronage of Resident Commissioner Robert Rede and American Consul James Tarleton. The piece she chose to perform was *Money*—an irreverent poke at the very foible that had led all these feverish lambs to the slaughter.[2] The Adelphi Players were in fine form. *Mrs Hanmer as Lady Franklyn, Miss Julia Hanmer as Clara, and Miss Stevens as Georgiana, sustained their well merited reputation*, wrote the GEELONG ADVERTISER. During the evening, Mrs Hanmer was presented with a gold watch and chain, as a *mark of respect for her private worth and public character.*[3] The watch was purchased from funds raised from the benefit Mrs Hanmer had previously held to free the alleged sly grogger Frank Carey. Carey had refused the money after his reprieve by Hotham. *Owing to the circumstances*, neither Tarleton nor Rede was present on this balmy night to see Mrs Hanmer receive her gift.

Had they been there, they might have wondered what sort of game this formidable woman was playing. Earlier that evening, the Americans had held a meeting at the Adelphi to determine what their position would be in the looming crisis. The atmosphere was considerably charged. Charles Ferguson was at the meeting. Tarleton had warned his countrymen to stay out of any impending conflict, but *others complained that we were doing nothing, while it was a matter of as much interest to us as to them, and began to accuse us of cowardice.*

Publicly, the Americans voted to desist. They would not be seen as instigators. *We regarded ourselves as foreigners*, recounted Ferguson, *and had no right to be foremost in an open outbreak against the government.* Privately, it was obvious that many Americans, notably Mrs Hanmer's friend Captain McGill, were taking pole position. The diggers could count on their support. Like other foreign nationals who were joining the drilling corps at the Stockade, they believed their actions were essentially defensive; a collective stand against a government that had proved at the Gravel Pits that it had no hesitation in *firing on the people*.

Sarah Hanmer was directing the proceeds of all her benefits to the Diggers Defence Fund. She was the war chest's principal contributor. Yet the shrewd theatre manager was still able to court the patronage of Ballarat's highest official and the honorary consul of the most influential immigrant group in the colony. Rede and Tarleton sponsored a benefit in her honour, despite the fact that within two days her theatre would be used to host the Ballarat Reform League's most important meeting yet. Why would these men flatter her with their sponsorship, legitimate her prestige? Did they think this leading lady, who commanded the respect and affection of the American diggers, would use her influence to act as a go-between? Her prima donna Miss Stevens had, after all, solicited signatures from 1700 people to aid Frank Carey's liberation. Did Commissioner Rede court Sarah Hanmer's power, hoping it would be used to his benefit? Or fearing it would be used against him?

Peacemaker or firebrand? Sarah Hanmer kept everyone guessing. Sometimes it pays to have one foot in both camps, adroitly straddling the line.

*

On Saturday morning, the people of Ballarat woke to a stiff southerly breeze. The cool change did nothing to ease tempers. *Business is entirely suspended*, wrote Charles Evans, *but one topic of conversation engrosses the attention of diggers and storekeepers.* Twenty-three-year-old Evans thanked his stars that, unlike so many of his fellow immigrants, he had not shacked up with a lass and planted his seed on Australian soil. *Those whose means enable them are sending their families away*, he wrote,

> while others whom poverty compels to keep their wives and families amidst the scene of threatening danger are awaiting the approach of events which feeling bachelors may bless their happy fortune in not being troubled with.

For months—in some cases years—shamefaced men had been struggling to put food in the mouths of their children, watching their women labour under a hot sun or wash clothes in the driving rain to keep their families from the (purely figurative) poorhouse. Now these same men had to worry about how to protect their loved ones from an army that would scatter bullets among anonymous tents.

They knew they could do nothing to stop a storm at sea or a baby taken by merciful Providence but, lord knew, a man could stand up to another man. As the BALLARAT TIMES said, *who was to blame?* The Camp was legally in the right, but the licence hunt on the Gravel Pits, argued the BALLARAT TIMES, was a deliberate plan to *transform indignation into open riot…an embryo rebellion.*[4] Could a man retreat from such wanton provocation?

There were at least 1500 people crammed into the Stockade by Saturday afternoon. Some had spent the previous night there, but most had slept in their own tents. The purpose of the Stockade, after all, was to prevent, by force if necessary, the arrest of unlicensed diggers. There had never been a licence hunt at night. But throughout the day on Saturday, more diggers kept rolling up, many coming from other goldfields, eager to add weight to the moral majority of resistance. The numbers were swelled by women who brought food into the Stockade, and at least one female sly-grog seller, who knew a captive market when she saw one and set up shop on the fringe of the palisade.[5] *We were of all nations and colours*, wrote Raffaello Carboni. *Great works! was the shout.* Great Work. Magnum Opus. The alchemic principle of forging base matter into gold. A process that involves three stages: *Putrefactio*, corruption, darkness. *Albedo*, purification, whitening, the moon: female. *Citrinitus*, yellowing, enlightenment, the sun: male. The Great Work is said to be the uniting of opposites. Great Work requires conflagration to forge a bond.

But the fire in the bellies of the stockade's inmates was hardly transcendental. *A very mutinous and excited spirit was prevalent*, wrote Alexander Dick, who had only arrived in Ballarat on 22 November. He could immediately see that his chosen destination was *rife [sic] for an explosion*. Peter Lalor, whose tent was inside the Stockade, could read the mood too. He needed to corral the energy, lest a purportedly disciplined 'army' disintegrate into a violent mob, as at Bentley's Hotel. Already there had been reports that there were gangs roaming the Flat demanding cash, firearms and provisions from frightened diggers and their wives. These thugs were not under his authority, but mere looters taking advantage of the situation.

Martha Clendinning was one of their victims. Martha was in her store on Saturday 2 December, *a date to be long remembered.* A group of eight miners marched up in military fashion. The leader claimed to be a representative of the diggers' *Minister of War*. He demanded any firearms she possessed. She said she had none, but was disbelieved. The leader moved to search her tent.

> I did not like the idea of such a visitation so I said, 'If you do not believe me, perhaps you would believe the Doctor if I called him to speak to you'. 'Yes, yes' he said at once, 'call him out' and he appeared much

relieved at having a man to interview instead of a woman!

Martha escaped harm or loss of her goods, but knew that Saturday was a black day of wanton robbery and pillaging. She fetched her brother to stay with her that night when Dr Clendinning was called away.

On Saturday afternoon, Lalor once again stepped forward to take command. Emerging from *the committee room* of Diamond's store, he mounted an old log and gave a *stump oration*. Alexander Dick was there to hear it. Lalor held a double-barrelled gun in his hand *which he fingered in a nervous manner*. His message was simple: *We must make this a country we can live in*. He had personal reason to project a future that included basic human and political rights for all its citizens, rich or poor, landed or roving. Peter Lalor was waiting to be married. Two days earlier, Lalor had written a letter to his fiancée, Alicia Dunne. In it, he explained his motives for putting up his hand to lead the rebel movement. This is what he wrote: *I would be unworthy of being called a man. I would be unworthy of myself, and, above all, I would be unworthy of you and your love, were I base enough to desert my companions in danger*. He urged Alicia to *shed but a single tear* should his efforts fail, for he would have died in the cause of *honour and liberty*.[6] Lalor wanted to hold his head high as his young Irish bride walked towards him in the chapel of St Mary's, Geelong in July the following year.

The central committee of the reform league must have been grateful for the timing of events. So far, there had been no grand plan. No strategy for gaining the upper hand. Every action had been responsive, protective, rearguard. The Stockade had been thrown up at random. *The flames did not devour the Eureka Hotel*, admitted Carboni, *with the same impetuosity as we got up our stockade*. The majority of the miners and storekeepers on the diggings were not overtly rebellious, nor prepared to take up arms. *We of the peace portion of the residents*, is how Martha Clendinning identified herself, though she was sympathetic to the miners' land hunger and tax grievances. Henry Mundy counted himself in that portion. *All reasonable people*, he wrote, *were willing to wait til the Commission had finished its labours and report.* Such people still had faith that Hotham would do the right thing by them.

But even the activists were divided. Some of the members of the Ballarat Reform League had sworn the oath of allegiance at Bakery Hill, but not all. Humffray refused to enter the Stockade. Henry Harris and Charles 'Ikey' Dyte similarly clung to the hope of a constitutional resolution. Some were for a republic; others, like Lalor, claimed that the diggers' resistance was purely defensive, designed to protect each other and protest against the misrule of Ballarat's officials. Vern, cranky that Lalor had stepped so blithely into the leadership, was holding his own meetings down at the Star Hotel. Lalor had been a late starter, not part of the original reform league elite. Not everyone trusted his motives.

Tomorrow was Sunday. By custom, the Sabbath was observed as a day of rest on the goldfields. There would be no digger hunts. It would be a time to step off the rollercoaster of November's events. Time to take stock. For some, time to pray. Father Smyth had personally entered the stockade and pleaded for those of his flock to be at mass in the morning. The meeting of the reform league was scheduled for 2pm at the Adelphi. At that meeting, the leadership would be able to discuss their policies and tactics. The majority of the 1500 people who were in the stockade to hear Lalor's afternoon oration felt free to leave. People began to relax. Saturday afternoon was regarded as a half-holiday. No one recollected a licence check on a Saturday afternoon. They could go back to their own tents, back to their families, back to the hotels and refreshment tents. As H. R. Nicholls later wrote, the desire *to turn out in good trim on Sunday had an effect which probably changed the fortune of war*. One after another, the diggers left the stockade *to get a clean shirt or to prepare in some way for Sunday*. A government spy dutifully reported the unexpected exodus from behind the barricades.

Nicholls himself went to one of the many shanties on the fringe of the stockade. There he and his mates *had drinks ourselves and conversed with a young lady, decidedly good-looking, who presided over the grog*. Nicholls stayed until midnight then returned to the stockade. Jane Cuming's husband Stephen also left the stockade that night on account of *all the carousing and singing*. He had urged Lalor to close the grog shops *because if they were allowed to remain open, I concluded that it would mean absolute ruin*. Stephen went home to Jane and Martineau and did not return.[7]

Swimming upstream was a contingent of Americans, led by James McGill. His Independent Californian Rangers had decided to defy Tarleton's pleas. They came now to the stockade, offering service. Many of McGill's troops had seen combat in the Mexican–American War. They bore arms like feathers in a cap. McGill himself carried a handsome sword, a gift of Sarah Hanmer—a precious heirloom, brought across the seas. In a dramatic flourish, McGill headed his troop of men with this sword drawn. All of the Adelphi Theatre's props—pistols, revolvers, sabres—had been distributed to the Californian Rangers. The actors themselves had swapped the stage for the Stockade. Was it as Carboni said—that the Stockade was nothing more than *our infatuation*, a higgledy-piggledy barricade containing a dozen family tents and sly-grog shops, defended by a handful of men brandishing theatre props?

By nightfall, about 1500 people remained in the Stockade, mostly those diggers and storekeepers like the Diamonds and the Shanahans, who lived in the captive tents; out-of-towners; and the sentries, chiefly Americans, posted to keep friends in and foes out.

There is another reason why so many of the men inside the Stockade on Saturday night might have gone home. There was a full moon. According to the principles of lunar menstrual synchrony, women are designed to ovulate on the full moon.[8] Female humans' biological blueprint is to release eggs when there is the most light in the night sky. Bleeding time thus corresponds to the new moon, a time of inward focus and self-nourishing.

The invention of electricity has changed this pre-modern prototype for human behaviour: now, not only do women menstruate at different times in the lunar cycle, but at different times from each other. However, most women are aware that when they live in close proximity to other women, their menstrual cycles start to coincide. With only candles and campfires for nightly illumination in the tents of Ballarat in 1854, women's menstrual cycles would very probably have synchronised. And they would have fallen into step with the phases of the moon.

When H. R. Nicholls rode in to Ballarat at the end of November and felt that *the whole place was electric*, could he have been reading the hormonal magnetism of the goldfield's five thousand women, a community in heat? The record is silent. Martha Clendinning was far too polite to discuss her bodily functions. Hobart Town Poll, who might have been relied on to call a cunt a cunt, didn't write her memoirs.

*

From the Camp, some two kilometres as the crow flies from Eureka, the Stockade site was a picture of abstract commotion. A dark ring in the centre, ragged lines of brown hats and blue shirts marching one way, then the other, then back again. A sea of white calico and canvas dots quivering in the breeze. A huge flag of blue and white rising from the ochre earth. The windlasses were still, the creeks and shafts abandoned. Distant figures darted in and out of tents. A moving canvas of conspicuous endeavour.

The details—faces, words, numbers—were a blur, but one thing was certain. Mining operations, domestic work, entertainment and commerce had ceased a day early. There were none of the usual Sunday pastimes: music, card games, bowling, shooting at targets, children playing quoits, women promenading in their finest clothes. Where was everybody? Only one person had been to the Camp to purchase a licence today—and that was a woman. Elizabeth Rowlands marched up to the commissioner's tent, clutching her baby Mary Ann, and bought herself a licence for £3. Then she took the licence back to her tent at Eureka and her husband burned it.

Was she a spy, checking the lie of the enemy's land? Perhaps the miners thought a new mother would get past the Camp's sentries. If so, they were right. This peculiar act, this unusual weekend limbo, must be a warning. A calm before the storm. An attack was surely imminent. Not if. No longer if. It was only a matter of when. The Camp was ready to fend off any assault. The territory was well and truly fortified. Sandbags, bales of hay, sacks of flour and wheat—all piled high around the most important buildings and along the front fence facing the diggings. Commissioner Rede had announced a curfew: no lights in neighbouring tents after 8pm, punishable by summary fire from the sentries.

The Camp was now under the jurisdiction of the military, which, according to civil servant G. H. Mann, *was rather awkward sometimes.* But still the troops kept piling in. Today, a contingent from the Castlemaine Camp. More backup—six hundred soldiers, plus munitions and cannon—were on their way from Melbourne, under the charge of the old warhorse Major-General Sir Robert Nickle, commander-in-chief of the forces in Victoria. Many of the soldiers at Ballarat had already been on twenty-four-hour sentry duty for days. They had passed several nights without a wink of sleep, hadn't washed or changed out of rain-soaked clothes. Over 540 edgy young men jostled for a place to lay their weary heads. But constant deliberate false alarms were given at night by Captain Thomas to keep the soldiers on their toes.

Huyghue described these men as *striplings…half weaned cubs of the Lion Mother*, newly arrived in Australia and disoriented by their long passage. Several of these boys—footsore, exhausted, unable to retaliate—had been violently ambushed as they entered Ballarat only two days earlier.

At the Camp, there were no longer any mother lions to give succour. Most wives and female servants, who helped with provisioning, had been sent away. Corporal John Neill's wife Ellen and their baby Fanny were an exception; they stayed put despite the privations and fear of attack. Rations were basic. All of the stores had been removed from the commissariat building and dumped outside, so as to vacate the space for shielding any remaining women and children, or the sick and infirm. Food was covered in grit, spoiled by damp. Water was in short supply, as the contracted carrier had not filled the week's order. Tradesmen either feared crossing the insurgents or were supporting them with an embargo on the Camp. The whole length of Lydiard

Street was an unbroken row of horses, tied to pickets, obliviously munching their fodder.

Samuel Huyghue was in the Camp on Saturday night. *An ominous and oppressive silence brooded over the deserted workings*, he later wrote. The full moon rose high in the cloudless sky. The breeze was gentle, still warm after the heat of the day. At 2.30am, Captain Thomas called on his troops to fall in. This time it was no false alarm. One hundred mounted and 175 foot soldiers assembled at the rear of the Camp, joined by a contingent of officers, police and civil commissioners. Police Inspector Gordon Evans handed around bottles of brandy to his men. They were told it was *for the benefit of all*.[9] The remaining 384 soldiers would stay to defend the Camp. At 3am, those chosen to fight slipped silently down the hill.

*

Military historian Gregory Blake has written a 240-page book about what happened next. The book offers a forensic dissection of the fifteen-minute gun battle to take the stockade. What follows here is a more impressionist account.

Corporal Neill, like most of his regiment, had slept in his clothes. He quietly fell in behind his sergeant, leaving Ellen and baby Fanny behind in bed. Captain Thomas, an old India man, led the troops the back way, down Mair Street, across Black Hill, past the Melbourne Road to the Free Trade Hotel. From here, detachments of the 12th and 40th regiments extended in skirmishing order. Part of the mounted force of military and police moved around the flank and rear of the slumbering Stockade. The idea was to get as close as possible without being seen. It was 4am on Sunday. No one was watching.

Of course, the question of who fired the first shot has been hotly contested for over 150 years. Both sides of the Stockade wished to claim the strategic immunity of self-defence. The moral economy of armed conflict requires an aggressor. Captain Thomas later reported to Hotham that when the troops were 150 metres from the barricade, he detected *rather sharp and well-directed fire from the insurgents…then, and not until then, I ordered commence firing*. Lalor wrote in a letter to the AGE on 9 April 1855 that, without warning or provocation, *almost immediately, the military poured in one or two volleys of musketry, which was a plain intimation that we must sell our lives as dearly as we could.* Blake reasons that on evidence and by logic 'there may have been several "first shots" within seconds of each other'. But from his extensive research and ballistic reconstruction, he is certain that the first shot came from within the Stockade.

Does it matter? The scene tells its own story. A sentry realises the Stockade is suddenly surrounded. Like mercury, in the magical hour of darkness between the full and waxing moon, the noose of the law has slipped around the stronghold.[10] A shot rings out, followed by deafening volleys. The sleeping residents of the Stockade jerk to attention at the sound of gunfire. Men scamper to get dressed, falling out of their tents with one leg in their pants. Women lie flat to the ground, folding their bodies around children and babies. Twenty-six-year-old Scotswoman Mary Faulds is in labour with her first child; her anguished cries cannot be distinguished from the frantic shouting around her. Bridget Shanahan hears the firing before her husband Timothy, who has not long gone to bed. She pulls him out of his cot, thrusts his gun in his hand, and tells him to go out. Timothy leaves the tent, but goes and hides in an outhouse. Bridget stays in the tent with their three children. Elizabeth Wilson, who keeps a store just outside the Stockade perimeter, loads rifles for her husband Richard. They have not bothered to change into nightclothes and are ready for action. Bridget Callinan distracts the soldiers while her wounded brothers Michael, Patrick and Thomas are helped away. (What did she do to divert the redcoats' attention? History does not record the nature of the distraction but a flash of thigh or breast might have done the trick.[11])

The exchange of fire went on for no more than fifteen minutes, until soldiers from the 40th Regiment strode over a low section of the barricade and the miners knew the jig was up. It was now a hand-to-hand fight between trained members of the British army and an undermanned team of zealous amateurs, their ardent wives and screaming children. *The entrenchment was then carried*, reported Captain Thomas, *and taken by the point of bayonet, the insurgents retreating. I ordered the firing to cease.*[12]

*

It's what happened after the surrender that really matters. It's what happened after the firing ceased that made contemporary observers call the Eureka clash a *massacre*, not a battle.

With the barricade breached and adrenaline surging, the lid was finally lifted off the simmering cauldron of military and police discipline. What bubbled over was a lethal stew of hunger, discomfort, exhaustion, boredom, insult, exasperation, sexual depravity, braggadocio, spite, homesickness, terror and relief. Charles Schulze, who operated a bakery on Bakery Hill and was an eyewitness to the violent outpouring of rancour that followed the rebels' surrender, could see what the weeks of Joe-ing had produced. *Jaded, tired, not allowed to return the insult*, he wrote, *you can imagine. That when the time came, they revenged themselves to the fullest extent.*[13]

It was the bayonets not the bullets that did the damage. Mayhem and carnage reigned, as the crazed soldiers and police thrust their blades into dead, dying and wounded miners. Gold lust gave way to blood lust as the Eureka line became a killing field. *It was a trooper that did it*, Anne Diamond later testified. *I know that my husband got three hurts from a sword on the back; he fell on his face and he got three cuts of a sword and a stab of a bayonet.*[14] Anne and her husband were fleeing from the Stockade when Martin was shot. *They treated the dead bodies very badly*, Anne reported twenty-two days after Martin's death. *The woman that laid him out could prove that.*

Some soldiers hacked at the bodies of those strewn on the ground. Others surrounded tents and sliced and jabbed at the bullet-riddled canvas. Ostensibly, they were on the hunt for prisoners; no insurgent should be allowed to escape. In effect, as the GEELONG ADVERTISER railed on 5 December, *those perfectly innocent of rebellious notions were murdered, fired at and horribly mangled by the troopers.* Outnumbered and trapped, many insurgents were literally butchered. One eyewitness later reported that:

> every body had a plurality of mortal wounds: the corpses of the slain had been hacked by the mounted troopers out of sheer brutality…It was a needless massacre. Not even at the siege of Sebastopol did British soldiers kill enemies who lay wounded and defenceless.[15]

The residents of the Stockade could not believe their eyes.

Those who were able began to run towards Brown Hill, at the rear of the Stockade where the palisade did not quite join. The scrub was thick and the ground broken, impeding the troopers' mounts. Brown Hill would shelter outlaws for weeks to come. Others jumped down mine shafts, heedless of deep water. Their bloated bodies were fished out days later. Some fled into neighbouring tents, where they clambered up sod chimneys or shimmied under cots. Some of the wounded within the Stockade found themselves cloaked by the shuddering bodies of women, pretending to mourn their dead in order that the soldiers would pass without further recrimination. Bridget Hynes threw herself over an injured man and cried, *He is dead! He is dead!* so that the troopers would not run him through. Bridget was two months pregnant with her first child, a honeymoon conception under a happier full moon. Peter Lalor, who had been shot in the shoulder, was dragged under a ledge and safely concealed. Henry Ross, mortally wounded, was not so lucky. At least he was spared the pain of seeing the *chaste* flag that he had sired dragged down from its mast by Constable John King and paraded before his fellow policemen as a trophy of war.

Officers remained silent as boy soldiers taunted and assaulted bystanders. The bodies of the dead were heaped together face up: mouths gaping, eyes fixed. *Several of them were still heaving*, an eyewitness reported to the GEELONG ADVERTISER, *and at every rise of their breasts, the blood spouted out of their wounds, or just bubbled out and trickled away.*[16] The victims of the frantic attack were not only the deceased. Standing by, tragically alive to the moment, were *poor women crying for absent husbands and children frightened into quietness.* Other women had bolted from their tents, leaving their husbands behind. Mary Curtain rushed out of her store in her nightgown with fifteen-month-old Mary Agnes in tow. Mary was eight months pregnant. *Such was the terror and hurry with which my family fled*, husband Patrick Curtain later claimed, *that they left behind them even their every day dress.*[17]

Another man woke on hearing the shots. He went out of his tent in his shirt and drawers. Seeing what was happening, he shouted at a trooper *For God's sake don't kill my wife and children. He was shot dead on his own threshold.*[18]

What more humiliating way to surrender? A dawn raid. On a Sunday. The miners caught with their pants down on their own doorsteps. Who would be swaggering now?

If the soldiers and police were perturbed by the presence of families in their frenzied midst, most did not show it. *A poor woman and her children*, reported a stunned GEELONG ADVERTISER correspondent,

> were standing outside a tent. She said that the troopers had surrounded the tent, and pierced it with their swords. She, her husband, and her children were ordered out by the troopers, and were inspected in their night clothes outside, while the troopers searched the tent.[19]

Some troopers demonstrated more compunction. Charles Ferguson, one of McGill's Californian Rangers, saw a woman come running out of her tent in her nightdress. She ran over to some soldiers who had captured her husband. She begged them to release him *but she was only pushed around roughly by the soldiers, when at last the commanding officer rode up and ordered them to deliver to the woman her husband.* Ferguson had the highest praise for this chivalrous fellow: *That was a manly officer.*

Not so fortunate was Rebecca Noonan. Thirty-two-year-old Rebecca ran a store one hundred yards from the stockade. Her husband Michael was a miner. The couple, natives of County Clare, had five children. As the family was attempting to escape from their burning tent, Michael was stopped by police and arrested. Michael pleaded that he was *a peaceable and loyal subject of Her Majesty and [his] Excellency's Government*, but was taken into custody regardless. Rebecca remonstrated. She was then *brutally assaulted by the foot police and her life threatened.*[20] Rebecca was four months pregnant.

Mary Faulds' predicament was extreme. When soldiers burst into her tent in the stockade she was lying on the ground, wedged between two cots with a blanket covering her, labouring to bring her baby into this mad world. The soldiers turned around and left her to her fear and anguish. Mary's baby Adeliza was born later that day.[21] Other women performed feats of remarkable courage. Richard Wilson fled his shop, leaving his wife Elizabeth behind. A miner raced up to her and said, *Look Ma'am, where can I hide?* She replied, *Right where you stand.* And with that she lifted her dress, pushed the man to the floor, stepped over him and swathed him in her hoop skirts.[22]

Women's clothing was in high demand. Frederick Vern, who had not been in the Stockade at the time of the attack, escaped Ballarat disguised as a woman. Captain James McGill also parted with his sex for a short season. He fled into the bush, where he was later met by Sarah Hanmer, who provided him with dress, shawl and bonnet—either her own or costumes from the theatre—and food for his journey into hiding.[23]

Other women risked their own safety to aid the wounded and dying. A defenceless man was cut and slashed on his body and head near the tent of Dr Leman, close to the stockade. Mrs Leman heard the man's cries and left the cover of her tent to assist him. *The cruel sight drew an expression of horror from her*, reported an onlooker, *which reaching the ears of one of the butchers he turned around and deliberately fired at her.*[24] The shot missed and the soldier fired again as Emma Leman fled back into her tent.

The man Mrs Leman risked her life to help was

twenty-three-year-old English miner Henry Powell. He had come from Creswick the previous day to visit William Cox, who lived with his wife Eliza on the Eureka, only a short distance from the stockade. Eliza was forty-four years old, the same age as Ellen Young, and had only been in the colony eight months. She had five children and Powell was keen on the eldest daughter, twenty-four-year-old Fanny. If Henry had come to ask for Fanny's hand, his timing was fatal. When he emerged from the Coxes' tent on Sunday morning, he was confronted by Arthur Akehurst, clerk of the police court, who promptly dashed the innocent Powell over the head with his sword and told him he was a prisoner. As Powell lay dazed and bleeding on the ground, Akehurst cut him several more times and fired at him, then mounted troopers arrived and trampled him with their horses. William Cox was arrested. He asked for a moment to put on his clothes but, according to Eliza who stood by, *they said no you bugger come along.*[25]

William Cox was corralled with the other 114 prisoners taken to the Camp. One of those arrested was Raffaello Carboni, who had been asleep in his tent at the time of the attack. Carboni was *dragged out, and hobbled to a dozen more prisoners outside, and we were marched to the Camp*. Another was Timothy Hayes, who was also at home with his family when the stockade was taken. He was making his way to the stockade to assist the wounded when he was arrested. On seeing the mounted troops leading her handcuffed husband back to the Camp, Anastasia rushed headlong between the horses and bawled out Timothy's captors. *If I had been a man*, she spat, *I wouldn't have been taken by so few as these.*[26] It's hard to know at whom the insult was directed.

The shameful fact was that the stockade was a shambles. It was a piece of theatre that broke loose from its script of cat-and-mouse local politics—the persecutors and the persecuted, hunters and the hunted—and spilled human blood. The weapons were real and the stakes were high: no less than manly honour and duty were on the line. Peter Lalor himself had admitted that he *would be unworthy of being called a man... were I base enough to desert my companions in danger.* But the very men who had been goaded into resistance, rendered impotent by a legal system that denied them rights and a taxation system that made them paupers, disappointed by a land that promised reward for honest toil but delivered instead disease, death and penury, hacking away at barren rock while their womenfolk found fertile ground for their skills and labour—these men could not even defend their wives and families from danger, let alone their companions, when push came to deadly shove. It was the final indignity.

The Ballarat miners had come to Victoria to be independent and free men, proud and virtuous colonists. *Modern Argonauts. Young Hercules*, as guidebook author Samuel Mossman had promised. Most had failed to feed, clothe or adequately house the families they brought with them or those they quickly started. And, finally, there was nothing heroic about watching your women be assaulted while standing in the dawn light in your drawers.

*

Not satisfied with the show of potency occasioned by the thrust of bayonets, the order was given to burn to the ground all of the tents in the Stockade and vicinity. The Camp had failed to stop a conflagration at Bentley's Hotel, and now it would generate its own apocalyptic ruins. Tactically speaking, fire would root out any insurgent hiding in civilian enclosures. In terms of theatre, nothing instils fear like fire. So, using a pot of burning tar, the troopers and soldiers set about torching every tent on the ground. *There was no system to regulate our search*, one police officer later testified. Another admitted that the police had no idea whether the occupants were in the tents before they fired them.[27] From the Camp, Samuel Huyghue listened to the *deep reverberations* of musketry *telling us that there was a real collision at last*, then ghostly silence. In a trice, he could see only *sheets of smoke and flame.*

In the Stockade, some of the blazing tents contained the bodies of the wounded or dead. Two men who burned to death in their tent had either passed out or were still asleep. The sight of their charred remains was so sickening that even the soldiers had to turn away. Patrick Curtain had managed to escape the Stockade without injury. He found Mary and little Mary Agnes, and delivered them to friends. *On my return after leaving my family in safety at a distance*, he later wrote in an unsuccessful claim for compensation, *I found my store all in flames without a chance of saving anything.*[28]

There was a knock at Bridget Shanahan's door. Timothy had not returned. He may still have been hiding in the outhouse. A trooper and a foot soldier barged in. *Shoot that woman*, ordered the trooper. The soldier begged, *Spare the woman.* The trooper hesitated. *Well, get out of this place*, he finally said, *the place is going to be burnt woman.* The men set fire to the tent, but Bridget managed to put it out before much was destroyed.[29]

The ring of fire extended out in cataclysmic ripples. Most of the surrounding tents were diggers' homes, stores and small grog shops. *Some of these*, marvelled Huyghue, *were actually defended by their occupants while burning, and several contained women and children who were with difficulty rescued from the flames.* John Sheehan's wife and children were huddled inside their tent when it was set alight.[30] And did not get out in time. The Curtains and Shanahans, being inside the Stockade, perhaps expected some retribution. But the Sheehans' tent was outside the barricade and being *strictly honest sober and industrious* and having *no part directly or indirectly* in the uprising, they did not anticipate the troops' vengeance. Other people had not even been in the neighbourhood on that Sunday morning, but similarly all lost their belongings in the wholesale torching. James Bourke and his wife and family had left their tent, unfortunately positioned next to the Stockade, on Friday night. When James returned on Sunday afternoon, *I found my said Tent and all my property therein consumed.*[31] Like the many other families who were completely dispossessed of their tents, stores, clothes, furniture, cash and personal items, the Bourkes received no compensation.

According to Huyghue, Lalor owed his escape to the fact that the soldier who saw him fall was *fully engrossed…in rescuing an old Scotchwoman and her family of children from her burning tent, a task of considerable difficulty which evoked an expression of fervid gratitude from the relieved parent.* The woman quickly snatched a piece of paper from the smouldering wreck of her home and asked her rescuer to write his name so she could remember *to whom she owed what doubtless seemed to her an act of remarkable generosity.*

As the moonlit night was gently displaced by iridescent morning, the reality of the situation became clear. It was not a bad dream. There was no silver lining. *Stragglers from the neighborhood of the stockade*, wrote eyewitness John Fraser, *some of them in a state of the greatest terror and excitement, came hurrying along close to the tents.* An Irishman approached Fraser for a drink of water. He had his wife and three little children with him.

The poor woman, crying bitterly, presented, to our

> mind, a picture of distress, as, nursing her infant in her arms, she bewailed in heartrending tones the loss of their little possessions—tent, clothes, everything—burnt and destroyed by the troopers.[32]

William Adams, who ran a store near the stockade, was shot three times while trying to flee his burning tent with his wife and child. After he emerged from a week in the Camp hospital, he estimated the loss of his family's worldly goods to be £937 10s. He had £4 10s in his pocket when he was taken to the hospital; the loose change was missing from his blood-splattered pants when he was released. As for the Eureka Flag, an anonymous eyewitness sent his account to the GEELONG ADVERTISER:

> The diggers standard was carried by in triumph to the Camp, waved about in the air, then pitched from one another, thrown down and trampled upon.[33]

Those participating in the victory dance then proceeded to cut off little pieces of the flag and tuck them away as souvenirs. Small patches of Prussian blue wool have been turning up in public collections ever since, roosting like pigeons scattered on the breeze.[34]

Commanding officers turned a blind eye to the brutal, petty and wilful misdeeds of their junior charges. As far as Hotham was concerned, it was simply a case of boys being boys.[35] But apart from arson, murder and pillage, what other spoils of war might these unbridled young men have seized? There are subtle intimations of still more 'unmanly acts' perpetrated amid the chaos and terror, acts that Victorian sensibilities preferred to consign to the reader's imagination. Thomas Pierson alludes to *hundreds of other cruel deeds done by these fiends that would strike any civilised person with horror*. Dan Calwell the young American, who, with his brother Davis, appears to have remained part of the peaceful faction, wrote home to his parents and sister reporting on the Stockade clash. The victors, reported Dan, *committed all the brutalities of the darker ages.* H. R. Nicholls recounted that a few nights after the Stockade, he visited the grog shop of the *young and pretty girl, who attracted much attention.* Her tent was close to the Stockade, but was inexplicably not burned down. The girl told him that on the morning of the attack her tent was *full of fugitives—some lying on the ground, some under tables, and all afraid that they would be discovered.* She stood outside the tent. Some troopers approached her. She told them she was alone *and hoped that they would not hurt her.* One *excited soldier* ran his bayonet through her dress, but his companions called him away and he didn't enter the tent. The Gold Fields Commission of Enquiry later found that *the scenes connected with this outbreak...as stated to the Commission, and as currently rumoured, exhibit some of those disgraceful inhumanities that are the customary feature of a social outbreak.* The commissioners acknowledged that the mounted police, in particular, had committed the sort of acts of indiscriminate violence displayed *in moments of ungovernable excitement* but *declined to elaborate this subject further.*

Anthropologist Roland Littlewood argues, in one of the few expositions of military rape, that sexual violence in warfare has occurred from Hebrew times through to the twentieth-century atrocities of Rwanda and Bosnia. Incidents, however, are rarely reported. Sexual assault by soldiers 'reflects badly' not only on the perpetrators but also 'on the victim, for an explicit justification frequently made by the soldiers who rape women is that it is to degrade and humiliate them'. Littlewood's research shows that most military rapes occur in house-to-house searches and reprisal attacks; sexual gratification is often rationalised on the grounds that the assaulted women were housing enemies of the state.

Here is the politics of sexuality inextricably linked to the sexuality of politics. Perpetrating male violence on the female body aims to do symbolic violence to the body politic. Just as the flag was symbolically trampled and souvenired, so Ballarat's women may well have been taken as a trophy of battle. As we have seen, women in Ballarat played an inordinately prominent role in mobilising and validating the social and political grievances of their community. If some soldiers did penetrate the sexual strongholds of Eureka's women, it made for a far more abject surrender than Eureka's men were prepared to concede openly.

*

It was all over by the time the sun scaled Mt Warrenheip.

For the troops and police returning to Camp at daybreak, the taste of victory was intoxicating. Still, they were given more rum—a reward, perhaps, or a timeless anaesthetic for the soul. When the soldiers were finally dismissed from duty, Huyghue tells us, *they rushed cheering and capering like school boys to their tents*. In his report to Governor Hotham the following day, Captain Thomas was pleased to advise that the behaviour of the troops and police, both officers and men, was *very good*.

Meanwhile, the people of Ballarat woke to the smell of burning canvas and the eerie sounds of mourning. Slowly people descended on the Stockade in silent fascination and horror. Lifeless and disfigured bodies had been laid out in neat rows, their clothes saturated with blood from those horrible bayonet wounds, with military guards standing over them lest they rise from the dead and scamper off.

During the next few hours, grieving relatives and friends retrieved the bodies, taking them home to be nursed or shrouded. Some diggers were dragged to nearby hotels turned into makeshift hospitals. Henry Powell was removed to the Albion Hotel, where the landlady Mrs O'Kell had only four months earlier brandished her gun at the murderous American Robert Clarke, peeved over a card game. She had by now passed the licence to Albert Goldstein. What was that Californian maxim about women and Jews? In Victoria, it was neither Shylock nor the shrew that blighted the limitless frontier; the British army took care of all that.

Thomas Pierson was not in the Stockade for the battle, but like most of Ballarat's residents, he either visited or knew those who had. The treatment of the prisoners and wounded was, in his opinion, *characteristic of English warfare. Most heathenish, blood-thirsty, disgraceful and cruel.* In nine years' time America would begin its own civil war, a conflict that would last four years and claim the lives of at least 650,000 soldiers and an unquantifiable number of civilians.

Charles Evans, too, was filled with disgust when he walked down to the Stockade on Sunday afternoon. That night he bared his troubled soul to his diary. *The brave noble hearts did not turn their swords on armed men*, he wrote, *but galloped courageously among the tents shooting at women, and cutting down defenceless men*. The young Shropshire lad's world had been turned upside down. *I did not guess that Englishmen in authority had made such savage use and cowardly use of their power as unhappily proved to be the case*, he scribbled, his hand trembling with fury and pity. *Newly made widows recognising the bloody remains of a slaughtered husband*, Evans went on, unable to stem the flow of his rueful outpourings. *Children screaming and crying round a dead father... cowardly and monstrous cruelties...It is a dark indelible stain on a British Government.*

Ballarat was in a state of shock. *Instead of the noisy mirth which usually characterises Sunday here*, Evans concluded his entry for 3 December, *an uncomfortable stillness prevails and many seem to think it is the lull before the tempest.* In fact, the storm had passed.

*

Now there was the clean-up.

All the unclaimed dead and wounded were brought to the Camp in carts that afternoon—three dray-loads full of maimed and lifeless bodies. Huyghue saw the mangled remains in the Camp hospital. The dead rebels' faces were *ghastly and passionately distorted.* Half-clothed, surprised from sleep, they remained frozen in a burlesque of battle. The nameless dead were unceremoniously buried at the cemetery on Monday. Regimental and civilian surgeons attempted to patch up the shattered limbs and ragged gashes of the wounded.

Four soldiers were dead: Privates William Webb (nineteen years) and Felix Boyle (thirty-two years) of the 12th Regiment and Michael Roney (twenty-two years) and Joseph Wall of the 40th (twenty years). At least nine more soldiers and police were wounded.

Captain Henry Wise, a twenty-five-year-old commissioned officer and the most popular soldier in the division, died of a gunshot wound to his leg on 21 December. He had only been in the country four weeks before he sustained his mortal injury leading the first line of troops into the Stockade. Before he died, Wise gamely announced that *his dancing was spoiled.* Henry Wise left a wife, Jane, to dance alone. Did she have a friend to comfort her at the Victoria Barracks in Melbourne, so forlorn, so far from home? Perhaps not; a Mrs Wise sailed for London in February 1855.

It is impossible to say exactly how many civilians died at the Stockade, in the surrounding tents or in the bush and the mine shafts where the dazed and wounded fled. There were many body counts that circulated in the following days and weeks. Peter Lalor famously published a list of the Eureka martyrs, in which he named twenty-two. Timothy Shanahan also counted twenty-two. Samuel Huyghue estimated thirty to forty. Dan Calwell reported to his American relatives a figure of thirty killed. In his diary entry for 6 December, Thomas Pierson noted twenty-five deaths. But some time later he scrawled in the margin, *time has proved that near 60 have died of the diggers in all.* Captain Thomas wrote in his official report that the casualties of the military action had been *great* but there was *no means of ascertaining correctly.* He estimated at least thirty killed on the spot, and *many more died of their wounds subsequently.* The numbers of injuries and fatalities, reported the GEELONG ADVERTISER on 8 December, were *more numerous than originally supposed.*

Among the known dead were Martin Diamond, Anne's husband; John Hynes, cousin to Bridget Hynes' husband; Patrick Gittens, who had been the best man at Bridget's wedding; Prussian Jew Teddy Thonen, the 'lemonade seller'; Llewellyn Rowlands, who was shot in the chest by troopers outside his tent, half a mile from the Stockade. He wasn't Elizabeth Rowlands' husband, but maybe the troopers thought he was and deliberately sought him out for his wife's presumed treachery the previous morning. So many people caught in the wrong place at the wrong time, collateral damage of bitterly unfriendly fire. G. H. Mann simply recorded that *an onerous number of funerals were frequently passing to the cemetery for many days.*

Of these funeral corteges, Charles Evans described only

one—the one that began our story. This is the coffin trimmed with white and followed by *a respectable and sorrowful group*. This is the coffin containing a dead woman, whose body was claimed but not named. This is the woman mercilessly butchered by a mounted trooper while she was pleading for the life of her husband. We don't know whether he was spared—whether she took the bullet or the bayonet for him. We don't know whether she left motherless children behind. We don't know how many other women may have been among the numbers of dead that could not be ascertained correctly. This is the woman who was slipped quietly into the earth by her weeping friends and loved ones, then slipped just as silently out of history.

*

The seismic front had passed, but there was one fatal aftershock. Directly after the riots, as the government would now refer to the storming of the Stockade, Ballarat was placed under martial law by order of Governor Hotham. There could be no light in any tent after 8pm. Reprisals were expected; the Camp was still jumpy as a cut snake. On Monday night, one trigger-happy sentry thought he heard gunfire coming from a tent close to the Camp. He opened fire. *Among the victims of last night's unpardonable recklessness*, wrote Charles Evans in his diary on Tuesday, *were a woman and her infant. The same ball which murdered the mother (for that's the term for it) passed through the child as it lay sleeping in her arms*. He also recorded that another young woman had a miraculous escape.

> Hearing the reports of musketry and the dread whiz of bullets around her, she ran out of her tent to seek shelter. She had just got outside when a ball whistled

> immediately before her eyes passing through both sides of her bonnet.

This is the Woman of '54, the one who would write to the papers in 1884 to tell of the night she almost lost her life, a tale she related as an antidote to the noticeably chauvinistic thirtieth anniversary commemorations. This is the woman who called Humffray a coward. Closer to the action, Charles Evans had no trouble attesting to *monstrous acts like these polluting the soil with the innocent blood of men women and children*.

One woman's terror was another's opportunity. In the midst of the chaos of renewed firing, screaming and panic on that Monday night, a lone figure stole out from the Camp. Clouds obscured the moon, waning now, and the person chose the moment to run down the hill, keeping close to the picket fence to avoid holes and tent ropes. *In an instant*, recalled Samuel Huyghue, *a dozen rifles were pointed at the moving object when a ray of moonlight befriended her (for it proved to be a woman) and she got off scatheless.* The soldiers were more discerning now than they had been the previous morning. *As soon as her garments revealed her sex the deadly weapons were lowered,* wrote Huyghue. *It was a close shave but perhaps she never realised to the full the danger she escaped.*

It's more likely this woman was fully aware of the risks of stealing into the Camp to see her husband, who was one of the prisoners. But Anastasia Hayes was nothing if not a risk-taker. She had five children and a newborn baby, but still she found the nerve to broker a *secret communication* with Timothy through the connivance of the lockup keeper, who was subsequently arrested for his perfidy. Huyghue's own suspicion was that Anastasia was working as a spy for the reform league and that part of her plan was to rescue the prisoners by creating a diversion.

Paranoia had gripped the Camp by now. For good measure, the prisoners were transferred from the 'logs' to the zinc-lined commissariat store. This means the women who had stayed at the Camp during the previous terrifying days, including Ellen Neill and baby Fanny, must have been moved out. Maggie Johnston recorded the week's bizarre arrangements in her diary.

> December 3 Sunday
> The awful day of the attack made at the Eureka at 5 in the morning.
>
> December 4 Monday
> All day long funerals passing.
>
> December 5 Tuesday
> Somewhat similar.
>
> December 6 Wednesday
> Mrs Lane staying with me for a week.

*

By the end of that train wreck of a month, the bulk of the funerals were over, the shops were once again open, mining operations were in full steam and the rattle of the windlass chimed in syncopated rhythm with squeezeboxes, street bands, shrieking children and barking dogs.

Peter Lalor, with the connivance of Stephen and Jane Cuming, was in hiding in Geelong, under the care of Alicia Dunne. Along with Lalor, Frederick Vern, George Black and James McGill also had a price on their heads. Thirteen men—including Timothy Hayes, Raffaello Carboni and the *nigger rebel*, African-American John Joseph—were on their way to Melbourne to be tried for treason. Henry Seekamp had been arrested in his home, with Clara and her children looking on, and would contest a charge of sedition.

The rest of the prisoners were released to the ruins of their burnt-out tents, grief-stricken kin and uncertain futures. Robert Rede's report for the last week of December noted a population increase of 855 women and 1955 children, and a decrease of 4130 men. *A better state of order is returning*, he wrote, *and the miners are resuming work…little gold has been raised.*[36]

Eureka Wright, whose parents Thomas and Mary Wright were in their tent inside the stockade when it was stormed, celebrated her first birthday.

Dear Jamie and I spent a quiet day all alone, wrote Maggie Johnston. *Our first Christmas after our marriage.* Her baby quickened.

A year earlier, Thomas Pierson had wondered what fate would befall him, Frances and Mason by the next Christmas. Now, he joined with thousands of other drunk and sunburnt people thronging the long Main Road that ran through the Flat to rejoice at the birth of Christ and other small miracles. It was a hundred degrees; the flies were as thick as Connecticut snow, and Thomas reckoned he would never grow accustomed to this strange country. Yuletide tells a story of birth, hope and promise in a spiritual sanctum, but for Thomas and Frances, after all they had seen, *the exiles dream of home is past.*

CONCLUSION

A DAY AT THE RACES

There was little work done in those last weeks of 1854. The aftermath of what soon became known as the Eureka Stockade—the AGE newspaper gave the bloody event this name on 20 December—took its toll on the usual bustling hive of end-of-year industry. First there were the funerals; then came the removal of incinerated tents, the stocktake of decimated business and the shelter of homeless families. There were preparations for Christmas too. And all under the blazing sun of a summer hot spell.

But there was another matter more pressing than the body count, the burnt-out ground of the Eureka or the baking of mince tarts. There was the matter of the races.

The races are the absorbing topic, noted the Ballarat correspondent of the GEELONG ADVERTISER on 27 December. The inaugural Ballarat Race Meeting had been planned for months. The event was intended to rival *the oldest and best regulated courses in this colony* and put the fledgling goldfields town on the sporting calendar. A weighing machine had been purchased at great expense, a track cleared some seven miles from the Camp, near Bald Hills, beyond Waldock's Station, and stewards appointed for the five-day meet, which was slated to commence on 12 December. Prize money had been collected for the Hack Race, the Maiden Plate, the Camp Purse, the Ballarat Town Plate, the Publicans Purse, the Gold Diggings Plate, the Consolation Stakes and the Ladies Purse: a rollcall of Ballarat's social taxonomy as clear as the blue sky itself.

But, according to the BALLARAT TIMES, the *recent disturbances were ill calculated to promote sporting affairs.* There was also the considerable complication that two of the stewards—Messrs Rede and Johnston—were more likely to be lynched than listened to should they appear before a drunk and festive public. Johnston, noted the BALLARAT TIMES, *always sounded as if he was insulting you*, adding generously that *perhaps he could not help it.* Rede, the paper conceded, was an *accomplished scholar* and *generous donor* to charitable causes, but *his manner* set everyone at odds. For their own safety, both Rede and Johnston had left Ballarat shortly after the Stockade clash.

So the first race day was rescheduled for Boxing Day and new stewards were appointed, neutral men unlikely to incite another riot. But still the fates were cruel to the sport of kings. Four thousand post-Christmas revellers walked the seven miles in scorching heat to the racecourse only to discover that the weighing apparatus had been accidentally damaged and the first race postponed indefinitely. *It is too much to expect large assemblages of people to remain patient under a scorching sun*, noted the TIMES. *Liquids of all kinds* were *eagerly sought for.* Ice sellers did a roaring trade, while pickpocket gangs swarmed from one *hard drinking* circle to the next. Sarah Hanmer was in attendance but got herself into *a difficulty* that soon gave rise *to a good deal of yabber…too private and intricate to publish.* By the time new scales had arrived and Mr Keating's bay horse *had it all his own way* in the Hack Race later that evening, the crowd was legless.

On day two, clouds of dust billowed in the arc of a northerly gale. The faces of punters looked *as if at a masquerade ball*, so besmeared with topsoil and sweat that you couldn't *recognize your most intimate friend*. Then the seven-mile stagger back to the diggings, only to repeat the trek the following day. One party, who had hired a horse-drawn conveyance to relieve the slog, had cause to regret their indolence when the buggy overturned, resulting in serious injury to several passengers.

Next the temperature plummeted and *a perfect deluge* flooded the track. *A sudden change of the weather*, noted the TIMES, *rendered a visit to the course more an act of martyrdom than pleasure*. By the end of the stormy third day, when the Ladies Purse (*presented by the Ladies of Ballarat and Creswick of not less than 100 sovereigns…1 mile and a half, 11 stone; gentleman riders*) was taken out by Mr Waldock's St Patrick, the people of Ballarat must have wondered whether they were being punished for something.

But their suffering was rewarded. *With Old Father Christmas*, concluded the TIMES, *five days' good racing, and a race dinner and ball crowded into one week, we ought to have enjoyed ourselves*. William Westgarth, who was in Ballarat as a member of the Gold Fields Commission of Enquiry established by Governor Hotham to investigate the root cause of miners' grievances, thought the races *a most absorbing spectacle*.[1]

A week-long holiday had scuttled the gold escort (the armed guard transporting gold to Melbourne) but done wonders for the morale of a community beset with trauma, *sickened by hope deferred*.

*

New Year's Day 1855 was ushered in by an even more absorbing sight than thousands of well-oiled race-goers. *To our readers,* beckoned the editor of the BALLARAT TIMES, *A happy new year to you all.* Clara Seekamp continued her leader:

> That you may have better health, more wealth, and much more justice this year than during the one just past, is the earnest prayer of your fellow labourer—the Editor.

With her husband awaiting trial on charges of sedition, Clara Seekamp took the reins of their family enterprise. She published the list of subscribers to the proposed Miners Hospital: topping the list was Sarah Hanmer with a generous £53 donation. (The second-largest contribution was from Robert Rede.) She published a letter from Jewish auctioneer Henry Harris, beseeching the Ballarat community to come to the financial aid of those *unfortunates who have innocently suffered from the late fearful entente on the Eureka [when] women became widows, children fatherless.* There is also a letter from 'Quartz', encouraging people to write to *the enquiry into the late massacre* and *make suggestions to the Commission on political questions.*

There are many remarkable features of the New Year's Day paper, but the most outstanding is by far the least prominent. Edition 45 of the BALLARAT TIMES, Monday, January 1, 1855, bears a small imprint in the bottom corner of the last column of its final page:

> *Printed and published by Mrs Seekamp, Ballarat.*

These seven little words encapsulate the other insurrection that had occurred in the watershed year of 1854.

When a few hundred polyglot gold miners hastily constructed a rough palisade around fifteen tents on the Eureka Lead, they intended to provide a place of armed refuge for unlicensed diggers against the legally sanctioned licence hunts designed to oppress, entrap and emasculate them. They raised a flag that would fly beside the French, German, American, British, Canadian and other standards that were customarily flown at public meetings. They called it the Australian Flag. Standing below that flag's simple, geopolitically specific design, they swore an oath to stand by each other to defend their rights and liberties. Those rights, they considered, were nothing more or less than their entitlement as free-born Britons to be treated like men. Not animals, serfs or slaves: men.

The miners were not disloyal to their sovereign, but rather had lost any shred of respect for the minions who served her. They did not want to change the system of government; they wanted to be included in it. At no time did they riot against or launch an assault on authorities. They were not insurgents. They were not revolutionaries. For the most part, they were British subjects denied the basic civilities of British justice. They were ethnic insiders being treated like outsiders. They rebelled against an unpopular and viciously policed poll tax when all peaceful means of protest had been rebuffed. They fought back when attacked by the military in a pre-emptive strike that was intended to restore the authority of a government that taxed but would not listen, a goldfields regime that postulated but would not protect, and an imperialist agenda that had promised so much but delivered precious little.

They sewed a flag and built a fence.

Flailing desperately to conjure a worthy enemy following bloody Sunday, Governor Hotham quickly determined that only *foreigners* could be responsible for such outrageous acts of perfidy. No one was fooled, least of all when Hotham declared an amnesty for any Americans involved in the affray. The Americans had been the only ones who, perhaps, truly did foresee a republican future and for whom insurrection against redcoats had already proved a successful political strategy. Clara Seekamp certainly was not duped by Hotham's scapegoating tactic. In her leader on New Year's Day 1855, she called Hotham to account:

> Who are the foreigners? Where are the foreigners? What is it that constitutes a foreigner?...Poor Governor Hotham! Could you not have found some other more truthful excuse for all the illegal and even murderous excesses committed by your soldiery and butchers?...Why did you disregard our memorials and entreaties, our prayers and our cries for justice and protection against your unjust stewards here, until the people, sickened by hope deferred, and maddened by continued and increased acts of oppression, were driven to take up arms in self defence?

That Clara's action—offering a political analysis of the Eureka Stockade—was genuinely revolutionary is evident in the general response. William Westgarth, opening his copy of the BALLARAT TIMES on New Year's Day, did not fail to notice the breathtaking hubris of its emancipated editor. The TIMES was *at war with the authorities local and general*, he surmised before adding smugly, *we amused ourselves with the violent style of the 'leaders'*. Tickled by his own sparkling wit, Westgarth made a pun of a woman aspiring to editorial governance. He forgot, perhaps, that with no representation in the legislature, the diggers could only make their voice heard through the press. In Ballarat, the only press was the BALLARAT TIMES, whose usual leader-writer was presently in prison on charges of sedition, with his wife stepping to the breach.

There is no extant copy of edition 46, but Clara was evidently still chafing at the bit. The BALLARAT TIMES *contains...a manifesto from Mrs Seekamp*, wrote a journalist at the GEELONG ADVERTISER (soon syndicated throughout the country), *as startling in its tone, and as energetic in its language, italics, and capitals, and the free use of the words 'sedition', 'liberty', 'oppression' etc as a Russian ukase would be.* The reporter had a novel solution to this remarkable situation:

> I only hope that Sir William a'Beckett will at once perceive that a lenient sentence upon Mr Seekamp and a quick return to his editorial duties, will relieve, at all events, the gold field of Ballarat from the dangerous influence of a free press petticoat government.

The Ballarat troubles had been caused, in part, by lack of judicial transparency and unchecked miscarriages of justice, yet the (pro-democracy) ADVERTISER's reporter was prepared to suggest that Attorney General William a'Beckett exercise his discretion to restore the status of the press as a bastion of masculine authority. He was not alone. Charles Thatcher, the famous goldfields balladeer, also had something to say about Clara's editorial style. In his popular ditty 'Ballarat Comic Alphabet', penned in 1855, Thatcher devoted 'S' to the imprisoned Seekamp:

> S is for Seekamp who I trust will be
> Released upon my life
> It will but save us from the trash
> Inserted by his wife [2]

The anomaly of Clara's pre-eminence at the masthead of the TIMES only served to affirm the general state of affairs that Thatcher lamented in other of his verses. *The gals that come out to Australia to roam/Have much higher notions than when they're at home,* he sang in 'London and the Diggings'.[3] Having women call the political race was clearly too big a hurdle for most people.

Nonetheless, Clara Seekamp and Ellen Young were not the only women to use the press as a route to the political influence otherwise denied them. On 7 December, Caroline Chisholm wrote a letter to the editor of the ARGUS. Vitriol was not her style. *Any thoughtful person who calmly views our present condition, either commercially or politically*, she wrote, would see the problem was underutilisation of *the rich and beautiful land God has given us.* With remarkable prescience, Chisholm concluded that *we are a nation of consumers instead of producers.* Pre-figuring the mining magnates of over a century later, she counselled Governor Hotham to *stop taxing and start ploughing*, a plea that echoed one of the miners' key grievances: unlock the lands!

*

In the weeks directly following the Stockade clash, miners formed yet another quixotic expectation: that justice would be done. By 15 December, there were calls for the exhumation of the bodies that had been swiftly buried in makeshift graves. The date is important. On 9 December, Henry Powell—the unarmed miner outside the Stockade who had been *dreadfully mangled* by a policeman despite the protests of Eliza Cox—died of his wounds. The following day, an inquest was held. The finding of the inquest, published on the 13th, was that the mounted police were culpable of *firing at and cutting down the unarmed and innocent persons of both sexes.* Powell's was the only coronial investigation of any death that occurred during or after the Eureka clash. Subsequent to his burial, the Ballarat correspondent for the GEELONG ADVERTISER predicted that all the bodies lately buried would be exhumed and inquests held. *It is said by those who are learned in law*, the ADVERTISER suggested, *that all those killed on the 3rd and who had died subsequently of their wounds should have been subject to Coroner's inquests.* Digging up the bodies would require political courage. It would also need a community determined to maintain its rage.

Charles Evans, for one, could not believe that the government would get off lightly. Surely the men who had perpetrated atrocities on blameless victims would be held to account by virtue of both natural and British justice. His diary entries keenly demonstrate his horror and disbelief at how far the British officials had strayed from their national and racial superiority as agents of civility and progress.

There were others eager to bear witness to the moral and jurisprudential implications of the slaughter, afraid that time would veil the unsightly wounds. On 15 December, an anonymous poem was published in the GEELONG ADVERTISER. 'The Mounted Butchers' aimed for documentary relevance.

> There go the 'Troopers' that slaughtered our men,
> When all fight and resistance was o'er:...
> By firing the tents, and cutting men down:
> And mangling and maiming the dead
> They barely upheld the old British Crown,
> That our fathers had fought for and bled.
> Women and children escaped not their fire...
> Like demons they rode and vented their ire,
> When the 'Red Coats' the skirmish had won.

The anonymous poet confirmed publicly what Charles Evans had scribbled privately in his diary: *The brave noble hearts did not turn their swords on armed men, but galloped courageously among the tents shooting at women, and cutting down defenceless men.*

Yet ultimately, local indignation could not be sustained.

When the dust settled, Henry Powell's would be the only inquest. The bodies remained in the ground. Only one man, Powell's killer, would be brought before the courts. But before that, smelling danger, the red-coated rats abandoned Hotham's ship in droves. Three soldiers deserted the 12th Regiment in November 1854. Nineteen more followed in December 1854 and January 1855. A further thirteen deserted in the early months of 1855. In total, thirty-five out of sixty-five soldiers of Ballarat's 12th Regiment deserted. In 1855, 165 soldiers in Victoria threw back the Queen's shilling, the highest recorded desertion rate in Victoria's history.[4]

Diggers and Redcoats alike had fought well and fierce, recorded Corporal John Neill after the stockade fight.[5] But some casualties were more equal than others. It was six months before death certificates were issued for miners who lost their lives at Eureka: a bulk lot issued by the Ballarat registrar on 20 June, identifying sixteen men who died of *gunshot wound* on 3 December 1854. Yet there was a paper trail of evidence and a mother lode of popular memory to inscribe the reality that at least a dozen more people, both women and men, had been the victims of government brutality on that fateful day.

*

Now fast forward one year to 3 December 1855. The trials of thirteen miners for treason had dissolved in farce, making a laughing stock of the government. No jury would convict their peers of a capital offence for which there was not a shred of evidence, save, perhaps, a mangled blue and white flag pilfered by one of the troopers in the ashes of the Stockade, and later returned to him by the Crown—more as souvenir than state secret.

Only one blow from the prosecution landed, and it was no more than an oblique backhander, intended to strike at the potency of the miners' worrisome popularity among city dwellers. Timothy Hayes was the butt of the joke: Lieutenant T. Bailey Richards of the 40th Regiment swore on oath that he arrested the Ballarat Reform League leader walking unarmed outside the Stockade after the battle. He then regaled the court with the tale of Anastasia's insult: *His wife came up afterwards and said are you taken, he said yes, she then said to him 'if I had been a man I would not have been taken by so few as these'.*[6] Laughter in the court at the Punch and Judy show, the spectacle of an untamed shrew more powerful than her mate.

By the time the courts ejected the last of the prisoners, the goldfields commission had also tabled its report. It ranked the miners' grievances in this order: the licence fee (*or more properly the unseemly violence often necessary for its due collection*); the *land grievance*; and *the want of political rights and recognised status* rendering the mining population *an entirely non-privileged body... without gradations of public rank.* The editor of the GEELONG ADVERTISER offered his own summary of events:

> Denuded of the rights of citizenship, and tabooed, regarded as inferiors, and forced to submit to insolence, annoyance, direct insult and a long course of petty oppression, without means of address,

the miners had no option but to act. Their treatment had been *repugnant to British experience and derogatory to the manly feeling of independence.*[7]

The commission's recommendations for alleviating these complaints were quickly adopted. The *mining royalty* was replaced with a miner's right. For £1 per year, it entitled miners to fossick for minerals, gave them access to a plot of land on which they could make capital improvements, and enfranchised them to vote in and seek representation on both a new local mining court system and the Victorian legislature. Women could purchase a miner's right, but were excluded from its political spoils. (Victorian women would not win the state franchise for another fifty-three years.)

The commission of enquiry, like the juries, came out on the side of the miners. But this did not get the victims of 3 December any closer to the compensation many had claimed from the government for property losses when the military set the Eureka ablaze. A board of enquiry found in mid-winter 1855 that the destruction of tents on the morning of 3 December was a *necessary consequence* of the *resistance offered to the military. Your Board lament the losses sustained by individuals*, read the report, *but cannot forget that if the sufferers were not actively engaged in an overt act of Rebellion they displayed no disposition to support authority.* Thus Anne Diamond, whose husband was shot inside their store before it was burned to the ground, found her claim for £600 rejected. In this the struggling miner's wife was no different from Catherine Bentley, the formerly prosperous publican's wife, whose claim of £30,000 for the loss of her hotel and the forced annexation of land held in her name, was brushed aside. It was a small taste for these new Australians of the bitter pill of dispossession suffered irretrievably by the old Australians.

By December 1855, Henry Seekamp was back at the helm of the TIMES, having served half of his six-month sentence for sedition. A massive petition raised by Clara, and reputed to bear thirty thousand names, had begged successfully for his release. Charles Evans had published and printed his own newspaper, the BALLARAT LEADER, with J. B. Humffray at the helm. It lasted seven editions, folding at the same time that Queen Victoria signed the

The Man Scoby Mentioned in the printed form
As killed was Hid in the Abbottsford Convent
During the riots Under the influence of Peter Lalor
Late Speaker of the Victorian Legislative Assembly
And his Cousin or Uncle one
Father Kennedy who had Charge
of the Catholics Church at Ballarat at the time of riots
[illegible] they caused the riots [illegible]

I am given to Understand that Scoby is living at
Dowling forest near Ballarat his two sons George
And James Scoby keeps (livery stables) at Ballarat
At the time of the riots Scoby was a young
Man unmarried he is about 60 years now
10th April 1892

Note written by Catherine Bentley on the back of a copy of the petition to free her husband. Dated 10 April 1892, the anniversary of James Bentley's suicide. Transcription p. 479.

The Bentleys' dreams go up in smoke, as witnessed by Charles Doudiet, 1854.

Anastasia Hayes.

'The Australian Flag' gets its first airing.
Charles Doudiet, 1854.

Original meeting placard, rallying 'the inhabitants of Ballarat generally' to Bakery Hill on 29 November 1854.

DOWN WITH THE LICENSE FEE!

DOWN WITH DESPOTISM!

"WHO SO BASE AS BE A SLAVE?"

ON

WEDNESDAY NEXT

The 29th Instant, at Two o'clock,

A MEETING

Of all the DIGGERS, STOREKEEPERS, and Inhabitants of Ballarat generally, will be held

ON BAKERY HILL

For the immediate Abolition of the License Fee, and the speedy attainment of the other objects of the Ballarat Reform League. The report of the Deputations which have gone to the Lieutenant-Governor to demand the release of the prisoners lately convicted, and to Creswick and Forest Creeks, Bendigo, &c., will also be submitted at the same time.

All who claim the right to a voice in the framing of the Laws under which they should live, are solemnly bound to attend the Meeting and further its objects to the utmost extent of their power.

N.B. Bring your Licenses, they may be wanted.

PRINTED AT THE "TIMES" OFFICE, BAKERY HILL, BALLARAT.

St Alipius Catholic Church with mass flag flying, as depicted by von Guérard in January 1854.

Eliza Howard née Darcy, seated between Patrick Howard and Ella Hancock's mother. Date unknown but probably 1890s.

Eureka veterans at the 1904 anniversary, Jane Cuming front row, third from right. Kind permission Ballarat Heritage Services.

bill that would give her eponymous Australian colony its first Legislative Assembly.[8] When elections were held under the new Victorian Constitution in November 1855, J. B. Humffray and Peter Lalor were elected as Ballarat's representatives.

By spring, Sarah Hanmer had sold the Adelphi and left Ballarat. After moving around various other goldfields, she and Julia were playing to packed houses at Coppin's Olympic Theatre in Melbourne. (She appears to have uprooted out of choice rather than necessity; Sarah was re-issued with a Ballarat theatrical licence in January 1855, despite her direct competitor, Stephen Clarke, objecting that he had *always been loyal to the Crown which cannot be said of the Adelphi Company under the direction of Mrs Hanmer.*[9]) Sir Charles and Lady Hotham were regular theatre-goers, perhaps to distract them from the shadow of incompetence that trailed the governor. They may have occupied a private box to see Sarah and Julia perform a *Domestic Tragedy*, a *Burlesque* and a *Farce*, before Mayor J. T. Smith, and American consul James Tarleton. The Hothams did not know, of course, that tragedy was soon to befall them.

*

And so by 3 December 1855, after a year in which life-changing events had surged forth with an urgent force of nature, it was time to stop and remember the dead. Raffaello Carboni had published copies of his memoir *The Eureka Stockade: The Consequence of Some Pirates Wanting on Quarter Deck a Rebellion.* (Its cover price of five shillings put it *beyond the reach of many interested in the regrettable events.*[10]) The eccentric Italian spent the day sitting at the Stockade site and reading from his book from sunrise to sunset. There was no formal commemoration of the day. In the morning a group of some hundred mourners walked to the cemetery to pay their respects. If there were eulogies spoken, tears shed, passions rekindled, the newspapers did not report them. For there was another conflagration to upstage the first anniversary of the Stockade and monopolise media attention. *Fearful Fire at Ballarat. Great Loss of Life*, screamed the headlines.

On 1 December, a fire ripped through the new wooden buildings that lined the street where a year ago tents flapped in the breeze. The locus of the Main Street inferno was the United States Hotel, radiating *a glare of light…that has never before been witnessed on Ballarat.* The blaze had spread to the Criterion Store, once owned by Charles and George Evans, the Adelphi Theatre, Moody's Store and several other business and grog shops. Moses and Sons' zinc-lined store stopped the flames spreading further in the Eureka direction. One male and one female body were pulled from the burning United States Hotel, owned by American Mr Nicholls, a former friend of Sarah Hanmer's. The bodies were identified. One stump of charred human flesh was Nicholls himself; Dr Clendinning later held a coronial enquiry identifying the victim.

It was Henry Seekamp who ran down from the TIMES office at the first cry of fire. He was too late to save Nicholls but, entering the inferno, he saw a woman with her head lolling to one side. As Seekamp later told Clendinning,

> I endeavoured to envelop the head of the female with a silk handkerchief to enable me to lay hold of it, but the head was so burnt that it crumbled into cinder; and I was obliged to leave from the heat.[11]

(A subsequent post mortem later exposed *two testicles complete*, revealing the headless woman to be a man.) Mr McGill, who, a year to the day earlier, had brandished Sarah Hanmer's heirloom rapier at the head of the Californian Rangers, now poured water on the smouldering remains. The capital damage was estimated at £50,000. Two more bodies were found.

Two weeks later, the worst floods on record inundated the town, leading the GEELONG ADVERTISER to conclude: *December is a fatal month in Ballarat—last year the sword, this year fire and flood are the agents.*

And then, on the last day of the year, Charles Hotham died after a brief but violent illness, with his lady by his side. They had been married just over two years. The only extant passages from Lady Hotham's diary pertain to the final days of her husband's life. She read to him, fed him, prayed with him. *He asked me to miss him*, she wrote,

> he put his left arm around my neck, and kissed me many times as if he wished to say good bye, but he did not speak…for a moment before he died his eyes resumed their natural expression, he seemed to be looking at me with intense affection.[12]

Some said Hotham had caught a chill in the freakish summer weather; other claimed it was a fatal bout of diarrhoea. Those who did not fear speaking ill of the dead swore he was broken in health and spirit through his own foolhardiness, *landing here with words of liberty upon his lips, but with the design of a despot.* For Lady Jane Sarah Hotham, twice widowed at the age of thirty-eight, there was nothing but grief.

*

1856 marked a turning point in the sexual politics of Victoria. When Lady Hotham sailed back to England in February of that year, she left behind her a colony struggling to contain the transformative forces it had both encouraged and feared. For if Eureka was a real time and a real place, it also became a metaphor for a moment of sweeping change when old and new regimes, attitudes, structures and aspirations collided head on.

Women had both stirred up and been carried along by that torrent of history. As the technology of gold digging was itself making the transition—from the early days of independent, alluvial mining, where individuals worked for themselves, to syndicated (corporatised) quartz mining, employing waged workers—so the initial phase of relative autonomy and liberation for women began to solidify into familiar structures of dominance and subservience.

The growth of towns, which the miner's right facilitated, led to the establishment of permanent hospitals, schools and churches: the longed-for feminisation of the frontier. An editorial in the BALLARAT TIMES from 12 June 1856, on the 'Progress of Ballarat', articulated the criteria for such improvement. A few years ago, it explained, Ballarat exhibited *the universal disorganisation of society*. Now, by contrast, *[we are] a peaceful, orderly people [showing] the decencies and refinements of civilised life*. Martha Clendinning affords a perfect barometer of the changes that such civility was supposed to entail.

By 1856 Martha had decided to shut the store that had given her such *satisfaction*. Her reason had nothing to do with economic imperative. She was a good businesswoman and did a profitable trade, despite increased competition and diminishing returns. *I was satisfied with the result of my work*, she declared. As Dr Clendinning had struggled to establish his own practice, she had worked to *supplement his income*.

After 1855, *Ballarat had become a settled township in which men came 'to stay' and with their wives and families make their homes there.* Once the feverish turmoil of the early diggings subsided, sex roles began to revert to their former ideological inertia. *The time had gone by*, wrote Martha, *when, even on the gold fields, a woman unaccustomed to such work could carry on her business without invidious remarks.* Fearful for her husband's reputation (she worried he might *be blamed from allowing me to continue at it*) she chose to shut up shop. The good doctor was himself *most anxious* about how her business activities would be viewed and was *greatly pleased* when she *retired.*

Dr Clendinning at once began building her a wooden house on Red Hill. *This put an end to all further remarks*, Martha conceded, *and allowed us to make our home fit for a lady and her doctor husband to occupy, and, in a little time, to add a small garden to their comforts.* The picket fence of Martha's newly constrained life was complete when she began the charity work that is the keystone of *civilised life.* Martha Clendinning, doctor's wife, was on the first committee for the Ballarat Female Refuge and a member of the Ladies' Benevolent Society of Melbourne. Like many former miners who later looked back on the roaring fifties with nostalgia, Martha remembered her years as an autonomous shopkeeper with affection and not a little regret.

Other trailblazers weren't prepared to go so quietly.

When Lola Montez toured Melbourne and its glistening hinterland in early 1856, she raised eyebrows for her outlandish claims to political influence as much as her saucy spider dancing. As we have seen, her tour was dogged by controversy, none more infamous than when she horsewhipped Henry Seekamp for giving her a bad review in the BALLARAT TIMES. *The coward who could beat a woman, ran from a woman*, thundered Lola in her curtain speech after thrashing Seekamp. *He says he will drive me off the diggings; but I will change the tables, and make Seekamp* de*camp!*[13] The stoush spilled from the theatre to the courts when Seekamp sued Lola for assault and Lola counter-sued for slander. PUNCH composed a twenty-seven-verse poem about the incident, facetiously titled 'The Battle of Ballarat', a direct allusion to the Eureka Stockade.

Come forth, come forth, thou vap'ring Erle
Thou scribe so rude and rash
And yield thee to the punishment
Of Lola Montes' lash.[14]

Imperial anxieties about the state of social flux in the colonies in general, and about the presumptuous, defiant behaviour of women in particular, are summed up in the satirical analogy between women whipping men and the military whipping the miners.

Lola's public incursions into the structures of power may ultimately have been viewed as a salacious sideshow, but in 1856 there was another struggle taking place between the forces of female aspiration and masculine privilege.

The organised movement for female suffrage in Australia didn't mobilise until the 1880s, but it is clear that women's political and legal rights, including suffrage, were part of the liberal democratic agenda of some gold rush visionaries, male and female. In 1856, this agenda butted up against the 'civilising' impulse to restore the status quo to Victoria's sexual politics. A letter to the editor of the BALLARAT TIMES in 1856 provides compelling evidence that there were women on the diggings who interpreted the rhetoric of political and social inclusiveness as an invitation to participate more fully in the decision-making processes that governed their lives.

On 8 September, Fanny Smith wrote this. It is an important enough document to be quoted in full:

> My Dear Sir—Will you be good enough to inform me if ladies holding the 'miner's right' are eligible to be elected as members of the Local Court? I have read the Gold Fields Act 18 Vic No 37, and find it silent as to sex. The point has been disputed, and I have thought of asking the opinion of Mr Chairman Daly, but I am told that he has stated he sees no objection to lady members, provided they possess the necessary qualification—are proposed, seconded and elected. Your opinion will be anxiously waited for by myself and many other ladies ambitious of a seat in the Local Legislature of Ballarat.[15]

Fanny's letter gives us many vital clues as to the political literacy and vigour of Ballarat's women. She is versed in the relevant legislation and the critical processes, she is using Chairman Daly's alleged support as a wedge, and she is letting it be known that she is not a lone voice, but simply the vocal tip of a looming iceberg of female ambition. Indeed, in February 1856, the ARGUS cautioned the *leaders of the 'women's rights' movement* against their *somewhat injudicious proceedings.*[16]

The miner's right had been the most tangible outcome of the Ballarat troubles. The newly constituted local mining courts, empowered to resolve mining and partnership disputes, were widely seen as a victory for self-rule. The miner's right was the gateway to participation: the 'necessary qualification' for voting or standing for office. Geoffrey Blainey has characterised the miner's right as 'probably the high tide of Australian democracy'.[17] And Fanny Smith was correct: there was nothing in the legislation to bar women from holding a miner's right. Indeed many women elected to purchase one to stake a claim on the land or were obliged to purchase one if they mined independently of husbands or ran their own businesses on the diggings, which many did.[18] But did the legislature anticipate that possession of the miner's right would also constitute legal sanction for women's participation in the other democratic functions promised by the municipal franchise?

Fanny Smith never got a straight answer on the issue of representation in the local courts. But her possum-stirring had an immediate effect. On 12 September 1856, another letter to the editor was published in the BALLARAT TIMES, by someone claiming to be putting herself up as a candidate in the imminent elections for state parliament for the seat of North Grant. Her platform? *All the crazy ideas going around*, including universal suffrage:

> Women's right: I am for their having the same rights as a man, and to allow them to go into the House and to the Bar; for I am sure there is many an old woman in both positions already.[19]

The later suffragists would, of course, become familiar with this form of mockery.

The same issue of the BALLARAT TIMES reported that twenty-six-year-old Thomas Loader would contest the seat of North Grant against sitting member J. B. Humffray in the 1856 Victorian Legislative Assembly election. There were clearly enough ambitious ladies in Ballarat to convince a young man to stake his political future on the improvement of their legal status. Although Loader did not expressly advocate the female franchise, his policy on law reform included *rights of women* and *simplification of divorce law... questions I have strong opinions upon the necessity of immediately reforming*. No other popular candidate in the 1856 election included such a radical policy as women's rights in their platform. At the election, however,

Humffray won by an overwhelming majority. Thomas Loader may have seen that there were special circumstances in gold rush Victoria that made certain social reforms, including women's rights, 'peculiarly requisite'. But even by 1856, he was swimming against the tide.

Small and scattered as they are, these nuggets of evidence that women's political citizenship was being advocated in Australia as early as 1856 are significant. They place the genesis of women's rights activism in that gold rush community of adventurers, risk-takers, speculators and freedom fighters who struggled for the more famous civic liberties often said to be at the heart of Australia's democratic tradition.

For Victoria's women, the window of golden opportunity that opened during the social flux and political tumult of the mid- to late 1850s was firmly slammed shut by the *Electoral Law Consolidation Act* of 1865, which finally inserted the word 'male' before the word 'person' in the voting qualification, thus ensuring that manhood suffrage was just that. By the time 'universal suffrage' became a hot political topic in the late 1860s, it was taken for granted that it was the rights and entitlements of property, not gender, that were at stake.

The baton of manhood suffrage—and its attendant values of independence, responsibility and human dignity—thus passed, in legend at least, from Eureka's miners to the shearers to the union movement to the labour movement to today's activists and idealists. The dynamic yet still disenfranchised proto-feminist women's rights movement of the 1850s dropped unceremoniously from public view.

To top it all off, by the time of the Ballarat Christmas Races of 1856, there was no longer a Ladies Purse.

*

1856 was also a watershed year for Eureka remembrance. On the eve of the second anniversary of the battle/riots/uprising/massacre (for all these terms were by now used interchangeably), a crowd of three hundred miners gathered *on the ground* and passed a resolution:

> that Wednesday 3rd of December, being the anniversary of the massacre of the Ballarat Patriots, be observed as a general holiday, in commemoration of the men who so nobly sacrificed their lives in resisting injustice and tyranny.

At 2pm the following day, a group of five hundred mourners met on the stockade site. Each wore a black gauze scarf tied around the left arm. Miner John Lynch read an oration, exhorting the crowd to: *Be true men all you men, like those we celebrate.* The mourners then formed a solemn procession to the cemetery. It was here that Dr Hambrook—who had not been anywhere near Ballarat two years prior—delivered his rousing graveside address, the eulogy that opened this book.

Morning dawns upon the land for whose happiness and independence the patriots bled, Hambrook boomed.

> Combine together for the common weal—maintain the right—protect the weak—give your determined opposition to injustice in every shape, and let others in future ages have the opportunity of pointing to this colony, and saying—'The men of Victoria were true to themselves'.

And with that, Eureka drifted into something more like a disturbed dream than an actual historical reality.

By 3 December 1857 there was no half-holiday. No crowds.

No black armbands and but one reference in the BALLARAT TIMES to the events of three years hence: *happily, those dark and dismal days are past forever*.

By 1858: *the stockade, with all the strong feelings then called up, is forgotten, save by a few*. Five Germans and two newspaper reporters were *all who met to do honour to the memory of the men who fell four years ago*. One reporter concluded, *The thought of races or apathy triumph over sympathy*.

*

So, yes: Geoffrey Blainey was spot-on when he said that Eureka is like a great neon sign with messages that flick on and off, selling different lessons to different customers according to the fashion of the day. It has been that way since 1856, when the second anniversary was used to underscore the colony's transformation from the wild and delirious nature of the 'early days' to the beginnings of a settled society. In the transition from rough to respectable, men's transgressions were celebrated. Miners became patriots, while women were erased from the frontline of the frontier.

But that's only part of the story. By 1884, pioneer women had fought back with the declarations that opened this book: the Lady Who Was There and the Female of '54 wanted that light to shine on them for one brief moment of historical remembrance. And then at the fiftieth anniversary of Eureka in 1904, when the old survivors were gathered together in the flash of the photographer's gaze, Jane Cuming took a front-row seat. The women of Eureka have always been there.

*

In her firecracker leader of New Year's Day 1855, Clara Seekamp took the temperature of her community and predicted a patriotic fever that would burn low but would not completely die.

> What is this country else but Australia? Is it any more England than it is Ireland or Scotland, France or America, Italy or Germany? Is the population, wealth, intelligence, enterprise and learning wholly and solely English? No, the population of Australia is not English, but Australian. Whoever works towards the development of its resources and its wealth is no longer a foreigner but an Australian, a title fully as good, if not better, than that of any inhabitants of any of the geographical dominions in the world. The latest immigrant is the youngest Australian.

It is one of the mental traps of historical imagination to conjure all people in the past as old. But make no mistake: Eureka was a youth movement. The inhabitants of Ballarat, like the youth of a century later, believed that the times they were a'changing. And like today's backpackers, the gold rush generation was transient, expansive, adventurous: in search of experience, questing for something more authentic, more precious than they could find at home, something that would transcend the familiar boundaries of custom and caste.

But there is a difference too: where today's backpackers might search for metaphysical transcendence, the 1850s gold seekers were fortune hunters. They took risks calculated to bring economic prosperity, not personal enrichment. Few had a return ticket or a line of credit. In this, they were more like refugees than tourists. And for them, independence was a political concept as much as a personal goal, quite distinct from the individualism that would drive later youth movements. Yet the conflict at

Eureka was inter-generational as much as it was intra-imperial. New expectations for who people could be and what they were worth collided with old structures for measuring value. The currency was liberty and, as with any liberation narrative, those with the prerogative of privilege resisted the incursion of those with a claim to entitlement.

Two months after Clara Seekamp issued her New Year's missive, Karl Marx, writing in the German-language newspaper NEUE ODER-ZEITUNG, characterised the Eureka Stockade outbreak as being but *the symptom of a general revolutionary movement in Victoria.* If there was a revolution at Eureka, it was not a political but a sociological one. The mining community of Ballarat did not intend to overthrow the British Crown, any more than it wanted to create an equal distribution of wealth or a global map without colour lines. Any republican feelings were as nascent as the proto-feminist sentiments that were stirred up, but ultimately buried, in the topsy-turvy whirlwind of gold rush flux.

More widespread was the desire to replace static power relations with a fluid, mobile social hierarchy based on merit rather than birth, breeding, rank, marriage or conventional sex roles. In this, the gold rush generation largely succeeded. A study of the life trajectories of gold rush immigrants reveals that most ultimately fulfilled their objective. They mightn't have struck it rich, but they built businesses, farms, families, towns and, ultimately, a nation. But this was all to come.

*

Karl Marx might more accurately have observed that the goldfields society was straining under the weight of its own internal contradictions. On the diggings, unsullied egalitarian urges vied with the tried and true reality of ethnic, racial and class schism. The land was vast and 'empty', but the places of habitation were cramped and squalid. The practical need for co-operation wrestled with the base drives of competition. Men could not move up and women would not stay down. Idealism and energy collided with brutality and death. And new beginnings ended abruptly in old sufferings. The certainty, as Clara Seekamp correctly foretold, was that these ambiguities and tensions would be Australia's own story, to tentatively assert or flagrantly deny.

Printed and published by Mrs. Seekamp
Ballarat.

EPILOGUE

Main characters

Martha Clendinning remained a keystone of the Ballarat establishment during her husband's long tenure as Ballarat's district coroner. When their only child, Margaret, married Ballarat's former resident commissioner, Robert Rede, in 1873, the wedding arrangements filled the social pages of the local papers. Dr George Clendinning, sixteen years his wife's senior, died in 1876. Martha moved to Toorak, where she wrote her memoirs, and lived until 1908. She was eighty-six years old. She was buried in Ballarat, not far from the place where she ran her first store.

Soon after Eureka, **Robert Rede** was transferred from his position as resident gold commissioner of Ballarat to sheriff of Geelong. In 1859, when Rede was forty-four years old, he married nineteen-year-old Isabella Strachan, the daughter of a member of the Legislative Council. They had a son, Robert, in 1861. The following year Isabella died of liver and kidney disease. In 1868, the widowed Rede returned to Ballarat as the town's sheriff. Four years later he fell madly in love with Margaret Clendinning, thirty-three years his junior. He wrote passionate love letters to Margaret and sent her pressed flowers in tiny envelopes, revealing another side of a man who had become renowned for his cold-hearted treatment of the Ballarat miners. They were married in January 1873. Robert Rede died at his home in Toorak in 1904, one year shy of his ninetieth birthday. Fairlie Rede, the youngest of Robert and Margaret Rede's six children, died in 1968. She has a hybrid tea rose named after her.

After appointing herself the Ballarat poetess in 1854, **Ellen Young** retired from public life to support her husband Frederick's career. Frederick gave up gold mining and returned to his profession as a chemist, becoming the first mayor for East Ballarat in 1862. Ellen appeared in print only one more time. In 1864 she wrote to the BALLARAT STAR to defend herself against insinuations made by Charles Dyte, who was also elected to the East Ballarat Council. Ten years after Eureka, Ellen reminded readers that she had *pleaded the cause of the oppressed from lawless law* and by doing so had won *the general acknowledged esteem of this community.* Frederick died in 1868, aged fifty-six, of apoplexy. Ellen died in 1872, aged sixty-two, of diarrhoea. They are buried in the Church of England section of the Ballarat Cemetery.

Peter Lalor remained in hiding until a general amnesty towards all Eureka participants was declared following the unsuccessful state trials in May and June 1855. He married Alicia Dunne on 10 July 1855 at St Mary's Catholic Church in Geelong. They had three children, the eldest of whom, Ann, was born in 1856. As an elected member of the Legislative Assembly, Lalor became known as a turncoat conservative and capitalist mine owner. Daughter Ann died of pulmonary phthisis in 1885 in the family's East Melbourne mansion and Alicia died in 1887. Peter followed two years later.

The marriage of **Anastasia** and **Timothy Hayes** did not survive the cauldron of the Eureka years. Perhaps his fiery wife's jibe, used in evidence against Timothy in his treason trial, was the last straw. Timothy abandoned his family and travelled to South America and the United States. Anastasia, left alone to raise their six children, continued working at St Alipius School but fell out with the Catholic Church after agitating for fair pay and a living allowance. According to Anne Hall, Anastasia's family was brought up to believe their father was a coward; subsequent generations inherited Anastasia's bitterness at being deserted by her husband and exploited by her church. Sharp of mind and tongue to the last, Anastasia Hayes died in Ballarat in 1892, aged seventy-four.

Brave **Catherine McLister** dared to expose the intimate underbelly of the Government Camp but she had a weak physical constitution and died in childbirth on 4 March 1858 at the age of thirty-two. The official cause of death was *phthisis*, more commonly known as consumption. Her baby son, James, lived for ten days, dying of *debility* in the Geelong home of his father, Robert McLister, whose profession was by then listed as *gold digger*.

The man who shew too much, Police Inspector **Gordon Evans**, was transferred from Ballarat to Carlsruhe soon after Eureka. In May 1855, he married Lucy Ann Govett, a squatter's daughter from Van Diemen's Land, ten years his junior. They had eleven children. Evans died of a stroke in South Melbourne in 1885, aged fifty-nine. His death certificate lists his occupation as *sharebroker*.

Sixteen-year-old **Anne Duke** gave birth to her first child, John, on the road between Ballarat and Bendigo, ten days after the storming of the Eureka Stockade. She and her husband George had eleven more children, most born in Woodend, where the family settled into a life of farming and breeding. Anne died in 1914, aged seventy-six. Her husband died four years later. Their youngest child, Annie, lived until 1948, only six years shy of witnessing the centenary of the Eureka Stockade.

James and **Margaret Johnston** left the Ballarat Government Camp on 4 March 1855. Their first child, Sophia, was born on 30 April, six weeks premature. On Sophia's birth certificate, former Assistant Gold Commissioner James Johnston is listed as a farmer. The couple went on to have fourteen more children, the youngest twin boys. In the 1890s, their eldest son, James, murdered his wife and children and attempted to kill himself. He was tried and hanged for his crime. Margaret Brown Howden Johnston died on 13 July 1888 at Buninyong, aged fifty-five. The cause of death was *exhaustion*. The eldest of her children was thirty-three, the twins thirteen. An 1855 dictionary of medical terms defines *exhaustion* as *loss of strength, occasioned by excessive evacuations, great fatigue, privation of food or by disease*. Giving birth to fifteen children in twenty years may well count as the *excessive evacuation* of human bodies. Margaret was buried in the Ballarat Cemetery with Presbyterian rites.

Frances and **Thomas Pierson** did not return to America. Nor did they have any more children in Victoria. Frances died in 1865, aged forty-five. The following year, her son Mason married Elizabeth Markham at Buninyong. They had four daughters: Frances Elizabeth, Elizabeth, Mary and Elizabeth. When

Mason's wife died, he married her sister Annie Markham, with whom he had another daughter, Frances May. Thomas Pierson died in 1881, aged sixty-eight, and Mason died in 1910, aged seventy-three.

Lady Jane Sarah Hotham returned to England on 20 January 1856. From the Hood family's home at Cricket St Thomas, she personally oversaw the design and construction of the memorial tomb to her husband, Sir Charles Hotham, which stands tall in the Melbourne General Cemetery. She spared no expense on the monument, using her own funds to supplement the controversial £1500 pledged by the Victorian Legislative Council to defray funeral and burial expenses. Jane wanted the sculptural decoration of the monument to closely resemble the native foliage of Australia, suggesting an affinity with the land that transcended the tragedy of her time in the colony. The monument was not fully installed until September 1858.

On 30 August 1860, at the age of forty-three, Jane married William Armytage, a captain of the Royal Navy. Together they went on the Atlantic Telegraph Expedition in 1866, and travelled extensively abroad, including a time in Malta in 1871. Jane continued to be known as Lady Hotham after her marriage to Captain Armytage, and kept up her court appearances. She divided her time between London and Devon. Armytage died in 1881. Lady Jane Sarah Hood Holbech Hotham Armytage died on 28 April 1907, aged ninety. She outlived three husbands, her sovereign Queen Victoria and the colonial rule of Australia.

Eliza Darcy married Patrick Howard at Ballarat's St Alipius Church in August 1855. Their first child, Mary Ann, was born in 1856 and died six months later. Over the next twenty-four years, the couple had eleven more children. The Howard family remained closely aligned with the Darcy family, farming in the Birregurra area. Eliza Darcy died in Geelong in 1920, aged eighty-four. Leo Howard, who died in 2010 aged ninety-three, was the son of Eliza and Patrick's second-youngest child, Daniel, born in 1880—and the father of famed Australian musicians Shane, Marcia and Damian Howard. Ella Hancock, Eliza and Patrick's granddaughter from their youngest child Alicia, is the oldest living Eureka descendant, aged ninety-seven in 2013.

Merchant and journalist **George Francis Train**, who dubbed the Eureka Stockade *Australia's Bunker Hill*, returned to the United States in November 1855. Here he was reunited with his wife, Willie Davis, and met their baby daughter. Willie had returned to New York in 1854 while pregnant, as George wanted his first child to be born in America so that he was eligible to become president. Train became a global transport magnate and himself ran for President of the United States as an independent candidate in 1872. He and Willie separated the same year. Train was the major financier of THE REVOLUTION, a newspaper published by women's rights activists Susan B. Anthony and Elizabeth Cady Stanton. He died, eccentric and alone, in New York City in 1904, aged seventy-five. Train is reputed to have been the inspiration for Phileas Fogg, the protagonist in Jules Verne's *Around the World in Eighty Days*.

Stephen and **Jane Cuming**, who sheltered Peter Lalor after his escape from the stockade, remained in Ballarat for the rest of their lives. They built a house on the site of their original house on Pennyweight Hill, where they mined and later grew fruit and vegetables. Jane and Stephen's daughter Martineau, who was six years old at Eureka, married Simon Andrew and later lived in Clunes at the time of the mining riots against the use of Chinese scab labour by the Lothair Mine, part-owned by Peter Lalor. Stephen Cuming died at the age of seventy-eight in 1898. Jane survived him by thirteen years, long enough to be present at the fiftieth anniversary of Eureka. She died at the age of eighty-eight, telling her great-granddaughter that for all the difficulties of life on the goldfields, *she felt freer than in Cornwall.* Martineau died in the Pennyweight Hill house in 1930.

Thomas and **Bridget Hynes** (née Nolan), who were married at St Alipius just two months before Eureka, had their first child, Kate, in 1855. After profits from shallow alluvial mining bottomed out in Ballarat, the family settled at Cardigan, where they farmed and ran a dairy. They had ten more children, all of whom lived to adulthood, before migrating overland to Terrick Terrick near Gunbower Island. Bridget's younger brother, Michael Nolan, gave up mining for shearing and later selected land in South Gippsland. He is remembered as a pioneer of Leongatha. Five of Bridget and Tom's sons and one of their daughters also settled in the Leongatha–Tarwin Valley district. Tom Hynes died in 1897 and Bridget in 1910, aged seventy-seven. Both are buried in the Leongatha Cemetery.

Charles Evans and his brother George established Evans Brothers Printers, Stationers and Booksellers, carving out a long-standing place in the commercial and cultural life of Ballarat. In 1859, Evans Brothers made the highly symbolic move from the flats of Main Road, East Ballarat, to the elevated Lydiard Street in the township. In 1858, twenty-eight-year-old Charles married a seventeen-year-old Scottish girl, Catherine McCallum. They had twelve children together. In the 1870s, Evans Brothers expanded its operations to a Melbourne office. Charles Evans died in 1881 in Emerald Hill (later called South Melbourne), just two months after the birth of his youngest child. He was fifty-four years old. George Evans had died two years earlier, of excessive drinking, also in his fifty-fourth year.

After selling the Adelphi Theatre in early 1855, **Sarah Hanmer** moved between the goldfields and Melbourne, with her daughter Julia in tow, playing to delighted audiences in headlining performances. Sarah was issued a publicans licence for the Ballarat Races of 4 December 1856. She prospered financially and owned properties in Ballarat, for which she collected rents through a broker. In November 1858, Sarah was sued by her rent collector, Mr Baker, in a libel case that kept Ballarat entertained for weeks. In court Sarah was variously described as *an actress who had made money* and *an actress who dealt in mining transactions*. The court found in Baker's favour, but only awarded him forty shillings (he had claimed £500). By 1864, Sarah had moved to Brisbane and started a new Adelphi Company. On New Year's Eve that year, she gave a benefit concert under the patronage of the governor, Sir G. F. Bowen. Sarah Ann Hanmer, widow of Henry Augustus Leicester Hanmer, Surgeon (sic), died in Adelaide of *fungus* on 9 August 1867, aged forty-six.

Julia Hanmer married William Henry Surplice in Ballarat on 8 December 1856. She was sixteen years old. William, the government surveyor, was thirty-two. On her marriage certificate, Julia is identified as Julia Ford and names her father as Frederick Ford, accountant. Her mother, Sarah, was present at the wedding in the Church of England schoolhouse. The business of Surplice and Sons, run by William Sr and Alfred Surplice, sold provisions to the military at the Government Camp in January 1855. Julia and William Henry had seven children, the first six of whom were born in Ballarat and the last in Sydney after the family moved to New South Wales in the mid-1870s. Julia and William lived in Suva, Fiji, for many years. Julia died in 1920, aged eighty, and is buried in the Waverley Cemetery.

Catherine Bentley may have been Eureka's longest-term victim. Her second child, Louisa, was born in February 1855, while James Bentley was incarcerated for murder. By late 1855, now raising two young children alone, Catherine had been brought up on sly-grogging charges in Maryborough. She repeatedly petitioned parliament for compensation for the loss of her hotel and land in Ballarat but to no avail. James was released three years into his sentence and bonded to remain in the Darebin Creek area of what was then outer Melbourne. Their daughter Matilda was born in March 1857.

By early 1859, when daughter Christina was born, the family were living in Newbridge, where Catherine was running a store. At the age of fifteen months, Christina ran out onto the street in front of the store and was hit by a horse and cart, her brains dashed out on the ground. She died in Catherine's arms. Four months later, baby Albert was born in Kingarra, only to die thirteen months later of diphtheria. The Bentleys' sixth child, Ada, was born in 1863. James Bentley committed suicide by laudanum poisoning in Ballarat Street, Carlton, in April 1873. At his inquest, Catherine testified that *my husband has never been quite right since he lost his property at the Ballarat Riots, he has never recovered from the effects of it, for the last two years he has never ceased to talk about it. He has been low spirited with despondency about his family—over their prospects.* Certainly the Bentleys never returned to the position of affluence and influence they held in 1854.

The effects of inter-generational trauma continued: Louisa Bentley had two children out of wedlock by the time she was twenty; Matilda Bentley had seven children before her death at the age of thirty-one; Ada died in 1934 in a mental asylum. Catherine Bentley remarried, to a farmer named Andrew Mayo, and moved to Neerim South. Catherine Sherwin Bentley Mayo died of apoplexy on 14 December 1906 at the age of seventy-five. She is buried in the Church of England section of the Neerim Cemetery.

Corporal John Neill of the 40th Regiment and his wife, **Ellen Neill,** remained in the Ballarat district for the rest of their trauma-scarred lives. John was discharged as medically unfit on 31 January 1856, after a previous court martial and demotion for drunkenness. On 19 March 1857, three-year-old Fanny Neill died. Three weeks later, her sixteen-month-old sister Agnes followed. John and Ellen's daughters are buried in the Ballarat Old Cemetery. Their gravestone enshrined John Neill as *Corporal in Her Majesty's 40th Regiment*, despite his recent discharge. Ellen Neill died in 1894, one year prior to her husband, at their home in Creswick. Her obituary in the CRESWICK ADVERTISER remembered Ellen thus: *Although favoured with a classical education she was in no way pretentious, and was respected by all who knew her.*

It was **Elizabeth Rowland**'s first child, born in 1854, who she took to the Camp when she bought herself a licence on 2 December. She and husband Thomas had eight more, the last born in 1876, when Elizabeth was forty-nine years old. The family lived out their days at Ballarat. Elizabeth died in 1914, aged eighty-seven.

After her husband was released from prison in June 1855, **Clara Seekamp** stepped down from her role as publisher of the BALLARAT TIMES. Clara's petition for Henry's early release had been successful but, following the trials and tribulations of 1854–5, culminating in cradling the crumbling head of a victim of the Main Street fire, he was fragile and unwell. In July 1856, following the courtroom dramas with Lola Montez, Henry Seekamp was successfully sued for libel by Lola's solicitor. Seekamp had called Mr Lewis *a dirty, pettifogging Jew informer*. Henry was ordered to pay Lewis £100. In October 1856, the Seekamps sold the BALLARAT TIMES due to Henry's *shattered health*. Business had also been affected when the government widened the Melbourne Road, removing five of the Seekamps' six houses and creating a twelve-foot-high cutting outside the TIMES office.

In 1857, Clara was reunited with her seven-year-old daughter, Clara Maria Du Val, who had sailed from Ireland to join her twin brother, Francis, and older brother, Oliver, in the Seekamps' Bakery Hill home. After Clara's years of petitioning the government, in October 1861 a select committee finally awarded her £500 compensation for loss of business income, property value and amenity associated with the road widening. She had wanted £3000. Asked by the select committee why her husband wasn't fronting the case, Clara replied that while her husband believed in writing letters, she preferred direct action. She summed up her circumstances like this: *We looked on the loss of business as the greatest grievance of all, and though we thought we could turn the ground into money, we were deprived of doing so.*

By 1862, Henry had moved to Brisbane, where he was offering French lessons as *Mons. Henri Seekamp, formerly Professor in the Institut Chatelain, Paris*. He died on the Clermont diggings in Queensland of *Natural causes accelerated by Intemperance* in

January 1864, aged thirty-five. Clara moved to Melbourne with her children. In 1873, she wrote to the Victorian Press Association requesting pecuniary assistance. In 1868, eighteen-year-old Clara Maria died of diphtheria at their home in St Kilda. Son Oliver died in 1884 of lead poisoning, aged forty-two. Clara Maria Lodge Du Val Seekamp lived to the age of eighty-nine, and died of senile debility and heart failure in the Pascoe Vale home of her son Francis. Clara's death certificate describes her profession as *housewife*.

3 December 1855, the first anniversary of the Eureka Stockade, was a day of torrential rain and flooding. The downpour came after three days of *burning north winds.* Most establishments on Main Road were flooded; the concert hall at the Star Hotel was swept away. These weather conditions inaugurated a tradition of the heavens opening over Victoria on 3 December. Inclement weather also marred celebrations on 3 December 1884, 1904 and 1954.

Other characters

Caroline Chisholm continued to be an outspoken advocate of democratic reform, championing the twin causes of unlocking the lands and universal suffrage. In 1866 she returned to England, where she died in poverty and relative obscurity in 1877.

Bridget Callinan, who distracted the troopers while her injured brothers escaped the stockade, died in 1897 from pneumonia, aged seventy-two. She lived in the Ballarat district her whole life and is buried in the Old Ballarat Cemetery. She never married.

Mary Ann Welch who, along with her son Barnard, testified against Catherine and James Bentley, died of a lung abscess at

Ballarat on 11 November 1860. She was forty-five years old. In the eight short years after Mary Ann sailed from England, she had cared for her seven children while her husband went to the goldfields, lost her only daughter soon after arrival, moved the remaining six children to Ballarat where her husband had established a storekeeping business, witnessed a murder, watched her home burn down in mass riots, acted as star witness at a notorious show trial in Melbourne, given birth to two more children and watched those children die before their first birthdays. Nine months after the death of their last baby brother, Mary Ann's remaining six sons were motherless.

Dr Alfred Carr, who performed the autopsy on James Scobie in the Eureka Hotel on 7 October 1854 and assisted the wounded after the stockade, returned to England to be reunited with his wife Louisa and two sons in March 1855. He was thirty-four. There he became *medically depressed* after the death of his mother. He returned to Melbourne in 1857, petitioned the government for compensation for medical services rendered at Eureka, and was committed to the Yarra Bend Lunatic Asylum on the grounds of *monomania*: what we would now call paranoia. As a patient, Carr campaigned against the brutal treatment of patients at Yarra Bend. He wrote home to Louisa, *Keep up your spirits and do not despair. Once out of this I do not think they will ever again succeed in getting me into an asylum again.* After years in and out of institutions, he was interred at the Ararat Asylum in 1887. His entry record notes that Carr was *full of delusional ideas as to identity, power and position.* Carr died as an inmate at Ararat in 1894.

Assistant Commissioner **Amos** and his family perished on the steamship *London* when it sank in the Bay of Biscay on its way to

Melbourne in 1866. Two hundred and twenty lives were lost.

Fanny Davis, the exquisite chronicler of life on board the *Conway*, married miner George Jones in 1862, four years after her arrival in Melbourne. They were married at the Wesleyan Church in Ballarat. Fanny had six children in nine years, all born in Buninyong. All survived infancy. Fanny died in 1882 in East Ballarat, aged fifty-two.

Jane Swan's family settled in Collingwood, where her father, Edward, worked in his trade as a painter and glazier. Her mother, Isabella, had two more children in Victoria: Ernest in 1857 and Isabella in 1859. Jane married William Davison the same year. Jane had three children: Isabella in 1860, Jane in 1861 and Charles in 1862. She died in childbirth with Charles. She was twenty-three. Jane's mother, Isabella, died in 1909 at the age of ninety-two.

Louisa Timewell and her young family disembarked in Melbourne in October 1852. Shortly after their arrival, Louisa contracted colonial fever and died. Her baby Kate was too young to grieve. Louisa's ship diary was sent back 'home'. The ship on which it was conveyed was wrecked. Some of the ship's mail was recovered from the wreck, and the sodden diary was returned to one of Louisa's sisters. Eventually, it found its way to Kate, who had married in 1869 and, by 1887, had eleven children of her own. The first seven were boys; the eighth a girl, Louisa. All eleven of the children survived childhood. Kate's elder sister Mary Louisa was not so lucky: six of her eight children died before their first birthdays.

Sarah Ann Raws stayed on in Victoria when the rest of her family returned to Lancashire in 1858. Twenty-year-old Sarah had married John Tomlinson, who she'd met while her family was at the diggings. The couple operated a butcher shop at Nuggety, near Maldon, where they had eight children. Later they took up land at Thyra, where they grew cereal crops and had two more children. When Sarah died she was remembered for her *nobility of character, justice and goodness.*

Solomon and **Ada Belinfante** bore twelve children, six of whom predeceased them. Their first three children—Rebecca, Raphael and Anna—all died before 1875, while Annie and Septimus both died in 1875, the year the last Belinfante child, Philip, was born. He died the following year. Solomon began his life in Melbourne as a garment trader, but by the time of Philip's birth he was a prosperous commercial broker. The family lived in Victoria Street, Collingwood. Solomon died in 1884 and Ada died in 1917. Two of their children died in 1954, the centenary of Eureka: Louis, aged ninety-four, and Amy, who never married, aged eighty-nine.

Eliza and **John Perrin** were eventually reunited. They operated a butchers shop together in Bungaree. Eliza's cousin never came to Australia.

Charles Dyte married Evelina Nathan sometime between his arrival in Victoria in 1853 and the birth of their first son, David, in 1854. Their marriage is not registered in the official Victorian births, deaths and marriage records, but it is likely they married in the Melbourne or Ballarat synagogue. Evelina gave birth to twins, Miriam and Teresa, in 1858, and two more daughters, whose births were not registered. Neither of the twin girls ever married. They died in Ballarat: Miriam, eighty-five years old, in 1943 and Theresa, eighty-one years old, in 1939. Charles Dyte died in 1893 aged seventy-six and Eve in 1899, also aged seventy-six.

Annie Hollander died in Ballarat in 1898, aged forty-one, after bearing sixteen children. She is buried in the Jewish section of the Old Ballarat Cemetery, along with her son Morris (died 1875, five hours old) and daughters Fanny (died 1874, three days old), Jane (died 1875, sixteen years) and Eva (died 1884, ten years).

Mary Faulds, whose baby Adeliza was born inside the Eureka Stockade on 3 December 1854, would have six more children with her husband, Matthew. They lived the rest of their days in Ballarat and Buninyong. Mary died in 1897.

Rebecca Noonan, who was assaulted by police on 3 December while pregnant, gave birth to baby Rebecca on 1 April 1855. Rebecca was born with a scar on her neck that corresponded with the bayonet wound on her mother's neck, inflicted during the stockade attack. On 26 December, and again on 19 February 1855, her husband, Michael Noonan, petitioned the government for compensation for the loss of his tent, store and all belongings on the grounds of the *dire disaster which he has encountered [which] has been all but ruinous to him…a married man with a family of five children, totally dependent on his industrious and unceasing industry.* His petition was put away.

ACKNOWLEDGMENTS

This book has been ten years in the making. A long road invites many debts. I give thanks and praise to all those who have helped me along the way, but in particular:

My colleagues in the History Program at La Trobe University, where I undertook the research for this book through an Australian Research Council-funded postdoctoral fellowship, and later completed the manuscript through a La Trobe University Humanities Bridging Fellowship. Special thanks to Judith Brett, Richard Broome, Marilyn Lake, Katie Holmes, Adrian Jones, John Hirst, Diane Kirkby, Gwenda Tavan, Alice Garner, Janet Butler and Alex McDermott for their intellectual support and companionship.

All the Eureka descendants who trusted me with their families' heritage. I could not include every story, but the spirit of your ancestors lives and breathes in the text. I am exceptionally grateful to the following people for their enduring support and patience: Don Walker, Ella Hancock, the Howards—Damian, Marcia, Shane, Eric and Adele, Andrew Crowley, Anne Hall, Ellen Campbell, Val D'Angri, Bill and Chris Hanlon, John Wilson and Lorraine Brownlie.

Staff at the State Library of Victoria—my second home. Special thanks to Shane Carmody for his boundless enthusiasm and Gerard Hayes for finding me the picture of the Adelphi Theatre interior. I also acknowledge the SLV's generous provision of images for this book, and thank Margot Jones for all her help.

The many people who have been fellow travellers on some leg of the journey: Anna Clark, Helen Garner, Jenny Darling, Donica Bettanin, Dot Wickham, Susan Kruss, Ron Egeberg, Roger Trudgeon, Peter Freund, Kay Gibson, Jan Croggan, staff at the Public Record Office Victoria, Paul Pickering, Katherine Armstrong, Gabriel Maddock and Kristin Phillips.

Barb Malmgren, Bernadette Hess and Barbara Burge for their expert care and counsel.

The kind souls who agreed to read the first colossal draft of the manuscript: Barry Jones, Fiona Capp, Ray Cassin, Tim Sullivan and Rick Kane. The final product was much improved by your judicious road testing. All errors of fact and judgment remain my own. Tim also gave crucial ongoing technical advice on mining technology in his role as Museums Director at Sovereign Hill.

Jacinta di Mase, my literary agent, for her quiet dignity and steely determination to make this book fly. You are a ripper.

The team at Text. What a dream it has been to work with you all. Thanks to Michael Heyward for bringing me into the fold, and to Emily Booth, Jane Novak, Rachel Shepheard, Kirsty Wilson, Shalini Kunahlan and Chong Weng Ho for bringing the book to life. Hats off to my editor, Mandy Brett, for her skill and fine mind. There are not enough thank-yous, Mandy.

Friends and family, so many of you, but especially Justine Sless and Katrina Carling for school pick-ups and sleep-overs on demand; Richard Perry for a lifetime of books; John Goldlust for lunchtime chats; Rachel Goldlust for sisterly swims; Madeleine and George Wright for their faith; and Ruth Leonards, mother extraordinaire, for letting a thousand kindnesses bloom.

Bernie, Noah and Esther Wright, my favourite people.

And Damien Wright, who has loved me and loved me and loved me through a lot.

ILLUSTRATIONS

All illustrations are courtesy State Library of Victoria unless otherwise stated.

Plate section one

1 *Queen Rose*: Ballarat Historical Society Collection.

2 Top: Eugene von Guérard, *Old Ballarat as it Was in the Summer of 1853–54*, 1884, oil on canvas. Collection: Art Gallery of Ballarat. Gift of James Oddie on Eureka Day, 1885.
Bottom: Eugene von Guérard, *Ballarat 1.8. Aug 1853.*

3 Top: John Leech, *Alarming Prospect, Single Ladies off to the Diggings, 1853*. Issued as frontispiece to *Punch*'s 'Pocket Book', 1853.
Bottom: John Alexander Gilfillan, *Travelling to the Diggings, the Keilor Plains. Victoria, 1853. Illustrated London News*, February 26, 1853. 'Sketches from the Victoria Gold Diggings'.

4 Top: S. T. Gill, *Lucky Digger that Returned, Victorian Gold Fields 1852–3.*
Bottom: William Strutt, detail from *The Girls the Diggers Left Behind, and What They Had To Do*, 1851. From *Victoria the Golden*, sketchbook. Victorian Parliamentary Library via SLV.

Plate section two

1 Top: S. T. Gill, *Zealous Gold Diggers, Bendigo July 1st /52.*
Bottom: S. T. Gill, *Sly Grog Shanty, Victorian Gold Fields 1852–3.*

2 Sarah Hanmer: courtesy Lorraine Brownlie.

3 Top: *Interior of Adelphi Theatre, Ballarat 1855*. Artist unknown.
Bottom: Thomas Ham (engraver), *Store at the Diggings, 1854.*

4 Top: S. T. Gill, *Subscription Ball, 1854* (sketch).
Bottom: 'A Very Just Complaint', from *Melbourne Punch*, 1856.

Plate section three

1 Top: Catherine Bentley's letter, written on the back of the petition to free James Bentley. Formerly in the possession of Andrew Crowley. Sovereign Hill Gold Museum Collection 97.0205.
It reads:

> The man Scoby mentioned in the printed form as killed, was hid in the Abbotsford Convent during the riots, under the influence of Peter Lalor late speaker of the Victorian Legislative Assembly and his cousin or uncle one Father Kennedy who had charge of the Catholics Church at Ballarat at the time of riots in fact they caused the riots. See officials report on Ballarat riots.
>
> I am given to understand that Scoby is living at Dowling Forest near Ballarat his two sons George and James Scoby, keeps (livery stables) at Ballarat.
>
> At the time of the riots Scoby was a young man, unmarried he is about 60 years now.
>
> 10th April 18/92

Bottom: Charles A. Doudiet, *Eureka Riot 17th October*, 1854, watercolour on paper. Collection: Art Gallery of Ballarat. Purchased by the Ballarat Fine Art Gallery with the assistance of many donors, 1996.

2 Anastasia Hayes: Public Record Office Victoria, Hayes Family Photographs, VPRS 12970. Courtesy State of Victoria.

3 Top: Charles A. Doudiet, *Swearing Allegiance to the 'Southern Cross'*, 1854, watercolour on paper. Collection: Art Gallery of Ballarat. Purchased by the Ballarat Fine Art Gallery with the assistance of many donors, 1996.
Middle: Bakery Hill Meeting Poster: Public Record Office Victoria, Eureka Stockade Historical Collection, VPRS 5527/P/4. Courtesy State of Victoria.
Bottom: Eugene von Guérard, *Katholisch Kapelle aus den Gravel Pit Lunis 3u Ballarat Januav 1854.*

4 Top: Eliza Howard née Darcy, Patrick Howard and family: courtesy Ella Hancock and Adele Howard.
Bottom: Eureka veterans at the 1904 anniversary: kind permission of Ballarat Heritage Services.

NOTES

PREFACE

1 A copy of Deegan's lecture, 'The Mining Camps of the Fifties', is held by the Royal Historical Society of Victoria.
2 Geoffrey Blainey drew the arresting word picture in a discussion with Tony Jones on the ABC's *Lateline* on 7 May 2001.
3 *Argus*, 6 December 1854.
4 The full speech can be downloaded from the Whitlam Institute's website.

INTRODUCTION: DUST AND RATTLING BONES

1 H. R. Nicholls published his account, 'Reminiscences of the Eureka Stockade', in 1890.
2 The number of miners killed during and after the Eureka clash is highly contentious. The conclusion to this book explains why. Twenty-seven men are listed as died from wounds received on 3 December, registered on Ballarat District Death Register on 20 June 1855. At least three bodies are known to have been buried at sites other than Ballarat: Ian MacFarlane, *Eureka from the Official Records* (Melbourne: Public Records Office Victoria, 1995), 104. Dorothy Wickham has also traced nine other civilians reported as dead of wounds inflicted at Eureka in other sources: Dorothy Wickham, *Deaths at Eureka* (Ballarat: Ballarat Heritage Services, 1996), 48. Peter Lalor listed twenty dead in his published account of the affray: *Age*, 7 April 1855. In 1892, this list was inscribed on a Ballarat statue in Lalor's honour, with the words *and others who were killed* tacked on the end. For the full text of the statue inscription, see Bob O'Brien, *Massacre at Eureka: The Untold Story* (Ballarat: The Sovereign Hill Museums Association, 1992), 132. Greg Blake has recently claimed that these 'others' may number at least twenty-one

unidentified casualties. Blake also concludes that there were many more military casualties than the four military officially reported. See Gregory Blake, *To Pierce the Tyrant's Heart: The Battle for the Eureka Stockade, 3 December 1854* (Loftus, ACT: Australian Army History Unit, 2009), 198–200. Some witnesses later reported up to fifty dead of wounds sustained during the battle. See chapter 12 of this book. The real figure may never be known.

3 The observations of Charles Evans are all drawn from his diary, written between 24 September 1853 and 21 January 1855. Until 2012, this diary was known as the 'Samuel Lazarus diary'. My research discovered that Charles Evans was the true author of the famous goldfields diary. For an account of the research journey that led to the official change in provenance, see Clare Wright, 'Desperately Seeking Samuel: A Diary Lost and Found,' *La Trobe Journal* 90(2012):6–22.

4 *Ballarat Times*, 3 December 1856.

5 These population figures are from Public Record Office Victoria (hereinafter PROV), VPRS 1189/95 M55/443, monthly returns of the Gold Fields Commission. Population statistics for Ballarat and the goldfields 1854 are also found in VPRS 1189/95 L55/1734, VPRS 1189/94 and VPRS 1085/09. These figures are sometimes inconsistent with each other, and occasionally change markedly from month to month.

6 This quote is in the Andrew Crowley file in the Montrose Cottage Collection held at the Gold Museum, Ballarat.

7 All observations of Maggie Johnston are drawn from this diary. Ellen Campbell has now lodged a transcript of the diary at the State Library of Victoria. Margaret (Maggie) Johnston. Diary, transcript, 1854 May 18–Oct. 17 1856, 1854. State Library of Victoria, Australian Manuscripts Collection MS 1641288.

8 *Ballarat Star*, 26 July 1884.

9 *Ballarat Star*, 28 November 1884.

10 *Argus*, 4 December 1854, 9. There is no registered death for Catherine Smith in 1854 or 1855. There is a Moyle family still living in Upwey, but my attempts to contact them have been unproductive.

ONE: A VIRGIN COUNTRY

1 Scottish journalist and politician Thomas McCombie had immigrated to Victoria in 1841. These observations are excerpted from McCombie's later writings, *Australian Sketches*, penned after his return to England in 1859. 'Sketching' Australia was a popular pastime, akin to today's travel writing, and there are many published *Australian Sketches*.

2 Henry Mundy wrote his remarkable 730-page memoirs sometime before his death in 1912.

3 William Howitt's famous work, *Land, Labour and Gold*, was published in London in 1855, on his return to England after two years in Victoria. William's wife, Mary Howitt, with whom he co-authored 180 published works of poetry and prose, did not accompany her husband and two sons to Australia.

4 It was quite common for a ship to have its own in-house newspaper, circulated by an enterprising editor who had brought a small printing press on board. Ship's newspapers contained news of births, deaths and marriages during the journey, shipboard gossip, notices for entertainments, advertisements for items being bought or sold, as well as editorial comments about what immigrants could expect in their new life in the colonies. The State Library of Victoria holds all ten volumes of the *Marco Polo Chronicle*, published by Francis Whitfield Robinson and edited by Dr Gillespie.

5 It is the conventional wisdom that Hiscock 'discovered' gold at Ballarat. See, for example, Robyn Annear, *Nothing But Gold: The Diggers of 1852*, (Melbourne, Text Publishing, 1999), 10. Note that in *The Rush That Never Ended*, Geoffrey Blainey attributes the first Buninyong finds in the Ballarat region to John Dunlop and his mate Regan. Geoffrey Serle also gives the guernsey to Hiscock in *The Golden Age*. All authors agree that small deposits had been found in other parts of Victoria prior to this date, but the Ballarat finds of August/September 1851 were the first significant discoveries. Meanwhile, Fred Cahir has documented the pre-existing knowledge of Indigenous people with regards to mineral deposits, including gold. Fred Cahir, 'Finders not Keepers: Aboriginal People on the Goldfields of Victoria', in *Eureka: Reappraising an Australian Legend*, ed. Alan Mayne (Perth: API Network, 2006).

6 John Capper wrote three guidebooks to Australia, published in 1852, 1853 and 1855. These observations are drawn from his 1855 edition. All three volumes are held by the State Library of Victoria.

7 Sarah Watchwarn's words are preserved in the 1934 collection *Records of Pioneer Women*, produced by the Women's Centennial Council to celebrate one hundred years since the establishment of the first long-term European settlement in Victoria. Note that Ellen Clacy used the phrase 'grass widows' in her 1853 account of her sojourn in Victoria. She said it was a mining term. Later linguists consider the expression to have a dual etymology. It can refer to the grass that was used to stuff the marital mattress, which has been abandoned by the departed husband. Or it can refer to the phrase 'the grass is always greener', suggesting the husband has left for more promising pastures. Historian Christina Twomey gives an excellent account of the lives of women left behind by the gold rush in her book *Deserted and Destitute: Motherhood, Wife Desertion and Colonial Welfare*.

8 Wathaurung language terms were collected and recorded by Charles Griffith in the 1830s. Griffith was an early civil servant and politician in the Port Phillip District. His diaries, including extensive vocabulary lists, are preserved in the State Library of Victoria. My thanks to Ballarat-based historian Fred (David) Cahir for pointing me in the direction of Griffith's work. Cahir's own extensive research on the Wathaurung is essential reading for any modern student or scholar of gold rush history. For details about Queen Rose and Caroline, see Dorothy Wickham's invaluable collection of biographical sketches, *Women of the Diggings, Ballarat 1854*.

9 William McLeish wrote his memoirs in 1914, when he was almost seventy years old. The manuscript is held by the State Library of Victoria.

10 Samuel Heape's diary, kept between October 1853 and March 1854, is held by the State Library of Victoria. The observations of J. J. Bond are drawn from his ship diary aboard the *Lady Flora*, departing Gravesend in April 1853. Bond's diary is held in microform in many Australian collections through the Australian Joint Copying Project.

11 *Newcastle Courant*, 9 January 1857, 6.

12 Walter Bridges, Travelogue, *The Travels of Walter Bridges*, c. 1856, Ballarat Library.

13 American prospector Charles Ferguson makes it clear that using Aboriginal guides was common practice. See Ferguson's memoir *Experiences of a Forty-Niner*. Fred Cahir also documents many instances of Wathaurung making the most of immigrants' ignorance of the land for their own financial benefit.

14 Cahir, 'Dallong', 38.

15 The words belong to artist William Strutt, who is most famous for his remarkable painting *Black Thursday, February 6th, 1851*, which hangs in the State Library of Victoria. Strutt is also responsible for the lovely sketch of Victoria's grass widows fending for themselves in the pursuit of daily chores ordinarily performed by men.

16 Wilhelmina (Willie) Davis Train's letters home to America are preserved in the manuscripts collection of the Royal Historical Society of Victoria under the misleading name 'Miller Davis Train'. George Francis Train's published accounts in the *Boston Globe* are compiled in the book edited by E. Daniel and Annette Potts, *A Yankee Merchant in Goldrush Australia*.

17 Weston Bate, 'Gold: Social Energiser and Definer', 7.

18 Or mistress! Mining magnate Alice Cornwell, who owned and operated lucrative gold mines in Ballarat in the 1880s, was known as Madame Midas. Her life is fictionalised in the novel of that name by Fergus Hume, who is credited as the author of the first Australian crime novel,

The Mystery of a Hansom Cab. Both novels were extremely popular with Australian and British audiences of the day.

19 Edward Bell, 'Blue Book' Report on Immigration, tabled 27 September 1854, Government Printer.

20 Dan and Davis Calwell were the great-great-uncles of Arthur Calwell, who as Minister for Immigration in the post-World War II era, was a staunch defender of the White Australian Policy while advocating the strategy of 'populate or perish'. Dan and Davis Calwell's letters are held by the Royal Historical Society of Victoria.

21 These statistics are gleaned from my own number-crunching of the Victorian Births, Deaths and Marriage registers, 1851–7.

22 The observations of Thomas Pierson are gleaned from his diaries (1852–64), held by the State Library of Victoria.

23 There is widespread confusion about the authorship of the anonymous book *Social Life and Manners in Australia by a Resident*, published in London in 1861. It is generally attributed to Elizabeth Ramsay-Laye, a writer and women's rights campaigner who wrote two novels about her time in New South Wales, as well as *Memories of Social Life in Australia Thirty Years Ago*, published in London in 1914. The authors of *Australian Autobiographical Narratives: 1850-1900*, Kay Walsh and Joy Hooten, conclude that *Social Life and Manners* was *not* written by Ramsay-Laye, as the anonymous author came to Australia 'in 1851 or 1852' with her husband and never went to New South Wales. Walsh and Hooten do not propose an alternative to Ramsay-Laye as the author of *Social Life and Manners*, but adding weight to their theory is the fact that the State Library of Victoria's rare copy of *Social Life and Manners* is inscribed as being authored by 'J. Massey or Massary'. My research shows that a James Massey and Mrs James Massey arrived in Victoria in October 1852 aboard the *Julia*. However, there is no record of a Mr and Mrs Laye (or Ramsay-Laye) arriving in either Victoria or NSW in the 1850s. On the basis of this evidence, I am inclined to agree that *Social Life and Manners* was not penned by Elizabeth Ramsay-Laye, but rather by Mrs Elizabeth Massey.

24 The observations of Alexander Dick are drawn from his exceptional three-volume reminiscences of his life in Victoria between 1852 and 1907. Dick died in 1913. The original manuscripts are held at the State Library of Victoria.

25 This traveller's account was published in *Murray's Guide to the Gold Diggings*, the Lonely Planet of its day.

26 The technology of mineral extraction at Ballarat is ably covered by Weston Bate in *Lucky City* and Geoffrey Blainey in *The Rush That Never Ended*. However, my deepest debt of gratitude for understanding the

geology of gold mining goes to Tim Sullivan, deputy CEO of Sovereign Hill.

27 Weston Bate calls the Ballarat Circus Jones' Circus. John Wilson, a Eureka descendant, names the circus's proprietors as Messrs Jones and Noble in his 1885 account. However, Raffaello Carboni refers to it at Rowe's Circus in his infamous 1855 eyewitness account. Rowe's American Circus was certainly in Melbourne in August 1853; Thomas and Frances Pierson rented a house opposite it. Pierson says Rowe made £20,000 with his circus and always played to packed audiences. Joseph Rowe and his wife, an 'equestrienne', are known to have cleared $100,000 on their Australian tour. They charged 50c per adult and half price for children and servants. See John Culhane, *The American Circus*, 80. Joseph Rowe and his family left Victoria in 1854 to return to San Francisco.

28 These vignettes are all drawn from Robert Whitworth's *Australian Stories Round the Campfire*, published in the Australian International Monthly in 1872.

TWO: DELIVERANCE

1 Genealogical research on the Nolan, Hynes and Gittens families was supplied by Bill Hanlon. Hanlon was raised by his grandmother, Bridget Hynes, Bridget Nolan's daughter. Additional information was provided by John Wilson, also a descendant of the Nolan/Hynes family.

2 There is a substantial literature about women and Chartism. Jutta Schwarzkopf's book *Women in the Chartist Movement* is the most comprehensive. Paul Pickering and Alex Tyrell's *The People's Bread* also gives an excellent account of women's political activism in this period.

3 A remarkable collection of letters between William and Caroline Dexter is held by the State Library of Victoria. See also Patrick Morgan's excellent dual biography of the Dexters, *Folie à Deux*.

4 A file of cuttings from the *Wilts and Gloucestershire Standard* is held by the Royal Historical Society of Victoria.

5 The observations of Fanny Davis are drawn from her ship diary, written upon the *Conway*, 3 June 1858–10 September 1858. The diary is held at the State Library of Victoria.

6 The best analysis of the nineteenth-century concept of 'manliness', which is quite different from today's notion of 'masculinity', is provided by Gail Bederman in her book *Manliness and Civilization*. My thanks to Marilyn Lake for pointing me in the direction of Bederman's work.

7 This fellow's words are recorded in Mrs May Howell's book.

8 These lines are all drawn from the *Marco Polo Chronicle*, 23 November 1853–21 January 1854. Thomas Evans, brother of Charles and George Evans, was on this ship.

9 For these letters and diaries to be found in Australia, either copies or original items need to have been repatriated to Australian collections. Copies of Lucy's letters are now held at the Gold Museum, Ballarat.

10 Graeme Davison discusses the English pastoral idyll, transplanted onto Victoria's rural hinterland, in *The Rise and Fall of Marvellous Melbourne*. Historian Helen Doyle has also written eloquently on this subject in her unpublished doctoral thesis.

11 This statistic is not derived from immigration agent Bell's reports. It is gleaned from the research of Pauline Rule. See her article 'Irish Women and the Problem of Ex-Nuptial Conception'.

12 In 1857, popular goldfields balladeer Charles Thatcher penned a song touching on the cultural anxiety about the sexual homogeneity of Chinese immigrants. Called 'The Fine Fat Saucy Chinaman', it included these lyrics: *Now John, with all his many faults/Leads an industrious life/ The greatest drawback that he has/Is that he has no wife . . . Now as he's getting lots of gold/I've not the slightest doubt/That ultimately Chinese girls/By thousands will come out*. For the full song, see *Thatcher's Colonial Songster*, 79.

13 On the Chinese regarding Europeans as inferior, see Keir Reeves and Andrew Mountford's work on the Chinese during the gold rush.

14 PROV, original papers tabled in the Legislative Assembly, VPRS 3253/53.

THREE: CROSSING THE LINE

1 The life of Louisa Timewell, including her first-hand accounts of the ship journey to Victoria, is honoured in the 1934 *Records of Pioneer Women*. I've supplemented the 1934 entry with basic birth, death and marriage research.

2 *The Marco Polo Chronicle*.

3 Céleste de Chabrillan was a French courtesan prior to her marriage to Lionel de Chabrillan, the French consul. She had written a scandalous memoir of her highly colourful life prior to her voyage to Australia. Her second book was her memoir of her journey to and time in Victoria, based on diary entries and published as *Un Deuil au bout du mond (Death at the End of the World)* some twenty years later. Shunned by Melbourne society due to her self-publicised shady past, the melodramatic but remarkably modern Céleste came to see her time in the antipodes as a sort of bereavement. An English translation of *Un Deuil* has been written by Patricia Clancy and Jeanne Allen as *The French Consul's Wife*.

4 Charlotte Spence's experiences aboard the *John and Lucy* in June 1854 are captured in her husband John Spence's diary. Agnes Paterson's observations are drawn from her ship journal aboard the *Lord Clyde* in 1859, held by the State Library of Victoria. Henry Nicholls' observations are

drawn from his 1852 ship diary. Henry and his wife Marian lost their baby daughter, Marian, eight days into this ill-fated journey. Marian was their fourth child. The Nicholls had five more children in Victoria. State Library of Victoria holds all of the these manuscripts.

5 The observations of Bethuel Adams are drawn from his ship diary, written aboard the *Van Marnix*, departing Gravesend in October 1853. The diary is held by the State Library of Victoria.

6 Quoted in Don Charlwood's *The Long Farewell*, 88.

7 The observations of Jane Swan are drawn from her Diary of a Voyage from Gravesend to Port Phillip on the *William and Jane*, 12 August 1853–2 December 1853, held by the State Library of Victoria.

8 An excellent account of the *Ticonderoga* tragedy and its aftermath can be found at www.mylorenet/Ticohome.html

9 Henry Nicholls gives us this insight.

10 James Menzies immigrated to Victoria in 1848. His shipboard diary is held by the State Library of Victoria.

11 Beelzebub, alias Lucifer, alias Satan, was sometimes held accountable for the demonic possession of young women. His name also comes up repeatedly in the Salem Witch Trials.

12 The observations of Alpheus Boynton are drawn from his diaries, kept between 1852 and 1856. The diaries are held by the Mitchell Library in Sydney.

13 Sarah Ann Raws' shipboard diary, kept between May and August 1854, is part of the Tomlinson Papers, held at the State Library of Victoria. Sarah's father had owned a cotton mill in England before trying his luck in Victoria. Sarah remained in Victoria after the rest of her family returned to England in 1858. Sarah married butcher John Tomlinson and lived on the Mt Alexander diggings. They had ten children.

14 Mrs William Graham sailed to Victoria on the *Marco Polo* in 1863. Her account of her journey is held by the State Library of Victoria.

FOUR: THE ROAD

1 John D'Ewes published his account *Ballarat in 1854* in London in 1857.

2 These statistics are compiled from the *Melbourne Monthly Magazine* vol. 1 no. 11 June 1855 and the Colonial Secretary's Office Inward Correspondence, PROV VPRS 1189/94. For Aborigines as a 'dying race', see William Westgarth's early history of Victoria, *Victoria and the Victorian Gold Mines*. Westgarth attributed the decline in the Aboriginal population to the practices of cannibalism and infanticide, particularly of first-born females.

3 Solomon Belinfante's ship journal, penned between 3 April and 21 June

1854, is held by the State Library of Victoria.

4 The observations of Martha Clendinning are drawn from her unpublished memoirs, *Recollections of Ballarat: A Lady's Life at the Diggings Fifty Years Ago*. The manuscript forms part of the Clendinning–Rede papers, held by the State Library of Victoria.

5 This lovely phrase belongs to Weston Bate, drawn from his essay 'Gold: Social Energiser and Definer'.

6 Janet Kincaid's letter is included in a collection of letters addressed to residents of Maryborough, Victoria, 1851–1902. The collection is held by the State Library of Victoria under the author/creator label *Maryborough*. The diary of American digger Silas Andrews is also in this collection of records.

7 Information pertaining to Eliza Darcy is drawn from the oral history and records of the Darcy/Howard families.

8 The passage is published in John Capper's 1855 guidebook.

9 The observations of Eliza Lucus are drawn from her reminiscences, written in 1913 and held by the State Library of Victoria.

10 Jane McCracken's anguished letters make for uncomfortable reading. From the physical and emotional symptoms she describes to her mother, it is likely Jane was suffering from postnatal depression. Jane's letters form part of the McCracken Family Papers, available on microfilm as part of the Australian Joint Copying Project. Jane's brothers-in-law, Robert and Peter McCracken, established the famous McCracken's City Brewery in 1851. McCracken's was one of the original six breweries that formed the cartel of Carton and United Breweries (CUB) in 1903.

11 John Capper cites these statistics.

12 Historian Geoffrey Serle relates these statistics in *The Golden Age*.

13 These are merchant Robert Caldwell's numbers.

14 William Kelly records these numbers in the 1860 edition of his book. William Westgarth's offers the same statistical analysis.

15 This forms part of Magistrate John D'Ewes' analysis of what went wrong in 1854.

16 Bonwick's *Notes of a Gold Digger* is the source here.

17 Blake's vision in turn came from Luke 3:2–6: *Prepare the way for the Lord, make straight paths for him. Every valley shall be filled in, every mountain and hill made low. The crooked roads shall become straight, the rough ways smooth. And all mankind will see God's salvation.*

18 The observations of Emily Skinner are drawn from her journals and memoir. These were written anonymously, the initials E. S. being the only clue to the woman who had immigrated to Victoria in 1854 to join

her husband. Writer Edward Duyker painstakingly traced Emily's identity and published the manuscript in 1995. The observations of Mary Bristow are drawn from her journal, kept in 1854, and catalogued as *Aunt Spencer's Diary* in the Royal Historical Society of Victoria's collection. Mary addressed her journal to her nephew. Mrs Mannington Caffyn's observations are included in the anthology of women's writing, *Coo-ee: Tales of Australian Life by Australian Ladies*, edited by Mrs Patchett Martin in 1891. Other contributors to the collection include the well-known writers 'Tasma' and Mrs Campbell Praed.

19 James Bonwick, *Australian Gold Digger's Monthly Magazine,* March 1853.

20 Margaret Watson's story is recorded in *Records of Pioneer Women.*

21 These stories are drawn from the Victorian *Police Gazette* of 27 February 1854 and 24 March 1854 but any given edition of the *Police Gazette* in this era will have similar details of runaway women and dead babies.

22 The physical description of Catherine Bentley comes from her prison entry record. Public Record Office Victoria, VPRS 521: vol. 2: prisoner no 2818. Descriptions of her temperament are from family oral history. Andrew Crowley, descendant, interview with author, 20 July 2004. Audio and video recorded. Description of James from *Victorian Police Gazette*, 20 March 1856.

FIVE: THE GOLD DIGGERS OF '54

1 PROV VPRS 1189/93, monthly returns January 1854.

2 Society for Promoting Christian Knowledge, *A Visit to Australia and Its Gold Regions* (London, 1853). This rare book is held in the Special Collections of the Baillieu Library, the University of Melbourne.

3 This is Jo Anne Levy's number. Susan Lee Johnson cites the proportion of women on the southern Californian diggings as three per cent in 1850 and nineteen per cent by 1860.

4 Susan Lee Johnson makes this point in *Roaring Camp.*

5 PROV, Colonial Secretary's Office Outward Registered Correspondence, VPRS 3219, E1483.

6 The quote is drawn from an undated article in the *Ballarat Star* entitled 'Reminiscences of 1851–4'. The article is in the Francis William Niven Collection held by the University of Melbourne Archives. MS 74/73.

7 Chris McConville used this expression in his speech at the launch of the collection *Deeper Leads*, edited by Keir Reeves and David Nichol, at the Ballarat Art Gallery in 2007.

8 Mary Ann Tyler (nee Brooksbank) wrote her memoirs of life as a female gold digger in New South Wales in 1909, six years prior to her death.

9 The *Advertiser* article is cited in Fred Cahir's PhD thesis, 'Black Gold'.

10 Records of shareholders date for 1857. Marion McAdie's CD ROM, *Mining Shareholders Index 1857–1886*, is an invaluable data set for tracing the shareholding activities of individuals and families. Her index is extracted from the Victorian Government Gazette 1857–86.

11 *Geelong Advertiser*, 10 June 1854.

12 *Star of the East* arrived in September 1853. Depending on whether Anne conceived on board, the baby could have been born as early as April 1854. The dead baby materialises on the certificate for Anne's second marriage. Anne Diamond (née Keane/Kane) married John Bourke in August 1856.

13 Quoted in Laurel Johnson's groundbreaking booklet, *Women of Eureka.*

14 Mary Davison King's story is relayed in *Records of Pioneer Women.*

15 Shandy-gaff was a mixture of pale ale and ginger beer, a forerunner of today's shandy of beer and lemonade.

16 Mr McMillan's evidence to the Gold Fields Commission, recorded in the Gold Fields Commission Report 1854–55.

17 Harriet's story is included in John Capper's guidebook.

18 For Mrs Fitchett's reports in the *Geelong Advertiser*, see, for example, 13 February 1854.

19 Victorian Census, 1857.

SIX: WINNERS AND LOSERS

1 PROV, Denominational School Board, Inward Registered Correspondence, VPRS 61/3.

2 All details of Sarah Skinner's death are drawn from her inquest files. PROV VPRS 24.

3 William Buchan, *Domestic Medicine; Or, A Treatise on the Prevention and Cure of Diseases by Regimen and Simple Medicine*, 1798 A. Strahan [etc.] cited in Rudy's List of Archaic Medical Terms. http://www.antiquusmorbus.com/

4 Jean Edois Carey Inquest. PROV Inquest Deposition Files, VPRS 24/18 (1854/103).

5 Observations of Charles Eberle are drawn from his diary, held by the Royal Historical Society of Victoria.

6 The observations of Martin Mossman are drawn from his 1853 letters to his Aunt Hetty. The State Library of Victoria holds the letters. Martin told Hetty that he was going to leave the diggings for New Orleans, but there is no record of his departure from Victoria.

7 Antoine Fauchery's *Lettres d'un Mineur* was originally published in Paris in 1857.

8 These numbers are drawn from Digger—Victorian Pioneers Index 1837–1888, available online at the National Library of Australia's eResources website. The figures are by nature conservative, as many itinerant gold seekers did not stop to register their newborns, particularly stillbirths.

9 David Goodman devotes a whole chapter to the concept of Excitement in his exemplary study, *Gold Seeking*.

10 The observations of Samuel Huyghue are drawn from his unpublished account, *The Ballarat Riots*, penned in 1884. The State Library of Victoria holds the manuscript.

11 Greg Blake has calculated the mean ages of the soldiers stationed at Ballarat. He does so in order to make a counterpoint: that the men of the 40th had significantly more experience as trained soldiers than Huyghue gives them credit for.

12 See, for example, Paul Kennelly's unpublished thesis, *Wives in Search of Servants*. Kennelly has compiled a particularly useful collection of data tables regarding female emigration to Victoria in the period 1848–54.

13 These statistics are drawn from my analysis of the Victorian marriage registers. There were many more common law marriages, like that of Anne and Martin Diamond and William and Sarah Skinner. The fact that wives were choosing de facto relationships over sanctified marriages is another indicator that women were hedging their bets, particularly in an era when divorce laws meant that *til death us do part* was the legal reality.

14 Henry Catchpole's observations are drawn from the book *Victoria Gold: The Everyday Life of Two English Brothers Who Were Diggers*, compiled by Kenneth Kutz.

15 Catherine Chisholm's brother's remarks are drawn from a rare collection of letters spanning 1854–75. The letters are all to Catherine from her tight-knit farming family in Scotland. The Chisholm family papers are held by the State Library of Victoria.

16 The Brownlow Medal is a annual award ceremony for Australian Rules football that has become infamous for the bared flesh and glamorous gowns of the players' wives and girlfriends. The event is held at Crown Casino.

17 Irvine Louden's extraordinary 1992 study, *Death in Childbirth*, looks at the evolution of systems of maternal mortality between 1800 and 1950 in Britain, the USA, Australia, New Zealand and continental Europe.

18 Janet McCalman, *Sex and Suffering*.

19 Henry Handel Richardson based her novel *The Fortunes of Richard Mahoney* on her father's life. Dr Richardson's statistics are quoted in the MA thesis of Ballarat nurse Desley Beechey.

20 Keith Bowden, *Goldrush Doctors.*

21 Observations of James Selby are drawn from his diary and papers, kept between 1852 and 1854. The State Library of Victoria holds these manuscripts.

22 Desley Beechey reveals these ghastly details.

23 Details of Mrs Hazlehurst's case are drawn from court reports in the *Ballarat Times*, 19 February 1858.

24 Harry Hastings Pearce (1897–1984) left an extensive archive of goldfields' history and memorabilia to the State Library of Victoria. Pearce's manuscript, *What It Was Like to Be a Miner*, provides these details about infant mortality.

25 The anonymous digger is quoted in John Capper's guidebook.

26 Jocelynne Scutt, *Even in the Best of Homes* (Ringwood: Penguin, 1983).

27 Isaac Batey referred to the *Hobart Town coat of arms* in his reminiscences of life on the goldfields. Batey's manuscript is held by the Royal Historical Society of Victoria.

28 The Williams case is reported in the *Bendigo Advertiser* 22 March 1856. Other examples of domestic violence cases are contained in the PROV series Court Records, including Petty Sessions Registers, 1854–1962, VPRS 289, and Court of Petty Sessions Record Book VPRS 5939, both series housed at the Ballarat Archives Centre.

29 Eliza Perrin's letters are held in the Montrose Cottage Collection at the Gold Museum, Ballarat.

30 The dirty picture scandal is recounted in the *Melbourne Monthly Magazine* vol. 1, no. 1 May 1855. The Sophia Lewis story is told in exhilarating detail by Melbourne criminal lawyer Ken Oldis in *The Chinawoman.*

31 See John S. Levi and G. F. J. Bergman's history of Jewry in the colonial era, *Australian Genesis.*

32 The first purpose-built synagogue was consecrated in November 1855 in Ballarat East.

33 There was a large Jewish Harris clan in Cornwall, many of whom emigrated in the 1850s. A number of Henry Harrises came to Victoria between 1852 and 1854, making Ballarat Henry difficult to trace. Ballarat's current synagogue was built in 1861.

34 Stories drawn from *Records of Pioneer Women.*

35 Keith Pearce and Helen Fry, *The Lost Jews of Cornwall.*

36 Dyte was so lauded by Nathan Spielvogel, a Ballarat historian who specialised in Jewish history. His lionising of Dyte appears in his article 'The Ballarat Hebrew Congregation'.

37 Quoted in Marise Lawrence Cohen, 'Caroline Chisholm and Jewish Immigration'.

38 Levi and Bergman make this point in *Australian Genesis.*

SEVEN: THE WINTER OF THEIR DISCONTENT

1 *Geelong Advertiser*, 25 May 1854.

2 *Melbourne Monthly Magazine*, vol. 1, no. 1, May 1855, 28.

3 Neither Ellen nor Frederick's death certificates list any offspring, but it is clear from Ellen's writing that she once had a son.

4 Note that average life expectancy in the 1850s was less than forty years, but this is largely because the high rates of infant mortality skew what demographers call 'the life table'. Having survived the first five years of life, many in the gold rush generation lived into their sixties, seventies and beyond.

5 The better-known Mary Fortune, for example, had journalism published in the Melbourne press from the 1860s under the by-line Waif Wanderer or WW.

6 Note, however, that there are Letters to the Editor of the *Ballarat Times* published from September 1854 signed by Justitia that could have been written by Ellen Young. I suspect, however, that they were penned by Clara Du Val Seekamp. Justitia, Lady Justice, was the Roman Goddess of Justice. She is often represented as a matron carrying a sword—the power of reason and justice—and a set of measuring scales. Justitia is considered an allegorical allusion to moral force within western legal systems. In art, aspects of Justitia are sometimes conflated with the goddesses Fortuna (luck), Tyche (fate) and Nemesis (vengeance).

7 Unsourced quotation in Laurel Johnson *Women of Eureka.* The Montrose Cottage Collection, now held at the Gold Museum but previously curated by Johnston for her now defunct Montrose Cottage Museum in Ballarat, includes a reference to Clara being interviewed by a journalist for the *Courier* on 8 January 1902.

8 Mr H. Brown noted these prices in a letter to his sister written in 1854. The State Library of Victoria holds the letter.

9 Noah's letter to his mother, written in 1854, is held by the State Library of Victoria.

10 Geoffrey Serle provides the figures for this analysis of the land problem in *The Golden Age.*

11 This observation was made by Reynell Everleigh Johns, who was a police magistrate on the goldfields. The State Library of Victoria holds an extensive collection of Johns' diaries, papers and scientific writings, as well as a fragment of the Eureka Flag in Johns' possession at his death in 1910.

12 English historian Anna Clark explains the literary genre of Chartist melodrama in *The Struggle for the Breeches.*

13 See the work of Jutta Schwarzkopf in particular.

14 The poem may also have been published in the *Ballarat Times*, but no copies of the *Times* are extant for this period.

15 *The Liberty Song* was written by patriot John Dickinson during the American Revolution. First published as a poem in the *Boston Gazette* in 1768, its lyrics contain the following sentiment: *Then join hand in hand, brave Americans all, By uniting we stand, by dividing we fall.*

16 PROV VPRS 1189/93 G54/7193.

17 PROV VPRS 1189/93 F54/5371, I54/5194.

18 John Bastin, 'Eureka: An Eye-Witness Account', *The Australian Quarterly*, vol. 28, no. 4, December 1956, 78.

19 Hotham's speech was reported in the *Geelong Advertiser* on 26 June 1854.

20 Of Jane and her four sisters, only one had any children, suggesting the Hood girls may have suffered from hereditary infertility.

21 The *Argus* report was widely circulated. See the Hobart *Colonial Times*, 5 July 1854.

22 PROV VPRS 1085/08, despatch to George Grey no. 112.

23 *Ballarat Times*, 2 September 1854.

24 The *Argus* correspondent also guessed that Lady Hotham was less than thirty: a gift, perhaps, of the English sun.

25 *Simplex Munditiis*—simple, neat attire. Ben Jonson wrote a poem called *Simplex munditiis*: (Still to be neat, still to be drest/As you were going to a feast…), a telling indication of the much-touted superiority of education and culture of many diggers. Thanks to Barry Jones for the translation and Jonson reference.

26 *Geelong Advertiser*, 12 September 1854.

27 *Ballarat Courier*, 3 December 1904.

28 Reported in the *Geelong Advertiser*, 12 September 1854.

29 See Paul Pickering and Alex Tyrrell, *The People's Bread.*

30 The petition claimed that coffee drinking caused impotence in men, who came home from coffeehouses with *nothing moist but their snotty noses, nothing stiff but their joints, nor standing but their ears.*

31 PROV VPRS 1189.245 A53/5241.

32 PROV VPRS 1189.244 L55/254.

33 PROV VPRS 4066.01. See also the letters and petitions contained in VPRS 4066.02/03 and VPRS 1189.244 and VPRS 1189.238–240.

34 VPRS 4066.02.

35 VPRS 4066.03.

36 VPRS 4066.02.

37 Esther McKenzie's letter was written on 13 January 1855 and Mrs O'Neill's letter is dated 15 January 1855. Both are found in PROV VPRS 4066.02.

38 *Geelong Advertiser*, 10 October 1854. When Ellen Young wrote directly to Governor Hotham on 10 September 1854, she made it clear that it was with her husband Frederick's *sanction* that she took the liberty. VPRS 4066.01.

EIGHT: PARTING WITH MY SEX

1 *Argus*, 18 May 1854.

2 *Geelong Advertiser*, 11 May 1854. A copy of the notice in the *Ballarat Times* was forwarded to the *Geelong Advertiser* by its Ballarat correspondent. The *Ballarat Times* began publication on 4 March 1854, but the earliest extant copies date from September.
The Adelphi was a famous theatre in London's West End. There was also an Adelphi Theatre in gold rush San Francisco. Sarah Hanmer may have worked at either of them.

3 The anecdote is relayed in Ferguson's *The Experiences of a Forty-Niner*, written on his return to America in 1888. Sarah Hanmer made enough of an impression on Ferguson to include her in a memoir penned forty years after the event.

4 *Geelong Advertiser*, 8 June 1854.

5 *Ballarat Times*, 2 September 1854.

6 PROV VPRS 1189.244 M55/735.

7 Quoted in Alice M. Robinson et al.'s edited collection, *Notable Women in the American Theatre* (Connecticut: Greenwood Press, 1989).

8 *Melbourne Punch*, 14 September 1855, p. 65.

9 Howard's essay is found in the fascinating collection *Crossing the Stage*, edited by Lesley Ferris. Laurence Senelick's *The Changing Room: Sex, Drag and Theatre* also explores the themes of subversion, transgression and transformation in the nineteenth-century theatre.

10 *Argus*, 3 August 1854.

11 For the full lyrics, see *Thatcher's Colonial Songster* of 1857. Thatcher himself was a critic of female suffrage. While in New Zealand in 1865, Thatcher wrote to a Dunedin newspaper mocking the idea of women having a legislative role. 'A female Town Board I *should* like to see/Oh fancy what fine food there'd be for me'. Thatcher Papers, State Library of Victoria.

12 See, for example, *Melbourne Punch*, 28 February 1856 and 29 May 1856.
13 Miska Hauser's letters from Australia have been translated and published by Colin Roderick and Hugh Anderson.
14 Catherine Smith and Cynthia Greig's extraordinary annotated collection of nineteenth-century photographs of cross-dressing in America, *Women in Pants*, graphically illustrates these points.
15 It is sometimes claimed that Henrietta Dugdale wore the bloomer costume, but Susan Priestley's biography of Dugdale sets us straight. She wore a simple divided skirt but not the full bloomer costume, patterns for which could be obtained from Amelia Bloomer's magazine by women, for women, *The Lily*, published in Seneca Falls, New York, but readily circulated in England and continental Europe.
16 'Females in Men's Clothing', *Bendigo Advertiser*, 20 September 1879, cited in Lucy Chesser's *Parting with my Sex*.
17 John Hargreaves gives this estimate in his study of Ballarat's hotels.
18 For a longer discussion of the legend and legacy of Big Poll, see my 2003 book, *Beyond the Ladies Lounge*. Folk singer Glen Tomasetti gives a rendition of Thatcher's song on her 1961 album, *Glen Tomasetti Sings*.
19 Melbourne correspondent to *Mt Alexander Mail*, 15 July 1854.
20 A copy of this document is in the hands of descendant Andrew Crowley. Catherine's signature can be clearly seen.
21 This extract from the *Ballarat Times* of 15 July 1854 is republished in John D'Ewes' memoir.
22 In Australia, Raelene Frances, with her 'hidden history' of prostitution, and Elaine McKewon, with *The Scarlet Mile*, have begun this important, if difficult, project.
23 This point is made by Bronwyn Fensham in her MA thesis about women on the Ballarat diggings.
24 PROV VPRS 289.1.
25 Statistics and quotes drawn from Richard Holmes' masterful book, *Redcoat*.
26 *Argus*, 8 February 1855.
27 *Ballarat Times*, 11 February 1855.
28 *Ballarat Times*, 3 September, 1858.
29 Raelene Frances makes this point clear in *Selling Sex*, 42.
30 Fred Cahir documents this experience in his PhD thesis, 'Black Gold'.
31 The quote comes from Charles Gattey's 1967 history of the dress reform movement, *The Bloomer Girls*.

NINE: BURNING DOWN THE HOUSE

1 In *Scandal in the Colonies*, Kirsten McKenzie notes that subscription lists were used as a form of social gesture to divide the respectable from the dishonourable. Who was put on or off the list could create scandal in a community.

2 PROV Original Papers Tabled in the Legislative Assembly VPRS 3253/60.

3 Details gleaned from the Select Committee on Bentley's Hotel. VPRS 3253/60.

4 *Diggers' Advocate*, 16 September 1854.

5 *Ballarat Times*, 7 October 1854.

6 *Ballarat Times*, 23 September 1854.

7 *Diggers' Advocate*, 16 September 1854.

8 *Ballarat Times*, 23 September 1854.

9 *Geelong Advertiser*, 11 October 1854.

10 *Diggers' Advocate*, 16 September 1854.

11 *Diggers' Advocate*, 16 September 1854.

12 PROV VPRS 1189/94.

13 'Col. Vern's Narrative of the Ballaarat Insurrection' was published in the *Melbourne Monthly Magazine*, no. 7, vol. 2, November 1855. It claimed to be the first account published by a miner. Vern accused James Johnston of bribery and said he was the most disliked officer on the goldfield. After the Eureka Stockade battle, Vern was spotted in Buninyong, disguised in female attire viz: black drawn silk bonnet, light shawl and light cotton gown. VPRS 937/10.

14 There is, however, a Victorian marriage certificate for a James Scobie in 1865. Andrew Crowley's theory is that another miner was killed that morning and a very alive James Scobie was transported in the dead of night, at Peter Lalor's behest, to the Abbotsford Convent, where he lay low. Crowley swears it was in fact a miner called John Martin who died from a blow to the head earlier in the day. Crowley believes Martin was the partner in James Scobie and others' gold claim, and that Scobie was involved in his murder. He argues that James Scobie then pretended to be 'Peter Martin' when testifying at the inquest of the dead body brought to the Eureka Hotel later that day. Crowley lays out his case on his website www.hereticpress.com/Dogstar/History/Bentley.html

15 Coronial inquest into the death of James Scobie. PROV VPRS 5527/01.

16 Court reporters followed the case in both the *Age* and the *Argus* from 23 October to 24 November. Witness depositions and petitions are held in the Eureka Historical Collection at PROV VPRS 5527/01.

17 This observation is drawn from D'Ewes' own account.

18 See John Molony's *Eureka*, 55.

19 PROV VPRS 1189/92.

20 *Argus*, 4 November 1854.

21 Alexander Dick describes the atmosphere of fear and alarm in Melbourne in his diary.

22 *Melbourne Monthly Magazine*, vol. 1, no. 1, May 1855, p. 41.

23 *Geelong Advertiser*, 18 October 1854.

24 *Argus*, 18 November 1854.

25 PROV VPRS 5527/02

26 *Argus*, 2 November 1854.

27 PROV VPRS 1189/468

28 McFarlane's account is based solely on the archival sources held by PROV.

29 Fifty years later, on 5 December 1904, Elizabeth Rowlands published a letter in the *Ballarat Courier* recounting her involvement in the events of 1854.

30 *Riot at Ballarat*, Victorian Parliamentary Papers.

31 My account of the burning of Bentley's Hotel is drawn from evidence given to the Select Committee, which began hearing evidence on 2 November and tabled its report to Parliament on 21 November.

32 Emily's story is recounted in *Records of Pioneer Women*.

33 PROV VPRS 3253/60.

34 Catherine sent petitions for pecuniary aid and compensation in late 1854, 17 May 1855 and 14 November 1855. She claimed a loss of £30,000. PROV VPRS 1189/95 M55/912, S55/14.772.

35 *Ballarat Times*, 2 September 1854.

36 Ellen owes her choice of words to the Great Litany of the *Book of Common Prayer*.

37 This is the document that Andrew Crowley showed me during our interview. He has since donated it to the Gold Museum, Ballarat. See plate section 3, and transcript, page 479.

38 *Argus*, 4 November 1854.

39 *Argus*, 13 November 1854.

TEN: HIGH CAMP

1 PROV VPRS 1189/153, K54/13.392. The submission was *not entertained being an anonymous communication.*

2 This unofficial census is drawn from the account of John D'Ewes.

3 PROV VPRS 1189/91, G54/6826.
4 *Geelong Advertiser*, 2 March 1854.
5 PROV VPRS 937/10. The letter is dated 20 March 1854. Unless otherwise stated, all quotes and details pertaining to the Camp are drawn from police reports contained in the PROV series VPRS 937/10.
6 PROV VPRS 1189/164 G54/10.805 and H54/10533.
7 Neill's diary is used in Neil Smith's book, *Soldiers Bleed Too.* The diary is in private hands. Smith's self-published book endeavours to 'put the case from the Redcoat view', concluding that 'these men fought honourably and with courage in what was a difficult and hostile environment'.
8 PROV VPRS 1189/92 K54/14.002.
9 PROV VPRS 1189/153, K54/13.392.
10 PROV VPRS 1189/92 H54/11824.
11 PROV VPRS 1189/92 H54/11824.
12 PROV VPRS 1189/92 H54/11836.
13 *Geelong Advertiser,* 10 March 1854.
14 All details of Catherine McLister's case are drawn from the PROV series VPRS 1189/153, K54/12.242.
15 Robert McLister's death certificate in 1874 lists his profession as 'constable', indicating a return to the police force at some time subsequent to his wife's death.
16 Note that Geoffrey Blainey has made the point that the Eureka story has conventionally been written from the perspective of the miners only in his essay, 'Eureka: Why Hotham Decided to Swoop'. For an unusual approach to the emotional lives of soldiers, see Joanna Bourke, *An Intimate History of Killing.*

ELEVEN: CROSSING THE LINE (REPRISE)

1 *Ballarat Times*, 11 November 1854.
2 *Ballarat Times*, 25 October 1854.
3 *Ballarat Times*, 25 October 1854.
4 *Geelong Advertiser,* 28 October 1854.
5 PROV VPRS 12882.1.
6 Gregory Blake puts this case strongly in *To Pierce the Tyrant's Heart.*
7 *Ballarat Star,* 6 December 1884.
8 *Geelong Advertiser*, 3 November 1854.
9 *Geelong Advertiser*, 28 October 1854.
10 *Geelong Advertiser*, 30 October 1854.
11 *Geelong Advertiser*, 30 October 1854.

12 *Ballarat Times*, 11 November 1854.
13 PROV VPRS 1095 box 2.
14 My thanks to Andrew Vincent for the Latin translation.
15 *Ballarat Times*, 8 September 1856.
16 See, for example, Edith Thomas's book, *Les Petroleuses*, translated in its English edition as *The Women Incendiaries*.
17 William Howitt reports the incident in *Land, Labour and Gold*.
18 *Ballarat Times*, 15 August 1856.
19 PROV VPRS 5527/01.
20 *Argus*, 1 November 1854. Detective Cummings later commenced legal proceedings for libel against the journalist, declaring that Mrs Bentley had not been handcuffed but rather had sat by the side of her co-accused Hance, who was cuffed.
21 *Argus*, 20 November 1854.
22 *Age*, 20 November 1854.
23 *Argus*, 16 November 1854.
24 *Argus*, 16 November 1854.
25 PROV VPRS 4066.01.
26 PROV VPRS 1085/08.
27 *Argus*, 29 November 1854.
28 PROV VPRS 30/P/37.
29 The observations of W. H. Foster are drawn from the letters to his parents held in the State Library of Victoria.
30 PROV VPRS 1085/08.
31 PROV VPRS1189/92 K54/13219.
32 Keith Bowden makes this point in his study of Ballarat's doctors.
33 *Ballarat Times*, 18 November 1854.
34 The context in which the word was used was ironic: *The rebels, as they are pleased to term us*, would not be conciliated while there was still corruption and double-dealing in the judiciary: *Geelong Advertiser*, 30 November 1854.
35 *Geelong Advertiser*, 1 December 1854.
36 *Geelong Advertiser*, 1 December 1854.
37 As reported by Howitt in *Land, Labour and Gold*.
38 Anne Beggs-Sunter, 'Contesting the Flag: The Mixed Messages of the Eureka Flag', footnote 12.
39 Dorothy Wickham et al., *The Eureka Flag: Our Starry Banner*, 11.
40 There is certainly evidence that in 1854 people visualised the Southern

Cross as a star-studded Latin cross. In Hevelius's influential *Firmamentum* (1690), the first star atlas to depict the southern skies, Crux was depicted under the rear legs of Centaurus as a curved-edge Latin Cross riveted with a star on each of its four extremities. In *Purgatorio*, Dante attributed the cardinal virtues of Justice, Prudence, Temperance and Fortitude to the four brightest stars of the Southern Cross constellation. And in Alexander von Humbolt's *Personal Narrative of a Journey to the Equinoctial Regions of the New Continent 1799-1804*, published in 1852, the popular scientist-explorer wrote:

> A religious sentiment attaches them [the Spaniards] to a constellation the form of which recalls the sign of the faith planted by their ancestors in the deserts of the New World.

Von Humbolt drew his Crux with five stars contained within an angular cross.

Another sign of faith might have influenced the design of the Eureka Flag. Its five stars are eight-pointed. It is possible that this is because, in pattern-making terms, an eight-pointed star is the easiest to cut out quickly. But it is equally conceivable that the number of points was chosen with a less pragmatic view. In Christian religious iconography, the eight-pointed star is known as the Star of Redemption. Eight traditionally represents regeneration, hence the octagonal base of the baptismal font. (Noah also saved eight people on his ark and Jesus was circumcised on the eighth day after his birth.) So perhaps the eight-pointed Eureka stars symbolised new beginnings too: a new home, a new start, and now, a new and redemptive relationship of the governed to the laws that governed them. Early Fenian flags, flown by Irish republicans in the mid-nineteenth century, also employed eight-pointed stars.

41 Kristin Phillips on Youtube, 12 May 2013: '2010 Eureka Flag Conservator Kristin Phillips on conserving an Australian icon'. In August 2013 she added this in an email:

> It would have taken longer than a couple of nights to make the flag. It is big. The cutting out and pinning would have been difficult without a reasonable space to work in. By my very rough calculation there are approximately twenty-nine metres of seams and the flat felled seam is double—requiring two rows of hand stitching—so that's effectively fifty-eight metres of sewing. Flat out, with the seam all ready to go and no pinning etc., you can sew at about a metre per half hour. So at best that would mean that the time it would take to hand sew the fifty-eight metres would be twenty-nine hours. But you have to cut it, pin it and work out how to physically fit the people around the flag, as you couldn't all be doing it at the same time. For example, as you sew around a star you need to move the flag around so your hand is in the right spot, which affects the other people working on it. I

would think that this would effectively double the time required, so sixty hours at the very least; and, again, this is not including the time to cut it out and pin it.

42 Artlab Australia, Condition Assessment, Eureka Flag, May 2010.

43 PROV VPRS 1189/92 K54.13.511.

44 *Geelong Advertiser*, 2 December 1854.

45 PROV VPRS 1085/08.

46 *Ballarat Courier*, 5 December 1904.

47 PROV VPRS 1085/08.

48 *Argus*, 11 April 1917. Frederick Vern later wrote that Lalor stepped forward because he was the only *public speaker* there at the time. Vern and Captain Ross were down at the Eureka.

49 John Molony claims that Kennedy's words are an old Scottish saying, 93.

50 Anne Diamond née Keane gave evidence to the Gold Fields Commission of Enquiry on 26 December 1854.

51 In his essay, 'Eureka: Why Hotham Decided to Swoop', Geoffrey Blainey also argues that the Eureka Stockade was a strategic disaster, but for another reason. He argues that if the miners had fought a guerilla war, fanning out among the hills, bush and tents instead of barricading themselves in like sitting ducks, they could have 'won'. Blainey takes too literal an idea of warfare here. The Stockade was symbolic, not strategic.

52 Vern claimed that although Lalor knelt down and swore to *protect each other*, he did not ask the miners to swear allegiance to the flag.

53 PROV VPRS 1189/92 K54.512.

54 PROV VPRS 1189/92 K54/13.570.

55 PROV VPRS 12882.3 no. 27.

56 Report of the Ballarat correspondent to the *Geelong Advertiser*, written at 5am on 1 December 1854.

TWELVE: BLOODY SUNDAY

1 The *Geelong Advertiser* (1 December 1954) noted that the *absence of drunken men* was *remarkable*.

2 *Money*, by Edward Bulwer-Lytton, was described at the time as *a play which, for pathos, unexaggerated sentiment and elegant sarcasm, stands unrivalled in modern dramatic literature.* It premiered at the Haymarket Theatre in London in 1840. *Hobart Courier*, 7 October 1854.

3 *Geelong Advertiser*, 2 December 1854.

4 *Ballarat Times*, 3 December 1854.

5 Eyewitness H. R. Nicholls revealed this detail in his 1890 reminiscences.

6 The letter is quoted in Molony, though no source is given.

7 Interview with Stephen Cuming in *Ballarat Courier*, 3 December 1897.

8 Menstrual synchrony among co-habiting women is widely accepted in the scientific literature. Lunar synchrony is more controversial but has its champions within orthodox science. See, for example, W. B. Cutler and C. R. Garcia, 'The Psychoneuroendocrinology of the Ovulatory Cycle of Women: A Review', *Psychoneuroendocrinology*, vol. 5, 1979, 89–111. In 'Menstrual Synchrony—An Update and Review', C. A. Graham concludes that although menstrual synchrony is widely documented in scientific studies, the precise mechanisms involved and the adaptive function of menstrual synchrony are still not understood. *Human Nature*, vol. 2, issue 4, 1991, 293–311. There is an extensive literature of women's health and spirituality devoted to lunar menstrual synchrony. See, for example, Lara Owen, *Her Blood is Gold: Celebrating the Power of Menstruation* (San Francisco: Harper, 1993).

9 Evidence of policeman Robert Tully at the state trials: *Geelong Advertiser*, 28 February 1855.

10 Blainey makes the point about the strategic benefit of this single hour of darkness for an advancing army in his essay 'Eureka: Why Hotham Decided to Swoop'.

11 An incident in an 1873 riot in Clunes, a mining town close to Ballarat, demonstrates that women did expose their breasts in times of conflict. William Spence, a miner turned union organiser, tells the story of the riot by striking miners and their families in his 1909 memoir, *Australia's Awakening*:

> Nearby was a heap of road metal, and arming herself with a few stones, a sturdy North of Ireland woman, without shoes or stockings, mounted the barricade as the coaches drew up. As she did she called out to the other women, saying: 'Come on, you Cousin Jinnies, bring me the stones and I will fire them'. The sergeant in charge of the police presented his carbine at the woman and ordered her to desist. Her answer was to bare her breast and say to him: 'Shoot away, and be damned to ye, better be shot than starved to death.'

12 Despatch from Thomas to Hotham, VPRS 1085/08.

13 The observations of Charles Schulze are drawn from his eyewitness account, held by the National Library of Australia. Schulze called the cry of Joe! *A kind of Masonic password.*

14 Anne Diamond, evidence to Gold Fields Commission of Enquiry.

15 *Geelong Advertiser*, 25 January 1855.

16 *Geelong Advertiser*, 6 December 1854.

17 PROV VPRS 1189.101 c55/11.052.

18 Charles Evans' diary.

19 *Geelong Advertiser*, 6 December 1854.

20 PROV VPRS 1189/240 54/J14453.

21 Story recounted in Laurel Johnson, *Women of Eureka*.

22 'Grandma hid miner under her skirt at Eureka', *Ballarat News*, 15 June 1983.

23 William Withers says James McGill met Sarah Hanmer at The Springs.

24 The observation is noted by Charles Evans.

25 The deposition of Henry Powell was reprinted in the *Argus*, 15 December 1854.

26 PROV VPRS 5527/P, unit 2, item 9.

27 Evidence of Thomas Millan and John Doherty, state trials, reported in GA 28 Feb 1855.

28 PROV VPRS 1189.101 c55/11.052.

29 The incident is recounted in R. S. Ross's 1914 account, *Eureka: Freedom's Fight of '54.* Ross was a socialist journalist and trade union organiser, born in Sydney in 1873.

30 PROV VPRS 1189/204.

31 PROV VPRS 1189/240 54/J14433.

32 The story was recounted to R. S. Ross.

33 *Geelong Advertiser*, 6 December 1854.

34 Martha Clendinning ended up with a piece of the flag. She said it was a gift from Dr Carr. It was among her papers donated to the State Library of Victoria.

35 PROV VPRS 1085/08.

36 PROV VPRS 1189/94.

CONCLUSION: A DAY AT THE RACES

1 The Gold Fields Commission of Enquiry was first instigated in late October 1854 with the purpose of sending men of high standing to the goldfields to hear and enquire into complaints against officials, particularly seeking out instances of corruption or maladministration. Instructions were issued to the chairman, Westgarth, on 16 November and commissioners named. However, no paperwork appointing members was signed and sealed by the governor until 7 December, after events in Ballarat precipitated government action.

2 Thatcher Papers. Thatcher's misogyny is only surpassed by his anti-Semitism.

3 *Thatcher's Colonial Songster*, 7.

4 Desertions were recorded in the Victorian *Government Gazette*.

5 Quoted in Neil Smith, *Soldiers Bleed Too*, 21.

6 PROV VPRS 5527/P/2/9. This is Richards' sworn deposition at the state trials. Anastasia's words have been quoted differently in many secondary sources.

7 *Geelong Advertiser*, 28 February 1855.

8 The bill was passed by the Victorian Legislative Council in 1854, leading some historians to argue that the Eureka Stockade played no part in bringing democracy to Australia. This is a view to which J. B. Humffray was himself partial. In 1884 he declared that it was a romantic nonsense to claim, as some did, that the Victorian Constitution was *cradled in the Eureka Stockade*. The constitution, he corrected, was drawn up by La Trobe and passed by the old Legislative Council, so that it was *already nursed, weaned and full grown* by December 1854. According to Humffray, it was a *complete delusion* to think that the Eureka Stockade riots had anything to do with the current Victorian Constitution. (*Ballarat Star*, 29 July 1884.) It was not a popular view. Geoffrey Blainey was to attract a similar level of public hostility when he proffered much the same thesis in *The Rush That Never Ended* in 1963.

9 PROV VPRS 1189/244, M55/735.

10 *Geelong Advertiser*, 3 December 1855.

11 *Hobart Courier*, 11 December 1855.

12 The extracts of Lady Hotham's diary are held in the Hotham Papers at Hull University in England. Lady Hotham transcribed these few pages of her diary, plus scores of condolence letters she received from individuals and associations in Victoria, into one neat volume in her precise and elegant hand.

13 Isene Goldberg, *Queen of Hearts*, 280.

14 *Melbourne Punch*, 28 February, 1856, 27.

15 *Ballarat Times*, 8 September 1856.

16 *Argus*, 5 February 1856.

17 Quoted in Charles Fahey, Heather Holst, Sara Martin and Alan Mayne, 'A Miner's Right: Making Homes and Communities on the Victorian Goldfields', in Alan Mayne (ed.), *Eureka: Reappraising an Australian Legend*, API Network Books, Perth, 2006, 202. Fahey et al. have interpreted the miner's right as the most important instrument in the social transformations that occurred in the wake of the gold rush.

18 For examples of miner's rights held by women, see George McArthur Collection, Special Collections, Baillieu Library, University of Melbourne.

19 *Ballarat Times*, 12 September 1856.

SELECT BIBLIOGRAPHY

A NOTE ON SOURCES

This bibliography contains the primary and secondary sources that most influenced my research and thinking in the writing of this book over the course of a decade. It is by no means an exhaustive list of published and unpublished material on the subject of the Eureka Stockade or the Victorian gold rushes.

The full references for material cited in-text and in the endnotes can be found here.

Note that the Public Record Office of Victoria (PROV) holds an extensive collection of archives related to the management and regulation of the Victorian goldfields in general and the Eureka Stockade in particular. Individual accession records for material cited in this book can be found in the endnotes.

PROV series most useful to this study are as follows:

VPRS 30	Office of the Crown Solicitor, Criminal Trial Briefs
VPRS 937	Victoria Police, Inward Registered Correspondence
VPRS 1085	Governor's Office, Duplicate Despatches from the Governor to the Secretary of State
VPRS 1189	Colonial Secretary's Office, Inward Registered Correspondence
VPRS 3219	Colonial Secretary's Office, Outward Registered Correspondence
VPRS 3253	Legislative Assembly, Original Papers Tabled in the Legislative Assembly
VPRS 4066	Governor's Office, Inward Correspondence
VPRS 5527	Attorney-General's Department, Eureka Stockade—Historical Collection
VPRS 7601	Licensing Courts, Licensing Register—Metropolitan
VPRS 11878	Legislative Assembly, Select Committee Records, Sessional Arrangement

VPRS 1288	Department of Crown Lands and Survey, Index to Applications Registers, All Districts, Section 42, Land Act 1865
VPRS 12882	Resident Commissioner for Crown Lands at the Goldfields Ballarat Inwards and Outwards Correspondence Regarding the Ballarat Riots
VPRS 289	Ballarat Courts, Court Records (includes Petty Sessions Registers 1854–1962)
VPRS 1011	Outward Correspondence Books
VPRS 61	Denominational School Board, Inward Registered Correspondence
VPRS 24	Registrar-General's Department, Inquest Deposition Files

PRIMARY SOURCES

(Vic), Maryborough. *Records, 1851–1902*, 1851–1902. State Library of Victoria, Australian Manuscripts Collection, MS 10943.

Adams, Bethuel. *Diary of Bethuel H. Adams*, 1853. State Library of Victoria, Australian Manuscripts Collection, H15970.

Adams, David, ed. *The Letters of Rachel Henning*. Ringwood, Vic.: Penguin, 1988.

Anderson, Robert. *Robert Anderson Diary*, 1851–56. State Library of Victoria, Australian Manuscripts Collection, MS 8492.

Andrews, Silas. *A True Story of Early Victorian Days from a Diary Written by Silus Andrews*, 1852–57. State Library of Victoria, Australian Manuscripts Collection, MS 10943.

Anon. *Craig's Royal Hotel, Ballarat*. State Library of Victoria, Australian Manuscripts Collection, MS 01/111.

Archer, William Henry. *Archer Papers*, 1854. University of Melbourne Archives, 64/10.

Austin, Anna. *Letter to Lizzy*, 1856. State Library of Victoria, Australian Manuscripts Collection, MS 10514.

Barrett, James. *Letter to Sister Betsy*, 1854. State Library of Victoria, Australian Manuscripts Collection, AJCP M866.

Batey, Isaac. *Isaac Batey Reminiscences*, 1910. Royal Historical Society of Victoria, MS 000035.

Belinfante, Solomon. *Ship Diary*, 1854. State Library of Victoria, Australian Manuscripts Collection, PA 98/76.

Bentley Murder Trial: Transcript of Evidence. 1854. Royal Historical Society of Victoria, MS 15327 MS 000283 (Carr).

Birchall, Lucy. *Papers*, 1855. State Library of Victoria, Australian Manuscripts Collection, MS 9328.

Bogg, Henry. *Letters to Mother*, 1854. State Library of Victoria, Australian Manuscripts Collection, PA 99/68.

Boldrewood, Rolf. *The Miner's Right: A Tale of the Australian Goldfields.* 1973 edn, Sydney: Sydney University Press, 1890.

Bond, John James. *The Diary of J. J. Bond*, 1853–54. State Library of Victoria, Australian Manuscripts Collection, AJCP M724.

Bonwick, James. *Australian Gold Digger's Monthly Magazine and Colonial Family Visitor.* 8 vols Melbourne: *Argus* Office, 1852.

——. *Notes of a Gold Digger and Gold Digger's Guide.* Melbourne, 1852.

Boynton, Alpheus. *Diary of Alpheus Boynton*, 1852–56. Mitchell Library, State Library of New South Wales, ML MSS 1058.

Bridges, Walter. *The Travels of Walter Bridges*, c. 1856. Central Highlands Library (Ballarat).

Bristow, Mary. *Aunt Spencer's Diary*, 1854. Royal Historical Society of Victoria, MS 23801.

Brothers, Lazarus. *Lazarus Brothers' General Almanac for 1866.* Melbourne, 1866.

Brown, H. *Letter to Sister*, 1854. State Library of Victoria, Australian Manuscripts Collection, MS 12255.

Bushman, A. *Sidney's Australian Hand-Book: How to Settle and Succeed in Australia.* London, 1848.

Caffyn, Mrs Mannington. 'Victims of Circe.' In *Coo-Ee: Tales of Australian Life by Australian Ladies*, edited by Mrs Patchett Martin. London: Richard Edward King, 1891.

Caldwell, Robert. *The Gold Era of Victoria: Being the Present and Future of the Colony in Its Commercial, Statistical and Social Aspects.* London: Orr and Co, 1855.

Calwell, Davis. *Calwell Family Letters*, 1853–55. Royal Historical Society of Victoria, MS 000476.

Cannon, Michael, ed. *The Victorian Goldfields 1852–3: An Original Album by S.T. Gill.* Melbourne: State Library of Victoria, 1982.

Capper, John. *Phillips' Emigrants' Guide to Australia.* Liverpool: George Phillip and Son, 1855.

Carboni, Raffaello. *The Eureka Stockade.* Edited by Geoffrey Serle. Melbourne: Melbourne University Press, 1855.

——. *Letter to W. Archer*, 1854. Royal Historical Society of Victoria, MS 000315.

Chisholm. *Chisholm Family Letters*, 1854–75. State Library of Victoria, Australian Manuscripts Collection, MS 10512.

Chisholm, Caroline. *Caroline Chisholm*, 1854. Royal Historical Society of Victoria, MS 000422.

Clacy, Mrs Charles. *A Lady's Visit to the Gold Diggings of Australia in 1852–53: Written on the Spot.* London: Hurst and Blackett, 1853.

——. *Lights and Shadows of Australian Life.* London: Hurst and Blackett, 1854.

Clancy, Patricia and Allen, Jeanne. *The French Consul's Wife: Memoirs of Céleste de Chabrillan in Gold-Rush Australia*. Melbourne: Melbourne University Press, 1998.

Clark, Seth Rudolphus. *Seth Rudolphus Clark Diary*, 1852–58. State Library of Victoria, Australian Manuscripts Collection, MS 10436.

Cleland, Robert Glass. *Apron Full of Gold: The Letters of Mary Jane Megquier from San Francisco, 1849–56*. California: Huntington Library, 1949.

Clendinning, Martha. *Recollections of Ballarat: A Lady's Life at the Diggings Fifty Years Ago*, 1892. State Library of Victoria, Australian Manuscripts Collection, MS 10102/1.

Council, Historical Committee of the Women's Centenary. *Records of the Pioneer Women of Victoria*. Melbourne: Osboldstone, 1937.

Council, Women's Centenary. *Records of the Pioneer Women of Victoria*, 1934. Australian Manuscripts Collection, State Library of Victoria.

Coyne, J. Stirling. *Wanted, 1,000 Spirited Young Milliners for the Gold Diggings: A Farce in One Act*, 1852. University of Melbourne, Special Collections, SpC/MCL L-D Coyne.

Cripps, James. *James Cripps Reminiscences*, 1906. Mitchell Library, State Library of New South Wales, MLMSS 1524.

D'Ewes, John. *Ballarat in 1854*. London: Richard Bentley, 1857.

D*L*. *The Digger's Hand-Book and Truth About California*. Sydney, 1849.

Dalway, Noah. *Noah Dalway Letter*, 1854. State Library of Victoria, Australian Manuscripts Collection, MS 8884.

Davies, Alice. *Recollections of Mrs Alice Davies*, Royal Historical Society of Victoria, MS 000992.

Davis, Fanny. *Ship Diary*, 1858. State Library of Victoria, Australian Manuscripts Collection, MS 10509.

Deegan, John Francis. *The Mining Camps of the Fifties*, 1889. Royal Historical Society of Victoria, MS 000825.

Dexter, Caroline. *Caroline Dexter Collection*, 1858–61. State Library of Australia, Australian Manuscripts Collection, MS 11630.

——. *Ladies Almanack, 1858, the Southern Cross, or, Australian Album and New Year's Gift*. Melbourne: Caroline Dexter, 1858.

Dick, Alexander. *Alexander Dick Diary*, 1854–56. State Library of Victoria, Australian Manuscripts Collection, MS 11241.

Dugdale, Henrietta. *A Few Hours in a Far Off Age*. Melbourne: McCarron Bird, 1883.

Duyker, Edward, ed. *A Woman on the Goldfields: Recollections of Emily Skinner 1854–78*. Melbourne: Melbourne University Press, 1995.

Eberle, Charles. *Diary of Charles Eberle*, 1882. Royal Historical Society of Victoria, MS 000034.

Esson, Louis. *The Southern Cross*. Melbourne: Robertson and Mullins, 1946.

Evans, Charles. *Charles Evans Diary* (Formerly Known as the *Samuel Lazarus Diary*), 1853–55. State Library of Victoria, Australian Manuscripts Collection, MS 11484.

Fauchery, Antoine. *Letters from a Miner in Australia*. Translated by A.R. Chisholm. Melbourne: Georgian House, 1965.

Ferguson, Charles. *The Experiences of a Forty-Niner During Thirty-Four Years' Residence in California and Australia*. Cleveland: Williams Publishing Co., 1888.

Foster, W. H. *Summaries 1851*, 1853–55. State Library of Victoria, Australian Manuscripts Collection, MS 11488.

Fraser, Frances, and Nettie Palmer, eds. *Centenary Gift Book*. Melbourne: Robertson and Mullens, 1934.

Fulton, Alexander. *Letters of Alexander Fulton*, 1858. Royal Historical Society of Victoria, 000394.

Gillespie, Dr. *The Marco Polo Chronicle*, 1853–54. State Library of Victoria, Australian Manuscripts Collection, MS 10862.

Graham, Mrs William. *Ship Account*, 1863. State Library of Victoria, Australian Manuscripts Collection, MS 10438.

Graham Smith, J. *Reminiscences of the Ballarat Goldfield*. Ballarat: Pick Point Publishing, 2000, 1899.

Green, James. *James Green Letter*, 1853. State Library of Victoria, Australian Manuscripts Collection, MS 9330.

Griffith, Charles. *Diary*, 1840. State Library of Victoria, Australian Manuscripts Collection, MS 9393.

Hall, Charles Browning. *Old Melbourne Notebook: 1852–54*. Northbridge, Western Australia: Access Press, 1996.

Ham, Mary. *Ham and Collings Family Papers*, 1851–70. State Library of Queensland, 1787 series 6.

———. *Ham Letters*, 1862. State Library of Victoria, Australian Manuscripts Collection, MS 10787 MS 10870.

Handel Richardson, Henry. *The Fortunes of Richard Mahony*. London: William Heinemann, 1917.

Hargraves, Edward Hammond. *Australia and Its Goldfields: A Historical Sketch*. London: H. Ingram and Co., 1855.

Hart, Lucy. *Letters*, 1852–3. Gold Museum, Ballarat, MS 8838.

Haylon, Leslie. *Blood on the Wattle: A Play of the Eureka Stockade*. Sydney: Angus and Robertson, 1948.

Heape, Samuel. *Ship Diary*, 1854. State Library of Victoria, Australian Manuscripts Collection, MS 10518.

Hopkins, James. *Diary of a Voyage*, 1855. State Library of Victoria, Australian Manuscripts Collection, MS 12435.

Howell, Mrs W. May. *Reminscences of Australia, the Diggings and the Bush*. London: W. May Howell, 1869.

Howitt, William. *Land, Labour and Gold: Or Two Years in Victoria, with Visits to Sydney and Van Dieman's Land*. London: Longman, 1855.

Hume, Fergus. *Madame Midas*. Melbourne: Text Publishing, 1999 (first published 1888).

———. *The Mystery of a Hansom Cab*. Melbourne: Text Publishing, 1999 (first published 1886).

Humffray, John Basson. *John Basson Humffray Diary*, 1853-54. State Library of Victoria, Australian Manuscripts Collection, MS 7822.

Huxtable. *Huxtable and Co's Commercial Directory of Ballarat*. Ballarat, 1857.

Huyghue, Samuel. *The Ballarat Riots*, 1884. State Library of Victoria, Australian Manuscripts Collection, MS 7725.

Jevons, William Stanley. *William Stanley Jevons Papers*, 1855. State Library of Victoria, Australian Manuscripts Collection, MS2633.

Johns, Reynell Everleigh. *Reynell Everleigh Johns Papers*, 1852–55. State Library of Victoria, Australian Manuscripts Collection, MS 10075.

Johnston, Margaret (Maggie). *Diary, Transcript, 1854 May 18-Oct. 17 1856*, 1854. State Library of Victoria, Australian Manuscripts Collection MS 1641288.

Keesing, Nancy, ed. *History of the Australian Gold Rushes by Those Who Were There*. Sydney: Angus and Robertson, 1971.

Kelly, William. *Life in Victoria in 1853 and 1858*. London: Chapman and Hall, 1860.

Knowledge, Society for Promoting Christian. *A Visit to Australia and Its Gold Regions*. London, 1853.

Kutz, Kenneth J. *Victoria Gold: The Everyday Life of Two English Brothers Who Were Diggers on the Victorian Goldfields 1852–67*. Darien, Connecticut: Gold Fever Publishing, 1993.

Lalor, Peter. *Lalor Family Papers*, 1853–55. State Library of Victoria, Australian Manuscripts Collection, AJCP M2039.

Lang, George Dunmore. *Letter to Mother*, 1854. John Dunmore Lang papers, Mitchell Library, A2224 CY 2177.

La Trobe, Charles. *Charles La Trobe Letters*, 1855–1864. State Library of Victoria, Australian Manuscripts Collection, misc—see LDA 2.

Levinson, Hyman. *A Record of Some Memoirs, Compiled for Her Children and Grandchildren by Augusta Levinson*, 1920. Royal Historical Society of Victoria, 22119.

Lucus, Eliza. *Diary of Eliza Lucus*, 1913. State Library of Victoria, Australian Manuscripts Collection, MS 12104.

Lyall, Charles. *Charivari*, 1854. State Library of Victoria, Australian Manuscripts Collection, MS 12221.

MacCartie, Justin Charles. 'The Eureka Stockade: Australia's Only Battle.' In *Battles of the Nineteenth Century*. London: Cassell, 1902.

MacKenzie, Eneas. *Memoirs of Mrs Caroline Chisholm with an Account of Her Philanthropic Labours*. London: Webb, Millington and Co., 1852.

Mann, G.H. *G.H. Mann Memoirs*, 1886. State Library of Victoria, Australian Manuscripts Collection, MS 9288.

McArthur, George. *George McArthur Collection*, 1859–1884. University of Melbourne Special Collections.
McCall, Elizabeth Wilkie. *Elizabeth Wilkie McCall Letters*, 1854. State Library of Victoria, Australian Manuscripts Collection, MS 9012.
McCombie, Thomas. *Australian Sketches: The Gold Discovery, Bush Graves Etc Etc*. London: W. Johnston, 1861.
———. *The History of Victoria*. Melbourne: Sands and Kenny, 1858.
McCracken, Jane. *McCracken Family Papers*, State Library of Victoria, Australian Manuscripts Collection, AJCP 1976.
McLeish, William. *Wlliam McLeish Memoir*, 1914. State Library of Victoria, Australian Manuscripts Collection, MS 11846.
Menzies, James. *Diary of a Voyage*, 1848. State Library of Victoria, Australian Manuscripts Collection, MS 10633.
Montez, Lola. *Lectures of Lola Montez (Countess of Landfeld) Including Her Autobiography*. New York: Rudd and Carleton, 1858.
Moore-Bentley, Mary. *Journey to Durran Durra*. Connells Point, NSW: Privately published, contact Jeanne Bow, 1983. Written 1935.
Mossman, Martin. *Letters to Aunt Hetty*, 1853. State Library of Victoria, Australian Manuscripts Collection, MS 13196.
Mossman, Samuel. *The Gold Regions of Australia*. London, 1852.
Mundy, Henry. *Henry Mundy Reminiscences*, 1909. State Library of Victoria, Australian Manuscripts Collection, MS 10416.
Murray's Guide to the Gold Diggings: The Australian Gold Diggings, Where They Are and How to Get at Them. London: Stuart and Murray, 1852.
Nicholls, H. R. 'Reminiscences of the Eureka Stockade.' *Centennial Magazine* 2, no. 10 (May 1890): 746–50.
Nicholls, Henry. *Henry Nicholls Diary*, 1852. State Library of Victoria, Australian Manuscripts Collection, MS 12432.
Niven, Francis William. *Niven Collection*, 1851–58. University of Melbourne Archives, 74/73.
Nugent Wood, Susan. *Woman's Work in Australia/by a Daughter of the Soil*. Melbourne: Samuel Mullen, 1862.
Pasley, Charles. *Charles Pasley Letters*, 1854. State Library of Victoria, Australian Manuscripts Collection, MS 6167.
Paterson, Agnes. *Logbook*, 1859. State Library of Victoria, Australian Manuscripts Collection, MS 9492.
Pearce, Harry Hasting. *The Causes of Eureka*, 1968. State Library of Victoria, Australian Manuscripts Collection, MS 9370.
Pearce, Harry Hastings. *What It Was Like to Be a Miner*, 1968, State Library of Victoria, Australian Manuscripts Collection, MS 9370.
Pierson, Thomas. *Thomas Pierson Diary*, 1852–55. State Library of Victoria, Australian Manuscripts Collection, MS 11646.
Potts, E. Daniel, and Annette Potts. *A Yankee Merchant in Goldrush Australia: The Letters of George Francis Train 1853–55*. Melbourne: Heinemann, 1970.

Procedings, Votes and. 'The Goldfields Commission Report.' edited by Legislative Council of Victoria, 1854–55.

Pyke, W. T. *Australian Heroes and Adventures: Bush Tales.* Melbourne: Coles Book Arcade, 1887.

Ramsay-Laye, Elizabeth. *Social Life and Manners in Australia.* London, 1861.

Raws, Sarah. *Tomlinson Papers*, 1854. State Library of Victoria, Australian Manuscripts Collection, MS 12275.

Read, C. Rudston. *What I Heard, Saw and Did on the Australian Gold-Fields.* London: T. and W. Boone, 1853.

Reilly, J. Gavan. *For Freedom at Eureka.* State Library of Victoria, Australian Manuscripts Collection, MS10987.

'Report from the Commission Appointed to Inquire into the Condition of the Goldfields.' Melbourne, 1855.

Roderick, Colin and Anderson, Hugh, ed. *Miska Hauser's Letters from Australia 1854–58.* Melbourne: Red Rooster Press, 1988.

Ross, Bryce. *Bryce Ross's Diggings Directory.* Melbourne, 1853.

Ross, R. S. *Eureka: Freedom's Fight of '54.* Melbourne: Fraser and Jenkinson, 1914.

Schulze, Charles. *Extracts from Eye-Witness Account of Eureka Stockade*, 1854. National Library of Australia, MS 9125.

Seeley, Mrs Leonard. *Mrs Leonard B Seeley Commonplace Book*, 1854. State Library of Victoria, Australian Manuscripts Collection, MS 13174.

Selby, James. *Diary and Papers*, 1852–54. State Library of Victoria, Australian Manuscripts Collection, MS 9866.

Sherer, John. *The Gold-Finder of Australia: How He Went, How He Fared and How He Made His Fortune.* London: Clarke, Beeton, and Co. 1853.

Smith, J. Graham. *Reminiscences of the Ballarat Goldfield.* 2002 ed. Ballarat: Pick Point Publishing, 1899.

Smyth, Patrick. *Letter to W. H. Archer*, 1854. State Library of Victoria, Australian Manuscripts Collection, MS 11491.

Spence, John. *Ship Diary*, 1854. State Library of Victoria, Australian Manuscripts Collection, MS 9326.

Spencer, Mrs. *Contract of Employment*, 1858. State Library of Victoria, Australian Manuscripts Collection, MS 3721(b).

Swan, Jane Ann. *Diary of a Voyage from Gravesend to Port Philllip on the William and Jane, 12 August 1853–2 December 1853*, 1853. State Library of Victoria, Australian Manuscripts Collection, MS 11465.

Tait, J. M. 'Oddfellows Christmas Annual.' *Australian International Monthly*, 6 July 1872.

Thatcher, Charles. *Thatcher Papers*, 1831–78. State Libarary of Victoria, Australian Manuscript Collection.

——. *Thatcher's Colonial Minstrel: New Collection of Songs by the Inimitable Thatcher.* Melbourne: Charlwood and Son, 1864.

———. *Thatcher's Colonial Songster*. Melbourne: Charlwood, 1857.
Thomes, William. *Gold Hunter's Adventures: Or, Life in Australia*. Boston: Lee and Shepard, 1864.
Train, Miller Davis. *Letters of Miller Davis Train*, 1854. Royal Historical Society of Victoria, MS 000134.
Tyler, Mary Ann. *The Adventurous Memoirs of a Gold Diggeress 1841–1909*. Wellington, NSW: Kate Gibbs, 1985.
Various. *Letters from the Wilts and Gloucestershire Standard*, 1851–56. Royal Historical Society of Victoria, MS 000095.
Vern, Frederick. 'Col. Vern's Narrative of the Ballaarat Insurrection.' *The Melbourne Monthly*, November 1855, 5–13.
Votes and Proceedings, Legislative Council of Victoria. 'The Goldfields Commission Report.' Melbourne: Votes and Proceedings, Legislative Council of Victoria, 1854-55, A-76, 1855.
VPP. 'Ballaarat Outbreak: Petition.' 1855.
———. 'Report from the Select Committee on Ballarat Compensation (Bentley's Hotel).' 1858.
———. 'Report from the Select Committee Upon Mrs Seekamp's Claim.' Melbourne: Victorian Parliamentary Papers 1860-61, 1861.
———. 'Riot at Ballarat: Report of the Board Appointed to Enquire into Circumstances Connected with the Late Disturbance at Ballaarat.' 1854-55.
———. 'Victorian Parliamentary Debates: Electoral Law Consolidation Bill.' 1865.
Watters, Charlotte. *Charlotte Watters Letter*, 1854. Royal Historical Society of Victoria, MS 000669.
Westgarth, William. *Victoria and the Victorian Gold Mines in 1857*. London, 1857.
Whitelaw, Eliza. *Reminscences*, 1900. State Library of Victoria, Australian Manuscripts Collection.
Whitworth, Robert. 'Australian Stories Round the Campfire.' *Australian International Monthly*, 6 July 1872.
Wilson, John William. *The Starry Banner of Australia: An Episode in Colonial History*. Brisbane: Brian Donaghey (first published 1885), 1963.
Withers, William. *History of Ballarat and Some Ballarat Reminiscences*. Ballarat: Ballarat Heritage Services, 1870 (facsimile edition 1999).
Woodbury, Walter. *Letters to Mother*, 1854. State Library of Victoria, Australian Manuscripts Collection, AJCP M1952.
Wyld, James. *Notes on the Distribution of Gold Throughout the World Including Australia, California, Russia and Great Britain*. London, 1853.

SECONDARY SOURCES

Anderson, Margaret. 'Mrs Charles Clacy, Lola Montez and Poll the Grogseller: Glimpses of Women on the Early Victorian Goldfields.' In *Gold: Forgotten Histories and Lost Objects of Australia*, edited by Iain McCalman, Alexander Cook and Andrew Reeves. 225–50. Cambridge: Cambridge University Press, 2001.

Annear, Robyn. *Fly a Rebel Flag: The Battle at Eureka*. Fitzroy, Vic.: Black Dog Books, 2004.

———. *Nothing but Gold: The Diggers of 1852*. Melbourne: Text Publishing, 1999.

Asher, Louise. 'Women on the Ballarat Goldfields—1850s and Early 1860s.' Honours, The University of Melbourne, 1977.

Barry, David. *Women and Political Insurgency: France in the Mid-Nineteenth Century*. London: Palgrave Macmillan, 1996.

Bate, Weston. 'Gold: Social Energiser and Definer.' *Victorian Historical Journal* 72, no. 1&2 (2001).

———. *Lucky City: The First Generation at Ballarat, 1851–1901*. Melbourne: Melbourne University Press, 1978.

———. 'Perceptions of Eureka.' *Victorian Historical Journal* 75, no. 2 (2004): 133–45.

Bederman, Gail. *Manliness and Civilization: A Cultural History of Gender and Race in the United States, 1880–1917*. Chicago and London: The University of Chicago Press, 1996.

Beechey, Desley. 'Eureka! Women and Birthing on the Ballarat Goldfields in the 1850s.' MA, Australian Catholic University, 2003.

Beggs-Sunter, Anne. 'Contesting the Flag: The Mixed Messages of the Eureka Flag.' In *Eureka: Reappraising an Australian Legend*, edited by Alan Mayne. Perth: API Network Books, 2006.

———. 'Eureka: Gathering the "Oppressed of All Nations".' *Journal of Australian Colonial History* 10, no. 1 (2008): 15–35.

Blainey, Geoffrey. *Black Kettle and Full Moon*. Ringwood, Vic.: Penguin, 2003.

———. 'Eureka: Why Hotham Decided to Swoop.' In *The Legacy of Eureka: Past, Present and Future*, edited by Anne Beggs-Sunter and Kevin Livingston. 1–6. Ballarat: University of Ballarat, 1998.

———. *The Rush That Never Ended*. Melbourne: Melbourne University Press, 1963.

Blake, Gregory. *To Pierce the Tyrant's Heart: The Battle for the Eureka Stockade, 3 December 1854*. Loftus, ACT: Australian Army History Unit, 2009.

Blee, Jill. *The Liberator's Birthday*. Briar Hill, Vic.: Indra Publishing, 2002.

Bohstedt, John. *Riots and Community Politics in England and Wales*. Cambridge, Mass.: Harvard University Press, 1983.

Booth, Michael R. *Theatre in the Victorian Age*. London: Cambridge University Press, 1991.

Bowden, Keith. *Goldrush Doctors at Ballarat*. Mulgrave, Vic.: Magenta Press, 1977.

Broome, Richard. *Aboriginal Australians: A History since 1788*. Sydney: Allen & Unwin, 2010.

Bourke, Joanna. *An Intimate History of Killing: Face-to-Face Killing in Twentieth Century Warfare*. London: Granta, 1999.

Burke, Keast. *Gold and Silver: Photographs of Australian Goldfields from the Holtermann Collection*. Ringwood, Vic.: Penguin, 1973.

Cahir, David. 'Black Gold: A History of the Role of Aboriginal People on the Goldfields of Victoria, 1850–70.' PhD, University of Ballarat, 2006.

Cahir, David (Fred) and Clark, Ian D. '"Why Should They Pay Money to the Queen?" Aboriginal Miners and Land Claims.' *Journal of Australian Colonial History* 10, no. 1 (2008): 115–28.

Cahir, Fred. '"Are You Off to the Diggings?" Aboriginal Guiding to and on the Goldfields.' *The La Trobe Journal*, no. 85 (2010): 22–37.

———. 'Dallong: Possum Skin Rugs.' *Provenance: The Journal of the Public Record Office of Victoria*, no. 4 (2004) 1–6.

———. 'Finders Not Keepers: Aboriginal People on the Goldfields of Victoria.' In *Eureka: Reappraising an Australian Legend*, edited by Alan Mayne. 143–53. Perth: API Network Books, 2006.

Cahir, Fred and Clark, Ian. 'The Case of Peter Mungett.' *Provenance: The Journal of the Public Record Office of Victoria*, no. 8 (2009): 1–19.

Cannon, Michael. *Lola Montes: The Tragic Story of a Liberated Woman*. Melbourne: Heritage Publications, 1973.

———. *Old Melbourne Town: Before the Gold Rush*. Main Ridge, Vic: Loch Haven, 1991.

Capp, Bernard. *When Gossips Meet: Women, Family and Neighbourhood in Early Modern England*. Oxford: Oxford University Press, 2003.

Charlwood, Don. *The Long Farewell: The Perilous Voyages of Settlers under Sail in the Great Migrations to Australia*. Ringwood, Vic.: Penguin, 1981.

Chesser, Lucy. *Parting with My Sex: Cross-Dressing, Inversion and Sexuality in Australian Cultural Life*. Sydney: Sydney University Press, 2008.

Churchward, L. G. 'Americans and Other Foreigners at Eureka.' *Historical Studies* Eureka Supplement (1954): 78–87.

Clark, Anna. *The Struggle for the Breeches: Gender and the Making of The British Working Class*. London: Rivers Oram Press, 1995.

Clark, Ian. *Aboriginal Languages and Clans: An Historical Atlas of Western and Central Victoria, 1800–1900*, Melbourne: Department of Geography and Environmental Science, Monash University, 1990.

Clendinnen, Inga. *Dancing with Strangers*. Melbourne: Text Publishing, 2003.

Cochrane, Peter. *Colonial Ambition: Foundations of Australian Democracy*. Carlton, Vic.: Melbourne University Press, 2006.

Cohen, Marise Lawrence. 'Caroline Chisholm and Jewish Immigration.' *Australian Jewish Historical Society Journal* 11, no. 2 (1944).

Collings, J. W. *Thomas Ham: Pioneer Engraver and Publisher*, 1945. State Library of Victoria, Australian Manuscripts Collection, MS 10870.

Collins, Diane. 'A "Roaring Decade": Listening to the Australian Gold-Fields.' In *Talking and Listening in the Age of Modernity: Essays on the History of Sound*, edited by Joy Damousi and Desley Deacon. Canberra: ANU E-press, 2007.

Corfield, Justin, Wickham, Dorothy and Gervasoni, Clare. *The Eureka Encyclopaedia*. Ballarat: Ballarat Heritage Services, 2004.

Culhane, John. *The American Circus: An Illustrated History*. New York: Henry Holt and Co., 1990.

Currey, Charles Herbert. *The Irish at Eureka*. Sydney: Angus and Robertson, 1954.

Curry, Jane Kathleen. *Nineteenth-Century American Women Theatre Managers*. Connecticut: Greenwood Press, 1994.

Curtin, Emma. 'Gentility Afloat: Gentlewomen's Diaries and the Voyage to Australia, 1830–80.' *Australian Historical Studies* 26, no. 105 (1995): 634–52.

D'Auvergne, Edmund. *Lola Montez: An Adventuress of the Forties*. London: T. Werner Laurie, 1909.

Damousi, Joy. 'Chaos and Order: Gender, Space and Sexuality on Female Convict Ships.' *Australian Historical Studies* 26, no. 104 (1995): 351–72.

Davison, Graeme. *The Rise and Fall of Marvellous Melbourne*. Carlton, Vic.: Melbourne University Press, 1978.

———. *The Use and Abuse of Australian History*. St Leonards, NSW: Allen & Unwin, 2000.

Deason, Denise. *Welcome Stranger: The Amazing True Story of One Man's Legendary Search for Gold—at All Costs*. Ringwood, Vic.: Penguin, 2005.

Dimmack, Max. *Noel Counihan*. Carlton, Vic.: Melbourne University Press, 1974.

Doggett, Anne. 'Beyond Gentility: Women and Music in Early Ballarat.' *History Australia* 6, no. 2 (2009): 37.1–37.17.

Doyle, Helen. 'Australia Infelix: Making History in an Unsettled Country.' PhD, Monash University, 2005.

Druett, Joan. *Hen Frigates: Passion and Peril, Nineteenth-Century Women at Sea*. New York: Touchstone, 1998.

Edwards, Laura F. *Scarlett Doesn't Live Here Anymore: Southern Women in the Civil War Era*. Chicago: University of Illinois Press, 2000.

Fahey, Charles, Holst, Heather, Martin, Sarah and Mayne, Alan. 'A Miner's Right: Making Homes and Communities on the Victorian

Goldfields.' In *Eureka: Reappraising an Australian Legend*, edited by Alan Mayne. Perth: API Network Books, 2006.

Fauré, Christine. *Democracy without Women: Feminism and the Rise of Liberal Individualism in France*. Bloomington: Indiana University Press, 1991.

Featherstone, Guy. *James Bonwick: An Australian Life*, 1972. Royal Historical Society of Victoria, MS 000338.

Fensham, Bronwyn. '"Right Handsome Girls": Women on the Ballarat Diggings in the 1850s.' MA, Monash University, 1994.

Ferris, Lesley, ed. *Crossing the Stage: Controversies on Cross-Dressing*. London: Routledge, 1993.

Fitzpatrick, David. *Oceans of Consolation: Personal Accounts of Irish Migration to Australia*. Ithaca, NY: Cornell University Press, 1994.

FitzSimons, Peter. *Eureka: The Unfinished Revolution*. North Sydney, NSW: Random House, 2012.

Fotheringham, Richard, ed. *Australian Plays for the Colonial Stage 1834–1899*. St Lucia, Qld: University of Queensland Press, 2006.

Fox, Len. 'Women and the Eureka Flag.' *Overland* 105 (1986).

Frances, Raelene. *Selling Sex: A Hidden History of Prostitution*. Sydney: UNSW Press, 2007.

Frevert, Ute. *Women in German History: From Bourgeois Emancipation to Sexual Liberation*. Translated by Stuart McKinnon-Evans. Oxford: Berg, 1988.

Frost, Lucy. 'Untrodden Dresses, Loose Trowsers, and Trailing Skirts: Walking through Colonial Space.' *Women's Writing* 5, no. 2 (1998): 201–12.

Glenn, Susan A. *Female Spectacle: The Theatrical Roots of Modern Feminism*. Cambridge, Mass.: Harvard University Press, 2000.

Goldberg, Isaac. *Queen of Hearts: The Passionate Pilgrimage of Lola Montes*. New York: John Day Co., 1936.

Goldman, Lazarus Morris. *The Jews in Victoria in the Nineteenth Century*. Melbourne: Lazarus Morris Goldman, 1954.

Goldman, Marion S. *Gold Diggers and Silver Miners: Prostitution and Social Life on the Comstock Lode*. Ann Arbor: University of Michigan Press, 1981.

Goodman, David. *Gold Seeking: Victoria and California in the 1850s*. St Leonards, NSW: Allen & Unwin, 1994.

Grimshaw, Patricia and Graham Willett. 'Women's History and Family History: An Exploration of Colonial Family Structure.' In *Australian Women: Feminist Perspectives*, edited by Norma Grieve and Patricia Grimshaw. Melbourne: Oxford University Press, 1981.

Haines, Robyn. *Doctors at Sea: Emigrant Voyages to Colonial Australia*. Hampshire: Palgrave Macmillan, 2005.

Halliday, Jon and Fuller, Peter, ed. *The Psychology of Gambling*. London: Allen Lane, 1974.

Hamand Venet, Wendy. *Neither Ballots nor Bullets: Women Abolitionists and the Civil War*. Charlottesville: University Press of Virginia, 1991.

Hancock, Marguerite. *Colonial Consorts: The Wives of Victoria's Governors 1839–1900*. Melbourne: Melbourne University Press, 2001.

Hargreaves, John. *Ballarat Hotels, Past and Present*, nd. Central Highlands Regional Library Corporation, Australian Research Collection.

Hill, David. *Gold Rush: The Fever That Forever Changed Australia*. Sydney: William Heinemann, 2010.

Hirst, John. *Australia's Democracy: A Short History*. Sydney: Allen & Unwin, 2002.

Holmes, Richard. *Redcoat: The British Soldier in the Age of Horse and Musket*. London: HarperCollins, 2001.

Horsfall, David. *March to Big Gold Mountain*. Ascot Vale, Vic.: Red Rooster Press, 1985.

Hughes, Robert. *Culture of Complaint: The Fraying of America*. Oxford: Oxford University Press, 1993.

Inglis, Ken. *Australian Colonists: An Exploration of Social History 1788–1870*. Carlton, Vic.: Melbourne University Press, 1993.

Ireland, John. *'Three Cheers for Mr Ireland': Towards a Re-Assessment of Richard Davies Ireland*, 1988. State Library of Victoria—Australian Manuscripts Collection, MS 12570.

Irving, Terry. *The Southern Tree of Liberty: The Democratic Movement in New South Wales before 1856*. Annandale, NSW: The Federation Press, 2006.

Johnson, Laurel. *Women of Eureka*. Ballarat: Historic Montrose Cottage and Eureka Museum, 1995.

Johnson, Susan Lee. *Roaring Camp: The Social World of the California Gold Rush*. New York: W. W. Norton, 2000.

Keane, John. *Violence and Democracy*. Cambridge: Cambridge University Press, 2004.

Kennelly, Paul. *Wives in Search of Servants; Youth in Search of Wives: The Assisted Emigration of Single Females to Victoria, 1848–54*, 1979. State Library of Victoria, Australian Manuscripts Collection, MS 10737.

Kiddle, Margaret. *Caroline Chisholm*. Melbourne: Melbourne University Press, 1969.

Kruss, Susan. *Calico Ceilings: The Women of Eureka*. Melbourne: Five Islands Press, 2004.

Kyi, Anna. 'Unravelling the Mystery of the Woah Hawp Canton Quartz Mining Company, Ballarat.' *Journal of Australian Colonial History* 6 (2004): 59–79.

Lacoue-Labarthe, Philippe. *Heidegger and the Politics of Poetry*. Madison: University of Wisconsin Press, 2007.

Lake, Marilyn. 'Feminist History as National History: Writing the Political History of Women.' *Australian Historical Studies* 27, no. 106 1996: 154-69.

Landes, Joan. *Women and the Public Sphere in the Age of the French Revolution*. Ithaca, NY: Cornell University Press, 1988.

Lawrence, Susan. *Dolly's Creek: An Archaeology of a Victorian Goldfields Community*. Melbourne: Melbourne University Press, 2000.

Lee, Vera. *The Reign of Women in Eighteenth-Century France*. Cambridge, Mass.: Schenkman, 1975.

Leonard, Elizabeth. *All the Daring of the Soldier: Women of the Civil War Armies*. New York: W. W. Norton, 1999.

Levi, John S. and Bergman, G. F. J. *Australian Genesis: Jewish Convicts and Settlers 1788–1860*. Melbourne: Melbourne University Press, 2002.

Levy, Jo Ann. *They Saw the Elephant: Women in the California Gold Rush*. Hamden, Connecticut: Archon Books, 1990.

Lewis, Jane. *Women and Social Action in Victorian and Edwardian England*. London: Edward Elgar, 1991.

Linnane, Rev. T. J. *Names in the Eureka Story*. Canberra: A. N. L., 1973.

Littlewood, Roland. 'Military Rape'. *Anthropology Today* 13, no. 2 (1997).

Loudon, Irvine. *Death in Childbirth: An International Study of Maternal Care and Maternal Mortality, 1800–1950*. Oxford: Oxford University Press, 1992.

Love, Harold, ed. *The Australian Stage: A Documentary History*. Sydney: UNSW Press, 1984.

MacFarlane, Ian. *Eureka from the Official Records*. Melbourne: Public Record Office Victoria, 1995.

Mackaness, George, ed. *The Australian Journal of William Strutt 1850–62*. Vol. XLI. Melbourne: Australian Historical Monographs, 1958.

Mannin, Ethel. *Women and the Revolution*. London: Secker & Warburg, 1938.

Mayne, Alan. 'Goldrush Landscapes: An Ethnography.' In *Deeper Leads: New Approaches to Victorian Goldfields History*, edited by Keir Reeves and David Nichols, David. Ballarat: Ballarat Heritage Services, 2007.

McAdie, Marion. 'Mining Shareholders Index, 1857–86.', 2006.

McCalman, Janet. *Sex and Suffering: Women's Health and a Women's Hospital*. Carlton, Vic.: Melbourne University Press, 1998.

McKenzie, Janet. *Noel Counihan*. Kenthurst, NSW.: Kangaroo Press, 1986.

McKenzie, Kirsten. *Scandal in the Colonies*. Melbourne: Melbourne University Press, 2004.

McKewon, Elaine. *The Scarlet Mile: A Social History of Prostitution in Kalgoorlie, 1894–2004*. Perth: University of Western Australia Press, 2005.

Molony, John. *Eureka*. Melbourne: Melbourne University Press, 1984.

Moore, F. Michael. *Drag! Male and Female Impersonators on Stage, Screen and Television*. North Carolina: McFarland, 1994.

Moore, Keith. 'The Role of the Local Catholic School Teachers in the Uprising at Eureka.' In *The Legacy of Eureka: Past, Present and Future*, edited by Anne Beggs–Sunter and Kevin Livingstone. 21–30. Ballarat: University of Ballarat, 1998.

Morgan, Patrick. *Folie à Deux: William and Caroline Dexter in Colonial Australia*. Quakers Hill, NSW: Quakers Hill Press, 1999.

Murphy-Lawless, Jo. 'The Obstetric View of Feminine Identity: A Nineteenth Century Case History of the Use of Forceps on Unmarried Women in Ireland.' In *Gender and Discourse: The Power of Talk*, edited by Alexandra Dundas Todd and Sue Fisher. Norwood, New Jersey: Ablex Publishing Corp., 1988.

Neilson Gattey, Charles. *The Bloomer Girls*. London: Femina Books, 1967.

O'Brien, Bob. *Massacre at Eureka: The Untold Story*. Ballarat: The Sovereign Hill Museums Association, 1998.

Oddey, Alison. *Performing Women: Stand-Ups, Strumpets and Itinerants*. London: Macmillan, 1999.

Oldfield, Audrey. *Australian Women and the Vote*. Melbourne: Cambridge University Press, 1994.

———. *The Great Republic of the Southern Seas: Republicans in Nineteenth-Century Australia*. Alexandria, NSW: Hale & Iremonger, 1999.

———. *Woman Suffrage in Australia: A Gift or a Struggle*. Melbourne: Cambridge University Press, 1992.

Oldis, Ken. *The Chinawoman*. Melbourne: Arcadia, 2008.

Pask, Edward H. *Enter the Colonies Dancing: A History of Dance in Australia, 1835–1940*. Melbourne: Oxford University Press, 1979.

Pearce, Keith and Fry, Helen. *The Lost Jews of Cornwall: From the Middle Ages to the Nineteenth Century*. Bristol: Redcliffe, 2000.

Pettman, Jan Jindy. 'Second-Class Citizens? Nationalism, Identity and Difference in Australia.' In *Gender, Politics and Citizenship in the 1990s*, edited by Barbara Sullivan and Gillian Whitehouse. Sydney: UNSW Press, 1996.

Philipp, June. *A Poor Man's Diggings: Mining and Community at Bethanga, Victoria, 1875–1912*. Melbourne: Hyland House, 1987.

Pickering, Paul. '"Ripe for a Republic": British Radical Responses to the Eureka Stockade.' *Australian Historical Studies* 34, no. 121 (2003): 69–91.

Pickering, Paul and Tyrrell, Alex. *The People's Bread: A History of the Anti-Corn Law League*. London: Leicester University Press, 2000.

Poulton, Jill. *Adelaide Ironside: The Pilgrim of Art*. Sydney: Hale & Iremonger, 1987.

Price, Roger. *The Revolutions of 1848*. New Jersey: Humanities Press International, 1988.

Priestley, Susan. *Henrietta Augusta Dugdale: An Activist 1827–1918*. Melbourne: Melbourne Books, 2011.

Pybus, Cassandra and Maxwell-Stewart, Hamish. *American Citizens, British Slaves: Yankee Political Prisoners in an Australian Penal Colony 1839–50*. Carlton, Vic.: Melbourne University Press, 2002.

Rhodes, Linda. *Two for the Price of One: The Lives of Mining Wives*. Perth: API Network, 2005.

Robertson, Priscilla. *Revolutions of 1848: A Social History*. New Jersey: Princeton University Press, 1952.

Rule, Pauline. 'Honora and Her Sisters: Success and Sorrow among Irish Immigrant Women in Colonial Victoria.' In *Irish-Australian Studies*, edited by Rebecca Phelan. 151–61. Sydney: Crossing Press, 1994.

———. 'Irish Women and the Problem of Ex-Nuptial Conception in Colonial Victoria.' In *Ireland and Australia, 1798–1998: Studies in Culture, Identity and Migration*, edited by Phillip Bull, Frances Devlin Glass and Helen Doyle. 113–23. Sydney: Crossing Press, 2000.

Rushen, Elizabeth. *Single and Free: Female Migration to Australia, 1833–37*. Melbourne: Australian Scholarly Publishing, 2003.

Russell, Geoffrey. *Water for Gold! The Fight to Quench Central Victoria's Goldfields*. Melbourne: Australian Scholarly Publishing, 2009.

Schwarzkopf, Jutta. *Women in the Chartist Movement*. London: Macmillan, 1991.

Scutt, Jocelynne. *The Sexual Gerrymander*. Melbourne: Spinifex, 1994.

Selzer, Anita. *Governors' Wives in Colonial Australia*. Canberra: National Library of Australia, 2002.

Senelick, Laurence. *The Changing Room: Sex, Drag and Theatre*. London: Routledge, 2000.

Serle, Geoffrey. 'The Causes of Eureka.' In *Historical Studies: Eureka Supplement*. 42–54. Melbourne: Melbourne University Press, 1954.

———. *The Golden Age: A History of the Colony of Victoria, 1851–1861*. Melbourne: Melbourne University Press, 1963.

Smith, Bernard. *Noel Counihan: Artist and Revolutionary*. Melbourne: Oxford University Publishing, 1993.

Smith, Catherine and Greig, Cynthia. *Women in Pants: Manly Maidens, Cowgirls and Other Renegades*. New York: Harry N. Abrams, 2003.

Smith, Neil C. *Soldiers Bleed Too: The Redcoats at the Eureka Stockade 1854*. Brighton, Vic.: Mostly Unsung Military History, 2004.

Sperber, Jonathan. *The European Revolutions, 1848–1851*. Cambridge: Cambridge University Press, 2005.

Spielvogel, Nathan. *The Affair at Eureka: The Story of '54*. Melbourne: Bread and Cheese Club, 1945.

———. 'The Ballarat Hebrew Congregation.' *Australian Jewish Historical Society Journal* 11, no. 6 (1946).

St John Williams, Noel T. *Redcoats and Courtesans: The Birth of the British Army 1660–1690*. London: Brassey's UK, 1994.

Stavely Baird, Patricia. *An Unlettered Girl: Her Life on the Goldfields*. Canberra: National Library of Australia, 2002.

Swain, Shurlee. 'Remembering Eureka: Is It a Boys' Own Game?' In *The Legacy of Eureka: Past, Present and Future*, edited by Anne Beggs-Sunter and Kevin Livingston. 31–36. Ballarat: University of Ballarat, 1998.

Talbot Cross, Mary. *Fortune's Fool: The Road Beyond Eureka*. Kew, Vic.: The Shalimar Press, 2001.

Thomas, Edith. *The Women Incendiaries (Les Petroleuses)*. London: Secker & Warburg, 1963.

Twomey, Christina. *Deserted and Destitute: Motherhood, Wife Desertion and Colonial Welfare*. Melbourne: Australian Scholarly Publishing, 2002.

Varley, James F. *Lola Montez: The Californian Adventures of Europe's Notorious Courtesan*. Spokane, Washington: Arthur H. Clark Co., 1996.

Walsh, Kay and Hooton, Joy. *Australian Autobiographical Narratives: An Annotated Bibliography: 1850–1900*. Canberra: National Library of Australia, 1993.

Walshe, R. D. 'The Significance of Eureka in Australian History.' In *Historical Studies: Eureka Supplement*. 103–27. Melbourne: Melbourne University Press, 1954.

Watson, Don. *Rabbit Syndrome: Australia and America*. Quarterly Essay. Edited by Peter Craven. Vol. 4. Melbourne: Black Inc., 2001.

Welsh, Lionel. *Vermilion and Gold: Vignettes of Chinese Life in Ballarat*. Ballarat: Montrose Historic Cottage, 2000.

Wickham, Dorothy. 'Blood, Sweat and Tears: Women at Eureka.' *Journal of Australian Colonial History* 10, no. 1 (2008): 99–114.

———. *Deaths at Eureka*. Ballarat: Ballarat Heritage Services, 1996.

———. *Shot in the Dark: A Pre-Eureka Incident, Being the Petition for the Compensation Case of Benden S. Hassell*. Ballarat: Ballarat Heritage Services, 1998.

———. *St Alipius: The Early History of Ballarat's First Church*. Ballarat: Ballarat Heritage Services, 1997.

———. *Women of the Diggings, Ballarat 1854*. Ballarat: Ballarat Heritage Services, 2009.

Wickham, Dorothy, Gervasoni, Clare and D'Angri, Val. *The Eureka Flag: Our Starry Banner*. Ballarat: Ballarat Heritage Services, 2000.

Wickham Koon, Helene. *Gold Rush Performers: A Biographical Dictionary of Actors, Singers, Dancers, Musicians, Circus Performers and Minstrel Players in America's Far West, 1848–69*. Jefferson, North Carolina: McFarland, 1994.

Williams, Margaret. *Australia on the Popular Stage 1829–1929*: An Historical Entertainment in Six Acts. Melbourne: Oxford University Press, 1983.

Williams, Paul. *The True Story of the Pikeman's Dog*. Ballarat: Eureka Stockade Memorial Association Inc., 2003.

Worthington, Vivienne. *Anastasia, Woman of Eureka: A Tribute to Anastasia Withers*. Ballarat: Vivienne Worthington, 2004.

Wright, Clare. *Beyond the Ladies Lounge: Australia's Female Publicans*. Carlton, Vic.: Melbourne University Press, 2003.

———. 'Desperately Seeking Samuel: A Diary Lost and Found.' *The La Trobe Journal* 90 (2012): 6–22.

———. 'The Eureka Stockade: An Alternative Portrait.' In *Making Australian History: Perpectives on the Past since 1788*, edited by Deborah Gare and David Ritter. South Melbourne: Thomson, 2008.

———. 'Golden Opportunities: The Early Origins of Women's Suffrage in Victoria.' *Victorian Historical Journal* 79, no. 2 (2008): 210–24.

———. 'An Indelible Stain': Gifts of the Samuel Lazarus Diary.' *History Australia* 6, no. 2 (2009): 45.1–45.5.

———. 'Labour Pains: Towards a Female Perspective on the Birth of Australian Democracy.' In *Eureka: Reappraising an Australian Legend*, edited by Alan Mayne. 123–43. Perth: API Network Books, 2006.

———. 'A Lover and a Fighter: The Trouble with Lola Montez.' *Overland* 195 (2009): 20–29.

———. '"New Brooms They Say Sweep Clean": Women's Political Activism on the Ballarat Goldfields, 1854.' *Australian Historical Studies* 39, no. 3 (2008): 305–22.

Yalom, Marilyn. *Blood Sisters: The French Revolution in Women's Memory*. London: Pandora/HarperCollins, 1995.

Youngdale, James. *Populism: A Psychohistorical Perspective*. New York: National University Publications, 1975.

INDEX